GRANTA BOOKS

THE VIEW FROM THE GROUND

Martha Gellhorn was born in St Louis, Missouri. In 1930, aged twenty-one, she talked her way into a free passage to Europe and arrived in Paris with seventy-five dollars in her pocket and the conviction that she could earn a living as a foreign correspondent. She returned to the United States in 1934 and two years later published her acclaimed book of four linked novellas on Depression-hit America, *The Trouble I've Seen*.

In 1937 she returned to Europe as a war correspondent, and for the next nine years she reported on the wars in Spain, Finland, China and finally Europe in World War Two. These experiences are collected in *The Face of War*. After 1946 her journalism became occasional and freelance, but she continued to report on whatever engaged her interest and concern, from Vietnam to the Middle East and the wars in Central America.

Martha Gellhorn is the author of five novels, two collections of stories, four books of novellas and three books of non-fiction. She lives in Wales.

MARTHA GELLHORN

The View from the Ground

GRANTA BOOKS
LONDON
in association with
PENGUIN BOOKS

GRANTA BOOKS
2/3 Hanover Yard, Noel Road, Islington, London N1 8BE

Published in association with the Penguin Group
Penguin Books Ltd, 27 Wrights Lane, London W8 5TZ, England
Viking Penguin, a division of Penguin Books Inc.,
375 Hudson Street, New York, New York 10014, USA
Penguin Books Australia Ltd, Ringwood, Victoria, Australia
Penguin Books Canada Ltd, 2802 John Street, Markham,
Ontario, Canada L3R 1B4
Penguin Books (NZ) Ltd, 182-190 Wairau Road, Auckland 10,
New Zealand

Penguin Books Ltd, Registered Offices: Harmondsworth,
Middlesex, England

First published in Great Britain by Granta Books 1989
This edition published 1990
1 3 5 7 9 10 8 6 4 2

Printed in England by Clays Ltd, St Ives plc

TO MY FATHER

"As life is action and passion, it is required of man that he should share the passion and action of his time, at peril of being judged not to have lived."

Oliver Wendell Holmes, Jr.
Justice of the United States Supreme Court

"All over the world, Moran decided, the past was being wiped out by condominiums."

Elmore Leonard, Cat Chaser

AUTHOR'S NOTE

This book is a selection of articles written during five decades: peace-time reporting. That is to say, the countries in the background were at peace at the moment of writing, not that there was peace on earth. The articles are reprinted as originally published (warts and all) in chronological order by date of publication except as follows: the time of the event in the first article, 'Justice at Night', 1931, places it, not the later date of publication. The second, 'My Dear Mr Hopkins', is not an article but a compilation of reports. In the seventies, 'Beautiful Day of Dissent' failed to find a publisher, and 'When Franco Died' was published by *New York* magazine and *The Observer* and both cut it for space, differently. Having lost the original copy, I pieced the two together to make what I hope is the whole. The translation of the testimony in 'On Torture' has been expanded. I have changed titles which were not my choice.

I decided to put my hindsight comments on the decades at the end of each period, leaving the reader alone with the articles before I intruded with explanations.

CONTENTS

THE THIRTIES

THE FORTIES

THE FIFTIES

THE SIXTIES

THE SEVENTIES

THE EIGHTIES

THE THIRTIES

Justice at Night

We got off the day coach at Trenton, New Jersey, and bought a car for $28.50. It was an eight-year-old Dodge open touring-car and the back seat was full of fallen leaves. A boy, who worked for the car dealer, drove us to the City Hall to get an automobile licence and he said: 'The boss gypped the pants off you, you should of got his machine for $20 flat and it's not worth that.' So we started out to tour across America, which is, roughly speaking, a distance of 3,000 miles.

I have to tell this because without the car, and without the peculiarly weak insides of that car, we should not have seen a lynching.

It was September, and as we drove south the days were dusty and hot and the sky was pale. We skidded in dust that was as moving and uncertain as sand, and when we stopped for the night we scraped it off our faces and shook it from our hair like powder. So, finally, we thought we'd drive at night, which would be cooler anyhow, and we wouldn't see the dust coming at us. The beauty of America is its desolation: once you leave New England and the industrial centres of the east you feel that no one lives in the country at all. In the south you see a few people, stationary in the fields, thinking or just standing, and broken shacks where people more or less live, thin people who are accustomed to semi-starvation and crops that never quite pay enough. The towns or villages give an impression of belonging to the flies; and it is impossible to imagine that on occasion these languid people move with a furious purpose.

We drove through Mississippi at night, trying to get to a town called Columbia, hoping that the hotel would be less slovenly than usual and that there would be some food available. The car broke down. We did everything we could think of doing, which wasn't much, and once or twice it panted wearily and then there was silence. We sat in it and cursed and wondered what to do. No one passed; there was no reason for anyone to pass. The roads are bad and mosquitoes sing too close the minute you stop moving. And the only reason to go to a small town in Mississippi is to sell something, or try to sell, and that doesn't happen late at night.

It was thirty miles or more to Columbia and we were tired. If it hadn't been for the mosquitoes we should simply have slept in the car and hoped that someone would drive past in the morning. As it was we smoked cigarettes and swatted at ourselves and swore and hated machinery and talked about the good old days when people got about in stage-coaches. It didn't make things better and we had fallen into a helpless silence when we heard a car coming. From some distance we could hear it banging over the ruts in the road. We climbed out and stood so the headlights would find us and presently a truck appeared, swaying crazily. It stopped and a man leaned out. As a matter of fact, he sagged out the side and he had a bottle in one hand, waving it at us.

'Anything wrong?' he said.

We explained about the car and asked for a lift. He pulled his head into the truck and consulted with the driver. Then he reappeared and said they'd give us a lift to Columbia later, but first they were going to a lynching and if we didn't mind the detour . . .

We climbed into the truck.

'Northerners?' the driver said. 'Where did you all come from?'

We said that we had driven down from Trenton in New Jersey and he said, 'In that old piece of tin?' referring to our car. The other man wiped the neck of the bottle by running his finger around

4

inside it, and offered it to me. 'Do you good,' he said, 'best corn outside Kentucky.' It was no time to refuse hospitality. I drank some of the stuff which had a taste like gasoline, except that it was like gasoline on fire, and he handed it to my friend Joe, who also drank some and coughed, and they both laughed.

I said timidly, 'Who's getting lynched?'

'Some goddam nigger, name of Hyacinth as I recollect.'

'What did he do?'

'He got after a white woman.' I began to think with doubt and disgust of this explanation. So I asked who the woman was.

'Some widow woman, owns land down towards Natchez.'

'How old is she?' Joe asked. Joe was in doubt, too.

'Christ, she's so old she ought to of died. She's about forty or fifty.'

'And the boy?'

'You mean that nigger Hyacinth?'

I said yes, and was told that Hyacinth was about nineteen, though you couldn't always tell with niggers; sometimes they looked older than they were and sometimes younger.

'What happened?' Joe said. 'How do you know she got raped?'

'She says so,' the driver said. 'She's been screaming off her head about it ever since this afternoon. She run down to the next plantation and screamed and said hang that man; and she said it was Hyacinth. She ought to of knowed him anyhow; he was working for her sometime back.'

'How do you mean; was he a servant?'

'No,' the driver said, 'he was working on her land on shares. Most of her croppers've moved off by now; she don't give them any keep and they can't make the crop if they don't get nothing to eat all winter. She sure is cruel hard on niggers, that woman; she's got a bad name for being a mean one.'

'Well,' Joe said, very gently, 'it doesn't look likely to me that a boy of nineteen would go after a woman of forty or fifty. Unless she's very beautiful, of course.'

'Beautiful,' the man with the bottle said, 'Jees, you ought to see her. They could stick her out in a field and she'd scare the crows to death.'

We bumped in silence over the roads. I couldn't think of anything to say. These men were evidently going to the lynching, but I didn't see that they were blind with anger against the Negro, or burning to avenge the honour of the nameless widow. Joe whispered to me: 'You know we can't just sit and take this. I don't believe the boy did anything to that woman. We can't just sit around and let a man get hung, you know.' I began to feel hot and nervous and I decided I'd like a drink even if it was corn whiskey. But I couldn't think of anything to do.

'How many people will be coming? A big crowd?' I asked.

'Yeah. They been getting the word around all evening. Some of the boys gonna go down and spring the jail. That's easy. Sheriff don't plan on holding that nigger till trial time anyhow. There'll be a lot of folks driving in from all over the county. They been telephoning around this afternoon and visiting folks and it gets around if there's trouble with a nigger. There'll be plenty of folks there.'

'But,' Joe said, this time desperately, 'you don't know that he did anything to that woman. You haven't any proof have you?'

'She says he did,' the driver said, 'that's enough for us. You gotta take a white woman's word any time before you take a nigger's. Helluva place it'd be if you said white folks lied and niggers told the truth.'

'But you said he worked for her,' Joe went on. 'You said she was mean and didn't give her share-croppers decent rations. He's so much younger than she is, too, and you said she wasn't any beauty. He may have been going to see her to ask for money for food and he may have gotten mad and raised his arm or something that made her think he was going to strike her . . .'

'Lissen, sonny,' the man with the bottle said quietly, finally, 'this here ain't none of your goddam business.'

We drove in silence, lurching against each other, and the driver took a drink, steering with one hand, and then the other man drank. They were sore, I could see that. They'd come out to get drunk and have a good time and here we were, asking questions and spoiling their fun. They were getting a grim drunk, not a laughing one, and they were sore about it. They didn't offer us the bottle any more.

The road widened and ahead we could see tail-lights. The driver stepped on the gas and the truck rattled forward. We passed a touring car with six men in it; I saw some shot-guns. 'That you, Danny?' the driver shouted. 'Hi, Luke, see you later.'

We were evidently going to an appointed meeting place. I asked about this. 'They'll bring him up from jail,' the man with the bottle said. 'We all are gonna get together at the Big Elm crossroads.'

There were more cars now and the road was better. 'Almost there,' the driver said, and for no reason at all the man with the bottle said, 'Attaboy,' and laughed and slapped his leg.

There was no moon. I saw an enormous tree and, though there were no doubt others, it stood by itself and had a curious air of usefulness. The roads forked and there were shapeless dark cars sprawled in the dust and men waiting in groups, laughing, drinking, and looking down the road for something to appear; something that would give this party meaning. I couldn't judge the crowd but there must have been about fifty cars, and these cars travel full.

Presently a line of cars came up the road. They were going as fast as they could over the ruts. They stopped and men poured out of them, not making much noise, apparently knowing what they had to do as if it were a ritual, or something they had practised often before. Some of these men seemed to be the poorest of white farmers: tenants or share-croppers themselves. Tattered clothes, the usual thin unhinged bodies, that soiled look of people who live in little crowded places. There were one or two men who seemed to be there on principle, as one would go to a dinner party because it was an obligation, but a very boring one, and a few men, rather more compact than the others, who directed the show. It was hard to tell in this light, but they seemed men of middle age mostly, householders, heads of families, reliable people. Joe was saying now, 'I'd like to kill somebody myself.'

I couldn't think of anything at all. I kept wondering why we were here. I hadn't seen Hyacinth yet.

But Hyacinth was there, surrounded by men. He had been brought in one of the last cars. I heard a man say: 'Hurry up before the bastard dies of fright.' Hyacinth was walked across the road, through an open space, to the great tree. He had his hands tied and there was a rope around his waist. They were dragging him; his legs curled under him and his head seemed loose and heavy on his neck. He looked small and far too quiet. They had torn off his shirt.

The men gathered around; they came without any commands and stood at a distance to give the leaders room to work. There was not any decisive noise, no cheering or shouting, but just a steady threatening murmur of anger or determination. The action moved fast, with precision.

A sedan drove up and stopped under the tree. A man climbed on to the top quickly. Another. They stood black against the sky. From beneath, a group of men, shoving and pushing, got Hyacinth's limp thin body up to them. Hyacinth half-lay, half-squatted on the roof. From the ground a length of rope sailed up, hung in the air, curved and fell. A man tried again and the rope caught and hung down from a limb. The noosed end was thrown to one of the men standing on the car-roof. He held it and shook Hyacinth. There were no words now, only vague instructions, half-spoken. The crowd stood still; you could hear the mosquitoes whining.

The other man held something in his hand; it looked like a great jug. He held it over Hyacinth, who shivered suddenly, and came to life. His voice rose out of him like something apart, and it hurt one's ears to listen to it; it was higher than a voice can be, not human. 'Boss,' he said. 'Boss, I didn't do nuthin, don't burn me Boss, Boss . . .' The crowd had trembled now, stirred by his voice, and there were orders to hurry, to kill the bastard, what the hell were they waiting for . . .

The two men held him up and put the noose around his neck,

and now he was making a terrible sound, like a dog whimpering. The minute they let go, he slacked into a kneeling position and his whole body seemed to shrink and dwindle and there was this noise he made. The two men jumped down from the roof: the rope was taut now. The car started and the silly sound of the starter failing to work, then the hesitant acceleration of the motor were so important that nothing else was heard; there were no other sounds anywhere; just these, and a moment's waiting. The car moved forward, fast. Hyacinth skidded and fought an instant—less than an instant—to keep his footing or some hold, some safety. He snapped from the back of the car, hung suspended, twirling a little on the rope, with his head fallen sideways. I did not know whether he was dead. There was a choked sound beside me and it was Joe, crying, sitting there crying, with fury, with helplessness, and I kept looking at Hyacinth and thinking: it can't have happened. There had been a noise, a sudden guttural sound as of people breathing out a deep breath, when the rope carried Hyacinth twisting into the air. Now a man came forward with a torch made of newspaper, burning. He reached up and the flames licked at Hyacinth's feet. He had been soaked in kerosene to make it easy, but the flames didn't take so well at first. Then they got on to his trousers and went well, shooting up, and there was a hissing sound and I thought a smell. I went away and was sick.

When I came back the cars were going off down the road quietly. And men were calling to each other saying: 'So long, Jake. . .' 'Hi there, Billy . . .' 'See you t'morrow, Sam . . .' Just saying goodnight to each other and going home.

The driver and the man with the bottle came back to the truck and got in. They seemed in a good frame of mind. The driver said, 'Well there won't be no more fresh niggers in these parts for a while. We'll get you to Columbia now. Sorry we hadta keep you waiting . . .'

9

My Dear Mr Hopkins

Washington, D.C.

11 November, 1934

My Dear Mr Hopkins:

I came in today from Gastonia, North Carolina, and was as flat and grim as is to be expected. I got a notice from your office asking about 'protest groups.' All during this trip in both Carolinas I have been thinking to myself about that curious phrase *red menace*, and wondering where said menace hid itself. Every house I visited—mill worker or unemployed—had a picture of the President. These ranged from newspaper clippings (in destitute homes) to large coloured prints, framed in gilt cardboard. The portrait holds the place of honour over the mantel; I can only compare this to the Italian peasant's Madonna. I have been seeing people who, according to any standard, have practically nothing in life and practically nothing to look forward to or hope for. But there is hope, confidence, something intangible and real: 'The President isn't going to forget us.'

I went to see a woman with five children who was living on relief ($3.40 a week). Her picture of the President was a small one, and she told me her oldest daughter had been married some months ago and had cried for the big coloured picture as a wedding present. The children have no shoes and that woman is terrified of the coming cold. There is almost no furniture left in the home, and you can imagine what and how they eat. But she said, suddenly brightening, 'I'd give my heart to see the President. I know he means to do everything he can for us; but they make it hard for him; they won't let him.' I note this case as something special; because here the faith was coupled with a feeling (entirely sympathetic) that the President was not omnipotent.

I have been seeing mill workers; and in every mill, when possible, the local Union president. There has been widespread discrimination against Union members in the south; and many mills haven't re-opened since the strike. Those open often run on such curtailment that workers are getting from two to three days' work a week. The price of food has risen (especially the kind of food they eat: fat-back bacon, flour, corn meal, sorghum) as high as 100 per cent. It is getting cold; and they have no clothes. The Union presidents are almost all out of work since the strike.

In many mill villages, evictions have been served; more threatened. These men are in a terrible fix. (Lord, how barren the language seems: these men are faced by hunger and cold, by the prospect of becoming dependent beggars—in their own eyes; by the threat of homelessness, and of having their families dispersed. What more a man can face, I don't know.) You would expect to find them maddened with fear, with hostility. I expected and waited for 'lawless' talk, threats, or at least blank despair. And I didn't find it. I found a kind of contained and quiet misery; fear for their families and fear that their children wouldn't be able to go to school. ('All we want is work and the chance to care for our families like a man should.') But what is keeping them sane, keeping them going on and hoping, is their belief in the President.

What the rights and wrongs of this are, I don't know.

But the fact remains that they believe the President promised them they would get their jobs back after the strike, regardless of whether they were Union or non-Union men. The President will see that they have work and proper wages; and that the stretch-out[1] will be abandoned. They don't waver in this faith. They merely hope the President will send 'his men' (the Labour Conciliators) quickly, because it is hard to wait.

These are the things they say to me: 'We trust in the Supreme Being and Franklin Roosevelt.' 'You heard him talk over the radio, ain't you? He's the only President who ever said anything about the forgotten man. We know he's going to stand by us.' 'He's a man of his word and he promised us; we aren't worrying as long as we got him.' 'The President won't let these awful conditions go on.' 'The President wanted the Code;[2] and they weren't sticking to the Code. The President knows why we struck.' 'The President said no man was going to go hungry and cold; he'll get us our jobs.'

I am going on and on about this because I think it has vast importance. These people will be slow to give up hope; terribly slow to doubt the President. But if they don't get their jobs; then what? If the winter comes on and they find themselves on our below-subsistence relief, then what? I think they might strike again; hopelessly and apathetically. In very few places, there might be some violence, speedily crushed. But if they lose this hope, there isn't much left for them as a group. And if this class (what marvellous stock they are, too) loses its courage or morale or whatever you want to call it, there will be an even worse social problem than there now is. With time, adding disillusionment and suffering, they might actually go against their own grain and turn into desperate people. As it is, between them and fear stands the President. But only the President.

[1] Heavily increased individual work load.
[2] Minimum wage.

To go on with the mills. The stretch-out is the constant cry of the workers. Needless to say, every mill owner angrily denies that there is a stretch-out and some of them asked what the word means. But I saw, by intention, some of his workers; a couple of them had quit his mill after the strike. (They were Union people, and also felt that as Union people they would be highly unwelcome there, when the mills re-opened.) They told me that during the summer two or three women a day fainted in the mill; a man of 35 died, between his looms, of heart failure.

Other cases: 'When you get out, you're just trembling all over, and you can't hardly get rested for the next day.' 'We don't know how long we can keep it up: it's killing the women and the men are all afraid they'll lose their jobs because they can't do the work.' I went to see one man in his home, and said, 'How are you?' 'Tired,' he said, 'tired and weary—like all the others; like all of us working here.' That sounds like something bad out of Dickens, but it was pretty grim, seeing the man. Their faces are proof of this statement; faces and bodies.

The people who seem most physically hit by this are the young girls, who are really in awful shape. I have watched them in some mills where the naked eye can tell that the work load is inhuman. They have no rest for eight hours; in one mill they told me they couldn't get time to cross the room to the drinking fountain for water. They eat standing up, keeping their eyes on the machines. In another mill I found three women lying on the cement floor of the toilet, resting.

Again (let us be just if possible) in some cases this speed-up is an academic question. It may be terribly bad but the mills only run two or three days a week; then you have the obvious complaint of not being able to live on what they earn.[3] And there is the mill owner's side, naturally. I've been looking at ledgers, written beautifully

[3] Wages: 7½ to 10 cents an hour.

in red. All of them tell me business is worse than last November, and they will have to curtail during the winter. In Gaston County, the leading mill owner told me there were 10,000 textile workers too many; there are 106 mills of which very few are running full time.

The workers tell me that things are worse since the Code; there is the stretch-out and part-time work, and the price of food is rocketing up.

What has been constantly before me is the health problem. To write about it is difficult only in that one doesn't know where to begin. Our relief people are definitely on below-subsistence living scales. (This is the unanimous verdict of anyone connected with relief; and a brief study of budgets clinches the matter.) The result is that dietary diseases abound. I know that in this area there has always been pellagra;[4] but that doesn't make matters better. In any case it is increasing; and I have seen it ranging from scaly elbows in children to insanity in a grown man. Here is what doctors say: 'It's no use telling mothers what to feed their children; they haven't the food to give.' 'Conditions are really horrible here; it seems as if the people are degenerating before your eyes: the children are worse mentally and physically than their parents.' 'I've just come in from seeing some patients who have been living on corn bread and corn hominy, without seasoning, for two weeks. I wonder how long it takes for pellagra to set in; just a question of days now.' 'All the mill workers I see are definite cases of under-nourishment; that's the best breeding ground I know for disease.' 'There's not much use prescribing medicine; they haven't the money to buy it.' 'You can't do anything with these people until they're educated to take care of themselves; they don't know what to eat; they haven't the beginning

[4] Vitamin deficiency disease, affects skin, proceeds to emaciation, paralysis, dementia, death. Easily cured by meat, eggs, milk, liver, yeast extract, etc.

of an idea how to protect themselves against sickness.'

The medical set-up, from every point of view, in this area is tragic. In Gaston County there is not one county clinic or hospital; and only one health officer (appointed or elected?). This gentleman has held his job for more than a dozen years, and must have had droll medical training some time during the last century. He believes oddly that three shots of neo-salvarsan will cure syphilis, and thinks that injecting this into the arm muscle is as good as anything. Result: he cripples and paralyses his patients, who won't go back. He likewise refuses to sign sterilization warrants on imbeciles; grounds: 'It's a man's prerogative to have children.' Another doctor in this area also owns a drug store. He was selling bottled tonic (home-made I think) to his mill worker patients as a cure for syphilis. This was discovered by a 21-year-old case worker, who wondered why her clients' money was disappearing so fast. When asked why he did this he said that syphilis was partly a 'run-down' condition, and that 'you ought to build the patients up.' Every doctor says that syphilis is spreading unchecked and uncured. One doctor even said that it had assumed the proportions of an epidemic and wouldn't be stopped unless the government stepped in, and treated it like smallpox.

I have seen three VD clinics only. One of them was over a store—three rooms; run by the county doctor, a nurse, and a coloured janitor who acted as assistant. I am told by these clinic doctors that most of the patients come in when the disease is in the second or third (and incurable) stage. That of course it is being spread regardless; and often they treat the whole family. That congenital syphilis is a terrible problem and practically untreated; nature kills off these children pretty well.

One doctor whose clientele was entirely mill workers showed me 50 Wassermans,[5] all four-plus. Not one of

[5] Blood tests for syphilis.

those people is taking treatment. All of them have families. As you know, these people sleep four in a bed; with the smallest children in the same bed with the parents.

Cases: a woman brought in a four-month-old baby; both of them looked deathly ill and the child was paralysed. The mother thought it was infantile; they were both four-plus Wassermans. But the treatment costs 25 cents a shot, and in that area the clinic is not allowed to accept relief orders for treatment; they were not being treated . . . Saw a family of four; everyone has syphilis. The boy was moronic; and the girl also had TB . . . A twelve-year-old girl with open syphilitic sores; her mother thought she had scratched a bite which had become infected.

In Camp Jackson Transient Camp 15 to 20 per cent have it. Here the problem is different; these men know what the disease is and definitely want to be treated; are willing to stay and work for their treatment. But amongst the Negroes syphilis is 'rheumatism.' And amongst the ignorant mill workers it is 'bad blood.' In neither case can any adequate job be done; partly because the people themselves are ignorant and careless. The doctors tell me that they have one child a year born to syphilitics, just as nicely as to the others.

Which brings us to birth control. Every social worker I saw, and every doctor, and the majority of mill owners, talked about birth control as the basic need of this class. I have seen three generations of unemployed (14 in all) living in one room; and both mother and daughter were pregnant. Our relief people have a child a year; large families are the despair of the social worker and the doctor. The doctors say that the more children in a family the lower the health rating. Likewise, the larger the family, the lower the intelligence rating. These people regard children as something the Lord has seen fit to send them, and you can't question the Lord even if you don't agree with Him. There is absolutely no hope for these children; I feel that our relief rolls will double themselves given time.

The children are growing up in terrible surroundings; dirt, disease, overcrowding, under-nourishment. Often their parents were farm people, who at least had air and enough food. This cannot be said for the children. I know we could do birth control in this area; it would be a slow and trying job beginning with education. (You have to fight superstition, stupidity and lack of hygiene.) But birth control could be worked into prenatal clinics; and the grapevine telegraph is the best propaganda I know. If it isn't done, we may as well fold up; these people cannot be bettered under present circumstances. Their health is going to pieces; the present generation of unemployed will be useless material in no time; their housing is frightful (talk about European slums); they are ignorant and often below-par intelligence.

What can we do? Feed them—feed them pinto beans and corn bread and sorghum and watch the pellagra spread. And in twenty years, what will there be? How can a decent civilization be based on a decayed substrata, which is incapable physically and mentally to cope with life?

As for their homes: I have seen a village where the latrines drain nicely down a gully to a well from which they get their drinking water. Nobody thinks anything about this, but half the population is both syphilitic and moronic; and why they aren't all dead of typhoid I don't know. Another mill village, which beats any European tenement I have seen: the houses are shot with holes, windows broken, no sewerage; rats. The rent for these houses is twice as high as that of fine mill houses. (Likewise, here, the company forces its employees to buy from the company grocery and make a 50 to 75 per cent profit. It is probable—and to be hoped—that one day the owners of this place will get shot or lynched. Their workers resemble peons I have seen in Mexico, who are eaten away by syphilis and pulqué.)

The houses in some mill villages are pretty good, and then there is a definite improvement in the humans who inhabit them. You can almost judge from a village what grade worker you will find there. But there is more than a housing problem, though I can't see much hope for people who have to 'pile up as best we can' in beds without blankets, and have to walk to a well for water, and dump their garbage wherever it's handy. However, there is a problem of education. (Do you know that the highest-paid teacher in a school in North Carolina gets $720 a year? You can pretty well imagine what they get in the way of teachers. This is not criticism of the teachers; it is downright woe.) But the schooling is such awful nonsense. Teach the kids to recite the Gettysburg Address by heart: somehow one is not impressed. They don't know what to eat or how to cook it. They don't know that their bodies can be maintained in health by protective measures. They don't know that they needn't have ten children when they can't feed one. They don't know that syphilis is destroying and contagious.

And with all this, they are grand people. If there is any meaning in the phrase *American stock* it has some meaning here. They are sound and good humoured, kind and loyal. I don't believe they are lazy; I believe they are mostly ill and ignorant. They have a strong family feeling, and one sees this in pitiful ways—for instance: if there is any means of keeping the children properly and prettily clothed, it is done; but the mother will be a prematurely aged, ugly woman who has nothing to put on her back. And the father's first comment will be: could we get shoes for the children so they can go to school (though the father himself may be walking on the ground.)

By the way, I get this constantly: talking to workers about a shut down or part-time mill, and saying the mill can't run because it has no orders. And they say to me wonderingly: 'But we haven't had any sheets for years and hardly any blankets. And no shirts or underclothes; and no towels. We could use the cloth.'

I hope you won't misunderstand this report. It's easy to see what the government is up against. What with a bunch of loathsome ignoramuses talking about 'lavish expenditure' et cetera. And all right-minded citizens virtuously protesting against anything which makes sense and sounds new. I'm writing this extra report because you did send us out to look; and you ought to get as much as we see. It isn't all there is to see, by any means; and naturally I have been looking at the worst and darkest side. But is is a terribly frightening picture. Is there no way we can get it before the public; no way to make them realize that you cannot build a future on destroyed basic material?

We are so proud of being a new people in a free land. And we have a serf class; a serf class which seems to me to be in as bad a state of degeneration (maybe, in this area, worse) than the lower class European who has learned self-protection through centuries of hardship. It makes me raging mad to hear talk of 'red revolution,' the talk of cowards who would deserve what they got, having blindly and selfishly fomented revolution themselves. Besides I don't believe it; it takes time for all things including successful rebellion; time and a tradition for revolutions which does not exist in this country. But it's far more terrible to think that the basis of our race is slowly rotting, almost before we have had time to become a race.

*

Boston, Massachusetts
26 November, 1934

My Dear Mr Hopkins:

This report will cover my ten days in Massachusetts (from 15 November through 25 November). I visited Boston, Lowell, Brockton, Lynn, Leicester, Oxford, Fall River, Lawrence.

I want to deal with a subject which is not included in our instructions. The subject is the administration of relief. In any report on Massachusetts you must have information about the administration, which is so definitely and blatantly bad that it has become an object of disapproval (if not disgust) for both the unemployed and the controlling classes (businessmen etc.). In the often repeated words of the unemployed, 'They're all in this together—the politicians and the relief people.'

It seems that our adminstrative posts are frequently assigned on recommendation of the Mayor and town Board of Aldermen. The adminstrator is a nice inefficient guy who is being rewarded for being somebody's cousin. Second: instead of having a unified FERA set-up which would care for both work and direct relief, the direct relief is handled by the Public Welfare which is a municipal biz and purely political in personnel. I can't very well let myself go as I should enjoy doing about the quality of these administrators; they are criminally incompetent.

In one town the FERA investigators (who are supposed to be doing some social work) are members of the Vice Squad who have been loaned for the job. Usually there is only one investigation at the office (followed by a perfunctory home visit) to establish the eligibility of the client for relief. I can't see that these questions do anything except hurt and offend the unemployed, destroy his pride, make him feel that he has sunk into a pauperized substrata, becoming merely a number; something anonymous who will presently be more or less fed.

I think this is a wretched job: wretched in every way. Politics is bad enough in any shape; but it shouldn't get around to manhandling the destitute.

Now about the unemployed themselves: this picture is so grim that whatever words I use will seem hysterical and exaggerated. I have been doing more case visiting here; about five families a day. And I find them all in the same shape—fear, fear driving them into a state of semi-collapse; cracking the nerves; and an overpowering terror of the future. These people are probably (by and large) more intelligent and better educated than the unemployed I saw in the south—which unfortunately isn't saying much. The price of this intelligence is consciousness. They know what they're going through. I haven't been in one home that hasn't offered me the spectacle of a human being driven beyond his or her powers of endurance and sanity. They can't live on the Public Welfare grocery orders. They can't pay rent and are evicted. They are shunted from place to place, and are watching their children grow thinner and thinner; fearing the cold for children who have neither coats nor shoes; wondering about coal.

And they don't understand why or how this happened. There are some cases in every locality of unemployables; people who have lived for two or three generations on the Welfare. (Why aren't there sterilization laws? All such cases are moronic, unequipped physically or mentally to face life—and they all have enormous families.) But the majority of the people are workers, who were competent to do their jobs and had been doing them over a period of years ranging from a dozen to twenty-five. Then a mill closes or curtails; a shoe factory shuts down or moves to another area. And there they are, for no reason they can understand, forced to be beggars asking for charity; subject to questions from strangers, and to all the miseries and indignities attached to

21

destitution. Their pride is dying but not without due agony.

I get these comments constantly: 'We can't live on that $12 [family of ten]—we're going to starve—and my husband can't find work—he's out every day looking—and I get afraid about him: he gets so black . . .' 'If anyone had told us a year ago we'd come to this I'd have said he was a liar; and what can we do.' 'It's a terrible thing when decent people have to beg.' 'We always tried to be as honest and decent as we could and we've worked all our lives; and what has it come to.' 'What's the use of looking for work any more; there isn't any. And look at the children. How would you feel if you saw your own kids like that: half-naked and sick.' 'It seems like we're just going backwards since the last two years.' 'We can't go crazy; we've got the kids to think about.' 'I don't want to ask for nothing. I hate this charity. But we haven't got any shoes; do you think you could get us something to put on our feet—just a pair of rubbers would do . . .'

I could go on and on. It is hard to believe that these conditions exist in a civilized country. I have been going into homes at mealtimes and seeing what they eat. It isn't possible; it isn't enough to begin with and then every article of food is calculated to destroy health. But how can they help that; if you're hungry you eat 'to fill up—but the kids ain't getting what's right for them; they're pale and thin. I can't do anything about it and sometimes I just wish we were all dead.'

Health: the Welfare nurses, doctors, social workers, the whole band, tell me that TB is on the increase. Naturally; undernourishment is the best guarantee known for bum lungs. The children have impetigo—as far as I can make out dirt has a lot to do with this. Rickets, anaemia, bad teeth, flabby muscles. Another bright thought: feeblemindedness is on the increase. Doctors speak of these people as being in direct degeneration from parent to child. My own limited experience is this: out of every three families I visited one had moronic children or one moronic parent. I don't mean merely stupid; I mean definitely below normal level intelligence, fit only for sanatoriums.

Again, due to unemployment and also to prevalent low wages (all these mill hands and shoe workers are working part-time; and their wages are not more—and often less—than relief), families are evicted from their homes. So they double up, in already horribly over-crowded houses. The result (my sources are labour leaders, social workers, doctors, nurses) is increased nervous disorders; and the nurses who work in the schools speak feelingly of low scholarship; the nervous state of the children—involuntary nervous gestures, sex perversions, malnutrition, increased TB.

Again I can only report that there are no organized protest groups: there is only decay. Each family in its own miserable home going to pieces. But I wonder if some day, crazed and despairing, they won't revolt without organization. It seems incredible to think that they will go on like this, patiently waiting for nothing.

The FERA relief cases do not feel that FERA is charity; it's work. Badly paid to be sure; but then it's only three days (or less) a week, and they're used to low wages for part-time. The Public Welfare cases, on the other hand, present a different problem. Where you have the shattered nerves, despair and fear (signs of life still) of the FERA people, you have apathy and listlessness in the Welfare people. I think this is due to the fact that their living standards are even lower; that they feel themselves irrevocably pauperized; that they hate the indignity and humiliation of the Welfare treatment, and that by the time they get around to applying for Welfare they have given up all hope and are pretty finished human material.

The labour leaders and social workers tell me there is

a distinct decline in living standards as from a year ago. I find that the foreign born (or one generation American) reacts better to hardship than the native. The reaction of the native to these circumstances is demoralization and nervous breakdown. (It's very interesting: what used to be a phrase for rich neurotic middle-aged matrons is now on the lips of all this working class.) Whereas the foreigner attempts still, despite homelessness and poverty, to maintain his home, and the women somehow keep alive their pride in what few possessions remain. This is not true of the lowest-class Latin worker, with a large family; but there I think economic conditions have (after a long struggle) beaten them out of a strong natural tendency to care for the foyer. The natives' homes are going quickly to hell; both from the material point of view (filth and decay) and from the moral point of view—the family ties melting under this strain.

I'm giving you this picture as I have been able to see it and through the eyes of the people (supposedly informed) with whom I talked. *Grim* is a gentle word: it's heartbreaking and terrifying. And I feel that as long as these people go on reproducing in such quantity, we can't begin to cope with the situation. Now, we are only feeding a third of the people needing relief; and inadequate food, bolstered up by odds and ends of clothing, and fuel, is all we can give. (Not always that.) Men of fifty and over have given up hope; for them there is no future. But what is most frightening is the young (between the ages of 18 and 25): they are apathetic and despairing, feeling there is nothing to look forward to, sinking into indifference. (By the way, the majority of VD cases in county clinics are patients of this age group and class.) I cannot write too feelingly of the physical condition of small children.

Concerning mills and shoe factories: (Lawrence is out of this—they scooped up about three million dollars worth of government orders and business is booming at the moment.) Labour relations seem quite good here. Which is a definite change from the South and from our point of view, as it concerns the mental state of the worker, this is cause for thanksgiving. There is none of the widespread Southern worker's persecution complex (largely justified there): fear of being fired for joining the Union, etc. But the mills are on their last legs: cost of production having mounted, so that market prices are below manufacturing costs; therefore no orders; therefore either shut down mills (the state is studded with factory and mill skeletons) or curtailment of hours. The workers do not get the Code weekly wage simply because they work two or three days a week. The mill owners here seem to feel very keenly the misery of their workers but they also feel there isn't much they can do. After a certain amount of red writing in ledgers, they are bound to fold up. (That's their story.)

The shoe industry is in a frightful state. The problem does seem to be unionized labour; which is to say that this being the stronghold of the shoe unions, the employers cannot compete with non-unionized factories in Maine, New Hampshire, etc., as sweat-shops, where the minimum NRA wage[1] is automatically the maximum. Factories are moving wholesale to Maine, New Hampshire and other non-unionized areas. The factories here are running erratically, often for a few weeks until an order goes through, then with several weeks' wait or time-marking.

It fills both the workers and the unemployed in this area with astonishment that there is nothing for shoe factories to do; but none of them have shoes to put on their feet and are facing winter with husks of shoes bound up in rags . . .

I'm not thrilled with Massachusetts.

[1] National Recovery Act

Camden, New Jersey
25 April, 1935

My Dear Mr Hopkins:

I have spent a week in Camden. It surprises me to find how radically attitudes can change within four or five months. Times were of course lousy, but you had faith in the President and the New Deal and things would surely pick up. This, as I wrote you then, hung on an almost mystic belief in Mr Roosevelt, a combination of wishful thinking and great personal loyalty.

In this town, and I believe it is a typical eastern industrial city, the unemployed are as despairing a crew as I have ever seen. Young men say, 'We'll never find work.' Men over forty say, 'Even if there was any work we wouldn't get it; we're too old.' They have been on relief too long; this is like the third year of the war when everything peters out into grey resignation. Moreover they are no longer sustained by confidence in the President. The suggested $50 monthly security wage seems to have done the trick. They are all convinced that $50 will be the coming flat wage for the unemployed, regardless of size of family. They say to you, quietly, like people who have been betrayed but are too tired to be angry, 'How does he expect us to live on that? Does he know what food costs, what rents are? How can we keep clothes on the children?'

Formerly everyone used to ask me about the President, used to speak admiringly of him. He is rarely mentioned now, only in answer to questions. Local labour organizers and local unemployed council leaders say that if he were up for election tomorrow he would lose. They explain this by saying that labour feels the NRA has let them down and the relief clients feel there is no hope for them; industry will not take them back and relief is going on, as a mere sop to starvation.

I bring this up not because I think the politics of it

will interest you (if in fact it has political significance) but because it is important in understanding the unemployed now. They used to be sustained by their personal faith: this belief made a good many things easier to bear and I think appreciably contributed to keeping them sane. Having lost that, their despair is a danger to themselves if to no one else.

I have been following the unemployed Leagues and Councils closely. First I must say that I think our local administrators are a droll bunch psychologically, in relation to these protest groups. Put any man in authority and he suddenly becomes an embryonic capitalist, an employer of labour. The similarity in relationships between relief administrators and dissatisfied relief clients and industrial magnates and dissatisfied labour would be laughable if it weren't sad and revolting. The Camden adminstrator now, in effect, is refusing to recognize the rights of labour to organize. (Humorous violation of 7A.[1]) He does not want to deal with the unemployed Councils or Leagues through their chosen representatives, but says that he will see any man individually, and discuss with him his personal complaint. There is a strike going on amongst the unemployed in New Jersey; I don't know the extent of this strike. Relief headquarters minimize it, and relief clients, in meetings, brag about it. The reason is that relief clients get a 20 per cent bonus for doing work relief, and they get their money in cash. The way they have figured it out, they are working for that 20 per cent bonus only and they regard it as sweated labour. The whole thing is hard to understand— you have to start from the original principle that society owes a man a living and that he has a *right* to relief. Therefore, his relief food order is not a gift, it's his inalienable heritage, not to be considered as part of his pay.

[1] Clause in the National Recovery Act guaranteeing the right to form and join labour unions.

They are very confused in their talk. (The Unemployed Council meetings are deplorably rudderless, but more of that later.) They talk about lowering the wage standard of their brothers in industry, by accepting these relief wages. They talk about the laxness of supervision on the work relief projects and say it isn't a job; it's an excuse to put in cash-paid parasites as supervisors, foremen, timekeepers, etc. They say that the object is to get as many men loafing on projects as possible, so that friends and political appointees can get these supervisory jobs with cash salaries. They talk of the waste of money and how it affects the taxpayer. (A long rambling speech about how 'we aren't taxpayers you say, but every time we buy food or clothing we are paying taxes, and our children will have to continue to carry this burden.')

The meetings themselves are an eye-opener. They are sad and dispirited, with the speakers trying very hard to get up a little enthusiasm from the audience. Obviously the principal lack is a lack of leadership. The men who head these organizations are all semi-literate (local boys, I don't know about the big shots, but am going to find out.) They are reasonable, baffled guys. With one exception: a sinister personage whose home I visited, a definite misfit (physically and mentally) in any society. It is to be noted that a large proportion of the unemployed have swung away from him saying he's 'radical.' Most of the reasoning and emotion of these people passes comprehension; why not be radical, for God's sake, they have every excuse. They are as Tory in their way as the Chamber of Commerce.

In all cases, the whole Unemployed Council performance seems particularly sad and futile; but I think it serves an admirable purpose. To wit: it gives these people something to do, keeps the leaders busy, gives the followers a feeling of belonging somewhere; someone is interested in them, they realize that they have neighbours, other people in the same miserable boat. This cuts the danger of helpless solitary stagnation, somewhat avoids the tendency to stay at home alone and rot in despair. The meetings take the place of entertainment (the movies, a pool room, a saloon), and are their only chance of having any social life.

At one big meeting I attended the high point of the evening was a prize draw: chances were a penny apiece and the prizes were food: a chicken, a duck, four cans of something, and a bushel of potatoes. At the risk of seeming slobbery, I must say it was one of the most forlorn and pitiful things I have ever seen in my life. These people had somehow collected a few pennies (what money was left over after the prizes had been bought was to pay for gasoline for a ten-year-old car which drove the chairman around to meetings.) They waited with passionate eagerness while the chances were read out, to see if they were going to be able to take some food home to the family. The man who won the duck said, 'No, we won't eat it, my little girl has been asking for a bunny for Easter and maybe she can make a pet of the duck. She hasn't got anything else to play with.'

There will, I presume, be a growing tendency on the part of those who administer relief to take sides either with industry or labour, depending on their personal prejudices, emotion and background. I have already noted this, in a haphazard way, and in Camden the issue came up clearly. A strike is pending in the New York Ship Building Corp. It will probably take place around May first, and will be a strike for higher wages primarily. The administrator was wondering what to do: should he give relief to the strikers, was their case really good, weren't they being paid enough anyhow? This somewhat clouds the original issue which is to give food to those who must have it and have no other means of obtaining it. One is tempted to point out the extent of FERA subsidization of private industry in that county, by the giving of supplementary relief to people employed in private industry but not making a subsistence living. One might also note that FERA preserves a fine labour market for these seasonal industries, which casually lay people off knowing they can always get them back when they need them. In fact, when I asked the manager of Campbell Soup how his workers lived during the long pull between tomato seasons (August to December work period approximately), he said, 'Oh, they go on relief.'

The administrator here tells me that business is in a bad way. The three big local concerns are Campbell Soup, RCA Victor, and New York Ship. Victor's has been laying people off steadily, and has closed down its print shop permanently. New York Ship is laying off and the strike will help. Campbell's is in its annual slack period, but will reach peak employment (about 4,500) in August, when tomatoes are in season. Campbell's, so I am told, has an annual payroll of about three million dollars and an annual profit of about ten million dollars. In any case, it is not in a bad way; but is the only industry that thrives.

As a source of employment, however, it is not brilliant. There is a gruelling speed-up (I can testify to this myself and I have backing for the statement from many sources). The tendency is to put two men on a job that requires four. Also, since the strike, one sees the now traditional and epic performance of Union workers getting laid off, never to return if the Campbell management knows it. One of the most fascinating angles of 7A is the slyness manufacturers have acquired to combat it. There were about 1,800 Union members in Campbell's. I should be surprised if any of these people had work there within six months. At least, if all of them stick to the Union—which they won't for the basic and cogent reason of hunger.

Now the Union people are still belonging to the

Union, though dues slip into arrears. I had a revealing talk with the local president of the Union, an American (most of the labour here is Italian, Polish or very illiterate Negro). He is a superior kind of man, intelligent, cynical, calm. He has of course been laid off. He says that the speed with which workers become demoralized is amazing. He expects that his own Union cohorts will stay in the Union for a few months and then drift into unemployed Councils or Leagues. He says also that it's terrible to see how quickly they let everything slide; it takes about three months for a man to get dirty, to stop caring about how his home looks, to get lazy and demoralized and (he suspects) unable to work.

This matter—the demoralization point—has interested me; I didn't originally bring it up, but found the unemployed themselves talking about it, either with fear or resignation. And a labour organizer with whom I spoke repeated statements they had made. (All of this voluntarily, no 'leading the witness.') For instance: I went to see a man aged 28. He had been out of steady work for six years. He lived on a house boat and did odd jobs of salvaging and selling wood and iron. He told me that it took from three to six months for a man to stop going around looking for work. 'What's the use, you only wear out your only pair of shoes and then you get so disgusted.' That phrase, 'I get so disgusted . . .' is the one I most frequently hear to describe how they feel. You can understand what it means: it's a kind of final admission of defeat or failure or both. Then the man began talking about the new works programme and he said, 'How many of them would work if they had the chance? How many of them even could work?'

Sometimes the unemployed themselves say: 'I don't know if I could do a real job right away, but I think I'd get used to it.'

The Union organizer, already mentioned, is connected with the building trades. There is some small municipal job on (I didn't see it) dealing with making a subway under the street. They have hired the unemployed to do it. He said they had more accidents on that job than they normally had on a big construction job, with men working on scaffolding and really having cause for accidents. He said, 'They get so clumsy; they forget how to do their job and then they seem just weak-like.'

I still believe that if men were offered a living wage and a good stiff piece of work which they could accept as work, they'd come across all right. But they regard work relief as made work; and God knows we aren't giving living wages. Americans don't work for love alone and precious few of them (after from four to six years of unemployment) work to keep their pride green.

Generalizing (probably accurately), the unskilled, uneducated labourer is probably getting used to relief. The middle-class white collar worker is taking it in the neck, horribly.

Housing is unspeakable. No doubt the housing was never a thing of beauty and general admiration around here; but ramshackle houses which have gone without repairs for upwards of five years are shameful places. There is marked overcrowding (and it is to be noted that TB is on the increase). I have seen houses where the plaster had fallen through to the lath, and the basement floated in water. One entire block of houses I visited is so infested with bedbugs that the only way to keep whole is to burn out the beds twice a week and paint the woodwork with carbolic acid, and even so you can just sit around and watch the little creatures crawling all over and dropping from the ceiling . . .

Household equipment nil. Apparently what goes last is the unused overstuffed furniture in the front room. Clothes nil. Really a terrible problem here; not only of protection against the elements (a lot of pneumonia among children: undernourishment plus exposure) but also the fact that having no clothes, these people are cut out of any social life. They don't dare go out, for shame. The men feel it in applying for jobs: their very shabbiness acts against them. I am now talking primarily about the white collar class.

Health: well, they seem to be getting a lot of service here in the system of calling their own doctor who is paid by FERA. The system apparently works here as elsewhere so that the best doctors do not take FERA clients (they do their own charity work in clinics) and some very canny folk, who solicit, get the trade. There are always stories about how badly this works: a man who got treatment at FERA expense for a year for rheumatism. He got no better and his wife asked if she chould change doctors. The new doctor had an X-ray taken and found the man had cancer of the hip. He died within six months.

But by and large, they are getting fairly good treatment I suppose, considering how lousy the medical attention for this class is, all over the country. They do, however, have a bad time getting the medicines prescribed by their doctors. TB is increasing; the hospitals for mental diseases (state and country) have over 1,000 more patients than in 1932, epileptics and feebleminded are increasing. Malnutrition seems prevalent among children but not among adults; and venereal disease is more or less static though an entirely different class is beginning to come to the free clinics.

It appears that the Depression is resulting in a lot of amateur prostitution. This is commented upon by the people who have to deal with the courts and care for delinquent children. The age limit is going down and unmarried mothers are very young. I was talking to a girl about this: she said, 'Well, the girls go out with anybody, you might say, just to have something to do and to forget this mess.' (She herself was on relief, getting something like $2 a week to live on.) I remarked that it was understandable, considering that at least they got a good square meal. And she said, very calmly, 'Meal? No, almost never. Sometimes they get a glass of beer.' It seems to me that this makes a picture, complete in itself. I've seen the girls. Obviously they want clothes, and a little fun. It's grim to think what they're getting for their trouble.

The young are as disheartening as any group, more so, really. They are apathetic, sinking into a resigned bitterness. Their schooling, such as it is, is a joke; and they have never had the opportunity to learn a trade. They have no resources within or without; and they are waiting for nothing. They don't believe in man or God, let alone private industry; the only thing that keeps them from suicide is this amazing loss of vitality: they exist. 'I generally go to bed around seven at night, because that way you get the day over with quicker.'

The Lord Will Provide for England

When you go to London you forget about war. Everything's the same. The high top-heavy buses rumble around with signs that extol laxatives and breakfast foods and inform you that a musical comedy called 'No Sky So Blue' is terrific. The people press against an iron railing before a house in a fashionable square, watching the young ladies and gentlemen inside dance to the tune of an expensive jazz band. In Regent Street, the jewellers' shops seriously display diamond tiaras, which will be seriously bought and actually worn. At the Admiralty Arch, their faces green and violet in the electric light and the coming dawn, stand men and women waiting to get a doughnut and a cup of coffee from the Silver Lady, a charity food van that serves the homeless every day. Red-coated guards pose like wooden Indians before Buckingham Palace and the gentry, in glittering evening dress, stream down Piccadilly while it's still day, on their way to the theatre. It's just as it always was. If you buttonholed every passer-by in Piccadilly Circus and asked: 'Do you think there's going to be a war in Europe?' ninety out of every hundred would say, 'No,' first, and if they stopped to think about it, they'd probably say: 'Well, not this year anyhow . . .'

England is prosperous, that's the thing to remember. Unemployment has dropped from 3,000,000 to 1,700,000. The great rearmament programme gives direct employment to 600,000, which means that families are out shopping again. People have money for a glass of beer or two on Saturday night, and a movie; there are cricket matches to watch on Sunday. People have pretty good homes and the rents are not high; if you work you can eat three times a day. And if the great London press, which sets the tone for the nation—the *Times* and the *Telegraph*, the *Mail* and the *Express*—avoids scaring the readers and agrees heartily with the government policy, that helps to keep people calm too. The radio is also discreetly advised not to underline troublesome issues, so you never tune in to hear of danger: you tune in on news programmes that are as neat and unexciting as the papers. And even the newsreels are trimmed, so that bombed China and bombed Spain are avoided, because the English public is not supposed to relish such horror.

It's all kept quiet, and you forget that across that choppy and uncomfortable Channel lies Europe, and you just think: I am in England, a fine green island, and everybody outside is a foreigner and very likely nasty, and here we'll tend to our own affairs, which means: Business as Usual.

Besides, England hasn't been invaded for a thousand years, and there is no terror to climb back into the memory of her people. In the last war, in all four years, there were only 1,414 people killed by aerial bombardment, and only 270 tons of bombs dropped on the whole country. For your information, it is estimated now that 200 tons of bombs could be dropped per day. And the English don't go in for imagination: imagination is considered to be improper if not downright alarmist.

There is a subway stop in London that rejoices in the name of Elephant and Castle. You buy your ticket and take a moving staircase deep down into the earth to the lowest tunnel, and wait on the platform for the train. All this time you (but only you) are thinking what sturdy bombproof cellars these subway stations make. As each stop comes, more people get out, until finally there are only poor people left. The Elephant and Castle station is in a slum packed with small dark factories: no one would go there for pleasure.

I was looking for Blackfriars Street, and a meeting I never

found. The workers of that neighbourhood were, supposedly, going to get together and talk about the danger of war, and I thought it would be a relief to see some other folk as worried as I was. I walked down many streets, all stony and treeless, between the two-storey houses that look painfully alike. In all the windows were shabby lace curtains, and against the light you could see from time to time a man or woman silhouetted, bent over a washbowl, or stretching and yawning, ready for sleep after a hard day. Children played noisily in the streets on homemade scooters, and it was as hot as Marseilles. The wrestling hall where the meeting was to be held was deserted, and finally, tired of walking about this barren place under the pale night sky, I stopped in at the Friar's Snack Bar.

It was a small dirty room with a wooden bar and a smell of fried fish, and crowded with the men from the neighbourhood. They were talking of the Schmeling-Louis fight. A fat pink boy named Basil burst in and ordered soda pop and started a whole new train of thought by calling for bets on greyhound racing. 'What we're interested in, Miss,' a man explained, 'is the fights, a bit of dog racing and a bit of horse racing.' This man, the wit of the crowd, stated that he had done two years and fifty-four days of the last war. 'I remember it,' he said 'All those bits of iron flying about, it fair gives me nightmares now.'

'Do you know Robert Taylor, Miss?' asked a young man who had just parked his bicycle outside.

I said I was sorry but I didn't.

'Hey, get back to politics.' This was an errand boy talking. 'I like discussing politics meself.'

'America's a silly kind of country, ain't it?' said Basil. 'Anyone can carry firearms, can't they? We read all about it in American detective magazines.'

And then, finally, wistfully, a thin boy in a mechanic's suit said: 'Is it true you kin earn $2,000 a week in America just repairing radios in your spare time?'

But no one had said anything about a future war; no one had said anything about Spain or Austria or China; no one had wondered about the $1,715,000,000 that's going into the English rearmament programme this year. No one said: what are we going to do with the guns and the planes and the tanks and the destroyers, when we get them?

I began to think, after a time, that anxiety was a luxury belonging exclusively to politicians. At least they talked about war in the House of Commons, and for once you didn't feel that the Channel was as wide as the Atlantic; for once you heard the danger named. The Opposition, sitting on the left of that narrow wood-panelled hall, began shouting: 'Where's the Prime Minister; where's the Prime Minister?' and there was anger in their voices. The galleries were jammed. Beneath the speaker's gallery was the great table where the speaker himself presides, and on the government side, Oliver Stanley had his long thin legs hiked up on the table, and farther down to the left was the handsome white head of Lloyd George and across from him, on the government side, was Winston Churchill, with the plump, witty face. Major Attlee, the leader of the Opposition, pale and thin, with a scholar's shoulders, rose to speak, and the House hushed: 'All of us would do anything we can to keep this country from war . . .' 'Hear! Hear!' from both sides of the room. 'If the Prime Minister says he cannot protect the lives of British sailors, he'll be the first Prime Minister in one hundred years to say it . . . The plain fact is that the Prime Minister has backed Franco to win . . .' They were talking about the bombed British ships, but what mattered was: is this government keeping us out of war, or getting us into it, worse and deeper? The place was tight with anger. Mr Chamberlain spoke carefully, not frankly, and suddenly from the public balconies, loud, surprising voices rose. 'We're sailors,' one of them shouted, 'and the Prime Minister says Franco can murder us.' 'We want justice,' another screamed. Then a man called out, with the attendants holding his legs and arms and muffling his mouth: 'Social Credit is the only way,' and laughter ran through the House.

Down in the Commons' bar, after the session, comments moved quickly among the journalists and MPs. 'Perhaps the government should just clean up the monuments and things and turn England into a tourist country.' 'Maybe we ought to grow bulbs and have galleries full of Rembrandts and be like Holland: they say Holland was a great maritime power once.' 'Did you ever see such a deplorable fizzle?' 'You people just want to get us into war: you're all Reds . . .'

Talking about the possibility of war is called 'war-mongering' and not a nice thing to do. But nevertheless all England speaks of air raid precautions. In England, you can easily prepare on a national scale against air raids, without talking or thinking about war, and wondering where the raids will come from, when or why.

The Home Secretary appealed for one million civilian volunteers to carry out the Air Raid Precautions plan. There are to be 600,000 A.R.P. wardens, citizens of over thirty, respected in the community, who cannot undertake active military service; their duty will be to direct the population of England and avert panic when the bombs begin to fall. These wardens are also liaison officers between all the other A.R.P. services. For instance, they must summon the A.R.P. fire brigade, which will help the regular firemen to fight incendiary bombs. (The English government seems to remember Guernica, and how it stood like a black skeleton in the Basque country after the Junkers passed over.) The wardens will also call the A.R.P. First Aid unit—250,000 doctors, nurses and ambulance drivers throughout the country— who are supposed to give immediate care to bomb victims. (But it's sorry work. When a city is bombed, houses collapse and there is little to do for the people who scream until they die. It is sometimes even hard to decide who the dead are, because the bombs make very big and very messy explosions. It's sad work for a doctor who has spent his life trying to fit people for a healthy life.) The wardens must also send the Evacuation and Decontamination squads to the places where they are needed. These squads are not volunteers, but trained municipal servants—street sweepers, sewer inspectors, garbage collectors, city workmen—who have the job of collecting debris after bombings, washing the streets after gas attacks, propping up the gutted and collapsing houses, and digging out the bodies of the dead. (And all the time you're digging, the planes are there, and it is strange how dark a city gets even on a sunny day, when the bombs fall, and it is horrible how slowly men work when they are trying to lift the bricks and cement, the granite and wood and steel of caved-in buildings off the bodies of still-living people. It is also very sad to prop up a house, while the people who once lived in it wait in tragic bewildered silence on the pavement, wondering where they will live next.)

England is gas-conscious. There are forty million gas masks already stored in government depots, and all over England people are being fitted with the ordinary civilian gas mask, which sells for about 75 cents and will be given away free in time of war. The ordinary gas mask is a small rubber affair, with isinglass over the eyes, a boxlike snout that contains the filter to keep out gas (but you can exhale tobacco smoke through the mask, which makes some people suspect that the masks are not exactly 100 per cent safe) and a narrow face-covering to keep the mask on. ('Of course you can get burned in it by mustard gas,' said the salesman, 'but then you can get burned in all of them.')

It is not sure at all that gas is a practical weapon against civilian populations, but it has been proved in Spain and China that a 500-pound bomb is a real horror. However, underground shelters against high-explosive bombs are not being built, because they are too expensive; and the main plan of A.R.P. is dispersal, which means that when the sirens howl out the warning, the citizens of England are supposed to go home and wait and try to think about something else. The people are told that they can make their homes gasproof by sticking old rags and strips of adhesive tape over leaky walls, and can keep their window-panes from shattering when bombs fall in the neighbourhood by pasting three sheets of cellophane over their windows. They are sold (for $7.50) with a sand bucket and a shovel and a small fire hose: the idea is that you hurry forth (perhaps wearing dark glasses against the glare of burning London) with the shovel and scoop up an incendiary bomb and plop it into the sand bucket and then turn on the fire hose. Seven booklets are put out by the Home Office, to teach people how to behave during the air raids, easy lessons for beginners. Also, you are informed in advance that—if you work in A.R.P.—you get $5,000 if you die or are blinded, or lose both feet or a hand and a foot. You get $2,500 if you are half blind or lose only one foot or hand, and so down the list of miseries.

In fact, A.R.P. is not the joke that people think and say it is, though as adequate precaution against air raids it is far from perfect. But the usefulness of it is propaganda: the people are being accustomed to the idea of war, after twenty years of excellent and effective peace propaganda on the part of pacifists and the League of Nations supporters. Also, the government very likely feels that a prepared civilian England cannot be terrorized into demanding a quick armistice. Moreover, this huge organization of personnel means that everyone in England will be under surveillance by some government authority, and when the air raid wardens are instructed to keep up the 'morale' of the people, it is no idle order.

Meantime classes go on all over England, teaching citizens how to act while being bombed. One particular class was being held in the home of a peeress, and the butler was very busy finding pencils for the ladies who had forgotten to bring theirs. You paid to join the class, thus insuring that no strangers would get in and worry you while taking notes. The lecturer was instructing the ladies (all attentive, the feathered hats and veils bowed over notebooks) on air raid warnings. His voice, cool and educated, droned over the pale green drawing room: "The alarm will be two minutes of a varying note on the sirens—the all-clear is two minutes of a steady note—have you got that?—the warning for gas attacks will be given by the police and the air raid wardens, who are to sound rattles. Of course you can't smoke in your shelter rooms, because of saving oxygen—it would be just as well to take tinned foods with you into your shelters, and as you're going to be down there for some little time, you might as well take games that can be played without physical exertion . . .' I thought of the people of Spain, the dark-faced women, drawn with hunger and anxiety, standing in doorways as the bombers passed over, silver and immaculate, dropping death. I thought of the crazy-eyed children running through the streets in hope of shelter and of the old people who could not run. I also thought that in Spain no one ever had time to think of panic, and that I had never heard anyone suggest taking games into a bomb cellar, where hundreds of desperately silent people wait for the planes to pass. I remembered how we stood on the balcony in the dawn in Barcelona and watched the searchlights hunting, and listened to the explosions, and never went anywhere for safety, believing that with bombers over a city you are lucky or nothing.

Reflecting on these things, I heard a voice and looked up to see a white-haired lady with small pearls in her ears, saying somewhat crossly to the lecturer, 'I do think ten minutes is an awfully small warning; it doesn't give you much time to turn off the lights and close the windows and get everything ready to go down into the shelter.' Whereupon the lecturer said apologetically, 'Well, I'm afraid you'll have to expect that.' The English are fortunate, I thought, they haven't any imagination at all. I asked the gentlewoman who was secretary of this course (and she stared at me) whether anyone here knew what was being talked about: had any of them considered Spain and China. Had anyone the remotest idea of the exhausting, persistent menace of death from the air. She said: 'You do lifeboat drill on a ship, don't you, but you don't expect the ship to sink . . .'

The poor are pretty indifferent to all this: they haven't the money to buy gasproof rooms and have no gardens in which to sink bombproof cellars, and besides they aren't told very much, because there's no use disturbing them. But at John Lewis, Silk Mercers, in London, you can get your sitting room gasproofed for a minimum of $60 and up to $2,500; you can buy an oilskin suit, like a fisherman's, that has been specially treated against gas, and in which you will look a fright but never mind, for about $15; you can buy a really efficient gas mask for the same sum, and you can buy special electric torches and air purifiers and all sorts of contraptions. Business is booming.

Another firm called Air Guard Limited will build you a cosy cellar against high-explosive bombs in your garden, where four people can be quite at home for $500. And if you have the money you can live in Bentinck Close, out near Regent's Park, a 'lovely location' as the agent will tell you, where there is a fine gas- and bombproof cellar provided for the tenants. The prospectus of this apartment house prints a map of the bombproof cellar with all details; there are lockers and bunks and shower rooms and special air purifiers. As the minimum rent is $2,150 a year, not many young people live there.

The organized Left complains bitterly about A.R.P. saying that the rich can buy individual protection in cities, or else leave for safer areas, but that the poor are stuck with three sheets of cellophane as protection against high-explosive bombs. Moreover, as Miss Ellen Wilkinson, Labour MP, asked, 'Is the government aware of how the women of the country feel at having this matter of grave importance to them all put entirely into the hands of society ladies and debutantes.' Besides this sort of comment, there are endless jokes: the young man-about-town who suggested that the next great scandal would be when a duchess, with inkstained fingers, was caught cheating at her A.R.P. warden exams . . . But despite talk, A.R.P. goes on, and it is the greatest peacetime effort England has ever made to prepare her people for the idea of war.

Obviously, no one, except the general staff and other responsible authorities, knows exactly what England will do in time of war. However, the main effort now is to protect England, the heart of the empire, and London, the heart of England. It is generally felt that if London were knocked out, by successive surprise air raids in the early days of a war, everything would go to pot. So the plans of England are defensive: England is going to protect itself first.

On authority, one learns that the east coast is protected by a triple line of defence: this defence consists of airfields, from which fighting planes can rise for immediate combat, anti-aircraft guns and searchlights. The air force, as far as can be determined, is 2,382 planes of which 1,500 are stationed in England. The latest fighter, called the Hawker Hurricane, is supposed to have a speed of 400 miles an hour and probably hasn't. At any rate, as various pilots point out, it is doubtful whether a man (and after all a pilot cannot be constructed but has only regulation heart and lungs) could fight at that speed. Everybody knows that pilots can and often do lose consciousness momentarily, rounding pylons. If a plane cruises at 400 m.p.h., it would be diving and manoeuvering at a superior speed. All this is speculation; the people who know about the Hawker Hurricanes are those who make them and run them. At any rate, this plane is the present flower of the combat air force, and one of the mainstays in the defence scheme.

The gun that is to bring down enemy planes is the famous 3.7 gun, of which there are supposed to be twelve in England, and about which talk rages in the press and Commons. A military authority estimated the ceiling of this gun at 40,000 feet; it is stated to have a shell-burst four times as great as that of the old 3-inch guns, and the time of flight of the shell between gun and target is supposed to be halved. All of which means that it's a dangerous gun, with the highest ceiling and the largest shell-burst of any now made, and if there are 1,000 of them, as desired, it would be extremely uncomfortable for enemy planes to fly over England. The air defence is being enlarged into five divisions, with a manpower of 100,000. The duty of these men will be to serve the anti-aircraft guns and work the searchlight barrage.

The searchlights are the third defence measure: it is planned to have England so organized that planes flying in from the sea would be caught in a beam of light immediately and would be carried, from searchlight battery to searchlight battery, in an unending band of light all the way inland. Presumably, this same system of airfields, gun and searchlight batteries would encircle important manufacturing cities and be cross-stitched across Great Britain. Coupled with planes, guns and lights are the sound detectors, located in greatest profusion along the east coast, from which direction the enemy will come; they will serve to warn both the army defence forces and the civilian population. The worry of all Englishmen who think about it is: have we enough planes, guns, searchlights, sound detectors, and men trained to handle these things? The answer they give is: No.

Germany is supposed to have 2,600 planes and an air force of 130,000 men. Italy is supposed to have 2,100 planes and 50,000 in its air force. So England is building planes like mad and trying to increase the personnel of her air force from its present 83,000 as rapidly as possible, and meanwhile England stalls, for all the world to see, and her people say: Well, in a year we'll be ready . . .

Various other defence measures are talked about. There is the famous and fantastic balloon barrage. The idea is to send up a fleet of small balloons, hitched together, which will float at a certain height. They could be a sort of fence along the coast, or a circular aerial wall above London, or both. Hanging from these balloons, which will be resting in the ether about 3,000 metres or more high, will be steel cables, like the railings on an iron fence but very long. If you hit a bird, going 400 m.p.h. in the air, it can be fatal. It is evident that if the balloon barrage stayed in place (and people seem to think it can be perfectly controlled) it would create a deadly obstacle. At best it would make night flying suicidal, and at the least it would keep enemy planes so high that they could not do accurate bombing.

There is also mention of the possible evacuation of London and the Channel coast, the moving of factories to the west coast, where supposedly they would be out of range of bombers. There is likewise talk of underground petrol and arms depots on the west coast. You cannot find out to what extent work has started on camouflaging or building underground munitions factories.

England needs 50,000 tons of imported food per day, and must control the seas or give up. When the new and rushed construction programme is completed, England will have an approximate 399 naval units: capital ships, destroyers, cruisers, aircraft carriers, etc. The fleet would probably again blockade the North Sea, but no one seems too concerned over the Mediterranean. You are told that after all, England hasn't always had the Suez Canal, and that commerce could be diverted around the Cape of Good Hope and be protected as it crossed the Atlantic (not hostile water anyhow, until nearing England) by the fleet. You are told that the Mediterranean could simply be bottled up, and there—you suppose—the Italian fleet would harry French communications with Africa, but that is the lookout of the French.

It is assumed that a blockade of the North Sea would greatly help England's allies (a very sound assumption, considering the last war) and that England would also send an air force to the Continent to aid her allies. You do not hear any plans for shipping a huge land army to the Continent, as was done in the last war, and Captain Liddell Hart, one of England's ranking military authorities, strongly warns against sending a large land army abroad. The English have always had the privilege of fighting their wars somewhere else, but now England is preparing to fight in her own air, over her own fields and cities, and the prospect is pleasing to no one.

The soundest reasoning of those who do not believe in an oncoming war goes like this: You bomb Sheffield, we bomb Cologne; you bomb Newcastle, we bomb the Saar. Who gets anything? It's equal, hopeless, crazy, and no one is going to start it . . . As one prominent military man said: 'No one can really win a war now. The only hope is to convince your adversary first that he certainly can't win it.'

We went to call on the swellest bit of army I ever saw. The Territorial Army is all volunteer, and in time of war it would be rushed into the defence of England. A thousand of these Territorials belong to the Honourable Artillery Company, which has its headquarters in the financial centre of London, the City, and drills on a smooth stretch of green lawn, whose turf is no doubt worth its weight in gold. You cannot get into the Honourable Artillery Company unless you are proposed and seconded, as if you were joining a swank club. It is really an officers' training school; in time of war more the 60 per cent of their men get commissions. At six o'clock in the evening the young stockbrokers begin drifting in with their rolled umbrellas, derby hats and stiff collars, and presently they emerge on the lawn in khaki mechanics' uniforms to drill. They must go to fifty evening drills a year for four years, and to two weeks' camp per year and then they are graduated, so to speak, and put on the reserve list. After an evening's drill, they meet in a long, low dining room and eat excellent food, and later go into the great hall, where their old flags hang in lacy blackened shreds from the panelled walls, and have their drinks and the comfortable snobbish feeling of belonging to the oldest military organization in the world.

Conversation ran like this. The colonel: 'There's been a great revolution in English thought in the last few years.'

I: 'Really?'

The colonel: 'Yes. A few years ago everyone was pacifist and soppy but now they're coming round to seeing reason.'

The lieutenant: 'Everybody's fighting disarmament. A really strong army will keep us out of war.'

The captain: 'We're twenty per cent overstrength right now. There was a rush of recruiting, after Hitler went into Austria.'

The lieutenant: 'We had some of those Nazi chaps over here last week. Gruppenfuehrer, I think they're called. Very nice people. Had a fine time with them. They thought our miniature gun range a marvel.'

But no one wondered whom England was arming against, or whom England was trying to stay out of war with, or what a war might be about.

The auxiliary air force, a civilian volunteer branch of the regular air force, consists of 13 squadrons, with airfields throughout England. One combat group has its planes and clubroom at Hendon and we went there to lunch with some young gentlemen who are pilots. Like the Honourable Artillery Company, this particular squadron is very chic. The gentleman pilots were delightful and would speak of anything but war. They come out and fly during week ends, and those who do not work fly almost all the time. There is a theory that boys of nineteen make the best pilots and some qualifications are whether you drive a fast car, ride to hounds or ski, all dangerous and expensive sports.

So England for one year alone spends $1,715,000,000 rearming. And young men volunteer for the land and air forces and civilians join the Air Raid Precautions work, and the regular army and navy recruit. But such questions as: Where is the war coming from, and why? When will it happen? What will bring it about, and can it be stopped? are not common questions at all. An old war horse, a retired colonel with a game leg, showing me gas mask depots, said: 'You just declare war and get together some redcoats and some brass bands and there'll be no trouble recruiting. People didn't know what they were fighting about in the last war, and they won't know in this one, and no one asks. Why should they?'

I drove north to Newcastle, through that smoky belt of cities where armaments are manufactured, through Coventry, Birmingham, Middlesbrough, Stockton and Sheffield. I believed that if I went where the planes and guns, the tanks and shells, the ships and bombs were being made, I'd find people thinking and talking, asking themselves what all this was about, this rush and boom, this prosperity built on destruction. I was, however, wrong.

In Coventry, they were having a parade with floats, to raise money for the local hospital. A lady with a huge muslin rose like a headlamp on her hat, standing in the crowd, started the conversation. A float had just passed called 'The League of Notions,' and thereupon she remarked that people who fought against bolshies were the only ones who were really trying to protect England. From that she went into A.R.P.; Lady Beatrice Something-or-Other, the local aristocrat, was apparently heading up the good work, and my friend remarked: 'I always think blue blood tells, don't you?' I said I knew very little about the subject. Then I spoke of recruiting, and she said: 'Of course, the young men all say they won't fight, but they will as soon as it starts.' And meanwhile the parade went on with gypsy floats and Snow White and the Seven Dwarfs and everything you can name, and Coventry is rich because cars are built here and planes, and everyone has work and money to spend and hoop-la for tomorrow.

In a Birmingham pub, the truck driver, with tobacco-stained stringy moustaches, said proudly, over his beer, 'The old country can't be beat.' A sailor came in and sat down at the next table with two women. The first woman said to the second, 'Don't your feet ache, dearie?' From that a discussion of the weather started that interested everyone. The second woman wore rimmed glasses and black cotton gloves and was fat and a charwoman, and full of spirit. She was ready to fight all England's enemies but wasn't clear as to who exactly had bombed those boats in Spain, anyhow it was a scandal. Two old people came in, sat down, ordered beer and drank it in total silence. They had very white hair and steady, unseeing blue eyes, both of them. This was Saturday night and the pub would stay open until ten and everyone was having a fine time. They all spoke to one another practically in whispers, very shy. No one was reading a newspaper, and no one talked politics. (Remember Czechoslovakia, the papers eagerly read and the speculation? We're on an island now, and the world is someplace else. This is England and tomorrow there is probably a cricket match.)

And all the way, forever and ever, the two-storey brick houses, growing straight out of the earth, each one like the last and all attached together. Fairly solid, fairly comfortable, quite cheap to rent, and horribly ugly. And the smokestacks against the sky, and the grimy town, and the pale factory people.

At Stockton, in the square, hemmed in by Penny's Bank and Barclay's and the National Provincial Bank, the Communist party was having a meeting. The speaker was hoarse and the crowd apathetic and it looked like rain. The dingy city lay in flat brick streets out from the square. 'The English flag does not protect English sailors,' the speaker shouted, but no one seemed to care. A young man in tweeds, selling Communist pamphlets, started a conversation. It sounded like a bad mystery thriller and was as depressing as the scenery: 'Germany could drop an army on to English soil from these new bombers, and if we were attacked we'd fight like the Spanish people. If we're going to be aggressors and sent over to fight Germany, then we'd join up and spread sedition in the ranks. The Communist party doesn't want war with anybody, even Germany.'

At Newcastle, a man who looked charmingly like Santa Claus, the president of a union of a million and a half shipwrights, told me: 'We go to the government and say: "You ask us to make these armaments, but what for? Who's the enemy? What's the danger?" All they'll say is: "We want two years' production in one. We don't know anything." ' With a great weariness he said: 'I address mass meetings and tell the workers that the peace of the world depends on our foreign policy and they begin to read the racing news.'

For three miles the Vickers-Armstrong plant stretches sootily along the Newcastle road. In a pub across from the factory gate, some workers were having a noonday beer. I asked an old woman with a frizzled permanent, who was drinking with them, if she had a gas mask. She roared with laughter and said she'd lived right here opposite the factory for twenty years and never had a gas mask and the only time she'd been gassed was on beer. The young cop on point duty outside remarked that he didn't mind whether there was a war or not; it'd be a bit of a change. He didn't think, however, that he'd see France; he thought they'd be going direct to Germany . . . And opposite the Vickers plant is a school, and all around are the homes of the workers, and everyone knows (or so you'd have thought) that munitions factories are targets for bombers—and there is Newcastle on the coast near the North Sea, but who was worrying?

The A.R.P. headquarters of Newcastle are in a fashionable neighbourhood, and formerly this was the house of a noble lord. Now the basement is full of gas masks, and trenches are being dug in the garden, and in the back courtyard is a little doll's house affair where you can practise being gassed, with your gas mask on. 'Nobody will start a war,' said the Air Raid Warden, confidently, 'because we shall be too strong.'

The shipyards are doing a huge business. The steel-grey director of one of the great firms received us, and was very surprised when asked whether he thought he was building these destroyers, cruisers, battleships for use or for looks. He hadn't bothered about it; that was the politicians' job. 'If a war started, we'd all march,' he said. 'But it's not my business to think about it.'

In Sheffield, having been politely but firmly removed from an arms factory, I went to visit the A.R.P. office. I heard such titbits as that builders were digging bombproof cellars into gardens to attract buyers to new houses, and that a large block of flats that catered to the clerk-employee class had a bombproof cellar but no one had asked to see it. 'People see how easy it is to protect themselves,' the A.R.P. official said, removing his pince-nez (after some more talk about cellophane), 'so they aren't afraid.'

'They'd better be,' I said. 'Sheffield is twelve minutes by air from the coast. And it's the biggest arms centre in England, isn't it, and what do you suppose bombers are after?'

'The government must know what it's doing,' he said, with dignity.

I remembered all the others in buses and bars and drawing rooms and clubs. I remembered the young man with a famous name, saying: 'Of course we run England but we do it very well. There isn't a war yet, is there? And if there is one, we'll win it.' The truck driver had also said: 'This country can't be beat.' Everyone who hadn't said it thought it. I remembered the cook, rather startling in a large black straw hat, coming to get the day's orders, and her comments on the world: 'I'm sure Sir Samuel Hoare—that's the Prime Minister, isn't it, Modom?—is doing his very best for us.' It didn't matter that Sir Samuel wasn't Prime Minister; after all, millions of her fellow countrymen shared her view. I thought of the lady MP remarking over coffee: 'All this A.R.P. talk is horrid, it just makes people war-mad. No one's going to bomb London. Nonsense. Why should they?' It rose from England like mist; it was as real as the London fog: *everything's going to be all right—somehow.* And at last I thought, well, they certainly believe it, so maybe it's true: the Lord will provide for England.

Obituary of a Democracy

On all the roads in Czechoslovakia, the army was going home. You would see them walking in small groups or alone, not walking fast and not walking well, but just going back from the frontiers as they had been told to do. Once in a while you would see a company, with its officer leading, marching along; but not the way an army marches to war. People would stand at the side of the road and watch them in silence. No one spoke and no one cheered, and the soldiers' faces were like the faces of the civilians, sad and bewildered and somehow hurt or ashamed. Sometimes soldiers would come by, with faded flowers in their caps, standing up in the commandeered trucks. But they were not singing, they were not calling to the girls. And then you would pass the artillery, the short-nosed, khaki-coloured, clean, strong guns, twelve of them, twenty of them, hauled by quick small cars; and the people watched the guns go by, in silence and despair.

At night, the headlights of your car would pick out a line of horses, three abreast, led by a cavalryman, forty horses, sixty horses, more than you could count, sleek and well-fed, being led back to the farmers who had given them to the army. In every village you could see the khaki-covered wagons, drawn up in a semicircle in the village square, and the soldiers, like gypsies, camped around their carts, waiting to move to the next place, farther from the frontier—home.

The rain-dark sky gleamed over the woods and in every

hollow there was a little lake. Peasants worked in the fields, kneeling to cut the sugar beets. The pale, cement-coloured villages lay in the ripples of the green land. And there on the road were the soldiers, like waifs, like hoboes, begging a lift.

A man waved to us and we stopped. He ran, banging his small suitcase against his legs. He was a corporal and wore thick glasses.

'Where do you want to go?'

'I'm going home,' he said without gladness. 'It is two villages farther down the road.'

He began to talk, all by himself, as if he had to say it to somebody whether he was understood or not. 'You realize we were all alone,' he said. 'England and France will see for themselves when it is Alsace-Lorraine he wants, or the colonies. Even the Poles will see when he wants the Corridor. And now we are going to be very poor. It will be hard for us to live and it will be hard for the Sudetens to live. But what could we do, as we were alone?'

'Your family will be waiting,' I said to cheer him up.

'I have one son,' he said. 'I am sorry for him'

They stopped you all along the road, everywhere. Trains weren't running: railroad lines that once led to their homes now ran through Germany; buses had been conscripted for the army. They walked very wearily and without haste, and they raised their arms, asking for a lift, but they did not seem to care whether you took them along or not.

The army scarcely knew where it was going. Men would ask you on the road if you knew whether such a village was German now, or Czech. Or had Poland taken it, or had it fallen to Hungary? They did not know where their families were. 'I live in Teplitz,' a middle-aged man said, and he held his trench cap tight in his hands, frightened and worried. 'But my wife will have gone with the children. She would not be safe there. But where would she be? Do you know where the people are from Teplitz?'

Those who lived in the part of Czechoslovakia that still remained did not know what work there would be, because so much had been lost: mines and factories and railroads and fields.

So where would a man work now? In a café near Tabor some soldiers were talking over the newspapers.

'There are going to be labour camps for the unemployed,' one of them said.

'There are no unemployed in Czechoslovakia,' another said.

'Yes, there are,' the first one said, leaning close to the paper and reading the small, smeared print. 'It says that in the months of July and August there were 160,000 unemployed in the whole state, but now of course there will be a great many, since the Germans have taken so much, and as we are poor we must now have labour camps.'

'Like Germany,' a third soldier said bitterly. 'Labour camps for the Czechs. As if we were Germans.' He spoke slowly in an angry, ashamed voice. Being a soldier was one thing—a soldier was a free man who fought gladly for his state. But to be herded into camps to work, when you had always worked proudly and freely, coming back at night to your home, your own things, your wife and your garden—that was another matter.

'We cannot help it,' the first one said. 'We cannot do what we like now.'

So there they were, everywhere, the army that never had a chance to fight. They had given up their fortifications that they would have held against aviation, artillery and infantry until they were dead. Their frontier had been pushed back, behind the mountains and the forests that they could have defended, and now the frontier was a mad zigzag across open indefensible country. All that remained to them was the third line of defence in the north, a neat double row of steel spools with barbed-wire twisted on them, a neat black row like cross-stitching cutting across the open fields, with here and there a camouflaged pillbox, looking like a haystack, with anti-tank guns in it. But the Czech army never thought it would be driven back to the third line; the army was proud and it was good.

It cost four million dollars a day to mobilize the army, and now it was going home. It cost four hundred million dollars to build the great Czech Maginot Line, a copy of the French defences constructed under French orders and on French plans, and now that was lost, and its secret, the secret of the French Maginot Line, belonged to the Germans. (But a Czech officer told me that when the Germans came to take over the fortifications he walked through them with a German officer, and the German looked at these defences with awe, and said, 'We would have lost hundreds of thousands of men getting through here, and maybe we couldn't have done it.') In two years it cost the people of Czechoslovakia seven hundred and fifty million dollars to arm themselves; in six weeks, just before the peace, they gave in voluntary contribution twenty million dollars to the National Defence Fund. They had never counted the cost because they were the outpost of France in Central Europe, they were a democracy, and they were prepared to fight with their allies for what they believed. But now all this meant nothing, the country was helpless, and the army was going home.

On 23 September at 4.30 p.m. there was a telephone call from London to the Czech Foreign Office, stating that England and France agreed they could no longer take the responsibility of counselling the Czechs not to mobilize. At 6 p.m. the same message came by telephone from Paris. At 9 p.m., therefore, on these instructions, the Czech government ordered mobilization for war. Eight hundred thousand men answered the call. Waiters in restaurants put down their trays and ran to their homes to get their equipment. Telegraph operators, taxi drivers, streetcar conductors, theatre ushers, newspaper vendors—all the people who worked at night left their jobs.

People raced through the streets. The mobilization was supposed to take six hours, and it took three. There was no singing, no hysterics, no war fever. But the Czechs were going to defend the land they had won back after three hundred years; they were going to fight for the democracy that they had spent twenty years patiently building. They were a fine army and they knew it; they were trained and disciplined and brave and they knew what they were fighting for. No women wept; no women held their men back; no women were afraid; though they knew that cities were like trenches: in war nowadays there is no safety anywhere, there is no rear guard. So the Czechs moved off in trucks and trains and private cars, and even on bicycles, to join their regiments.

And when they came back it wasn't like a retreat—because a retreat is fierce and alive, and all during a retreat you know that somewhere the army will stand and hold. But there was nothing to hold now: the land had been given away without asking them. They had never fired a shot; they were not allowed to die for their country. They were sent home. It was defeat without battle.

The soldiers weren't the only people walking without purpose, but always inland, away from the frontier. They weren't the only people waiting hopelessly in villages, not knowing where to go or what to do. In the north you got a feeling that the whole country was moving, lost, fleeing. On the road you passed a peasant's cart with a blue enamel pail hanging from it, with a funeral wreath of dead flowers sitting up on top of the mattresses. Four people walked beside it—an old man and an old woman and a younger couple. The women were eating dry bread: they had two slices apiece in their pocketbooks. They did not speak to each other and they walked with great weariness. They had been walking since before dawn and now it was late afternoon; they wanted to go as far from the frontier as they could before they stopped.

They were Czechs; poor people, not what you would call dangerous people; but the new Germany proved unhealthy for all Czechs and they were getting out. Many of their friends had been threatened or had already disappeared. They did not understand what had happened to their country; but their home was lost, their fields lay behind them, work and safety were gone. You could always tell the refugees by the way they walked, though most of them were empty-handed; they had left home too fast and in too great fear. You could tell the refugees by their shoulders, by how they held their heads and by the weariness.

Louny is a town near the new frontier: a stiff little stone city with some factories, some shops, schools. The peasants came here from the rich Bohemian plain to buy and sell; it had a quiet orderly life before all this. There were 11,000 people here in normal times and there have been 7,000 refugees shuttled back and forth in the last days. In the Sokol house, where the Czechs used to practise gymnastics, the refugees sleep. In a room are the bicycles that some of them rode in on; freshly washed stockings and underclothes dry from the upturned legs of desks and tables; straw is piled in the corners to sleep on, some people have mattresses. There are as many as sixty people in a room. They all had homes before; they were people who built their homes solidly to last forever because they believed in them.

Just to look at their faces is enough, but they will talk if you wait. A man of forty is sitting on a table holding his little yellow-haired daughter in his arms. He has a dark face that has grown bitter in this room. He was a mechanic, a German Sudeten.

'Everything is left behind,' he says, 'my tools, the shop, everything.' The child seems still frightened and he holds her gently; it is a strange thing for children to be waked in the night and hurried over the dark roads in silence.

'We were democrats,' the man says. 'Look, I have always lived here; I am a Czech citizen. But I cannot speak Czech and neither can the child; she went to the German school, I did my work always in German, my wife speaks German. I do not think you can say we were very oppressed.'

A man in a cap crossed the room and asked if I knew whether they would be allowed to emigrate to Canada. They say the names of these distant places hopefully, not sure what the country is like or where it is, but maybe there will be safety for them there. Canada, they know, is a safe country for people who believe in democracy.

They have gathered around in a crowd, and a thin, sick-looking man elbows his way into the centre; there are tears on his face. But by now you are used to this, you have seen so many people—men and women—weeping as they talk, not like people who pity themselves, but with helplessness and anger.

'What good does it do if we can go to Canada?' he shouts.

'I have lost my wife: I cannot find my wife and the two children. What are they going to do then—send us to Canada and not send the women? Are we ever to see our families again?'

'Where is your wife?' I said.

'I don't know,' he said; 'in Germany. When we first crossed the frontier coming here, they shipped us all back. Back to Germany, you understand. I had fought with the Czech gendarmes against the Henleinists[1] when they started to terrorize our town. But I was sent back. There were 1,200 of us and when the train got to Chomutov, the Henlein people came and took us all, took us prisoner. I lied and said my home was in Dux, and we got into another train. Then at Dux I escaped. I came back here on foot alone—my wife made me. We saw what the Henleinists were doing to the people who were against them. But I know nothing of my wife. And who will find our families for us?'

His voice had risen. The Red Cross nurse who was in charge here was standing away from them with a stricken face. She kept saying, 'It is worse than sickness; it is worse than death; the poor people.'

There was a woman by the window. She had not spoken. 'Ask her,' the others said, 'ask her what happened to her.' I could see she was weeping. But when she turned to speak her face was carved with anger. 'Look,' she said 'the Henlein police go about the street; they own the street and the village and the country. And so you are walking on the pavement. So one came up to me like this,' and she drew back her arm, 'and struck me across the face, and said I was a dirty Czech and they would make the Czechs, all the Czechs, so small,' her hand reached to the ground, 'in concentration camps. I had seen it before, and I feared for my child. I came here with her, walking, with nothing but the clothes on our backs, and there she is. My daughter has no home, no school, no country. Are the French and English happy now?'

At Kladno, a small, dismal town halfway between Prague and the new frontier, the refugees were all over, wherever there was

[1]Sudeten Nazis

room. They had housed a few hundred in the old people's home. The refugees wandered about among the old women with their kerchiefed heads and the old pipe-smoking men, lost and bewildered. The old people did not care any more: this home was their safety against a mad, uncertain world. But the refugees slept on straw in the clean, bright basement, and worried about tomorrow.

'They cannot send us back to Germany,' a grey-haired Czech said. 'I cannot go. My son was a soldier in the Czech army. He went home after the demobilization with three comrades. He did not know I had escaped. He walked into the house to see me and get clothes, and they arrested him. Only one of the three got away. He has told me. No one is safe,' he said, 'none of us; they cannot send me back.'

The refugees from the German occupied territory were also in the German school at Kladno (there were even German schools, it seems, in these preponderantly Czech towns), Czechs and Germans mixed together, closely bound by disaster, fed by Czech women, and no one cared about their nationality or politics. I have seen the way refugees live in America when the Mississippi rises and drives them from their homes. These people were fleeing too, from something they had not made, as innocent as the people who escape the danger of the rising river.

There were two tiny blond children, too small to speak, who bumbled around on fat legs and got in everyone's way, and everyone loved them. They were called Hansel and Gretel because their names had got lost in transit. They had come here with their blind grandmother, who was now in a hospital with pneumonia; no one knew where their parents were. There was a tall green-eyed boy who kept his shoes neatly shined, who somehow kept his hands and face washed and his shirt clean. (Sleeping on straw, of course, washing when and as he could, waiting in line for his daily soup). His green eyes were sad and he was very alone. His mother was sick and had to stay behind in German territory; his father was in Prague.

'What is your father?' I said, meaning what is his trade.

'A liberal,' the boy said, like saying, 'A man doomed.'

The boy was living there and waiting. He was a student of chemistry. The school was in this town; it would have to open again sometime. He said, with a quick flash of obstinacy, standing there alone against a world that was upside down and mad and cruel, 'I will sleep on hay and I will eat soup and I will be dirty and without my family and without my friends. But I will finish my studies. I am going to learn.'

And at Postelberg I got a look at the frontier. You couldn't believe it: it didn't make sense. Just barbed wire stretched across an open road, and on one side was Czechoslovakia and on the other side what had suddenly become Germany. A crowd of Czechs stood on their side of the barbed wire and stared; they were like people who doubted a dream. One young German soldier leaned on his rifle on the other side of the fence. He was very embarrassed by all these eyes; he tried to look confident and only looked awkward and uneasy, shifting from foot to foot. So the Czechs stood there staring into that land that had been theirs and was now no longer theirs, a land that had suddenly filled with darkness and terror for them.

It was not easy for them to understand. They knew that there were four new concentration camps already on what used to be Czechoslovakian soil where a concentration camp could never have existed: two near Carlsbad, one at Eich, another at Elbogen. And that people like them were already in these camps. They knew that the Henleinists roamed their new territory, drunk with power and the strange brutality that can come over men but which the Czechs do not understand anyhow. They knew that Czech women were forced to clean the village town halls and barracks on hands and knees, bullied and insulted by Henlein women (but how can it be, they thought, that women are so different?). They knew that Czechs were made to kneel before the statue of Masaryk, and defame the statue of the man they loved most, and swear allegiance to an alien conquerer. They knew (with shame and with disgust and with fear) all the miserable record of beating, abuse and torture that went on. They knew that men who believed as they did were in desperate danger on the other side of a piece of barbed wire.

And they stood like people stunned, and somehow it was terribly frightening.

Because the land was as green across the fence, the smooth Bohemian plain. The fields were as neat, the villages as sober, practical and grey. But there was something going on over there that horrified them, and you felt yourself that no one was safe any more. One strand of barbed wire cannot keep a whole system of life away. On one side of the fence was a life they knew and believed in: freedom and justice and truth and the right of every man to say what he thinks. But for how long, they thought, how long? Hitler is not a man to these people. He may be a god to the Nazis, but to the Czechs he is the power of darkness, and they have no arms left to fight him.

'The German soldiers were very correct,' a woman said to me, standing there with the barbed wire between us and the dark young German and his rifle. 'The Henleinists and the Gestapo have done all the cruelty, but the soldiers have not aided them.'

'No?' I said.

'No,' she said. 'Of course they do not help our people, but at least they do not strike them.'

'That is fine,' I said.

But the heart is heavy and the brain refuses to accept these things. The day before in Prague they brought a young girl out of a hotel on a stretcher; she had killed herself in her room, after her husband had been arrested in German territory. A newspaper editor and his wife who ran a German liberal paper swallowed veronal, but they did a bad job and it took them three days to die. A man I knew came up to me in a hotel lobby in Prague and said, whispering as if he were afraid to hear it, 'I took a girl out to dinner; I used to know her father—he was a lawyer in the second zone.' The second zone, I thought, what a way to name a piece of land: the second zone of invasion. 'But he didn't get out before the Germans came and she said she was wild for a time, but tonight she was very gay, oh, very gay.'

'Her father is all right, then?'

'No,' my friend said. 'But she has eight poison tablets in her purse, that she bought, and she says no one will ever get her into a concentration camp.'

'Listen,' I said, 'I've heard enough, so don't tell me any more. I can tell you names of Jewish doctors and Social Democrat lawyers who committed suicide in the Sudeten territory; I can tell you stories about beatings and brandings and executions with names and addresses attached to them. I know of simple people who had neither the money nor the information to use poison, so they just threw themselves under the trains that were supposed to take them back to Sudetenland. I've seen an old man with his front teeth knocked out and his ribs almost showing through a mess of red meat on his side and his arms black and swollen from the beating, and I can't bear to hear any more, see?—not for a while anyhow.'

So I stood at the frontier with the woman and we looked over into that new country across the barbed wire.

Prague is a beautiful city. Do you know Prague? The Hradsin Palace on the hill where Benes lived glowed against the night, and the cathedral spires beside it went up like lances into the sky. The bridges shone over the river, and parliament and the great white opera house were cut out of the darkness. (But the city does not shine this way any more, because the main electric power station of Prague is now in German territory.) In the old town you saw the great baroque buildings hugged against the hill, the narrow streets pierced with arcades, the flower market, the small cobbled squares with the houses flat and quiet around them. People were very happy and at ease in Prague, never noisy because the Czechs are a sober people, never elegant or dazzling because they dress in a practical, enduring way, but well fed and serene and busy and at home.

In the grey early morning you watched the people going to work in the new town. It wasn't the way you remembered it. Nothing had changed in the city: the automats were the same; the Bata shoe store stood where it always had; the same handsome leather goods were on display; the same clothes dummies posed in the windows, draped in masses of glittering cloth as they always were. But the people looked different. There was something new in Prague: fear.

They were afraid to talk in restaurants because who knew what kind of person was listening at the next table? Their mail was censored, and their newspapers. They could not take their money from the bank; they could not leave the country without permission. The foreign consulates were crowded with people begging for visas. As a foreigner, everyone you met spoke to you about leaving—could a man find work in America? They had loved their country and worked to make it fine. But now they hoped to get out before their country ceased being a republic, even in name. Already anti-Jewish demonstations had begun, the old ugly story of broken windows and shouted idiotic slogans; already whispering campaigns ran through the city, against Benes, against democracy. The Liberal and Left parties are outlawed; certain newspapers cease to print; politicians and public figures whose democratic faith was strong are already in flight. It is all coming, as it had to come. Even the taxi driver had said, with what sorrow, 'Democracy is dead. We have a dictatorship here too.' Czechoslovakia is no longer an independent state. People are afraid.

You began to add up the disaster. The military defences were gone and the country was now utterly helpless. The army was demobilized, and without the defences could never be used again. Over one million Czechs who had lived in their own country in September and had been citizens of a republic now found themselves, not through choice, citizens of Germany or of Poland or Hungary.

There was no way of telling how many refugees there were, but hundreds of thousands of Sudeten Germans had never belonged to the Henlein party and now they were either in concentration camps or fleeing toward a brief uncertain safety in the remnant of Czechoslovakia. The Czechs from the annexed territories were also moving, crossing the frontier at night; no one knows how many have come or how many will still find their way back to the homeland. There are 10,000 Austrian and German exiles, all of them marked men and women, most of them escaped from prison or concentration camps, who had been safe in the republic of Czechoslovakia. But Czechoslovakia cannot protect these people. Even Benes was not safe. And, besides, this small mutilated state cannot even temporarily house and feed and clothe hundreds of thousands of refugees. The economy of Czechoslovakia is as shattered as its military defences.

The great executive didn't look his part: he was of medium height, slender, neat, very accurate and shy. He received me in a board room that was furnished in huge mahogany and the walls were covered with maps. New maps, with incredible erratic crayon lines drawn on them: he showed me the frontier with a strange smile and did not comment.

Then he began to talk in a grey, matter-of-fact voice. He spoke like a professor, making his points on the map. There were only two ways that people spoke in Czechoslovakia, and this was the second way. When they talked they all spoke with terrible and violent control; but later, as the story went on, the control snapped, and people—these serious, quiet, inarticulate people—wept as they talked, with fury and helplessness. Or else they talked coldly, stating facts, trying to keep their voices and their minds dead.

So his hand moved over the map and his voice went on: '40 per cent of the metallurgical industry lost, 60 per cent of the soft coal lost, 63 per cent of the textile industry lost, 100 per cent of the porcelain industry lost, 57 per cent of the glass industry lost, 30 per cent of the sugar industry lost, 40 per cent of the chemical industry lost, 63 per cent of the paper industry lost . . .' All the work gone, the twenty years of patience and effort come to nothing.

'What will you do?' I said.

'Start again.'

'How?'

'Somehow,' he said, weary and proud. 'Somehow.'

The railroad lines were in red on the map, and you could see how it worked out, as if you were watching a movie, as if you saw the trains pulling the freight cars through the flat fields and the pine woods. Now the two railroad lines that linked northern and southern Czechoslovakia were cut: they both ran through the new Germany. You looked at it again, to make sure, and suddenly you realized there was no communication. It was as if the railroad from New York to San Francisco were cut at Chicago. He showed me Morava Ostrava, a great iron and steel town, stuck up foolishly on the side of Czechoslovakia, entirely surrounded by the new Germany and the new Poland.

'The iron comes from the Slovakian fields,' he said, and his finger traced an oval to the south, in the centre of the country. 'But you see the railroad is cut. The iron ore must be changed five times, on to five different trains, before it gets from the fields to the factory at Morava Ostrava.'

It went on and on, from a millionaire manufacturer to an economist, to a farm leader, to an exporter, an advertising agent, down to simple people who only knew their own small corner in the world, their own pigs and flax and hops, their own tiny shoe store or paper shop. A million hectares of timber land gone: hops, flax, fruit, vineyards, tobacco land ceded to Germany.

So you saw it, not as statistics, not as railroads lost and mines and factories gone, but in terms of human life. You saw it as unemployment and a falling standard of living and as labour camps and diminished wages and hardship and homelessness. You knew that not only had a democratic military power been wiped out, but you saw that a flourishing and successful trade rival had been destroyed. It was a very thorough job. I remember the boy who had been sitting with friends in a Prague restaurant; they were bowed over a map and were working with pencil and paper figuring up the losses. He was a boy who would normally play football and be deeply interested in having a motorcycle. And suddenly he rose from the table with a white face and furious eyes, and shouted out for everyone to hear, 'If we had fought alone and been defeated, it could not be worse.'

The German frontier is now three miles from the Skoda works at Pilsen. They will never make armaments for the Czech army again. Skoda transports the coal from what mines remain to them by truck because the railroad has been cut between Pilsen and Klatovy. Workers who lived in the Klatovy section, a sort of suburb to Pilsen where they had small homes and gardens, used to commute into Pilsen, a trip of two hours. Now that trip takes ten hours, having to make a wide semicircle to avoid the new Germany, and so workers must move to Pilsen or lose their jobs.

Outside the factory two men were leaning on their bicycles. One of them had cleaned up and wore a bright blue shirt without a collar, held in place by a shiny brass collar button. The other was grease-stained and dark. They seemed in no hurry to leave. They were going home into Germany. A week before they lived in Czechoslovakia and were Czechs and now they lived in Germany and had to get a printed permission from the German military authorities to cross into Pilsen to work. When they got on their bicycles they sailed down the fine concrete road past the bridge, on their way home, as they always had, but when they started to pedal up the hill they were stopped by two German soldiers in steel helmets, who asked for their papers. Just suddenly, there on the road, their country ended. Where they lived it had always been Czech.

They were talking together and the foreman translated for me.

The worker in the blue shirt was talking. 'I tried to get my wife across with the little girl yesterday but I'm not allowed.'

'Why?' I said.

'I do not know,' he said. 'We are not Germans, but they will not let us take anything away with us, and when we try to leave, even leaving the mattresses and the pots and pans and the bed clothes and our winter coats and everything there, they will not let us come. We have no politics either. But we are Czechs.'

The unwashed worker, who seemed very tired, said he was not easy in his mind. It seemed that he knew an old peasant named Janisek who had three sons. The sons had fled into Czechoslovakia before the German invasion. But the oldest son was the father's heir and the old man needed help on the farm. The oldest son was guaranteed safety if he returned, and so he came back. He was arrested as he entered the door of his father's house and taken away. They had not seen him since; they did not know where he had gone and they were afraid to ask.

'The old man is crazy,' the dark worker said. 'And he cannot do the work alone.'

'You see how it is.' The foreman made sweeping zigzagging movements with his hands. 'Our frontier. Crazy, isn't it. It has nothing to do with races or minorities, all that stuff. But is it not crazy? The country is cut up to ruin it. And there is already that trade agreement with Yugoslavia. They have to sell everything they have to Germany, and they may not even buy goods that are not manufactured in Germany, without Germany's permission. They are not invaded, but they are slaves too. There is that offer to Lithuania of fifteen years' non-aggression in return for another of these trade treaties. Treaties!' he said, with fury.

'Do you see how it is now? From the Baltic to the Black Sea he will run us all, with money, with commerce, with what people live and die by. We will all be good or we will starve.'

On that morning Edouard Benes drove from the Hradsin Palace for the last time. He stood up in the open car, with his wife beside him, and the car went slowly through the great stone courtyards out through the carved gates. The citizens of Prague had come to say goodbye. They stood along the curb and waited for this man who was a symbol of their state and their freedom. When he passed, they bowed their heads as people do for the dead. The crowd wept. Madame Benes held her head high and looked at the people, but her face was marked with tears. The president stood in the car and saluted his people and they did not speak or wave or cheer; they had come to say goodbye and they wept for him and for all that was lost. Below them the city lay in the autumn mist, grey and silver with the dark fine steeples of the churches rising into the grey sky. The car drove slowly into the country.

Eduoard Benes went to Lany to Masaryk's tomb. You drive through slender pine woods, past carefully cultivated fields. The last line of defence, the black steel spools with barbed wire on them, has been pushed back to leave the road clear, but the barbed wire stretches over the hills until it is lost against the sky. He drove through the small square town to the cemetery on the hill. It is just a country cemetery like others in Czechoslovakia. There is the tombstone with two doves on it, the tombstone with an urn. On all the tombstones are pictures of the dead, as is the custom in this country. The peasants and the little shopkeepers of the district are buried here.

And in a corner of the cemetery is the grave of Masaryk. You would know all about the Czechs from Masaryk's grave. A low wooden fence shuts it off from the others. There is a wide green mound of grass. And at the head of this stands a plain short granite block with a storm lantern on it. The light burns always in the storm lantern and simple people have come and placed on the grave bunches of flowers for the founder of their state. There is no name on this grave, no mark, no noble words. There is grass and a lantern that always burns and the flowers of peasants who loved Masaryk.

Edouard Benes knelt at this grave and prayed for his people. It was the last thing he did before he went into exile. Kneeling there, he knew surely what his people know now: that this is no peace, there is no safety and no justice and no permanence in it. The Czechs believe that they were not only betrayed, but betrayed in vain. Perhaps Benes felt that it was more than the liberty of his people that had been lost, or the life of his state. The founder of Czechoslovakia's democracy was buried here: perhaps Benes prayed in mourning for the democracy of all Europe.

The Thirties

The Thirties were a doom decade.

The New York stock market crashed in October 1929 and suddenly, mysteriously, the economic system in America and western Europe fell apart. Banks, industries and businesses collapsed. People who thought they had a lot of money or comfortable money lost it in an international panic. The enduring effect of the Great Depression, fully underway by January 1930, was unemployment. Millions of men and women were thrown on a giant rubbish heap of the unwanted. No government had foreseen this catastrophe, no help had been planned.

By 1933 Hitler ruled Germany. In 1936 the Spanish Civil War started, the shape of things to come, a Republic attacked by united Facism. Facist Italy completed its conquest of Ethiopia in 1937. The League of Nations, once a hope for sanity, was by now meaningless. In 1938 British and French governments allowed Hitler to dismember Czechoslovakia. Russia, far-off, hardly known, was locked in domestic agonies, millions dead from Stalin's handmade disasters. In the Far East, Japan was fiercely on the move, occupying Manchuria, then invading China in 1937. Having liquidated his top generals, Stalin signed a non-aggression pact with Hitler in August 1939.

As long predicted, the Second World War finally began on 1 September, 1939, though it started slowly with the defeat and division of Poland between Germany and Russia. At the end of the decade, the Finns alone were still fighting off the attack of their overpowering Soviet neighbour. In the last months of 1939 and the winter months of 1940, people who had never understood Nazi Germany and never thought about Japan were calling it the phoney war.

My life began in February 1930. I got ready in the summer of 1929, by leaving college at the end of my junior year, against my father's will, and running through two jobs, proof that I could make my way and pay for it if I didn't mind a diet of doughnuts and pawning my typewriter to tide me over weekends. 1930 was the real thing. I persuaded the Holland America Line to give me free passage in steerage, then described as Student Third Class, in return for a glowing article to use in their trade magazine. Aged twenty-one, with a suitcase and about $75, I set off for Paris where I knew nobody—a joyful confident grain of sand in a vast rising sandstorm. I had visited Paris twice before and it was not my dream city but I intended to become a foreign correspondent within a few weeks, and Paris was the obvious place to launch my career.

The launch lacked a certain *savoir faire*. The flower stalls at the Place de la Madeleine suited my liking for a pretty neighbourhood. On a nearby sidestreet I found a hotel, no more than a doorway, a desk and dark stairs, and was gratified by the price of the room. The room was smelly and squalid and I thought it impractical to have a mirror on the ceiling but perhaps that was a French custom. There was an amazing amount of noise in the corridors and other rooms but perhaps the French did a lot of roaming in hotels. I could not understand why the man at the desk grew more unfriendly each time he saw me, when I was probably the friendliest person in Paris.

Having checked the telephone directory, I presented myself at the office of the *New York Times* and informed the bureau chief, a lovely elderly Englishman aged maybe forty, that I was prepared to start work as a foreign correspondent on his staff. He had been smiling hugely at my opening remarks and mopped up tears of laughter when he learned where I lived. He took me to lunch—and my enthusiasm for free meals was unbounded—and explained that I was staying in a *maison de passe*, where rooms were rented by the hour to erotic couples. My new English friend insisted that I change my address, and bribed me with an invitation to report next week, again at lunch. He suggested the Left Bank; I would be safer in the students' milieu.

The private life of the French was their own business and no inconvenience to me, but I was offended by the unfriendliness of the man at the hotel desk. I got off the Métro at St Germain des Prés, thinking it would be nice to live in fields if not near flowers and was sorry to find no fields but did find a charming little hotel on the Rue de l'Université, which no doubt meant a street for students. This hotel was also cheap and a grand piano, with a big vase of flowers on it, filled the tiny foyer. My windowless room had a glass door opening on to an iron runway. The bath, at extra cost, was four flights down in the courtyard. I thought it remarkable that young men, the other residents, cried so much and quarrelled in such screeching voices but I liked the way they played Chopin on the grand piano and kept fresh flowers in the big vase.

An ex-Princetonian, studying at the Beaux Arts, a throw-back to my college days, came to collect me for dinner one night and was ardently approached by a Chopin pianist, and scandalized. He explained homosexuality, since I had never heard of it. I pointed out that I could hardly be safer than in a homosexual hotel and besides I was sick of people butting in on my living arrangements. I won and lost jobs without surprise and saved up, from my nothing earnings, so that I could eat the least expensive dish at a Russian restaurant where I mooned with silent love for a glorious White Russian balalaika player.

The years in France and adjacent countries were never easy, never dull and an education at last. Unlike the gifted Americans and British who settled in Paris in the twenties and lived among each other in what seems to me a cosy literary world, I soon lived entirely among the French, not a cosy world. The men were politicians and political journalists, the students of my generation were just as fervently political. Money depended on age; the old had it, some of them had lashings of it; the young did not.

I was astonished, a few years later in England, to meet young men who neither worked nor intended to work and were apparently rich. A combination of the English eldest son syndrome and the time-honoured method of living on debts, charm and hospitality. They were much more fun than the French but I thought them half-witted; they knew nothing about real life. Real life was the terrible English mill towns, the terrible mining towns in northern France, slums, strikes, protest marches broken up by the mounted Garde Républicaine, frantic underpaid workers and frantic half-starved unemployed. Real life was the Have-nots.

The Haves were sometimes enjoyable, generally ornamental and a valued source of free meals and country visits. I did not recognize the power of the Haves. Because of my own poverty, fretting over centimes, make-do or do-without, keeping up my appearance on half a shoe string, I absorbed a sense of what true poverty means, the kind you never chose and cannot escape, the prison of it. Maybe that was the most useful part of my education. It was a very high-class education, all in all, standing-room at ground level to watch history as it happened.

During the French years, I returned to America once in 1931. This period is lost in the mists of time. I know that I travelled a lot and began the stumbling interminable work on my first novel. (When it finally appeared, in 1934, my father read it and said, rightly, that he could not understand why anyone had published it. I have, also rightly, obliterated it ever since.) With a French companion in the autumn of 1931, I made a long hardship journey across the continent from the east to the west coast. It was all new and exotic to him, not to me, and I remember very little. I remembered 'Justice at Night' suddenly; it emerged intact, from its burial in my brain, and wrote itself as if by Ouija board one sunny morning in London in the summer of 1936. I don't know that it belongs here since it is not direct reporting; recollection in tranquillity four and a half years late. Recollection is not infallible.

I was cadging bed and breakfast from H. G. Wells; cadging room from those who had it was a major occupation of the moneyless young in those days. Wells nagged steadily about my writing habits; a professional writer had to work every morning for a fixed number of hours, as he did. Not me. I dug in solitude like a feverish mole until I had dug through to the end, then emerged into daylight, carefree, ready for anything except my typewriter; until the next time. I had just finished my book on the unemployed, *The Trouble I've Seen*, and spent the London nights dancing with young gentlemen of my acquaintance and was not about to adopt Wells' nine-thirty a.m. to twelve-thirty p.m. regime. Not then or ever. That morning, to show him I could write if I felt like it, I sat in his garden and let 'Justice at Night' produce itself. Wells sent it to the *Spectator*. I had already moved on to Germany where I ceased being a pacifist and became an ardent anti-Facist.

Late in 1934, in Paris, it dawned on me that my own country was in trouble. I thought that trouble was a European speciality. America was safe, rich and quiet, separate from the life around me. Upon finally realizing my mistake, I decided to return and offer my service to the nation. Which I did on a miserable little tub of the Bernstein Line, price of passage $85, arriving in New York on 10 October. By 16 October I was enrolled in the service of the nation.

In Washington, a reporter friend introduced me to Harry Hopkins, who was then the Director of the Federal Emergency Relief Administration, the FERA, the first national American dole. Mr Hopkins was hiring a few people to travel around the country and report back to him on how FERA worked in practice. I told Mr Hopkins that I knew a lot about unemployment and was a seasoned reporter; the first was true enough, the second not. I had been writing anything I could for any money I could earn, and the childish first novel; scarcely star rating. I think I remember a smiling blue gleam in Mr Hopkins' eyes at that interview.

I wore the only clothes I had, a Schiaparelli suit in nubbly brown tweed fastened up to its Chinese collar with large brown leather clips, and Schiap's version of an Anzac hat in brown crochet work adorned by a spike of cock pheasant feathers. I could not afford to buy clothes in the ordinary way and dressed myself in *soldes*, the bargain discarded outfits that the models of the great couturiers had worn in their last collections. Also I painted my face like Parisian ladies, lots of eyeshadow, mascara and lipstick, which was not at all the style for American ladies then and certainly not for social workers in Federal employment. Mr Hopkins may have been entertaining himself. He could sack me at any moment and was not delving deep into the public purse, though to me the job meant untold riches: $75 a week, train vouchers and $5 per diem travel allowance for food and hotels.

For three weeks short of a year, as closely as I can figure, I crossed the country, south, north, east, midwest, far west, wrote innumerable reports and kept no copies, the chronic worst habit of my professional life. A few years ago, someone found six of my early reports in Mrs Roosevelt's papers at the Hyde Park Roosevelt Library. I have cut and stuck three together in 'My Dear Mr Hopkins' because I think they are a small but vital record of a period in American history. They were not written for publication, they can hardly be called written; banged out in haste as information.

After a few months, I was so outraged by the wretched treatment of the unemployed that I stormed back to Washington and announced to Mr Hopkins that I was resigning to write a bitter exposé of the misery I had seen. I did not pause to reflect that I had no newspaper or magazine contacts and was unlikely to create a nationwide outcry of moral indignation. Instead of telling me not to waste his time, Mr Hopkins urged me to talk to Mrs Roosevelt before resigning; he had sent her my reports. I walked over to the White House, feeling grumpy and grudging. Mrs Roosevelt, who listened to everyone with care, listened to my tirade and said, 'You should talk to Franklin.'

That night I was invited to dinner at the White House, seated next to the President in my black sweater and skirt (for by then I was rich enough to buy ordinary clothes) and observed in glum silence the white and gold china and the copious though not gourmet food, hating this table full of cheerful well-fed guests in evening clothes. Didn't they know that better people were barefoot and in rags and half-starved; didn't they know anything about America?

Mrs Roosevelt, being somewhat deaf, had a high sharp voice when talking loudly. She rose at the far end of the table and shouted, 'Franklin, talk to that girl. She says all the unemployed have pellagra and syphilis.' This silenced the table for an instant, followed by an explosion of laughter; I was ready to get up and go. The President hid his amusement, listened to the little I was willing to say—not much, suffocated by anger—and asked me to come and see him again. In that quaint way, my friendship with the Roosevelts began and lasted the rest of their lives. Mrs Roosevelt persuaded me that I could help the unemployed more by sticking to the job, so I went back to work until I was fired, courtesy of the FBI.

I think I know what happened now, though I had a more grandiose explanation at the time. In a little town on a lake in Idaho called Coeur d'Alene, pronounced Cur Daleen, I found the unemployed victimized as often before by a crooked contractor. These men, who had all been small farmers or ranchers on their own land, shovelled dirt from here to there until the contractor collected the shovels, threw them in the lake, and pocketed a tidy commission on an order for new shovels. Meantime the men were idle, unpaid and had to endure a humiliating means-test for direct dole money to see them through.

I had never understood the frequent queries from Washington about 'protest groups.' I thought Washington was idiotic—they didn't realize that these people suffered from despair, not anger. But I was angry. By buying them beer and haranguing them, I convinced a few hesitant men to break the windows of the FERA office at night. Afterwards someone would surely come and look into their grievances. Then I moved on to the next stop, Seattle, while the FBI showed up at speed in Coeur d'Alene, alarmed by that first puny act of violence. Naturally the men told the FBI that the Relief lady had suggested this good idea; the contractor was arrested for fraud, they got their shovels for keeps, and I was recalled to Washington.

I wrote to my parents jubilantly and conceitedly: 'I'm out of this man's government because I'm a "dangerous Communist" and the Department of Justice believes me to be subversive and a menace. Isn't it flattering? I shrieked with laughter when Aubrey [Williams, Mr Hopkins' deputy] told me; seems the unemployed go about quoting me and refuse—after my visits—to take things lying down.'

While I was collecting bits and pieces from my seldom-used desk in the Washington FERA office, the President's secretary rang with a message from the President. He and Mrs Roosevelt, who was out of town, had heard that I was dismissed and were worried about my finances because I would not find another government job with the FBI scowling, so they felt it would be best if I lived at the White House until I sorted myself out. I thought this was kind and helpful but did not see it as extraordinary, a cameo example of the way the Roosevelts serenely made their own choices and judgements.

Everyone in the FERA office was outdone with the stupid interfering FBI cops; I treated the whole thing as a joke. Naturally, the Roosevelts, the most intelligent people in the country, knew it was all nonsense though, being the older generation, they considered the practical side. I had saved enough money for time to write a book, but had not planned where to work and the White House would be a good quiet place to start. It was too, but I needed the complete mole existence for writing and departed from the White House with thanks and kisses as soon as a friend offered me his empty remote house in Connecticut. Being fired was an honourable discharge in my view, not like quitting; and I was very happy to work on fiction again. When I finished the book, I went back to Europe, having done my duty by my country.

That was the time when I really loved my compatriots, 'the

insulted and injured,' Americans I had never known before. It was the only time that I have fully trusted and respected the American Presidency, and its influence on the government and the people. Now it is accepted that Franklin Roosevelt was one of the rare great Presidents. While he was in office, until America entered the war, both the Roosevelts were daily vilified and mocked in the Republican press, and both were indifferent to these attacks. Mrs Roosevelt was in herself a moral true north. I think the President's own affliction, crippled by polio at the age of thirty-nine, taught him sympathy for misfortune. They were wise. They had natural dignity and no need or liking for the panoply of power. I miss above all their private and public fearlessness.

Born to every privilege that America can offer, they were neither impressed by privilege nor interested in placating it. The New Deal, the Roosevelt regime, was truly geared to concern for the majority of the citizens. I am very glad that I grew up in America when I did and glad that I knew it when the Roosevelts lived in the White House. Superpower America is another country.

I had gone to Spain in March 1937 and become a war correspondent by accident. From then on, until 1947, I wrote no journalism except war reports apart from four articles in 1938. *Collier's,* my employer, cabled me in Barcelona asking me to go to Prague. In war, I never knew anything beyond what I could see and hear, a full-time occupation. The Big Picture always exists, and I seem to have spent my life observing how desperately the Big Picture affects the little people who did not devise it and have no control over it. I didn't know what was happening around Madrid and certainly not what was happening in Czechoslovakia but now I had suddenly at long last become a foreign correspondent.

I went to Czechoslovakia when the Czechs were mobilized and determined to fight for their country against Hitler; I went the second time after the Munich Pact. In between, at *Collier's* request, I went to England, because my editor wanted some idea of the English reaction to oncoming war. I had already done a similar article about France. 'The Lord Will Provide for England' shows that I found the mental climate in England intolerable; sodden imagination, no distress for others beyond the sceptr'd isle.

Three days before he flew to Berchtesgaden to sign away the life of Czechoslovakia, the Prime Minister, Neville Chamberlain, a stick figure with a fossil mind, addressed the nation by radio, speaking to and for the meanest stupidity of his people. 'How horrible, fantastic, incredible it is that we should be digging trenches and trying on gas masks because of a quarrel in a far-away country between people of whom we know nothing.' Then he came back from Germany, waving that shameful piece of paper and proclaiming 'peace with honour' to cheering crowds. This same government had starved the Republic of Spain through its nefarious Non-Intervention Treaty, while Hitler and Mussolini were free to aid Franco. I thought the only good British were in the International Brigade in Spain; I was finished with England. Never set foot again in the miserable self-centred country.

Instead of which, since 1943, London has been the one fixed point in my nomadic life.

At the end of the decade in December 1939, I was again in Paris on my way home to Cuba from the Russo-Finnish War. Czechoslovakia and Spain were lost and I knew I was saying goodbye to Europe. I did not think it was a phoney war, I thought it would be a hell-on-earth war and a long one. Having started off in this city, so merry and so ignorant almost ten years before, here I was despairing for Europe and broken-hearted for Spain. The powers of evil and money ruled the world.

Now brave men and women, anti-Fascists all over Europe, would be prey for the Gestapo. I had not then taken in the destiny planned for the Jews. Perhaps this was because in Germany in the summer of 1936 there were no startling signs of persecution, not when Nazi Germany was host to the Olympic Games, and on its best behaviour. I was obsessed by what Hitler was doing outside his country, not inside Germany. To me, Jews and anti-

Fascists were the same, caught in the same trap, equally condemned. Passports were the only escape. None of the people I knew and cared for had passports, nowhere to run. I saw them all as waiting for a sure death sentence, unsure of the date of execution.

Paris was beautiful and peaceful in the snow, peacefully empty. Men I had known in the early thirties, now important people, ate in grand restaurants and told me not to be so sad and foreboding. Cheer up, we have the Maginot Line. I owned an invaluable green American passport. I was perfectly safe, I even had some money in the bank because *Collier's* paid generously. I felt like a profiteer, ashamed and uselss. By geographical chance, the piece of the map where I was born, I could walk away, I had the great unfair advantage of choice.

Unconsciously, I think I learned the last lesson from those educational years. I had witnessed every kind of bravery in lives condemned by poverty and condemned by war; I had seen how others died. I got a measure for my own life; whatever its trials and tribulations they would always be petty insignificant stuff by comparison.

THE FORTIES

Journey Through a Peaceful Land

For several weeks now we have been driving through the American Way of Life. For a time, in New Jersey, Pennsylvania and Maryland, the American Way of Life looked like the tender memories of GI's, homesick songs, politicians' promises and the unattainable dream of all the homeless and hungry of Europe. Between the dogwood and the lilacs and the redbud and the flowering chestnuts, the fields lay combed and sleek, and the clean farmhouses stood inside their screens of old trees. The little towns were lovelier than one remembers American towns can be, faded brick and white wood, the tall, cool trees, and life sleeping there. Perhaps this is the Old World now. These people seemed to believe in peace and feel safe inside their houses and their habits. It is amazing how permanent a place can look, and how rooted and unchanging the populace, when there are no burned tanks beside the road, no buildings split in half, no fields scooped by shell fire.

We stopped at a tourist camp in Gettysburg, just opposite Pickett's Charge. The man who owned the eight small frame boxes appeared in white overalls and said, 'You'll have to excuse me looking like a working man. I been fixing things up a little.' We accepted this assurance that he was middle-class, the way we are, and the way all Americans seem determined to be. Gettysburg sprouts memorial monuments like cabbages; and throughout this county indestructible markers brief you on every event and personage connected with the War Between the States. This makes one wonder about Americans, who retain such mothering reverence for their own death and destruction. Have the people of Gettysburg any imagination for, let us say, the people of St Vith, over whose town a nameless battle raged briefly, leaving them without any town at all and no interest in putting up monuments? Or do they imagine that war could ever return to Gettysburg? It seems unlikely: history has given Gettysburg a nice little asset—a small trade in guides and guidebooks.

Everywhere along the perfect highway were places to eat, shining and comfortable, with copious—it seemed to me superb—uniform food. Inside the dapper Howard Johnson restaurants we kept seeing an American phenomenon: middle-aged women travelling in twos, threes and fours. Their maroon, turquoise, green and black sedans waited outside. Meanwhile they sat, featureless behind their eyeglasses, cement heavy, topped by ornate, microscopic hats, eating with precision and at length. These, no doubt, were some of Philip Wylie's Moms. It is hard to see what wisdom and delight they can bring to their families and their communities, but they appear to be contented, even gay, over their girlish cocktails and their ice-cream. The world's fat is badly divided. I think perhaps the American horror of age has prevented all these women from acquiring faces: it is a conspicuous lack. But the ice-cream is wonderful and why fret over the American tendency to look incompleted.

After Virginia, the American Way of Life goes largely to pot. Now it is the sandiness and the unvarying pines of North Carolina, and the Negroes. The Negroes look to me like Polish slave labour in Germany, and in the same way seem not to be living anywhere. We came to a place called Rocky Mount, where train tracks bisect the main business street and the gutters are sodden with refuse. After dark, the young take over the streets, racing along before the brilliant shop windows full of claptrap unnecessities, hurrying to drink more Coca-Cola. They shout, 'Hi, y'all,' to each other, and all look alike. The older people visit from front porch to front porch. The radios go on and on. Behind their invisible barbed wire, the Negroes watch, marked by poverty as by disease.

A curious thing happened in this place. In the movie house, during the newsreel, the citizens of Rocky Mount talked cheerfully to each other, filling time until the feature began. A rather stale bit of photography, showing the Arab delegation to the UN, unrolled on the screen. A voice mentioned the Palestine debate and there was a picture of Abba Hillel Silver and some remark about his being the Jewish spokesman. The high-school-age audience groned in unison: a strange sound, something mocking, something contemptuous, unplanned, not lasting, but spontaneous.

After that they settled down, lovingly and sweatily intertwined, ate popcorn, and watched the feature with exclamations of delight.

Farther down the Carolina coast at Myrtle Beach we re-found the American Way of Life, walking in handkerchief-size bathing suits, beautiful and slim and healthy, chatting away with passion about things: 'I'm gonna get me one of those cute little sunsuits they got in the window at Markey's . . . That green on the eighth hole is a mess . . . Did you ever try Sunray? You oughta. It'll keep you from gettin' red like that . . . I like those new Studebakers. Boy, that's a neat car . . . Y'all comin' to the movies tonight . . . comin' dancin'?' Is this people trembling for its safety from foes without and within, as our Public Figures would have us believe? If so, the trembling must be done behind locked doors. I have yet to hear one of them even mention the news they read over their morning cereal, eggs and bacon, hot cakes with syrup.

During this time there was a trial of lynchers, an escaped lynchee, and several of those mysterious Southern crimes called 'attempted rape.' In the North, one might have imagined this people with blood-shot eyes and grim mouths, snarling about white honour and keeping the niggers in their place. In Europe, where we always read of these horrors, Europeans would question us slyly or with disgust about our democracy.

But here, where it was all happening, no one seemed to notice it. Some 200 miles away, a historic trial was fizzling into predetermined failure. It did not cause one raised voice over the breakfast table (the only time a newspaper was visible), either in protest or approval.

Perhaps some of the Negro servants spoke of it, perhaps they suffered for the man who broke loose, heard the bullet hit the tree alongside him and hid for two days and nights, starving in the woods. They did not speak of it—not where you could hear them, in any case.

But the whites were not hiding their opinions; they simply did not have any. Contented, contented; genial decent people, playing with their children, enjoying the sun and the sea, wishing evil to no one.

Inland, after the swamps, and the mud creeks and the starved, dusty fields and the slumping Negro shanties, there is an Army post. A division which I had seen living recklessly, efficiently and with a style all its own in various parts of Europe, now lived on this red-clay and pine plateau in South Carolina, in peeling, white wood barracks, on fiercely geometric streets, with the sun pouring down, and one day following another world without end. Army posts are not places that born civilians can ever quite understand, any more than atheists would feel easy in seminaries or those who are sickened by the smell of ether could adjust to hospital life.

On an Army post all ranks speak of the world beyond their military square miles as 'the outside.' There is no fence around them, but the wall is felt either as oppression or protection, depending on taste. Some of the finest young combat officers are still here. They are no more surprised by the American attitude toward its Army than is a doctor who finds people unwilling to pay his bill once they are cured. For the fine ones are dedicated men, not vain, greedy or lazy, as it is popular to believe when their services are no longer essential. And on 'the outside,' people forget how knowledgeable a man must be to command in a modern army and how ceaselessly he must work to keep that knowledge sharp.

This division acquired much wisdom on the long journey

from Sicily to the North Sea. It learned that all people are not like Americans, and are not criminal for being different. The division left roots in Europe and the veterans inquire anxiously whether there is now glass in the windows and coal in the cellars at Nijmegen; have they been able to fix up those smashed villages along the Volturno; has anyone come back to Trois Ponts yet, if there was anything to come back to; and are the people in Leicester, England, getting enough to eat?

All those who truly earned their foreign travel (as opposed to racketeers, slobs and the ones who never had it so good) have this knowledge of suffering and want. You find them everywhere, the travelled Americans, who saw the world from two-and-a-half-ton trucks, in convoy, going from one ruined place to another. It is a tragedy that they are apparently so voiceless. We need their memories, which go something like: 'We used to take our rations in to this family in Reems, it was an old French lady and her husband and their kids, and they'd cook us up a real meal and treat us just like we was at home . . . I bet they weren't more'n 17, or less, they looked like it anyhow, and these guys walked, I mean walked, from Stalingrad. Looked like they dumped their wounded in some old furniture van and brung 'em along . . .' 'You'd see those Eyetie women out between the lines . . .' The travelled Americans found that everywhere they could get on with someone. They don't seem to listen much to their elected representatives, nor do they bother with their newspaper, on matters of foreign news and foreign policy: it must be some other Europe than the one they knew, that everyone's bitching about now.

Many veterans left this division at the end of the war, and then, after a short sojourn in the 'outside,' returned. On the outside they became unskilled labour with no chance to learn skills, uncertain men who believed themselves easily robbed, and their pride was attacked by the feeling that the home folks, bored now with heroes, regarded them as suckers to have wasted their lives fighting in Europe. So they came back and are solemnly appreciative of medical care for their young wives and new babies, and of four-room houses on the post that rent for $27.50 a month, and of being treated as if they were specialists in something. They are terribly young, because their branch of the service necessitates jumping from airplanes, and sometimes they even look young. Though the physical difference between a 22-year-old who had two years of combat and a 22-year-old who didn't is in itself a fairly complete comment on war.

Alongside the wise and practical veterans, there are the new soldiers who enlisted after the war, as if joining the Army was a bigger form of Bingo night. The GI Bill of Rights, instead of a full set of china dinnerware, was the lure; and the kids planned to sweat out their 18 months and then go to college free. As one of them said, 'I guess college is kind of a fad around now. Shoot, I'm having as much fun in the Army as I would in any old college somewhere.'

We drove through places called Old Hundred, Hamlet, Pee Dee. The main streets seem to have been ordered from a firm that mass-produces main streets for small Southern towns and there is nothing charming about the invariable drugstore, movie house, Woolworth's and the stucco gas stations on the crossroads. On the best streets, there were old or oldish houses, large, white and private behind soft trees. The other houses were dateless and styleless, but everywhere rich in roses and wisteria and clumped about with bright hydrangea bushes. And every street was a cool underwater green, shaded by arching live oaks: the towns are anchored in place by the magnificent trees. The trees remind you that America is not brand-new.

Why should anyone living here be in a flap about John L. Lewis or the German peace treaty? They manufacture their lives locally; they are self-sufficient. It is certain that when an itinerant man of God arrives and speaks darkly of Nineveh, for instance, he is talking about something more immediate and interesting than if Leland Stowe, perhaps, arrived and talked about Greece. There is a lot of religion, one way and another, in dignified, pillared Baptist churches and in epileptic gospel meetings, and one must assume that the conditions in heaven and hell are more absorbing, to people who plan to spend time in one or the other, than are conditions beyond the confines of Old Hundred, Hamlet and Pee Dee.

On a dusty street in Monroe, North Carolina, Harrison and Mr Pete were repairing shabby automobiles. Before this, Harrison repaired airplane motors in Calcutta and Karachi; and Mr Pete worked for the Navy in those small craft that landed the Army on the coast of North Africa and at Anzio. They bent over their busted automobiles and Mr Pete said to Harrison, 'How's the situation?' 'Situation well in hand,' Harrison replied. It is as if they had something wonderful between them, for they are home where they want to be, and Monroe is finer than any place on earth.

There is no moral to driving through America. There probably isn't any conclusion. Except the obvious one: America is not what it sounds, Americans are not those people you read about in newspapers and magazines. I know what a disgust America seems to those who read its own report of itself and are too far away to check the facts against the truth. America sounds greedy, righteous and afraid, and full of threatening sounds. We are not loved abroad and I see no reason to expect love, but our exported picture of ourselves is a disaster.

I do not believe that picture any more, though I see it daily, painted in words by our Public Figures. One day the local papers front-paged the report of the presidential advisory commission, which stated that 'weakness is an invitation to extermination,' and that war 'could come at any time' and that we have only four to ten years' immunity from atomic 'sneak attacks' on our cities. To avoid these calamities, we should immediately spend $1,750 million on defence. (One can imagine how that sounds to those threatening foreigners who are concerned with the fact that hunger is an invitation to extermination.) Alongside that story, these comfortable small-town papers printed the picture of an eleven-year-old local girl who won a national spelling bee. People hereabouts, average Americans, were not discussing the commission's picture of a strong, intact, well-fed nation loud with fear before the world's poor; they were talking about Mattie Lou's triumph.

The country goes on, being beautiful and strange.

In the mountains of North Carolina there is a clear, irregular piece of water, poured between green hills, and called Lake Lure. It compares favourably to Annecy or Garda, but did you ever hear of it? There are the Great Smoky Mountains piled on each other in huge, blue-green waves; the red land of Georgia and the pines; the dunes of Santa Rosa Island like a low chain of snow mountains with the sea glass-green and purple before them; the wild dark forest around Lake Pontchartrain: a land going on for ever, changing and lovely.

And the countryside is strange with its own life, and with its lightly anchored, restless people. At the edge of the Great Smoky Mountains National Park, some tamed, scrubbed Cherokees live on a reservation that looks like a sanitarium, and sell knick-knacks to tourists. The passing white Americans, mainly Southerners, regard the Indians as a picturesque tourist attraction. I wonder if the Indians ever go to a shapeless neighbouring town in order to stare at the picturesque whites. They would see the young palefaces waiting around a jukebox until someone produced the requisite nickel for music and then, silent and with expressionless faces, launching themselves into their tribal jitterbugging. These mysterious, not gay, complicated gyrations are obviously a ritual dance. The dancers, instead of feathered head-dresses, wear uniforms: the girls in shorts that cover only what is essential by law, and with long, loose shirts; the boys in T-shirts and trousers rolled above their ankles. Why travel to Yucatan or Bali when the natives dance so exotically in every American village?

In Charlotte, a brigade of ladies calling themselves 'Does,' who seem to be the female branch of the Elks, were holding a convention. The whole performance, and above all the ladies' faces, was scarcely credible. There are times when American women seem to form a third sex, something entirely apart, or perhaps they make another race rather than a sex. Dressed in printed silks and often bunched with orchids, they were given over to a fierce and purposeful activity, and the town, a little frightened, made way for them. From Baltimore to Houston, the cities seemed crawling with conventions. Why isn't this the American system of fiestas, substituting some improbable club or fanciful business for a saint's day?

You are never really let alone in the South. The loudspeakers that carry, on to the streets, unwanted music, advice and recitative are replaced—on the open road—by commanding signs. Drink Fosko (the South surely swallows more coloured, sweetened horror than is consumed with safety elsewhere in the world); or Sit on Spratline's Seat Cushions; and finally, and often, one is warned: Prepare to Meet Your God. Preparing to Meet God is no light event. In some unmemorable hamlet, on a stringy main street lined with dusty cars, a man of God stood outside the drugstore and exhorted sinners to step up and be saved. He did this in the blaze of Saturday afternoon, and from a distance he sounded as if he were having a fit or being tortured. Closer to, he made no sense at all and his voice was terrifying as he screamed, threatened and groaned. A young farmer in blue jeans, lounging unconcerned near this dreadful exhibition, opined that 'people can get crazy on God just like on likker. Seems they sit alone and think too much and they just get crazy on it.'

At Florala, in Alabama, a freckle-faced veteran owned and operated the bus-stop café. He remembered eating baked octopus in Naples and he remembered Switzerland, where 'they had everything under control. They didn't have no black market until the American soldiers came. You couldn't eat more than your share even if you had the money.' He had left a fine, $80-a-week job at Niagra Falls, because of the housing, and returned to Florala, where he was born. He worked from seven in the morning until nine at night, and that way 'kept from getting restless.' For restlessness is a disease as definite as malaria and must be steadily fought with all possible sanity precautions.

There at Florala too, on the edge of another delightful unknown lake, a very fat man and his agreeable wife were opening
a new hotel. It was the eighth which he had bought, rebuilt,
furnished, opened, operated and sold in the course of six years.
You could not think they were principally interested in bettering
themselves, for each hotel had been a success and offered a life
of security and ease. They were interested in moving; or they were
impelled to move.

It is charming the way everyone in the South says, 'Come
back.' This is the regulation farewell at gas stations, soda fountains,
general stores, tourist camps. 'Come back,' they call, 'come back.'
Do they feel marooned in one place, lost, needing to believe
someone will return to share their exile on the similar main streets,
in the varied but always new-looking land?

And everywhere, from the beaches of North Carolina to Biloxi
and Lake Pontchartrain, the not-rich people were vacationing.
Americans have a habit of thinking that foreigners do not work,
that some hereditary laziness prevents them becoming rich and
thus causes them to stir up endless trouble. But I have never seen
any country where so many people took so much time off to have
fun.

We are a wildly energetic people in our pursuit of pleasure,
let alone in our pursuit of money, and we are very odd to look
at as we go about our lives. Someday, no doubt, foreigners
will come to watch us, as—in our time—we streamed from
Oberammergau to Pekin, watching them. They will find the
country beautiful beyond belief and the natives peculiar enough
to make the trip worthwhile.

We were impressed by the number of schools, perched along
the roads, all spanking new, with fine hygienic windows, and the
playground loud and bright with children. The road signs say
'School—Slow,' with great frequency; and the school buses chug
about in laudable numbers. This wealth of schoolhouses does
not correspond with the Jeeter Lester preconception of the South
any more than does the striking prosperity.

Besides the schools, there are many colleges, looking like spreading country houses under their old trees. It would seem that people in the South are hipped on education and, judging by buildings alone, they ought to be a very learned set of people. This would scarcely appear to be the case. I have the impression that reading is an occupation suitable only for the sick or bedridden; and that the expression of ideas, the effort for articulate thought, is considered unnecessary. Most of the citizenry have not troubled to study grammar, despite the pretty schools. They speak English, on the whole, as if they were still learning it with some difficulty.

On the other hand, we saw two institutions of learning which seemed remarkable because the students evidently felt their education was a great and serious privilege. These rarities were Black Mountain College and Tuskegee Institute.

Black Mountain College, if nobody has bothered to tell you, is a collection of unattractive and scarcely confortable buildings set alongside a bright, small lake, with mountains ringing it, and a lovely morning mist and purple-soft evening sky. The young who attend this place are as lively a bunch as I ever saw, very merry with their Borsodi-communal life, wonderfully earnest about the world they live in and as intellectual as all get-out. I suppose their great human experiment is the mixing of coloured and white students, in the heart of the lynch country. But it seemed to me, perhaps inaccurately, that there was a self-consciousness about this, an excessive consideration for the Negro students because of their colour. The experiment will become successful when they can all treat each other with cheerful, friendly rudeness, irrespective of pigmentation. Obviously the white students and faculty cannot forget their sense of outrage against the injustice that is visited on the Negroes, economically and socially, since they live in constant contact with this injustice. When we were there, little groups of white students were walking the streets of Black Mountain, getting signatures to a petition for space for coloured people in the local movie house. It is certainly an inalienable right of Americans to go to the movies, even if only in Jim Crow seats.

In a rural way, Black Mountain is the nearest thing I have seen in America to the café life of students in Europe. By this I mean that it has been a long time since I heard young people talking steadily and with such passion about Art, Love, Life and Politics. I think these kids will turn out to be fine, if slightly unhappy, citizens. Not for them the abiding love of things and the comfortable herd minds of their countrymen. It would be interesting if they would settle, like human time bombs, in the South.

Tuskegee is a big, rich, handsome place: the Negroes have made their own world here and made it fine. George Washington Carver's laboratory is open to the public and it was moving to see, not only because of the audacious, selfless and determined mind that worked there, but because it is a shrine. Two stout, brightly clad coloured ladies, panting in the heat on the laboratory steps, gossiped together in the lovely voices Negroes have. They were not of the privileged group which studies here—they were the poor ones without education—but they had the joy of ownership and the right to admire. Coloured school children, looking awed, obedient and bored, filed through the big room, shepherded by their teachers. Young men studied the exhibited test tubes, with reverence. Everyone was proud: Dr Carver was theirs; this great campus was theirs; and—freed of the intolerable condescension of the whites—they seemed to stand straighter, walk faster and to be happy, not in the way of the poor Southern Negroes, a mindless, chuckling happiness that is almost resignation, but happy because their world looked good. The young people who graduate from Tuskegee also will become fine, if slightly unhappy, citizens. The country has not grown up to them.

At Orange, on the Sabine River, we entered Texas. At once, you felt that every man was out for himself and in a hurry about it. All charm disappeared, to be replaced by cactuses, oil wells and a climate like living under a vast hair-drier. There is too much land here and it could do with an influx of new blood. When you think of all the people rotting in DP camps, it seems a crime that southern Texas should waste under the sun.

We fled through Texas, through Beaumont and Houston,

with its outer fringe of Luna Park and gaudy tourist camps, its oil-boom crowdedness, through all the ugliness and grab, longing to be gone. But in Houston there was a man who should be mentioned—he seemed a phenomenon; he was kind. He ran a parking lot and enjoyed doing kindnesses to strangers. In this he was well out of the swim, for no one else in that part of Texas would have had time for such fantasy. He was loaning money to a woman, a hitchhiking waif who needed an operation; helping repair a shabby car belonging to some travellers who could not afford a garage mechanic; and trying, in an unaccented, easy way, to be decent to his fellow men. They should elect him mayor, for my money.

After all the miles and all the weeks, there is still no conclusion to draw from driving through America. It is beautiful and strange. It has also a great quality of unreality, because the reality of most of the world now is hunger and desolation, gutted houses and factories, the car that lies pocked with bullet holes and rusting at the side of the road, the burned-out tank, the ration tickets, the devious anguish of black markets, the hopelessly repaired clothes, the cracked shoes and the wretched allotment of coal. I do not see how anyone can make that reality clear to Americans, because they have not felt it and experience is not communicated through the mind. But if Americans could understand and feel that reality, someone should tell them to be generous quickly, to be impractically and imprudently generous, since it is not safe for one nation alone to be so blessed.

Cry Shame

The fierce lights of the newsreel cameras beat on a bald head and a pudgy, bewildered face; a photographer crouched four feet away; the press crowded at tables to the right; on the left sat the counsel and his aides; above, the four inquisitors lolled in reasonable and comfortable shadow. It looked like a cluttered stage set up there in front, but the rest of the big House Caucus Room was empty except for a few dozen people who seemed to have wandered in, casually, as one might into a Trans-Lux theatre between trains. And it was quite a show, and free too: the Un-Americans putting on a flawless travesty of justice.

Robert E. Stripling, the permanent counsel for the House Committee on Un-American Activities, was the chief actor. Stripling, of the sharp voice and sick, spiteful face, did most of the talking because Hanns Eisler, the other leading character, was not allowed to cross-examine, or call witnesses, or even suggest witnesses, or read a statement: so naturally he did not have as much to say. For a while it was rather dull and then suddenly the word 'communism' was pronounced. The four Un-Americans, sitting on their raised dais, woke up, moved, leaned forward. For now we had the clue, the thing the plot hung on, the horrid syllables that gave everyone his position and his fame and his power and his swelling sense of virtue. We had, in short, the delicious smell of blood.

And Stripling made a point: 21 years ago Eisler had applied

for membership in the German Communist Party. Eisler said he had not paid his dues (maybe he forgot or didn't have the money), nor gone to meetings (how boring a musician would find political gatherings with nothing to listen to but voices), and had, in effect, never been a 'real member' of the party. Stripling clearly did not believe this; he would have no possible way of understanding the emotions and actions and spontaneities and carelessnesses of a man who loves music. Nor would Stripling know, or try to imagine, what Germany was like in 1926. Stripling was obviously enjoying himself with this dumpy, perspiring foreigner who speaks such accented English.

Stripling, like all the Un-Americans, is a devoted and exclusive reader of the *Daily Worker*. (No other newspaper is seemingly credible enough to be cited in evidence.) He produced an antique pre-war clipping from his favourite paper; a picture of Eisler being greeted by a band of people—students, musicians, or someone— all giving the clenched-fist salute, and Eisler affably giving it back. Eisler observed that really this was the salute of all kinds of European workers and always has been, but Stripling, impatient of such balderdash, told Eisler curtly to identify himself in the picture. Then Stripling said, show the committee what you were doing; and innocently Eisler raised his arm with the fist clenched. The cameras clicked like teeth snapping shut, there was a ripple of triumphant amusement in the Caucus Room, and Stripling turned away with a sly and satisfied smile . . .

I had then seen as much of the show as I could stand, and I left. Besides, I had seen this show done before, but by real professionals; here in the Caucus Room it was after all a little Peoples' Court for beginners.

The one legal accusation against Hanns Eisler is that, in 1940, he evaded the law which excludes from permanent entry into the United States such aliens as advocate, or belong to organizations which advocate, the overthrow of the United States Government by force or violence. This statute has been construed by the State Department and the Un-Americans to embrace Communists and the Communist Party. But no one has proved that Hanns Eisler was a Communist in 1940, or at any time subsequent to the wandering application for membership in the German Communist Party in 1926.

However, the committee apparently feels it can discern what goes on inside a man's heart, despite what the man may say to the contrary. To prove their divining-rod theory that Eisler has 'communistic beliefs,' they submit as sole evidence some flattering excerpts from the Communist press, the fact that Eisler has written 'Red songs' (not titled by him; he is a musician only) which were sung by many anti-fascists as well as Communists, and the undeniable existence of his, shall we say, awkward brother. This is all, this pitiful and ignorant gossiping.

When Eisler said he had never been a 'real member' of the Communist Party, that is exactly what he meant. His technically false answer (that 1926 application for membership) will perhaps fix Eisler in the end. Yet those of us who are only human beings and not law-givers can understand this: that a person, driven by despair, hope or anger, makes a brief gesture, changes his mood, wanders off, forgets. And if the Un-Americans were realists, instead of a hunting pack, they would recognize that to be a 'real member' of the Communist Party, you have to earn your C by Communist standards, which no one has ever denied are both long and tough and highly unsuited to men who are chiefly interested in sonatas, cantatas and the theory of counterpoint.

However, as Norman M. Littell, lawyer for George Messer-smith, stated: if the committee thought Eisler was a Communist, the evidence should be turned over to the Justice Department for prosecution. For there are laws and courts of law, and an accused man has the right to a fair and free trial: at least as long as this country stands on rock. But the Un-Americans are not a law court, and do not have to prove anything. They can say what they like, armoured with subpoenas and safe beind their extraterritoriality which spares them suits for slander. So it was possible for Stripling to announce that Eisler is the Karl Marx of the music world, a remark of such grotesque and childish silliness that anywhere else it would make people yawn or laugh their heads off. It was also possible for Representative John E. Rankin (D, Miss.) to say that testimony indicated that 'Mr Eisler certainly is following the Communist line and serving the Comintern just as effectively as if he were a member of the Communist Party.' In the minds of the Un-Americans, We the People must be a bunch of fools or cowards, for we are seriously asked to shiver at the thought that Eisler's songs menace our way of life: on a note of music, apparently the whole structure will topple to pieces. If We the People do not believe our nation and system of government to be more secure than that, we ought to migrate like the lemmings, plunging solemnly into the sea . . .

Supposedly, an agent of the Comintern does something; he can't just sit around telling himself in a sinister fashion that he is an agent. But no one bothered to say, let alone prove, what Eisler, the alleged servant, has been doing in this country since 1940 to undermine us all. Eisler had visited Russia long before the war; the committee forgets that in the almost unimaginable past a lot of people went everywhere and it was not regarded as criminal. There even used to be, if you can believe it, plain commercial tours to the Soviet Union and anyone who had the fare could go, provided they wouldn't much rather have a bang-up time rollicking around Paris, France, and Rome, Italy, and other places which were also easy to reach. The committee says that Eisler was one who planned the International Music Bureau, apparently a dream on paper, which got its letterhead (and never went farther) in Moscow when Eisler was not there to consent or advise. But oddly enough, in those distant days before the war, music and books and painting flowed around quite freely between all except the fascist nations and this used to be considered a good thing.

Furthermore, as the committee neglects to note, we have only recently been at cold war with Russia: in the years between 1933 and 1939, a German anti-Nazi could conceivably have been grateful to the Russians for keeping him outspoken company in his hatred of Hitler. Since the committee's evidence seems principally to concern the period between 1929 and 1939, it is only proper to remind them of history.

But this is beside the point: if Eisler broke a law, if Eisler is a servant of the Comintern masquerading as a sincere composer of music, these facts can be proved by established courts of law and handled by the fixed penalties of law. What is intolerable is the free and easy process of defamation, replacing the careful and weighty process of justice.

There was an extraordinary feature of this case, which seems to have passed unnoticed. The State Department had a dossier on Eisler, saying that Eisler was 'communistic' but not a member of the party. Which leads one to brood, in sorrow of spirit, on the making of dossiers, and to ask oneself whether intuitive and arbitrary deduction is adequate evidence for governmental bodies.

The Un-Americans, after three days of sordid and pointless baying over Eisler, decided to turn his case over to the Justice Department, and ultimately to a court of law, which is where it always belonged and the only place it belonged. If Eisler in fact did break the law, it must be proved beyond a reasonable doubt, and if proved he will stand the penalty, and that is exactly how it should be. But as it is now, the Un-Americans have terminated another of their travesties of justice; nothing is proved though anything is stated; and Eisler departs, free as air, and at liberty to be boycotted in his profession and starve at will. This is not the great terror which we watched during the long hateful years; this is not the secret arrest, the questioning with torture, the returned box of ashes. This is just a little terror, calculated to frighten little people. It works. Without recourse to law, a man can be well and truly destroyed.

One asks oneself, finally, what these people wanted with Hanns Eisler. They proved nothing; they learned nothing. One can recognize the Un-Americans to be evil, but surely not half-witted; and they cannot expect anyone to believe that Eisler, writing background music in Hollywood for a living, is at the head of some large furtive movement of music-lovers, vowed to plunge us all into communism. There is a limt to possible public gullibility.

Of course, in pawing over Eisler, they had the joyful chance of trying to besmirch what is absolutely and finally unassailable: the character of Eleanor Roosevelt. And there was also the pleasure of being able subtly to scold and condescend to very important public figures. This must be a deep satisfaction, but it is amazing that the public figures do not rise, with dignity and good sense, to condemn these dingy tactics.

Still, none of this is enough, and one must wonder whether there is a plan in this shabbiness, and whether Eisler, who is not himself important to them, has importance as a test of strength. For perhaps these men in the House Caucus Room are determined to spread silence: to frighten those voices which will shout no, and ask questions, defend the few, attack cruelty and proclaim the rights and dignity of man.

A man with a family will think many times before speaking his mind fearlessly and critically when there lies ahead the threat of an Un-Americans' investigation, a publicized branding, and his job gone. It is small consolation to know that you cannot be put in jail for your opinions if your opinions, freely expressed, end by starving your dependents. And if you can ruin a musician's livelihood, before a court has determined whether he is indeed a law-breaker or not, pretty soon you can ruin a painter and a teacher and a writer and a lawyer and an actor and a scientist; and presently you have made a silent place.

If these things should come to pass, America is going to look very strange to Americans and they will not be at home here, for the air will slowly become unbreathable to all forms of life except sheep.

The Children Pay

You really wouldn't know, everyone says, there'd been a war here. It's too good to be true, they say; these Italians are the luckiest people on earth. And life is so pleasant and easy and, furthermore, cheap. You sit at a sidewalk café on the Via Veneto and have a drink before lunch and watch the people passing, and all the women look pretty and all the men look elegant and nobody hurries and everyone seems to be smiling, and around you there is Rome, ochre-coloured and soft in the sun.

Wherever you turn, you find beauty—the climbing stone splendour of the Spanish Steps, banked with flower stalls; the pillared courtyard of St Peter's; the great trees and ancient statues in the Pincio gardens. As for the shops, well, this is authentic luxury. You can buy anything from seductive pastries to diamonds, not forgetting leather goods and silks and antiques and whatever else you covet.

If you think Rome is wonderful, then wait until you see Venice. You loaf away the afternoon in St Mark's Square, eating the world's best ice-cream, looking at that marvel of light, the domed church and the high rectangular frame of palaces, watching children feed the pigeons and lovers saunter past in a state of beatitude, while two comic orchestras play off key. After which, you take a gondola to dinner or the opera. Tomorrow you can hire a speedboat and go to the Lido to swim. Why should one ever leave this blissful spot?

But you'd be bewitched by Siena, too, and Ravello and Florence and any place else you name, and you ought to drive because the countryside is a dream. Once in a while, of course, you see ruins—bomb damage, most likely—but there is so much else unspoiled, unique, that you hardly notice these mementos of war. Besides, the Italians don't moan over what's smashed. You can't argue; it's a plain fact. Italy is pre-war, perfect, the nearest thing to heaven.

The word has gone out, and tourists flock to Italy by the hundreds of thousands. Swedes arrive in sumptuous blue buses. Austrians, wearing leather shorts and green-felt hats, ride around on the motor launches which are Venice's street cars. Even some well-dressed Germans nibble chocolate bars on the first-class train to Naples. The French, always chic, contemplate somewhat enviously gay Rome, this new rival to Paris. The English eat with joy and patiently figure up, afterwards, how many lire in a pound sterling and how much of their rationed money is left for the trip. And there are Swiss, and Indian ladies in saris and, everywhere, Americans. The Italians do not snarl at foreigners. The Italians seem delighted to share the wonders of their country.

Naturally, not everyone can be happy; you do see some beggars on the streets. But, as everyone says, there always have been poor people in Italy—it's pathetic but it's not news. So you give them 100 lire—about fifteen cents—and they smile and thank you. The kids who beg look like little imps, very picturesque in their rags, and they seem to be begging for fun as if it were a jolly new game.

If you happen to drive through the slums, by accident, they are so quaint and lively, with washing hanging across narrow streets, and a red mattress alongside pink geraniums on a window ledge, and everyone shouting and talking and running around, that you can't feel too upset. Besides, the Marshall Plan is pouring money into the country, and Italy's industrial production is 98 per cent of the 1938 peak, which is marvellous, isn't it? And they actually sell thousands of sewing machines to the United States where the sewing machine was born, and every country in Europe owes them money, and God knows there must be enough food, judging by the amount you see in the markets and the grocery stores and in all the restaurants. It's impossible to believe that five years ago Italy was a shambles, rotted with war. But whatever the war was like, it's over and done with now. Everyone says, merrily, that only two countries won the war, the United States and Italy, and it's more fun in Italy.

All of this seems like a fairy story or a travel advertisement. The astonishing thing is that it is largely true. Probably there is a reasonable explanation for the recovery of Italy, but it looks and feels like a miracle. Those who know Italy and Italians would agree that the miracle is built into the people. For here is a race which has been overrun, devastated and conquered since the beginning of history—and nothing can defeat their love of life. The result is that they go on living and working like a nation of beavers. And apparently an Italian has to be an optimist, and have faith in the future, or die. If you love life enough, it would seem you can force life to be good. They have survived the war and risen from the ruins with incredible speed.

But the war cannot be forgotten. It was a terrible war, inching over the land from Sicily to the Alps. Two armies fought here slowly. The retreating army, in bitterness and failure, had plenty of time to destroy the country and the people, as it moved north. The victorious army had plenty of artillery and aviation to destroy the country and the people as it advanced against the enemy. Someone must pay for this. The dead have paid their share and are quits.

Someone does pay.

In terms of life, the price falls most heavily where it is least deserved and least noticed—on children. Neither the enchanted foreigners nor the fairly privileged Italians visit the shuttered buildings that are orphanages, the prisonlike reform schools, the hospitals and rest homes crowded with tubercular and under-nourished children. Why should anyone trouble to inspect a dank school where thin, white-faced children are too hungry to concentrate on their books? No one wants to remember the torment of war. And certainly no adults want to watch children paying the price of adult cruelty and folly. But the children are there, scattered and hidden behind the pleasant appearance of everyday life. They go on paying for the war with their lives—they, at least, will never forget what the true cost is.

The port of Naples was a military target. Behind it, the crowding stone tenements of the poor got smashed as well. Two little boys, barefooted, ragged, bony, about nine years old, were walking in front of this giant rubble heap which is their neighbourhood. They were waiting for a ship that was due at two o'clock; then they would sneak past the gate into the dock area and beg food from the sailors. It was a pretty good system; they could figure on one meal a day. They had last eaten twenty-four hours before.

As the ship was late, they decided to show us where they lived and led us down a dust path into the ruins. Here the bombs had carved out a barren square which became a playground, full of children—there never were so many children as live in the slum streets of Naples. A man had built a swing of old crates and was charging a penny for a ride; he did not like to take money, but he was an unemployed dockworker and had three kids of his own. Our two little guides spoke to various chums, who were sorting old nails and tin cans and other objects they had salvaged for sale, and then took us into a street like a canyon. At this point the second child vanished into a black doorway. He evidently feared we were the police.

Luigi, the smaller, blond one, lived here in one windowless room with his mother and sister and two brothers. His father went to the war, he explained, and did not come home; his mother was out all day trying to find work. He seemed to think the room was very nice, and indeed he had part of a bed to sleep in and, although damp, the room was warmer than the streets. The second brother, a boy of thirteen, sat on the edge of the lumpy, unsavoury bed and stared from a strange, closed-in face. Luigi announced, in a matter-of-fact way, that his brother had much fear ever since the bombings—he had become a little stupid in the head, and his sister coughed all the time. Another brother begged uptown with a group of friends; he was the one who brought in money.

Now Luigi had to return to the docks to see about the ship, so we pushed our way through an enormous crowd which had gathered, children and women and the jobless men. Perhaps we had come to offer work? Or food? Or could we do something about this baby—a grey package—or this one, another grey package covered with sores? On the streets by the docks we met a pal of Luigi's—this was a very small, dark boy; it is hard to tell the ages of such undersized children—who was collecting cigarette butts. He remarked bitterly that he could do nothing in this wind; rain or wind made the business bad. But on a good day if you worked hard you could sometimes pick up twenty cents' worth of butts.

The cigarette merchant informed Luigi that mutual friends were sitting behind that fence over there, playing cards. These five busy little gamblers, aged seven to twelve, had made some money in the morning, pooled it, bought bread and cheese, so now they were fed for the day and could take it easy, playing an improvised card game on a heap of cement that was the crushed wall of an apartment building. Luigi did not know where they lived. Three of them had no parents, so he guessed they lived someplace different every night. Then he said 'So long,' and slipped through the iron gate into the docks to continue his daily search for food.

No one knows how many children in Italy exist like this, and it is a mystery how they manage. They do not go to school because they have no shoes and they need their time to find food, and besides there aren't enough schools. They do not come under the care of any agency because war disrupts social services quite as thoroughly as it does dock installations and rail terminals. In Italy a child is considered an orphan if he has lost one parent, and this is a sound definition—one parent cannot maintain a home. So these children roam in the adult world's jungle, cheated of everything that would make a decent childhood.

But they are not the unluckiest children. The unluckiest are the ones who get thrust into orphanage prisons like the Hotel of the Poor in Naples, where everything has been silenced by terror and misery, except the children's eyes. The unluckiest are the girls, not criminal, only homeless, lost, who are locked into a certain convent reform school in Rome, where they are made to feel ugly and despised and forever outcast. The children of the streets hold on to their freedom as long as they can, but what catches up with them is sickness, principally tuberculosis, that great legacy of war.

Through no fault of the Italian authorities, statistics on children are unreliable. They are guesses based on some known facts, and these figures are apt to be underestimated rather than overestimated. A private report of the Ministry of the Interior estimates that 300,000 children are predisposed to tuberculosis, and of these, 6.5 per cent are helped. If a child happens to be in this 6.5 per cent, he is better off than a healthy orphan, for the care in the TB preventoria, as they are called, is gentler than in most orphanages, and the child will receive a little extra food— perhaps more powdered milk—and have a clean bed. He will be allowed to stay in the sun for at least an hour a day and, if very young, some hours longer. He might even have a toy. In Naples there is one such TB rest home for 300 children that seemed cheerfully human because the walls were freshly painted, trees grew in the courtyard, the little girls had hair ribbons, which they loved, and a unit of the United States Air Force, having bombed the building by mistake, now sends the children dolls.

A delicious little girl, with curling brown hair and a bright-red hair ribbon, showed us her doll and thanked us for it. As we were Americans, she assumed we would know the other Americans who gave it to her. She had colour in her cheeks and smiled, and one thought, *At last, a happy child*. She probably was, too, because she knew no other life. When she was two years old, her mother had been killed during a bombing raid. Someone found the sick baby later, and she was put in here to pass her childhood with other children even less fortunate than she because they were even sicker.

On the seacoast, just above Ostia, Rome's summer resort, is a village called Fiumicino. Behind the dunes, in a large shabby villa, is an orphanage for eighty children. You will find such small institutions everywhere. But this one has a garden, and the children can play on the beach, so it is a fine place. The children are babies, aged two to five, and this day they were sitting on the sand in a large circle, singing their heads off. They were comfortably dirty and all wore absurd little white-and-blue-striped cotton caps because nuns usually feel that sun is perilous stuff.

The Superior, a young nun with an intelligent face, started to call out names. Suddenly a little bowlegged mulatto toddles toward us, followed by a little mulatto girl with kinky brown hair. A pale golden-blond child joined them, and another little girl with freckles and flaming red hair. They were four of the prettiest children imaginable.

'Mixed races,' the nun said, and gestured toward the whole circle. 'The soldiers left them behind.' These four had American Negro, German and Scots fathers—but all the nations that fought in Italy were here represented in their children. The babies went back to their places and began to sing again, very loudly, in Italian.

It is not known how many thousands of these children there are, illegitimate and abandoned, destined to spend their lives moving from institution to institution until they are any age between sixteen and twenty-one. They do not stay in one place and so grow up at least with borrowed roots, the same adults to look after them, the same house to live in. They move from a foundling home when they are two years old, and again when they are six, and again when they are twelve; and when they come of age they will receive identity papers stating that their parents are unknown. Thus they are guaranteed never to feel safe anywhere.

Italian children are a special race. It is difficult to destroy their natural quality, which is bright-eyed, not rowdy, liveliness. They seem very sure of themselves, and this gives them a charming, comic dignity—they are a constant pleasure to look at. You have to shave their heads, as is done to boys in many institutions, and put the girls in hideous shapeless greyish uniforms, and regiment and discipline them to death before you can ruin them. Whereas Italians have a superb talent for making their own homes happy places to grow in, their institutions are too often factories to break the great spirit of the children. The worst of these asylums where children must live are sickening echoes out of Dickens and the darkest, heartless past. The average are dismal and chilling, under the grey shadow of poverty. The best are the best because kindness and sun have entered them—not because they are rich enough to provide plentifully for a child's needs. None can afford that. You are reading only of the best.

On the hills outside Rome, surrounded by terraced vineyards, is a handsome modern building, with sun decks and balconies, wide windows and big airy rooms, that Mussolini ordered some years ago as a hospital for unmarried mothers. Monte Rotondo is now an orphanage for the children of Partisans, the men and women who died fighting Fascism. Three hundred little boys and girls, the boys wearing blue-and-white-checked pinafores, the girls in red-and-white ones, were playing on separate sides of the long cement roof. They sounded like a congress of birds and looked like a flower garden, and they were inventing their own games because they had only two rubber balls for toys. They seemed healthy and gay and as children should be.

Without warning, the illusion of happiness cracked. A nun led up a small brown-haired boy with beautiful but frightened eyes. He would look at no one and kept turning away his head, and you could see the cords standing out in his neck. He was mumbling or whispering something. Then I realized that this child was telling how the Germans came to arrest his father, a Partisan, but his father was not home and the Germans were angry, so they took his mother and his aunts and his grandmother into the streets and shot them. He was with his mother, but she fell on top of him and he was hidden by her skirt and the Germans thought he was dead, so they went away.

Now, on the other side of the low railing which divided the boys' playground from the girls', a very small boy started to wail in high screaming sobs. This was the brother of the child who was speaking; he imagined that his older brother, the only family he had left in the world, was being taken away from him.

Grown-ups came and asked questions and then surely they would put his brother in an automobile, and he would disappear and there would be no family anywhere. The little one sat on the cement floor, his face buried in his hands, and cried his heart out.

It was impossible to stop this needless torture. Among other things, Italy needs a loan of experienced child psychiatrists to instruct the men and women who have charge of these children. Now a nun, with perfect kindness and perfect insensitivity, presented a ten-year-old girl, blond-haired, slim and straight, with a fine, clever face. Quite clearly, as if she were talking of someone else, she told how her father came down from the hills, where he lived with a band of Partisans, to visit his family; and that day the Germans stopped in the village and rounded up many men and took them into the woods and stood them in a row and shot them. She was hiding behind the trees and she watched her father being killed. The sunny roof took on the aspect of a nightmare; one imagined child after child, in a blue or red pinafore, being led forward to recite the memory of horror. The only way to prevent this was to flee.

As we left, the nun said all the children had seen very terrible things, so they were 'more nervous' than ordinary children. For the least little reason, she said sadly, they were frightened and they cried.

The Villa Savoia is the former home of former King Umberto of Italy. Now the front part of the building is the Egyptian Legation, and the back part houses thirty-five mutilated children. The garden is wonderful, large and overgrown and full of secret places, and the rooms are bright and shining with sun. The children here are a living roll call of the battles of the war; they come from Cassino, blind; from Pescara, legless; from Frosinone without an arm; from Sicily, another blind. One of them found a curious round object on the beach, and he rolled it along like a hoop. It proved to be a mine and when he woke up in the hospital he had two stumps for arms and no eyes. A two-year-old boy was romping with his sister in a field. Under the grass something exploded, and she is dead and he is burned, with lidless eyes and twisted fingers.

And there is Giovanna, all softness like a deer, with brown hair and brown eyes. Her mother was running through the streets, pulling the child with her, during a bombing, and when she was killed she still held in her hand the right arm of her daughter. Giovanna spends her spare time knitting, with great effort, scarves for the stray cat that lives in the garden.

The blind children are very quiet. The little maimed ones guide the blind and tell them what they see. They all love the zoo and the movies, and the blind have marvellous notions of what the animals look like and what happens in the movies. They listen to the dialogue and make up the stories. In these stories there are always fine houses and lots to eat and beautiful parents and many happy children, and no one is blind.

But in cold weather they are all miserable, and a little boy will say his hand hurts, although he has no hand; and a little girl will complain of pain in a missing foot; and the blind are depressed by dampness and rain. Then, too, since they are growing, the bones push through the stumps of their arms and legs, and they must undergo more and more operations.

There are children with mutilated minds, too, who were so brutally shocked by the war that their minds can no longer direct their bodies. Some of them are in institutions; most of them are not. There is no room. You could learn about these children by walking through any bombed area and asking casual questions. In this way, by chance, near a Rome railway station I found a family which had been buried under their collapsing house during an air raid in 1944. There were four of them and they were dug out alive. The youngest boy was wounded in the head, but he was sewed together and he lives, hideously scarred, goes to school and seems fine. The government pays him $1.80 a month pension, which is the only fixed money coming in to the family. They moved back to the patched remnants of their house—where else could they go? The older brother, a boy of twelve, sits in their scabby room, year after year, doing nothing. He has never spoken since the night he was pulled from under the bricks of his home.

There are a few institutions for such children, of which the oldest must be the Gaetano Giardino Home, as it was founded as a shelter for mentally deranged children after World War I, and is naturally full up again after World War II. It is a beautiful old fort, on the rim of Rome, whitewashed and thick-walled, and a pitiful and alarming group of children live here behind the ancient moat and drawbridge. If, in this tragic crowd, you see what looks like a normal child, you ask: Why should she be here, that little one over there with long brown hair? Only because she has convulsions, as a result of the bombing of Velletri. But why that kid, doing carpenter work, the one wearing the lopsided glasses, the one with the nice grin—why is he here? Only because every so often he gets an unbearable headache, and then, for three and four days at a time, he loses his mind and lapses into a still blankness. But he is better than when he came, because then he was badly burned and his left arm was paralyzed too.

The estimated number of physically mutilated children is 15,000, but this is certainly an incomplete figure. About 15,000 men is a full-strength infantry division, so you can picture how many children this is when you remember the victory parade on Fifth Avenue, and how long it took one division to pass the reviewing stand. Only 3,000 of these wounded children can be taken care of. One does not know how the others live. There are approximately as many mentally deranged children as all American forces landed in Normany on D-Day, 45,000. But only 5.5 per cent of them can be helped in suitable institutions. The counted war orphans would fill twelve infantry divisions, 180,000 children, and twelve infantry divisions was the maximum size of the United States fighting army in Italy. As for the school children who are also often orphans and wounded and incipient TB cases, a government report states that 2,000,000 of these are needy and undernourished. Some 900,000 whose hunger endangers their immediate health receive food each day through the combined contribution of the United Nations Children's Emergency Fund and the Italian Government. They are given about 900 calories. What 900 calories look like is a small plate of rice with tomato sauce, a small piece of bread with some corned beef on it and a tin cup of powdered milk.

It goes on and on; it is a whole world of children who will never, as long as they live, stop paying for our grown-ups' war. Their eyes are hard to meet. They could so easily be full of laughter, but instead they are bewildered, wary, frightened, sad.

Many people in Italy are fiercely aware of the tragedy of these children. There are countless women of real good will who devote their time to volunteer work, and trained social workers who do an admirable job, especially in the Organization for Maternity and Infancy and the Red Cross; priests and doctors and nuns and teachers; the staff of the United Nations Children's Emergency Fund, who cannot be praised too highly; a young American social worker, Edna Weber, who runs, on almost no money, the happiest, most hopeful small orphanage I have seen; an inspired judge of the juvenile courts, Doctor Colucci, and others too numerous to list and name. They deserve unlimited respect because it takes a steady, faithful mind not to give up in despair before so overwhelming a task when you have so little means for handling it. No Italians can be happy that the state of our world forces them to spend one third of their national budget on military expenditure—including the care of cemeteries from two wars— while the children, the richness and future of their race, must be neglected for lack of funds.

It would be impossible to explain the last war to these children, let alone preparations for another. They really know about war and what it does to life. They must be the most convinced pacifists on earth. And not just these children, but all the others like them, throughout Europe, who know of war only that it comes into your street and onto your farm, and when it has gone you are left behind and have nothing you want, nothing you can count on, nothing a child has a right to. Adults could not persuade these small survivors that it is always necessary to make the world safe for democracy, but never safe for children.

Meantime, the fields of Italy are neat and lovely as gardens. The cities are bursting with people and bustling with buying and selling. The Italians, undaunted, struggle hard along the road to recovery and have strength left over to love life as they go. The foreigners, unanimously, admire a people who can make such a good thing of peace, and, unanimously, love Italy. It is one of the most beautiful countries in the world and, all things considered, one of the happiest. The sorrow and hardship of a few million children scarcely show.

The Forties

This book is not about war and I have written, in fact and fiction, all I want to write about the Second World War. I remember in hard detail the day and night of 7 May, 1945, the end of the war in Europe. After that, for two drifting years, I have snapshot memories. It is time to make a statement about my memory. The chronology of public events can be verified. My personal chronology cannot, being based on scant, usually undated letters and a few of those page-a-day diaries evidently scrawled as a sort of penance: self-discipline. I have never before tried to figure out when I was where (why I was where is another question) and I am finding it hard to do, and mortifying. I search my memory and discover black holes, depthless chasms, vast reaches of impenetrable fog. A good for nothing memory. Dates are correct as near as I know, the best I can manage.

When peace broke out, the general notion was to settle down. London was the only place I could imagine as possible to settle in. London had been undesirable real estate for six years and was strewn with empty neglected houses, going at cut-rate prices. I bought a pretty little house in South Eaton Place more carelessly than I would buy a book. It was a charming invalid; it ailed everywhere, from the roof to terminal dry rot. Though I owned it for two years, after it was patched up I lived in it no more than six months at most, between travels.

My restlessness was out of control. I made an unenthusiastic effort to report the final stage of the war in the Pacific; the war and my effort ended with the A-bombs while I was visiting my mother in St Louis. I spent time in Berlin with the American army of occupation, time in Portugal working badly on a war novel, time in France doing the same, time in Java reporting that dismal little colonial war. Sometime in London, Virginia Cowles and I wrote a frivolous play about war correspondents which made audiences laugh in the West End and folded overnight in New York. If I felt at home anywhere in this strange struggling peace, it was in London.

London looked sad. Weeds and wild flowers grew on bombsites everywhere, and great beams shored up the sides of half-destroyed buildings. There was no paint to freshen the face of the city. Rationing stayed strict. People were tired. Winter felt colder. My friends were as aimless as I was. We no longer had the imposed occupations of war, and nothing anyone specially wanted to do; or so it seemed. Limbo time.

One day I saw a pre-war English friend, a survivor from the early-thirties group of handsome young men-about-town, sitting alone in a big velvet chair in the Dorchester hotel foyer. He had been a prisoner of war since the Battle of Britain. With a strained smile and anxious eyes, he was watching strangers, listening to the babble of talk. I did not speak to him. I knew he was trying to get used to how people behaved who had not spent nearly six years behind barbed wire.

There were many parties; we made merry; no one talked about the war nor about those who were missing. The Chelsea Arts Ball at the Albert Hall, the rowdiest annual masquerade jamboree, had been suspended during the war and now, on New Year's Eve 1946, people could again romp around the huge floor, light-hearted, amorous and silly. Another English friend, whom I had met in Brussels wearing khaki, turned out to be a kind rich man when wearing mufti; he took a box for the great ball which I filled with Poles, former officers in the Carpathian Lancers, met in Italy. Costumes were put together from scraps. The Poles wore rented chef's hats and aprons; I was a gypsy based on brass hoop earrings and a red sash. Food remained scarce but not drink, I don't know why. Tight as ticks, hundreds of us danced until morning. I remember it happily as the best dance ever; it convinced me that the war was over.

My favourite Polish ex-officer, a funny glamorous absent-minded nobleman, soon to begin his career as a door-to-door salesman of brushes in the north, brought his cousin to my little house where we huddled around an electric fire. She was the last living member of his family, a lovely girl, with shy demure manners, dark blond hair and grey eyes. She had a tattooed number on her arm, having returned from Ravensbruck via a displaced persons camp. He told me later that she was fine, very cheerful: of course she had a few little problems. My housekeeper, who actually could not cook or clean any more than I could, was a sombre German Jewish refugee with diabetes. Everyone seemed to understand and accept everyone else; in all our different ways we had shared a common experience. I wondered what I would do with the rest of my life.

In this bustling jokey void, a letter arrived from my mother. She observed without emphasis that if I did not come home soon I would be an expatriate. The word appalled me, proving the power of language. Apart from a few visits and my year as a Federal employee and the following months in Connecticut, I had not lived in my homeland since 1930. I took myself for granted as a writer and an American, something that never changed. I lived where I liked or where it was convenient. Expatriate had a seedy decayed sort of sound. I sold my little house and returned to America in the spring of 1947.

The beginning was a treat. In a second-hand car, which by pure luck worked, my mother and I drove across America and Mexico to Acapulco. Part of this long happy trip is 'Journey Through a Peaceful Land.' As I wanted to sit still for a bit and grind on my war novel, we rented a house in Cuernavaca, a gentle village with dirt roads and flowers and superb trees and few foreigners, which enchanted us both. However, the object was to become a patriate and I chose Washington, remembered as a city of

117

bearable size and besides, where better to become a patriate than in the nation's capital.

A war-time friend had found a house for me in Georgetown. It was available to rent that September because it belonged to a beautiful former actress, a liberal Congresswoman from California who had lost her seat after a smear campaign—pink leaflets branding her as a 'pinko' et cetera—to a new man named Richard Nixon. I did not know this and it presents a fascinating question: can an omen be an omen if it is invisible? Georgetown was quiet and pretty with its brick dolls' houses and, as I was working on my novel, it made little difference where I lived my mole existence. On the other hand, I ought to take note of the nation's business, at least once in a while. I was favourably impressed on learning that anyone could walk into Congressional hearings and share the process of government as a spectator. Three cheers for American democracy.

I walked into a hearing of the House Committee on Un-American Activities, and wrote 'Cry Shame' in a greater passion of anger and disgust than shows in the article. Eisler was either deported or chose to leave, it hardly mattered which; he would never again find work in America. Though I had not seen or heard of him before the awful day of the hearing, I have a confused memory of going to wherever he departed (but when?) with a bunch of yellow roses for his wife, and imploring the baffled little man not to believe that all Americans were as loathesome as those Congressmen in Washington.

I could not accept the goings-on in that caucus room; they stewed in my mind. Why weren't the great American newspapers filled with condemnation? Why had the other Congressmen and Senators allowed this outrage? Why didn't everyone protest against the sinister wrongness of these horrible Congressional oafs? They denied the meaning of the war; they were practising the same kind of ugliness that flourished in Germany. No one I knew shared my fury and my prophetic fear; I seemed to be exaggerating.

The Un-American Activities Committee never unearthed a

single victim guilty of any criminal act. It was formed as a temporary group in 1938 to search out extremists in government posts but ignored American Nazis or Fascists. After the war, the Committee concentrated on trying to destroy the liberal spirit of the Roosevelt years, the New Deal. Their ill-begotten offspring, Senator Joseph McCarthy, succeeded beyond belief. America was entering its own particular Dark Ages when lives and livelihoods were ruined because a few Congressmen and later the heinous Senator denounced people as Communists or communistic, security risks. Proof was not needed; accusation did the job. The American reign of terror; no concentration camps, no gulags, no executions, just cowardly ostracism and unemployment, and it was enough.

About a month after the Eisler hearing, the Hollywood contingent arrived in Washington. Later famous as the Hollywood Ten, the chosen victims of the Un-American Activities Committee were a producer, two directors and seven scriptwriters, talented men employed in the making of commercial Hollywood films. They were accused of inserting communistic ideas in their work. I knew one of them, Alvah Bessie, who had fought in the Abraham Lincoln Battalion, and though I do not remember the hearings I visited them often in their hotel. I was relieved to share my anger. Sometime in those three days I made a broadcast on local radio, denouncing the Committee. My page-a-day diary describes this as a poor effort, too quickly written and not improved by the way my voice rose in rage. A feeble blow struck for freedom.

Ten decent citizens went to jail for contempt of Congress, refusing to answer questions, to 'name names' that would implicate and destroy others. Their careers were finished. The only way to save yourself was to toady to those ignorant inquisitors, the Un-Americans, elected representatives of the people. The only way those Congressmen could stay in business was to find more victims, thus justifying their charade of protecting the nation from Red enemies.

If this kind of contemptible and dangerous blackmail was an accepted part of the American system, I wanted no part in it.

I burrowed into my work until I had used up the lease of the Georgetown house, about four months in all; then moved to a cabin in a rural motel in Florida, the handiest sunshine area. There I lived in solitude until the book was done. I have always felt antipathy to it because Max Perkins, the great Scribner's editor, had talked me out of my working title, *Point of No Return,* saying it was too bleak. Overtired, as one is at the end of the job, I caved in to his remembered authority, for he was by then dead. I leafed through a Gideon Bible in the motel and came up with a senseless title that I abhor, *The Wine of Astonishment.* Since then, I will not budge on so much as a comma. But at any rate the work was finished, I mailed it to the publisher, I was free; and departed for Mexico, back to enchanting Cuernavaca.

I had been a patriate for less than a year. I would now revert to being a writer and an American; nothing changed that. Besides, I was a foreign correspondent; logically foreign correspondents lived in foreign countries. The world was wide and much of it very lovely; I intended to suit myself from now on and if that made me an expatriate, see if I cared. Not my problem. America was big, rich and safe and could look after itself.

The editor of *Collier's,* my splendid boss since 1937, died before the Second World War ended. Disliking his successor, I resigned and never again had a solid abode as a journalist. I decided I would use journalism, as a free lance, to pay for a fun trip or a chance to see whatever interested me. Not much journalism either, a few months in the summer, in Europe. My own work, fiction, came first; but my own work did not reap sheaves of gold and, though I knew that small is beautiful before it became a fashionable idea, still I had to earn enough to support a modest life behind high garden walls. The solution scared me, I was afraid that I would corrupt my mind and my writing, but thought that if I only wrote three short stories, fakes with happy endings, for popular American magazines, in three weeks each year, my immortal soul would not be irremediably tarnished. I called these stories 'bilgers' and having found some of them lately, I am delighted by them; they are stylish junk and I marvel that I was once so clever.

The four sweet years in Mexico were my private golden age. I lived in one of the most beautiful places on earth before it was spoiled—and this is a permanent good fortune in my life, to have reached the wonder places in time—and every summer I wrote my way to Europe and to London. 'The Children Pay' came from one of those early summer trips, a serious subject. Usually I chose unserious subjects—Capri, Eton—that amused me. I was taking a long leave of absence from the troubled world, except for a quick exciting visit to brand-new Israel.

A friend in Cuernavaca asked me how I could live without ever reading a newspaper. I said no doubt someone would telephone me if war was declared. Someone did: the Korean War. I know nothing whatever about the Korean War, never read about it in the papers, never read a book about it. If the people who ran the world could not run it without wars and if the people who lived in the world did not rebel against such deadly incompetence, I personally declared a separate peace. I was more contented than I had ever been, but still too young for contentment.

THE FIFTIES

The Most Unheard-of Thing

The Senate Caucus Room, a large imitation of Roman baths, tends
to echo and boom, and there are gong and wind sounds high up
in the four marbled corners. The American public knows this room
well, having seen it daily on television while Senator McCarthy
and the US Army disputed each other's veracity. The room,
however, looked quite different then, and so did Senator
McCarthy. Now the Senate Select Committee, which in fact is the
House Committee of the Club, is sitting in judgment on Senator
McCarthy, and there are no TV cameras and no agile
photographers and no radio engineers, and the procedure is strict
and orderly and quiet and fair.

The chairman of the Select Committee is a thin white-haired
man of 60 years, a Mormon from Utah, who speaks in a dry,
stubborn voice and has suddenly, not by his wish, become St
George. The other five Senators match him. They are the Senators
no one ever hears of, who do the work, who are steady, serious,
not brilliant men; and here they are, called to this unpleasant task,
and behaving in a way which restores considerable credit to the
Senate and to universal suffrage.

When these six men have written their report, all 96 Senators
will return to Washington, and sit down and decide in a special
session whether or not to censure Joseph McCarthy, or whether
to censure him a lot or a little. No one knows what the Senators
will say; but the hearings of the Select Committee have already

harmed Joe McCarthy, seriously and for the first time. He could not afford to have the country know that his Club suspects him of being unrespectable.

McCarthy is charged with contempt for the Senate or a Senatorial committee, with encouraging government employees to violate their oaths of office or Executive orders, with receiving and using confidential or 'classified' information from Executive files, with abusing his Senatorial colleagues, with abusing General Ralph Zwicker of the US Army.

The testimony against McCarthy is not new but it never fails to startle. There are the letters McCarthy wrote to Senator Gillette, chairman of another committee which was investigating McCarthy's activities in a Senatorial election in 1950. This was the famous election in which Tydings of Maryland was defeated after a picture, proved fraudulent, was circulated showing him in cosy converse with the American Communist leader, Earl Browder. McCarthy was held to be connected with that skulduggery; he would never appear before the Gillette committee to answer questions. Instead he accused the committee of stealing tens of thousands of the taxpayers' money in order to investigate his, McCarthy's, past, without proper authority. The entire episode sounded most unseemly, as it was read out before this quiet, dignified group of Senators.

The incidents which illustrated the first three charges against McCarthy were all noisy, scandalous, and megalomaniac; they are all well known; and the main feeling they produce now is one of great embarrassment. The offending Senator, who used to throw his weight around in such a successful and terrifying way, was obliged to sit quietly and listen, or testify in a strange metal-clanging monotone (with muted flashes of defiance. 'I said it then, I will say it now,' etc.) or retreat awkwardly through his cross examination. The committee saw to it that the hearings on the first three charges were thorough and dull.

The fourth charge against McCarthy was that he abused his colleagues in the Senate. Senator McCarthy has always spoken with remarkable force about anyone who disagrees with him. One of the men he abused is Senator Flanders, who is over seventy years old, and a Republican from Vermont. Of Senator Flanders, McCarthy remarked, 'I think they should get a man with a net and take him to a good quiet place,' having previously accused the Vermont Senator of 'senility or viciousness.' But it is because of this 'senile' old man that McCarthy found himself in the witness chair, a changed McCarthy, who insults no one.

It is hard and heavy work for Joe McCarthy to be this careful new man. Once, when the chairman silenced him McCarthy rose from his place at the witness table and walked slowly away across the room. He was taking deep breaths and he seemed to be holding his body rigid. The chairman watched, not moving, as one would watch a wild animal which is out of its cage. The public was quiet in the back of the room. McCarthy returned to his place and the hearing went on.

Even in the hall, where the familiar brilliant TV lights awaited him, and chummy commentators stood with ready microphones, McCarthy was no longer the one they used to know. He could here, with perfect freedom, be as loud, disdainful or threatening as he had been in the first few days of the hearing. But he was careful, careful, even refusing to comment on his prospects but only saying, 'I would rather the committee spoke about that.' And when his admirers, most often ladies of fifty and upwards, seized his hand and murmured praise, he was diffident, shyly smiling, and always careful.

When Senator Johnson said to his colleagues on the Select Committee, 'The Sentor's political life is at stake in the question before this committee,' neither McCarthy nor anyone else objected to the dramatic and final sound of those words. McCarthy hurried through a feeble defence of his manners towards his colleagues, claiming simply that when he was charged with being abusive he was enjoying his right to free expression. But his voice grew heavy with anger when he testified about General Zwicker, for the General was a needless and perhaps fatal mistake.

The case in which General Zwicker was involved is one of the most grotesque of the the McCarthy cases. The Army had a dentist and they thought the dentist was perhaps a Communist or had been, but they had no way of forcing him to tell, and they decided the best thing to do was to get him out of the service. They had no grounds for a court martial, and the only way to rid themselves of this perilous dentist was to give him an honourable discharge. Which they did. The dentist was not a threat to national security by any standards; except by McCarthy's.

McCarthy heard about this dentist as he hears of everything, through his private network of informers, and he moved in to attack. General Zwicker was the dentist's commanding officer. McCarthy called the General to explain why the dentist had been honourably discharged, and asked questions which were as silly as they were malicious; and Zwicker would not be bullied. Finally McCarthy, who considers people who are not to be bullied 'arrogant' and 'evasive,' told General Zwicker he was not fit to wear his uniform. Since the General had been wearing an Army uniform ever since his graduation from West Point, about thirty years ago, and had been decorated for gallantry in action, this treatment by McCarthy caused a general outcry and above all infuriated the Army. This mistake of mistreating Zwicker led to the Army-McCarthy hearings, and that long, disorderly and alarming show led to this last hearing, the quiet hearing, the one McCarthy cannot afford.

The only new piece of evidence which appeared was that McCarthy's famous spontaneous denunciation of General Zwicker had been pure theatre. Under cross-examination, McCarthy admitted that he had known, before he saw Zwicker, that the perilous dentist was going to be honourably discharged, so he could hardly have been shocked or surprised into blaming the General. McCarthy had put on his rage for the day, for the Press, for television, inventing the day's sensation as if he were writing a radio script. The story looked very mad indeed, spread out there before the Select Committee: mad and meaningless. It served only as a reminder that, in four years of Communist scourging, McCarthy has not brought one single Communist to trial by law, for any offence whatsoever.

On the first day of these hearings, McCarthy tried one of his usual harassing tactics. This is the technique of the irrelevant fact given irrational importance; and it can be a way to drive people dotty with helpless anger. McCarthy insisted that he had a right to know whether a sentence Senator Johnson, a Democratic member of the Select Committee, had allegedly spoken in an interview with the 'Denver Post' on 12 March was or was not correctly quoted. Chairman Watkins would not stand for this nonsense. He ruled McCarthy out of order three times; then he said, 'We are not going to be interrupted by these diversions . . . the committee will be in recess.' And banged his gavel and cleared the room.

McCarthy had never been treated in this way. He rushed into the hall where the TV cameras and microphones waited, and he stepped into the spotlight and said furiously into the amplifiers: 'This is the most unheard-of thing I ever heard of!' That made people laugh. They have not laughed at Joe McCarthy before. Of course, if they ever really start laughing, that will be that.

On the other hand, McCarthyism is alive and flourishes, and there are many able exponents, or even rivals, to take it over should some mishap befall the Senator from Wisconsin. No one has yet suggested censuring McCarthyism.

It Don't Matter Who Gets in, Dear

If we dare believe what we read, the eyes of the world, you know, *those* eyes, were fixed upon England, at the end of the second week of the great General Election campaign. This magnificent nation allows 20 days for electioneering, thus presenting us, the efficient Americans, with the finest possible example of a time-and-sanity-saving device. Six hundred and thirty men and women are elected as Members of Parliament. During the first week of the campaign it was hardly obvious that anyone wanted to be elected at all. In the second week it was very tepidly 'hotted-up,' a slang expression much in favour hereabouts. They are calling this the Dull Election. Nobody minds the dullness a bit.

At the beginning, if you wanted to know what was happening you telephoned the Central Office of the Labour Party and asked where election meetings would be held. Where indeed? Who knows? Try the London Office. The London Office said you better try the agents (the permanent party organizers) in the various London constituencies; they probably know. You telephoned to a few of them; they are not having many meetings, perhaps three in Battersea, one or two in Clapham, anyhow not until the very end. People don't want to go to meetings any more, now they can sit at home in comfort (the nights are unduly cold this May, also often quite wet) and listen to the radio or look at TV. After many polite, friendly telephone calls, you are sent a mimeographed list of constituencies, with the addresses of local party headquarters:

anyone with gumption can do his own work by telephoning to all 42 of them.

The Conservative Party was a lot sharper and brisker than this. Yes, of course, they say, and the next day you get a mimeographed list of speakers, and the date, hour and place of the meetings. This superior organization is evident throughout; the papers note it with a sort of admiring wonder. The Conservatives are out to get the vote. They have neglected none of the traditional aids; the roaming car with loud-speaker, the street-corner or village pump meetings, the house-to-house canvassing, complete with party handbills (so useful for starting the household fires), the small discreet window posters, the indoor meetings, the transport arrangements for getting voters to the polls.

The important point about this election is: everyone wants the same thing—peace and prosperity; it depends how you mean to get the one and keep the other, and who you want to do the job. The fiercest election controversy for a time was an argument as to which side has been misquoting the prices of bacon and tea and cheese. But then the deplored, unofficial dock and railway strikes obliterated tea, bacon and cheese. Meantime talk of food well overshadowed talk of the H-bomb. One thing can be safely said about the H-bomb: it hardly fits into daily life, does it? And their own private daily lives are the main concern of the people in this country. What is the use of winning a war and slogging through austerity for long years after the victory if, at last, you cannot think about chintz curtains and football pools and wage raises, summer holidays and schools for young Timothy?

I managed to find three meetings. They resembled nothing we do and nothing anyone does, except the English. The first I found was in Peckham, one of the many Londons, a solid brick wilderness along the edge of the vast city. It was a Conservative meeting in a permanently Labour constituency. The young Conservative candidate was making his campaign purely as a matter of sport, or for experience, or to keep the blue Conservative rosette flying in enemy territory. The meeting took place in the chilled brick basement of a local school. (Tacked to the wall a homemade crayon flower drawing, labelled helpfully, 'Tulip.') There was a Union Jack on the Speaker's table and above it the election poster of Eden, looking handsome, bland, boneless, with the slogan, 'Working for Peace.' This is a patently true statement, calm and sincere in tone, which is the Tory style for this campaign.

The audience, dressed in those peculiarly English variations of brown, looked exactly like a Labour audience; there were more women than men. The meeting began with a kindly prologue, in refined Cockney, by the chairman, a local Conservative businessman and big shot. He spoke respectfully of the incumbent Labour Member for Peckham and said it didn't matter who got elected as long as Peckham was well represented, which is odd election talk by the standards of any other country.

Then, true to a glorious English streak of dottiness, they presented a refugee Czech. The Czech spoke, with conviction, a heavy accent, and as if to himself, about the dreadful things happening in his country; he traced in detail, including unpronounceable names, the steps that had led to the Communist *coup d'état* in Prague. The tiny audience was restless. A rosy, husky old man stood up and announced he didn't come to hear about Czechoslovakia but about England, he didn't know nothing about Czechoslovakia nor nowhere else and he didn't want to; he thought they was coming here to be told what the Tories would do if they won and he was disgusted, that's what, and he was now leaving and he'd come back when they got talking about England. Enjoyable uproar. The Czech resumed. Another voice announced he was disgusted, he didn't come to hear about Czechoslovakia either. No one had, of course; it was quite incredible to find the poor Czech here on this occasion. Behind us sat a small, bright-eyed, unshaved, poorly-dressed man, who pulled back his raincoat to show a red enamel star pinned to his lapel. 'Are you a Communist?' asked the Conservative lady next to me, as if asking about some new kind of dahlia. He nodded and smiled. We looked forward to a merry meeting with good noisy heckling. But the Communist listened to the Czech in silence, and then left; bored, obviously.

After this drab beginning, which cleared the room of the opposition, who went to a neighbouring pub and never returned, Sir Beverley Baxter addressed the gathering. According to regular electioneering form, great party names, or as great as can be found, speak for lesser men; they steal the thunder and use the time; the candidate frequently finds himself obliged to repeat or say nothing.

Beverley Baxter, a famous journalist and long-time Conservative MP, gave a classical English speech: rambling, disorganized, good-natured, cosy; and everyone felt happy. In the course of this talk and for no special reason, he told the finest joke of the week; it concerned Mr Attlee. Sir Beverley had gone to report a Labour Party convention and was present at a meeting where one Bevanite after another, eight in all, was elected, with thunderous applause, to the party executive committee. While this fire raged around him, Attlee sat on the platform, doodling. At last, he had to speak. The Bevanite triumph was a grave blow to him and to his branch of the Labour Party; Baxter and others, filled with sympathy, could not imagine what the old leader would find to say. Attlee rose into the partisan clamour, and in his unvarying voice began his speech. 'We live in a small island with scarcely any resources except coal and fish.'

Nothing else of any value happened at Peckham that night. We agreed that the Conservative candidate was a fellow who could talk you to death. Peckham was safe for Labour as of yore.

Then there were two meetings in one night, in Hammersmith, nearer the heart of London, but a working-class sector on the whole. The first, a Conservative meeting, took place in Hammersmith town hall, a modern brick edifice, costly and grand. The speakers, Conservative Minister of Transport and the young pretender, spoke calmly and sensibly, giving many facts on the successful Conservative regime just ended; 300,000 houses a year, the end of rationing, peace in Korea and Indochina and top level talks on the way, the sad and dangerous division within the

Labour Party (Aneurin Bevan is the Tories' best un-secret weapon), the proved value of Sir Anthony Eden as a leader. They droned pleasantly on in their educated voices, and everyone listened as if in church. The audience was modest-income Conservative, with surprises. In front of us sat a coloured couple: African, West Indian? The backs of their heads were superbly un-English; they sat with their shoulders tightly touching and did not move a muscle for nearly two hours.

The second meeting that night was a great Labour Rally in a Hammersmith theatre. Whether it was news to everyone or only to your reporter, this meeting proved to be a reunion and chumming up, on one platform, of Aneurin Bevan and Mr Attlee. There was a huge, active, jolly crowd. In the lobby, election posters showed Mr Attlee, looking almost tipsy-sprightly, with the inscription, 'You Can Trust Mr Attlee.' Which is also a perfectly true statement and no one, certainly not the Tories, would dispute it. The vital question, in and out of the Labour Party, seems to be: do you trust Mr Bevan too?

On the stage, amongst a suitable platform crowd, was Mr Bevan, with his striking grey head and strong red face. The Hammersmith candidate talked away, to an accompaniment of amiable heckling and encouragement, and no one seemed interested. Suddenly there was a straggling effort at 'For He's a Jolly Good Fellow,' and scattered applause. Mr Attlee, due to arrive and make his third election speech that night, was in the house. But where? It is hard to give a man an ovation if you know he's around somewhere but you can't see him. Anti-climax piled on anti-climax, until the whole meeting turned into a delicious disorganized joke. A plank had been laid from the stage box to the stage; the idea was, perhaps, that Mr and Mrs Attlee would walk this plank into the waiting and welcoming arms of Mr Bevan. Apparently Mr and Mrs Attlee did not like the looks of that improvised plank; they tried to find their way backstage. Nothing happened. Each member of the party on the stage went in search of them, one by one; the rest stood waiting; the audience applauded, craned necks, laughed. Mr Bevan looked at his watch, giving the clear impression of a man doing a foolish and irritating duty. At last Mr and Mrs Attlee were hauled on stage. This wonderful disarray must have lasted nearly 10 minutes.

Mr Attlee began to speak in a most energetic manner; he was sure that Labour would win this election. Everyone felt cheered and bucked up. But he soon settled down; good and admirable generalities and a few facts about education or pensions; there was heckling, which he hardly noticed. The speech cannot have excited anyone, but no one expects to be excited by Mr Attlee. He is less like a politician than any politician of his stature anywhere in the world; it remains one of the permanent English mysteries that this quiet, bourgeois, peace-loving, uninspiring man has for so long been the leader of the only English revolutionary party.

Mr Attlee finished; you knew this had happened because he stopped talking. He hurried away, accompanied by Mrs Attlee who looked pretty in black and white, not a bit stylish, and who wore an expression of loving and anxious pride. On his way out, Mr Attlee shook hands with Mr Bevan. The quickest and least dramatic handshake possible. Loud applause. The meeting broke up. No one ended it. A sense of theatre, in politics, is most un-English.

Those are typical meetings. Quiet everywhere. How can you work up excitement when there are no issues? A Tory peer remarked, the other day, that it was certainly a contrast to the fine bad days of 1945, when the unfortunate candidates started by saying 'Ladies and Gentlemen' and that was the last thing you heard. Now, he went on, if Attlee and Morrison were taken into the new Conservative government which will (all agree) surely be elected, they would be unnoticeable, and probably a lot happier than in a government of their own.

This year, as an added attraction to the muted meetings, we have TV. Mr Macmillan, Mr Attlee, Dr Edith Summerskill (who started the one and only excitement, about bacon), Sir Anthony Eden and a panel of cabinet ministers being questioned by a panel of editors. The TV shows are deadly. The press never stops saying how deadly they are. The public hardly seems to notice, but perhaps they are not listening to what sounds like a sleepy affable mumble. (Except, of course, for food prices.) When sitting before their TV sets, they look, not listen. And, in a general spirit of good nature, they seem to like everyone. Mr Macmillan is handsome and Etonian, as befits a Tory Foreign Minister; Mr Attlee looks very nice with his pipe, and Mrs Attlee very nice and wifely; Sir Anthony Eden looks weary but pleasant, and his ministers all smile a lot and look confident and like good family doctors; the editors are suitably unfashionable and wordy and look oddly like working reporters, not editors. It is doubtful whether a single vote has been won or lost by these docile TV shows.

In the end, in England, when you want to find out how people are feeling, you always go to the pubs. It was in the pubs, at the height of the blitz, that people were saying, 'Little ole 'Itler can't take much more of this.' There is always a quiet shapeless flow of talk in the pubs, slow talk over slow beers, and this talk may rightly be considered the pulse of the nation.

These people, in the working-class pubs, look as if they had been invented by Charles Dickens and Carol Reed, and they talk their own dialect with the tongues of angels.

In Highgate, a woman of 65, out on a birthday party with a lady friend of hers, also 65 (three gins to celebrate), declared that no one could afford these new Council houses the Tories had built; they cost 21 and 24 and 28 shillings a week, no working-class person could, anyhow. They'd put her in one, not a new one, and it cost 14 shillings a week. 'What's it like?' I asked, expecting a blast. 'Quoite noice,' she said, 'Reely very noice. Two rooms and a scullery. I can't complain.' Still, she was a Labour woman. Still, 'we wouldn't loike to lose Anthony Eden, would we? He's a fine peaceful-living man.' Her friend said they had more money now than they'd ever had, and it didn't mean a thing; but she seemed neither surprised not upset by this gloomy conclusion.

In another pub a subway conductor, soft-spoken, gentle, remarked, 'There's no difference between the parties now, that's why no one's interested.' 'How about Irish Partition?' asked a happy drunk Irishman who had been offering all of us beers. No one accepted his offer, since he would miss the money in the sober morning. 'It's not an issue this time,' the subway man said. 'I fought in the English army and the American army,' the Irishman said, 'and I can prove it. What did I fight for? The freedom of small nations, that's what. Why the hell can't they start near home with the freedom of small nations? That's what I'm asking you.' This seemed good stuff, like election speeches, but it could not go far, considering that no party had mentioned the subject, except the Communists who favour a free Ireland, and since the Irish are all Roman Catholics they are not going to vote Communist, so that is that.

The pub keeper, a man who owns a car, said, 'It don't matter who gets in, dear, they cawn't do much.' He went on to say that no one was talking about the elections, 'We English don't like a fuss and arguments,' and besides 'everything is pretty good now, very good, you can say. There'll always be grumblers but with the wages people are getting, what is there to talk about?' What they have been talking about steadily, before, during and after is the Cockell-Marciano fight, apparently the one subject of great international interest. A sturdy housewife, clutching a paper parcel of fish and chips, departed, saying, 'Well, God bless, boys. Don't get excited.' As if they would, not about politics this year anyhow. An old man, with the kind of good serene face you so often see bent over a half pint, said, 'There's going to be a slump, if the Tories or the Socialists get in. Unless something happens, there's a bumb going to drop here and a war starts or somepin.' No one was a bit worried, either by the thought of a slump or a bumb, but all had another round of that remarkable flat beer.

Farther down in Camden Town, at another pub, a picturesque and shabby character announced, 'The English are a very slow class of people,' and went on to say that 'We English, we believe in every man making up his own mind, like. We want to buy our paper and have a bit of a read and think about it and then we want to go and put in our vote. In my bit of a house, my wife's Liberal and my niece what lives with us is Conservative and I'm Labour and we got a biggish window so we got all three of them posters up.' A dock worker from East Ham also spoke of freedom. 'You'll never find the English going Communist,' he said. 'We don't like it. It's not true Communism, it's dictatorial. We want to say what we think. I'm a republican myself and I don't like the Royal Family. They all look as if a good day's work would kill them. But most of the people like them, so we got them; but I can say what I think about it. You ever been to the Channel Islands? I'm going there for me holidays, I go every year. It's paradise.' 'How do they vote there?' I asked. 'Oh vote,' he said, 'It's a feudal system, like; you woudn't understand it.'

We moved to a scruffy little coffee bar, after pub closing time, and sat at a smeared table and tried to drink the nastiest coffee on earth, and talked about the election, and the calm of it, and whether the pub chaps were right in thinking that the Tories would win a bigger majority if election day was sunny, because Labour doesn't mind getting wet when it votes but Tories do. Beside us a small man with an illuminated smile and ill-fitting spectacles and a foul-looking meat pie, listened and then remarked, 'I believe that everything that happens to us is meant to happen to us, so we can learn from it. There's a reason; all we have to do is find out the reason. And I think that everyone in the world has intelligence and some kind of gift.' We stared at him with admiration and pleasure, and, wanting his opinion, I asked, 'Are you interested in the election?' 'Not particularly,' he said. 'I'm interested in learning.'

Rubbing together, as they have for centuries, in their small island, sustained by coal and fish, the English have become inextricably united, although totally un-uniform. No party can rule for one class of the population. The rulers have less and less choice, it would seem: each party is forever saddled with the others' successful reforms, each must rescue the others' mistakes. And any government must provide what all England wants: peace, not an ideal peace, but a possible workable peace in an un-ideal world, and prosperity, nothing flashy, no sudden riches, but this gradual betterment which gives everyone a bit of his own kind of ease, and time and chance for a reasonable joy in life.

Spies and Starlings

The House of Commons loves to laugh. The Members' jokes are debaters' quips and have a special flavour, like all jokes made between intimates. The *Times* reports of the Commons' proceedings are studded with parentheses, saying: Ministerial Laughter, Ministerial Cheers and Laughter, Laughter. Perched in the press gallery, the most usual community sound one hears, rising from the chamber, is a brisk bark or a merry bellow. Men laughing with or at each other are guaranteed sane chaps. In less fortunate countries, politicians on occasion throw benches and fight; they have been known to take pot shots at each other. In even less fortunate countries, politicans orate interminably in the very accents of pompous falsehood. In the House of Commons no politician talks for long without begging patience, and a very good excuse for 'imposing on the time of the House.' And he can expect to be rewarded or punished with mirth at any minute. The effect of this is a welcome and immediate sense of reality. Actual people are talking about actual things, in first-rate conversational English. No one is sacred and no one can swell to undue, unhuman size, for there is always the bark, the bellow, the roar, the giggle of laughter, and the Speaker's splendid Scots voice booming over the gaiety, saying, 'Orrrder, Orrrder, Orrrder.'

Since the Commons returned from the summer recess, and began its autumn session on 25 October there has been much laughter and one day which was outstanding because no one laughed at all. On the opening day, vast merriment attended an event which was so funny as to seem impossible: two Members had been elected from Ulster, Northern Ireland, but were unable to take their places in the House of Commons owing to the fact that they were in jail. They were in jail for helping in a hold-up of a British arms depot in order to get weapons for the Irish Republican Army. A second election was held; the two, in jail, were re-elected. This raised a fascinating dilemma: whereas you may not vote, in jail, you may, evidently, stand for Parliament. The winners were however still in jail, and the Courts decided that the two runners-up, in the second election, were the rightful members of Parliament. The runners-up were both Tories; Labour had a lovely time trying to argue them out of their seats. The two new members arrived at the bar of the House; one was a very small Irishman with reddish hair who looked terrified; the other was a more obviously cool and Parliamentary type. The argument went on, with bursts of audience laughter, largely between Mr Sidney Silverman, a Labour member, and Mr Speaker. Mr Silverman, like many MPs, cannot say *r*; the Speaker's *r*'s are a treat. The *r*'s had it.

On the second day of the Budget debate, the laughter was rather fierce, like tigers laughing over a nice fresh carcass. Mr Gaitskell, the former Labour Chancellor of the Exchequer, rose to eat alive Mr Butler, the incumbent of that office, and to tear to shreds his new and unexpected budget. The two men faced each other across the great table, where the Mace of Parliament lies, and gusts of Labour laughter blew Mr Gaitskell on as he mocked his opponent's use of metaphor and accused him of having made an electioneering budget last summer, and of having to buy it back now. Mr Butler was obliged, by the conventions of this place, to sit where he was and smile as best he could while the spiked points were driven against him. There were very harsh words too. 'An addict to half truths,' said Mr Gaitskell of Mr Butler. ('They aren't allowed to call each other liars, you see,' said the press gallery attendant, a man in a dress suit wearing a large gold plaque on his shirt front.) 'He began in folly, continued in deceit and ended in reaction,' said Mr Gaitskell of Mr Butler. This went down quite well at the time with the more blood-thirsty Labour members, but created a certain unease; people suggested that Mr Gaitskell had gone too far, this is not the usual tone of the House, there seemed to be personal venom in Mr Gaitskell's remarks, almost hate; in the end, it may not prove a successful speech at all.

Three days later, Mr Butler answered this attack. There was even more laughter, and a better humoured less personal tone; it was felt that in the duel-debate, Mr Butler had therefore won. Mr Butler pointed out that when Mr Gaitskell was Chancellor of the Exchequer in 1951, dollar reserves poured away, and the only step Mr Gaitskell took was to save $40 million in cheese imports. 'This marvellous roaring lion is a miserable little mouse who could only gnaw at a bit of cheese,' said Mr Butler of Mr Gaitskell, who sat and smiled sportingly while the House rocked with laughter at the joke. 'Socialists, sir,' said Mr Butler, addressing the Speaker, 'are connoisseurs of incompetence.' In turn, Mr Attlee and Mr Gaitskell, sitting with their feet on the Ministerial table, joined in the mirth, as three days before, Sir Anthony Eden and Mr Butler, slouched in the same privileged way, had laughed when they were discomfited.

At last came the long awaited day when Parliament was to discuss the case of Burgess and Maclean. The House adjourned itself, in order to become a sort of hearing-not-deciding body, and settled down in attentive seriousness, to learn the inside dope on this mystery. Many people had wondered about the possible results, but perhaps no one had foreseen that this day would turn into a triumph for the House of Commons, which reaffirmed itself, on the basis of a stale story of treason, the absolute upholder of civil liberties, and of the sanity and sanctity of law. It was a great day, although the tone was one of mourning, and speakers on both sides of the House repeatedly declared their sadness at having to deal with such a matter as the treason of Englishmen.

*

Nothing new was said about Burgess and Maclean; either there are no revelations or the revelations are still considered dangerous by the Security Service. What was new to our ears these days, and thrilling to hear, was the steadiness and justice of those who spoke, the absence of panic or exaggeration, the quiet insistence on legal processes as opposed to trial by suspicion. McCarthyism so repelled the English that they take special care not to be infected by it.

Mr Macmillan, the Foreign Secretary, opened the discussion and it was brilliantly his day; his grave dispassionate manner set the style for all that followed. And he made clear at once the questions of principle which concerned the House more deeply than Burgess and Maclean. 'Action against employees, whether of the State or anybody else, arising from suspicion and not from proof, may begin with good motives, and it may avert serious inconveniences or disasters, but judging from what has happened in some other countries, such a practice soon degenerates into the satisfaction of personal vendettas or a general system of tyranny, all in the name of public safety . . . It is not fair to bring in an atmosphere of today when judging events of the 1930s. How can the interests of security be maintained without damage to our traditional liberties? At what point do reasonable and necessary security measures become the repugnant attibutes of the police state? For it would indeed be a tragedy if we destroyed our freedom in the effort to preserve it.' (Cheers, from both sides of the House.)

Uniformly, although less eloquently and unreservedly than the Conservatives, Labour speakers rejected any form of witch-hunting. But several days before this discussion, using the immunity of the House, a Labour MP had named a private individual, Mr H.A.R. Philby, as being the man who warned Burgess and Maclean of impending arrest. By doing so, the Labour MP, Lt Col Lipton, aroused profound and vocal distaste on both sides of the House; he became a sort of villain in the piece. His action was regarded as McCarthyism. The Foreign Secretary took great pains to remove from Mr Philby any shadow of suspicion, and was approved for doing so. But Lt Col Lipton was unrepentant, and spoke again, again refusing to disclose sources, but casting suspicion, and this behaviour outraged the House. A Conservative back bencher, speaking after Lt Col Lipton, said, 'We must have constant and difficult decisions to make as to how far any action is justified on suspicion. After listening to the honourable and gallant Member [Lt Col Lipton], one is at least quite clear where he stands on that. He is in favour of acting on suspicion, of smearing on suspicion, by directing public suspicion on to an individual against whom nothing at all has been proved. We must leave it to his own conscience to straighten out what that may cost in personal suffering to the wife, children and friends of the person involved.'

This one instance was the only whiff of McCarthyism in the whole handling of the Burgess and Maclean debate; three days after the debate, Lt Col Lipton printed a retraction and apology to Mr Philby in the newspapers; and there lies, quickly mouldering, the shape of an injustice which Americans know too well.

The Prime Minister in closing the debate, repeated the key-note of the entire discussion. 'British justice over the centuries has been based on the principle that a man is to be presumed innocent until he can be proved guilty. Are we going to abandon that principle? Perhaps, worst of all, are we going to make an exception for political offences?' There was no laughter that day.

Within a day, the House was back to normal at Question Time, that excellent first hour when Cabinet Ministers must answer large and small inquiries about their duties. An honourable gentleman (Conservative) wanted to know what the Minister of Works was doing about the starlings in Trafalgar Square, those loud delightful birds which deposit filth on Nelson's Column and the passers-by equally; was the Minister doing anything to scare the birds away? The Minister said no humane and effective way could be found, although research was continuing. They had under construction a device called an ultra-sonic vibrator. (Laughter on both sides of the House.) Another honourable gentleman said that Birmingham had a device for scaring starlings which would scare any MP but left the starlings unaffected. (More laughter.)

The English are very proud of their Parliament, and week in, week out, century after century, they have pretty good cause to be.

Weekend in Israel

The beach runs the whole length of Israel. It is wild, golden, and dangerous. Now on a hot Friday evening after-sundown bathers are still lolling in the strong soupy breakers, while behind them along the shore front the citizens of Tel Aviv eat, drink and listen to a variety of hand-made music. The cafés and restaurants are all open and noisy, with shirt-sleeved singers delivering Hebrew love songs and shirt-sleeved violinists playing what sound like Hungarian jigs and the customers babbling busily in many tongues.

This is apparently a classless society. Everyone dresses alike, in cotton shirts, in cotton dresses, everyone looks comfortable if far from stylish, and everyone looks very much at home. If you have the price of admission you can go anywhere; and everyone must have the price of admission to something enjoyable, for all pleasure places are crowded and envy seems an unknown emotion. There is an aristocracy, I am told: the workers on the communal farms, the kibbutzniks, who are the poorest members of the State, are considered the top aristocrats. After that there is a small world of early settlers who feel a pride of precedence, but no one else minds or notices this private satisfaction. And the intellectual, in Israel, is honoured. On the other hand, first names alone are used, manners are affable pioneer style, no one is really rich, no one is in want, and life is universally hard.

Hard but good, they would say, and all theirs. They look

happy, which is perhaps the biggest surprise of all. There are eagle-faced Yemenites licking ice-cream cones, Nordic giants in shorts gobbling shashlik on sticks, young khaki-clad soldiers, male and female, joking on benches beside ruminative old men wearing Orthodox side-curls, glamour girls with Hollywood hairdos dancing at an outdoor café where, remotely, old ladies in shawls eat whipped-cream pastries and gossip about grandchildren. The people of Israel come from 62 nations and the first thing they had to do was learn Hebrew so they could talk to each other. (Only the children speak Hebrew with perfect ease). But here they are, a fantastic mixture, and they have made themselves into something new on the face of the earth.

On Saturday morning, the Sabbath, I went to the Gaza Strip. In a foreign country you should always study the speciality of the place. In Greece, ruins; in Italy, churches; in England, Parliament. In Israel the speciality is survival; the obvious place to see that is along the frontiers, where they are surviving actively all the time. Isaac, the driver, called for me at eight in the morning. In Poland, in 1937, Isaac was a medical student; then he became a soldier in the Polish Army and was captured by the Russians. In due course he escaped from the Russians and so, by devious routes, via China, he arrived in Israel 14 years ago; too late for medicine but not for the good life. Isaac, in his assured tough-guy way, speaks six languages. It is par for Israel.

Even at this hour it is hot, and even at this hour we discuss current events. Isaac's views on world politics are crisp and disabused. The Arabs have the oil. No claim Israel can make on the good sense or conscience of the world matters a hoot. Israelis will if necessary fight for their country to the last man, woman and child; they have no other choice and no other desire. They can only rely on themselves; that is the way things are. The Arabs have the oil. Isaac is not alone in this viewpoint.

We collected three others, an old man who is a Tel Aviv journalist, a young Englishwoman who is a social worker, and a young government guide. We drove south while the weather became more and more like a giant hair-drier. Presently, Isaac pointed to a low range of dunes a mile or so to our left: the Egyptian frontier, the Gaza Strip. The road now took on that classical emptiness and air of waiting which belong to all dangerous roads in war. Isaac remarked irritably that he hated this road, and took a pistol from the glove compartment. I said, 'Surely not in broad daylight?' 'Those bums sometimes come over and shoot from right behind those bushes,' said Isaac, nodding at the thin, hopeful beginnings of eucalyptus trees planted at the roadside.

At a cross-roads, also tediously empty, the rear axle broke. The problem now became less one of unfriendly Egyptians and more one of sunstroke. Presently an army patrol, sunburned and eating grapes, arrived in a command car. Two soldiers jumped out, making room for four of us; Isaac remained with them to guard our car. The army drove us merrily to a frontier kibbutz called Ein Hashelosha. A kibbutz is a communal farm, built from scratch by a group of people who have decided to join together in this way of life. They own nothing, they earn no money; they live by the immense sweat of their brows, building themselves places to live and play, rearing their children, caring for their cattle, tilling the fields. Tilling the fields is the miracle here because this is the Negev, the southern desert of Israel. Life in the end depends on a pipeline of water.

These kibbutzim are the only places I know where a daily practical effort is made to follow the teachings of Christ. That statement is calculated to annoy both Jews and Christians, but I think it is true. There are, consequently, not many of us who could manage to live on a kibbutz.

Ein Hashelosha is five years old and was founded by Jews from Argentina and Paraguay. A towering, stout, blond man escorted us around the premises; he looked, as they all do, like a hard-working poor farmer, dressed in faded shorts and shirt, sandals, a crushed canvas hat. He came from Buenos Aires. As we passed the small cement houses and wooden shacks, the scattered mess of farm machinery and building materials, the barbed-wire barricades and watch-towers, all hard, hot, and harsh, I said, 'It must be quite a change for you.' 'More or less,' said he.

We walked away from the huddle of dingy buildings and barns, across the sand to their outer fortifications, a system of slit trenches and dug-outs built around the water reservoir. It was intelligently planned and well made. The frontier is a mile off, over open farmland, ideal tank terrain. At night automobile headlights shine on the fields around them; there are two walls of barbed wire to enclose the buildings; men go to work in the fields, night and day, in pairs and always armed. They have to add regular sentry duty to their already backbreaking farm jobs.

And night after night Egyptian marauders, trained and armed men, penetrate their land. The night before we came, 70 metres of aluminium irrigation pipe were stolen: you have to see the burning land to know that anything to do with water is vital. The same night after we left, there was shooting in the fields. It is a permanent, nagging harassment; the purpose is to exhaust the people and disrupt the work. In conditions of perfect peace, life on this place would be an endurance contest. It seemed beyond endurance to have one's men shot at, one's children endangered, one's crops burned, one's precious animals and equipment stolen. Were they ever able to rest and be happy? 'When it is time to fight, we fight,' said the man from Buenos Aires. 'When it is time to dance, we dance.'

The fortifications had impressed me, but not for military reasons. Surely they realize what they are up against? 'We will handle up to tanks,' said the big man. 'After that, our army will take care.'

This simple statement sounded like a heroic poem, considering who said it and where it was said. The plain facts are that the Egyptians alone have more than 500 tanks— Shermans, Centurions, Stalins and the new Russian medium tanks. The Israelis have only Shermans and a few light French tanks which are really self-propelled guns. The Israelis obviously do not tell the exact amount of their inferior equipment, but it would be safe to guess something near a hundred tanks in all.

The Egyptians have 350 new MiG fighters, 30 to 40 English World War II bombers, which are still effective here, and 30 to 40

148

Ilyushin jet bombers. Against this array, as really modern planes, the Israelis have 24 French jet Mystère fighters, and the promise of 24 more jet fighters from Canada. They have nothing at all that can touch the Russian Ilyushin bombers, no planes that can fly high enough, no anti-aircraft guns that can reach so high into the sky. It will take seven minutes for Egyptian bombers to fly from their fields to Tel Aviv.

And though the Israelis have intense confidence in themselves and can mobilize 250,000 men and women within 36 hours, the Arab League, according to Israeli military intelligence (which is apt to be correct), have 340,000 men under arms at this moment. It should be remembered that Israel is only 14 miles wide in the centre, has an enormously long and difficult-to-protect frontier, and five other hostile states besides Egypt to reckon with.

Meantime, the farmers at Ein Hashelosha and at all the frontier kibbutzim build their small sandbagged fortifications and plan, without fuss, to defend them if necessary.

I dined that night with a young Army major and his wife. They live outside Tel Aviv in a small bungalow, very American, in a row of bungalows where prams and tricycles clutter the front lawns and everyone has the same little grassy, flowery back garden to sit in in the cool of the evening. They are native-born Israelis; it is difficult to describe them, but they are nearer in manner and appearance to Americans than to any European people, yet they are not American at all. They have a kind of freedom and simplicity that goes with a young nation, a natural ease, but they are quieter, more earnest than Americans. They are given to using their minds, and their command of languages is, as usual, a marvel. We ate a picnic supper in the garden; the children, aged four to six months, slept in the house beside us; the pretty, young mother passed plates and discussed war. It was, I think, a typical Israeli evening party.

They feel, they say, 'the tension.' Since Nasser has grabbed the Suez Canal they think the Arab-Israel war is postponed. But because like everyone else in Israel they believe Nasser will get away with this grab, they feel the war is only postponed and has now become inevitable. Nasser can use extra time to train his air and tank crews in their new Russian equipment and the Suez triumph will soothe Egyptian nationalism and keep the Egyptian populace happy, proud and excited temporarily. However, as there is no real bread for the Egyptian or any Arab people, there will have to be more circuses. Perhaps Nasser will partition Jordan first, as a minor circus. Israel is certainly the great show. All they can do is make guesses about Nasser's timetable. Israel's turn will come next spring, perhaps?

New Jersey is the same size as Israel, although New Jersey has four times Israel's population. The bordering states are New York, Pennsylvania, Delaware and Connecticut, and their combined population is equal to the population of Israel's neighbours, Egypt, Syria, Lebanon and Jordan—about 28 million people. But one cannot think of oneself, sitting in one's garden in the suburbs of Trenton, the children sleeping in the house, and discussing with friends calmly (for one must be calm, what else is there to be?) the fact that New Jersey is alone, cannot feed itself, is terrifyingly outnumbered, does not own the minimum of defensive arms, while there—encircling it—are the four neighbour states, rich, well-armed, able to buy more arms, and proclaiming their hate, determined to destroy New Jersey, boasting of their sacred mission to rid the North American Continent of citizens of New Jersey. No, there is no way to transfer oneself into the Israelis' position. But one can at least understand that these young Israeli parents, in their Tel Aviv suburb, would with reason feel 'the tension.'

The sharav has arrived. The sharav is the hot wind from the desert. It is quite as nasty as reported; one feels both murderous and tearful. In this weather I went with six other sufferers, by taxi, to Jerusalem. Jerusalem the Golden is a grievous disappointment. Perhaps the Old City, over there behind the great wall, is lovely; I do not know; I cannot go and see. The total Arab blockade of Israel extends to foreign tourists. (But poor Arabs shuffle through the Mandelbaum Gate in the Old City, every day, to cross into

Israeli Jerusalem, to get free treatment at the Israeli Hadassah Hospital.) Jerusalem is not only a disappointment but also a relatively unsafe frontier; to be shot at from the walls of the Old City, when walking home from dinner, is not unusual. I had not come to see Jerusalem but to get transport to a kibbutz on the near-by Jordan border. This kibbutz was briefly famous because a hand grenade had been thrown into their children's house.

A tall, lean, relaxed, ugly ex-Pole, who has lived there for 20 years, showed me, without comment, the open bathroom window through which the grenade had been thrown, the hole in the hall floor, and the startling fragmentation of the grenade, which had pocked all the surrounding walls and doors. Luckily the doors were closed into the bedrooms where 12 small boys slept. Any one of those sharp flying fragments of red-hot metal could have killed, blinded or maimed a child.

'I wonder why the fellow did it,' the tall man mused. 'Mostly they steal.'

'Steal what?'

He laughed. 'Anything they can get. Sometimes they come to the verandas of the houses and steal the washing.'

'But,' I began.

'What can we do? We have our work. We cannot pass our life fighting against stealers.'

'And if the stealers are also killers?'

'We still have our work.'

Supposedly there is an armistice between the Arab States and Israel, but from 1950 to July 1956, the Israeli Government has registered with the United Nations Mixed Armistice Commission a total of 6,261 attacks on Israeli citizens and property by Egypt, Jordan, Syria and Lebanon. Israeli casualties, for the same period, were 1,127 killed and wounded. Do these figures make any impact on the imagination? In July of this year, for instance, there were only 71 Arab attacks of some sort, only four Israelis killed, and 10 wounded. The 71 'armistice violations' included theft, sabotage, shots fired at farmers in fields, people on roads or in the streets of Jerusalem, kidnapping, a plane shot down, road mines laid, hand grenades thrown, the usual thing: a light month. Last April there were 19 Israelis killed and 59 wounded: a heavy month.

Since Nasser's Suez grab the Egyptian frontier has been relatively quiet; the main burden of daily harassment has passed to Jordan. In August, that began with Jordanian 'marauders' shooting up a bus in the Negev, killing a woman and a few men who were going home from Beersheba. It went on, in the familiar rat-bite way, day after day; little death, little destruction, too numerous, too small, and above all too routine to be reported in the world's press. Finally, Israeli archaeologists were killed while studying a site, and a woman was shot while picking olives in a kibbutz. The Israeli Government (after there has been enough of this deadly small stuff) orders an Army attack in force, usually on a military objective, as has been done just now in Jordan. The Israeli reprisal is always newsworthy. The number of such reprisals, by the Israel Army or by frontier kibbutzniks, from 1950 to July, 1956, was 24. The United Nations Mixed Armistice Commission states that the Arab dead and wounded resulting from these reprisals for that period totalled 252.

When the Israeli Government orders a reprisal attack it does so in order to slow down the daily Arab attacks along any given frontier. To date this has worked. At the same time, Israel receives the censure of world public opinion and of the United Nations. Israelis do not feel this is just, since the world and the United Nations fail effectively to condemn the perpetual and cumulatively heavier 'armistice violations' of the Arabs, but Israelis also feel that justice is a rare if not unobtainable commodity. Ben-Gurion, speaking for his whole people, never stops saying that he will meet the Arab leaders anywhere, any time, to talk peace. It is obvious that the Israelis must crave peace, but peace is not what they have got. They have not got war either, as yet. They have this, and they live with it.

And somehow they live well; not comfortably, not easily, and not—heaven knows—'graciously,' but well in a way that has something to do with the heart and the spirit. Driving to the airport, I asked the taxi driver his opinion of life in Israel. (No foreigner can resist the Israeli taxi drivers who, among an international breed of talkers and philosophers, are pure champions.) He said, 'It is all very bewteefool, very hoppy.'

Home of the Brave

The man was tall, very thin, with a fine emaciated face and two round indented scars in his cheek, bullet wounds or worse. Since everyone in Poland looks ten years older than his age, he may have been thirty-five, perhaps younger. He wore something shabby in the way of sweater, windbreaker, greyish trousers. Poor and ugly clothing is routine; what matters is that the clothes seem sleazy and no protection against the cold. Where there are few material signs of position, people declare themselves by their faces and the tone of their minds. This was a man of breeding and education, and of special courage, and he was one of Cardinal Wyszynski's Catholics.

He said, 'Our young people are so against doctrine that it even works against us. They say that they agree with us in some things, we have an ethical sense, we believe in the individual and his freedom and his soul, but then we have dogma too, and they hate dogma . . . No one, not the young nor us nor anyone, except some very old people who have understood nothing, wants capitalism again; that is over. We want the future, though we are not sure of its form. But that future must make room for and allow the dignity of the individual.'

No label that I knew fitted this man. I told him that he did not sound like any other Catholic I had talked to, outside Poland.

'We are Catholic humanists. We are only concerned with the freedom of the individual in this or any future society. We often feel closer to liberal Communists than to some totalitarian-minded Catholics—those who believe in a small ruling group, a strong government, and in telling the people, who are considered as a mass, what to do.'

I had come to see this unusual Catholic to check what I thought I had learned about young people in his country. In something over two weeks in Poland, I had listened at length to forty-eight people, all met by chance and luck; no one selected for me, no one supervised, and I had been guided to this tiny fraction of a fraction by my own special curiosity. I was interested in the young who live by their minds, because I wanted to see what a lifetime of war and Communism had done to their minds. I shall report here only on the intellectual young; the brain workers, not the manual workers.

Nothing and no one in Poland is as expected; and our yardsticks do not apply, for none of us has had to live as Poles have, through twenty merciless years. We belong in different worlds. Seen from Poland, the West seems very far away, an almost insanely luxurious dream. And Poland feels like a dream too, a heroic nightmare. One's sense of reality is dislocated. One needs a new vocabulary to think with.

Even flat terms that we imagine we can define, like 'Catholic' and 'Communist,' have not the tight meanings we give to them. There are Communist-sponsored Catholics, the totalitarian-minded believers that the thin man spoke of, and active Catholic humanists, supporters of the Cardinal. Then there are the younger Catholics who go to church because formerly it was one way to protest against the regime, and the church is linked to patriotism, and 'in hard times, religion is the only way to be free in your soul,' and churches are beautiful, and you are there with friends; but they do not obey any of the rules of the church. As for Communists, there is a type described, always laughingly, as a 'real, fanatic Communist'—these are hard to find, and I did not manage to see one; there is someone else described as 'very Communist'; and someone milder called 'quite Communist'; and there is a 'member of the Party,' which does not necessarily mean that he is a true

Communist at all. A man might have joined the Party during the war, because the Communist underground resistance was the most efficient against the Nazis; this is a frequent reason and accepted as laudable. Or a man might become a member of the Party after the war, because he had to, to do the work he wanted or to hold his position; not laudable perhaps, but understood. And then there is a massive condition, known as being 'communisant.' A graduate student, our equivalent of a man studying for his Ph.D. who consistently fails to write his thesis, explained that 'all our young people are communisants. It is not the *idea* we are against; we see it as more modern than capitalism.'

'Then you are Party members?' I asked.

Four of us were packed into a small hired car at the time, driving through the flat smoky Silesian countryside. 'No!' they cried out in shocked voice, 'no, no!' The party was 'administrative' and they had nothing to do with that sort of thing.

I told the Catholic with the wounded face about our Silesian outing. In the morning I had hired a soiled hotel car and collected my chums haphazardly in the street. This was in Krakow. My young new friends were free to go anywhere at once; they are always on the move, searching for an odd job, a chance meal, a permission from a government bureau, a book, fun, anything. A student has a stipend of four dollars a month; this is calculated on the real value of the *zloty*, the black market value, not the pepped-up official exchange. If lucky, he gets food parcels from home, and he does whatever jobs he can find or sells anything he may have, to survive. But a successful grown-up man having two jobs—one would not be enough—might earn thirty dollars a month and support a family, and this is considered very good money not by what it can provide, but simply good money to get. Poverty among intellectuals (all I know about) is universal; there are only degrees of worse and worse.

We were going to an industrial village in Silesia to see a Polish primitive painter whose work I had heard of. Riding in a private car is a treat, and since I was there, with my old-fashioned tendency to eat now and again, I would buy food if we could find it, so it was a real party.

One boy, aged twenty, was studying singing; another, aged twenty-two, was an accomplished scene designer and painter, a senior student; the third was the art-historian non-Ph.D. aged all of twenty-seven, a Pied Piper figure who leads the young to make fun for themselves. They and their friends run a little cabaret in a derelict cellar. Their stage is four battered kitchen tables in a row, scenery is painted on the wall of the cellar, costumes are tacked together out of borrowed odds and ends. If people have money, they pay to see the cabaret; if not, they see the show anyhow. The cellar had been closed for months; the band of young amateurs was suspect because of making political jokes. (At one time they did a strip-tease of a statue of Stalin, not tactful but much appreciated.) They had promised to make no more political jokes. Every night now, helpless with laughter, they rehearsed—in their filthy, freezing cellar—a take-off on the Romantics. Romanticism, with its emphasis on lovesickness, *mal du siècle*, and personal drama, strikes them as high comedy. The cabaret uses their talents and keeps their private hope alive.

In the car, Julek, the Pied Piper, began to remove his various coats. He always wears everything he owns, beat-up turtle-neck sweater, suit, overcoat, because he has no room of his own, sleeps wherever he can find a bed, and carries his property on his person. Suddenly loud warbling cries issued from the singer, while the painter shook with laughter. The painter said. 'This is an interesting boy. He shows me now what is the Russian school of *bel canto*.' Roaring with laughter at Russians is a mad Polish speciality; and the young I saw, who were all absorbed in the arts, laugh like billy-o. Unless they are telling you, with disgust, of the long period when their working lives were dominated by the theory of Socialist Realism, that Pollyanna version of art which makes everything sentimental and over-life-size, a whooping-up propaganda. Officially, until 1956, they had to be taught that Socialist Realism was real art. On the whole they despised and rejected this teaching by pure instinct.

Julek and I looked at the awful landscape, a synthesis of industrial ugliness, and Julek observed, 'If you cannot pay people to work, you must use terror. There is no other way. We were all made equal in poverty and that was necessary. Our country was destroyed by the war and hopelessly poor. If only the West could help us to get on our feet, then people could be paid to work; but no. Russia would not allow that. It is so awkward, isn't it, our culture goes West and our economics goes East.'

'Is it only poverty that makes Rysio [the painter] and Pavel [the singer] seem so discouraged for themselves?' I would have settled for that; you feel poverty as if it were a suffocating smell in the air.

'All the young are in despair, *a priori*. There is no future for them, and they know it. My life, for instance, is terribly important to me; but I see that it has no importance in the great thing of history. They will shut up our cellar one day, perhaps soon. Official opinion thinks we are reactionary because we make jokes. That is idiotic, but that is official opinion. It will be hard for us because it is easier when you have a little group to laugh together. But we will be stopped, and I understand it. I don't *accept* it; I understand it.'

Rysio, in a fury that was close to tears, said, 'I am a painter. I do not care whether a private man or a government runs a shop. What difference does it make? I only want to live in peace and paint. But who will ever buy my paintings? Who has money for that? Oh, I would give my paintings, my drawings, all; I have nothing, but everything I have, if only I could go to Italy and look at the beautiful Renaissance pictures.'

'If you had the money and were free, would you go for good?' I asked.

'No. No. I could not ever do that.'

I had asked all the young I saw whether they would leave Poland permanently, if able to, if a living could be earned elsewhere, and each one said: No.

And after this, to my surprise, it turned out that they were communisants.

'It's not the theory, then, that they object to,' I asked the Catholic humanist, 'but the practice?'

'Ah, the practice. It's so much better now, since 1956, you can have no idea.'

His smile lighted up his drawn, scarred face. Leon, a newly met journalist friend who had brought me here, and I said good-bye and went out into the slimy streets of Krakow. 'That's a good, sane man,' Leon said. I could place Leon, a little, because a few days before he had told me that he was 'partyless. I don't think I could belong to any party, even if I agreed with it.'

'The country seems full of good, sane people,' I said, 'And Krakow seems a good, sane city.'

For five hundred years Krakow has been a university town and a centre of art, but it was founded in the tenth century, and the ancient castle of the Polish Kings and the cathedral where they are buried rise on a hill above the city and the curving river. Herr Franck, a little man with pink-and-white skin and a pursed rosebud mouth, the monstrous Nazi King of Poland, lived and ruled in that castle and thus insulted the Poles' passionate love of their history. Narrow streets wind from the castle to the market square, with its arcaded town hall and flower stands and pigeons. The reconstructed statue of Poland's greatest poet stands in this square. The Nazis, determined to destroy the culture of the Poles as well as their bodies, dynamited this monument. All during the Nazi occupation, little bunches of flowers appeared on the dynamited rubble. But for twenty years now the people of Krakow have had no money to paint or refurbish their city, and it is dirty, worn-out, like a very old, very tired beauty.

Leon is young by my standards but not by Polish standards, as he is thirty. A man of seventy might have learned how to keep Leon's tolerant distance from life, by becoming a spectator. However, if you are a soldier at fifteen, in an underground army, and fight a final losing battle for your country, and are afterwards buffeted around Europe alone for eight years, perhaps you become seventy quickly.

'You know,' Leon said 'the truth is that most young people are only interested in politics as it affects their freedom.'

'But politics affects everything,' I said. 'Like an incurable disease. It spreads everywhere; it never leaves you alone.'

'We know we have the best we can get, and we are glad of it and only hope to keep it. This much freedom. And perhaps it will get better; maybe if the Russians grow richer. There would be less terror everywhere . . . People don't hate the Russians, you know, it isn't that. The Russians exploited us after the war, and they were always forcing us to love them. That was awful, but they've let up. With time, with time, it *has* to get better. Let's go and drink some vodka.'

They all drink a lot of vodka and who wouldn't and why not? The young ones exaggerate how much they drink; they haven't the money to drink steadily. In plays and stories they use vodka, drunkenness, as a symbol of bitterness and brutality. Drinking to forget, and becoming beastly as a result. This is touching; they are such unbeastly young.

We had a merry time in Krakow. We waltzed and tangoed at what is considered locally a depraved night club for low-class people. It was a big, plain, well-lit room with nursery-pink walls, and looked to me like a respectable dance hall for lower-middle-class families. The band was a delight. The Poles adore jazz, and it is the worst jazz I have ever heard. Cheap vodka is the diet in this dance hall; most of the women were tarts—hefty, scout-leaderish tarts. All the men, as everywhere else, kissed hands. At the end of each dance, with an elegance which would have been fine at Versailles, hands are kissed; when meeting or leaving a lady, hands are kissed. In the muddy street, under the drizzling sky, you see a woman dressed in baggy clothes and a beret and run-down shoes, and her face weary, pale, unpainted, having her hand kissed by a man who looks as if he had just come from a day's heavy road-building. The way to address waiters is to call softly, 'Please, Monsieur.' ('Mister' is not the right translation.) Chambermaids are 'Madame.' And even 'very' Communists, I am told, cannot bring themselves to say 'Comrade,' and they kiss hands too. The manners of the young are glorious, as are their voices; all voices, in fact. By their voices alone, you would say this is a nation of cultivated people. But how did the young learn? These manners, in this desolate *mise en scène*, have nobility and magic.

We went to the theatre; everyone goes to the theatre; seats are cheap. Krakow is a town of half a million people and has ten legitimate theatres, an operetta company, and a Philharmonic. The first play I saw there was written by a very young writer; it was modern (the characters dressed in blue jeans, floppy skirts), yet allegorical too. And imagination, in the theatre, proves an excellent substitute for money. Here, on a tilted, cleverly lit stage, furnished only with three symbolic bench swings, we were in the miserable crowded Warsaw room of two young men. Vodka played a prominent part in the plot, which was the story of the denial of love, the heartless treatment of a young girl. The playwright was attacking what he feels to be an attitude of his contemporaries; cynicism and self-hate, born of hopelessness, working itself out as vengeance on the innocent.

The other play was in the Workers' Theatre at Nowa Huta, a modern steel town built in five years on the outskirts of Krakow. One hundred thousand people live in these giant cement sardine tins, and only the theatre is graceful, and it is crowded every night. I saw, there, Camus's allegory against dictatorship, called *Siege of the State*. The costumes were dazzling in colour and shape, made of cheesecloth or cheap rayon stuff; the single décor was strong architecture; the crowd scenes were as beautiful as ballet. You could hear yourself breathe in that audience. This play, among us, would be considered highbrow and difficult. The workers of Nowa Huta like it best of the repertory, which includes, oddly enough, *The Rainmaker* and *Of Mice and Men*. A young woman less than thirty years old directs this theatre. I asked if anyone had seen the play in Paris; how did they get their ideas for costuming, staging? No one had seen it anywhere. This fresh, compelling production came straight out of their own heads. And there never was a clearer denunciation of tyranny.

My young pals agreed that the government was quite glad to let allegory past the censor; you can't have a political quarrel, with a powerful Eastern neighbour, over allegory. And it is entirely true that anyone can *say*, if not print, film, or act, what he likes. The freedom of speech is terrifying to an outsider, who fears that at some later date, when perhaps things have tightened up, this freedom will be paid for retroactively.

One night we went to a students' theatre, again a derelict basement which the young had fashioned into a tiny playhouse with their own hands. This play was also an allegory, having to do with prison—'Polish undergraduate Ionesco,' Julek said. The stage was set with ominous spindly black bars, cages, ladders. The theatre was a rabbit warren of handmade cement stairs with a small room, not more than twelve by eight feet, at the top. The director, an alarmingly thin boy, sleeps here on a short sofa and also uses his bedroom as the theatre office. We sat where we could in this room, the troupe and some other young ones, with a bottle of vodka and time nonexistent.

I don't know how the talk came to Auschwitz, that greatest of all memorials to dictatorship. A young musician said to me, 'But they don't know about Auschwitz in the West, do they? They don't believe it?'

'Yes, they do, they do.' Only of course, I thought, they don't know, they cannot visualize it, they cannot feel it. You have to go yourself; you have to see the mountain of women's hair, the mountain of dead children's shoes, the mountain of pulled-out teeth; you have to pick up a handful of mushy soil near the crematoriums and touch the rotting lumps of white bone in it. A man who had been a prisoner in this place for four years—from the age of twenty-one to twenty-five—guided me over the huge camp. We passed through the execution yard where his father, and tens of thousands of others, had been shot. He led me down narrow stairs to the torture cells beneath and told me in a flat voice what had happened here. There were bunches of field flowers on the doors of some cells, mementos left to the dead.

That day I had seen groups of gypsies, nuns, Polish peasants, a few Frenchmen, a few Dutchmen moving silently and with stunned faces around the crude brick buildings. Suddenly, in that dark, empty cellar my guide shivered but said nothing.

On four hundred and thirty-seven acres of swampland (an area smaller than La Guardia Airport), behind this barbed wire, the Nazis murdered four million men, women, and children by hunger, disease, medical experiments, poison gas, shooting, hanging, and injections of phenol to the heart.

No one who has seen Auschwitz will ever forget it. It is a sin that the twenty-eight nations (including our own) whose citizens were killed here do not preserve this prison and raise a noble monument to the dead. Auschwitz should never be forgotten; it is a warning for all mankind.

We stopped talking of Auschwitz because we could not bear it; but still we could not leave the war. The war is always with you in Poland, and even these very young people are incurably scarred by it. One said that they had had such 'grave' childhoods, 'it is better now to forget.' At ten years of age, he was carrying secret papers for the Home Army in Warsaw, perfectly aware of what the Gestapo did to children too. His parents died in Auschwitz. Another said that as a boy of nine, coming home, he saw German soldiers collect all the people from a big apartment house, line them up against the wall of their home, and mow them down with machine gun fire. 'When I was going home,' he said 'just across the street. I remember how afraid I was.' These memories burn in every brain. No one, in Poland, except the very very young, is free of such knowledge. And no one has had ease and safety, in the peace, to heal the memories a little. The wonder of all is the lion-hearted gaiety of these people.

Nothing I know of the war is as appalling as what they know and have lived through, but I have my special heroes and I spoke of them: the Polish Corps in Italy. Suddenly a young actor said, 'Words. Nothing but words. The Poles are always brave; they know how to die. They die everywhere, especially well in foreign wars. It is very nice for you; you can admire us. It is useless and it must stop. Better not be brave and live; better be like the Czechs and live. *There has been too much dying.'*

I said that I knew people in the West who believed that nuclear war was preferable to living under a totalitarian dictatorship, a Russian dictatorship obviously. The whole roomful of them, the quiet gentle girls, who need good food and a hair wash and a rest, and the tense, fiercely alert boys, cried out, 'No! No! Not ever!' One said, 'Haven't we had enough, in the name of God? Let us just *live*, no matter how we have to do it. You can do something about life, a little anyhow, or have some fun, if you're still alive.'

The youngest there, an actor of twenty, with a face like a Botticelli angel, said, 'Oh, stop it now. Stop talking about war. We have nothing but war films and war books, and we hear about it from our fathers and our brothers, and we can see what it was, any time we go anywhere. Stop. Talk about the future.'

'Good,' I said. 'What about the future?'

'Well,' he said, shy now with everyone listening, and this a matter of such importance, 'what is the student theatre like in America?'

Warsaw frightened me at once, a haunted city, and I never got over a feeling of dread, depression, an irrational anxiety for everyone. Warsaw was destroyed by the Germans in 1944, block by block, using dynamite, fire, bombs; doggedly, the Poles are rebuilding it. Warsaw looks or feels as if the war had ended last week, not some thirteen years ago. There is the wide weed-grown flat where once the ghetto stood; there are everywhere gaping holes in place of buildings; there are other buildings shored-up, half-burned, and slashes and holes from shellfire on peeling walls. There are the skinny new trees.

Poland was defeated by the Nazi and Soviet armies in the month of September, 1939; but conquered Poland remained one of the cruellest battlefields of the war, and six million Polish citizens were killed in the five and a half years of World War II. Statistics are always cold, but perhaps if one compares numbers, the statistics take on their true size: the total of dead and missing of the United States Armed Forces in World War II was 407,828.

In Warsaw, you also remember that you are in a Communist-controlled country, though by all accounts the control now is humane and lenient, judged by what it was and what it is in other satellite countries. Still you do hear the incompetent echo in the tapped hotel telephone; you do notice that people look over their shoulders when talking in restaurants—the secret police are dormant but not forgotten; you feel in your bones, as you would feel a threatening change in the weather, every change in Russian mood or action. This is not an air we have ever breathed; I doubt if we would be strong enough to resist such a climate and stay as healthy in spirit as the Poles.

The Old Town of Warsaw has been entirely rebuilt and is an enchanting seventeenth-century village, with pale-painted house fronts, carved doors, squares, small churches. The Poles needed this lovely reminder of their past, for if man does not live by bread alone, Poles particularly do not. I met a few young artists who were lucky enough to be allotted garrets in the Old Town as studio homes. They were adorable children, as tidy and domesticated and content with their attics as very old people who have at last retired to their dream bungalows in Florida.

One boy who paints fairy-story illustrations (the complete, determined escape) told me something of his life. When he was eleven, he was orphaned; he did not say (one never asks) how his parents died; they were both thirty-six at the time. His fifteen-year-old brother was deported for slave labour in Germany and never again heard of. An unknown family took him in; he stayed with them until he was fourteen. Then he returned to Warsaw alone, frail (he is frail now), and made his own way, working, scrounging, starving, to get an education, to go to the Beaux Arts. At twenty-three, he married. His wife, also a painter, is like a little furry woodland creature, so shy that she cannot speak without blushing, and never in a voice above a whisper. They were married for four years but had no place to live together. Now they have a home, made gay and pretty by their taste, their economies, and their skilful hands. At night they have their evening meal of tea and cookies, sitting together in a garret radiance of love. This is such joy, this safety and peace inside four walls, that they think of nothing except how to earn enough to keep what they have. In their lives they have made one trip, for three days to Dresden in East Germany to look at pictures in the museum; they said the pictures were wonderful.

A friend of theirs, a girl who works in a museum, is married to a painter and is also blessed with a garret, spoke of the destruction of Warsaw; she was twelve years old at the time. 'It took perhaps thirteen hours to walk through the city, when the Germans drove us all out. There was a great crowd of people, old ones and sick and wounded and children, and the Germans with their guns standing along the streets and saying, "Hurry up, hurry up." If anyone fell, they had to be left behind, and families got lost from each other. You could hear nothing except the fires and the sound of burning beams falling from houses. Happily, in these circumstances, one has no imagination.'

There is nothing cruel, insane, ugly that they have not seen; and it has made them strangely quiet. Another young man in this group, trying to explain their outlook, spoke of the difference between them and *les jeunes*, which means people younger than themselves. They are twenty-six, twenty-eight, and do not consider themselves young. He said with pity, with impatience too, 'The young have complexes which they *show*.'

These young ones have had enough and more than enough of politics, the wicked mess their elders have offered them. They believe in art and in their love for each other; they are not like old married couples, they are like Hansel and Gretel clinging together in a hostile world. They are absolutely private individuals and 'realists,' as they say. Maybe they feel that having homes, they have more than most and more than they dared hope for, and they hope no further.

Another day I talked with two successful young literary men in the Writers' Club. Each intellectual craft has its own club, a few modest rooms where you can eat and drink. They wanted to know about good writers in England and America, and I told them what I could, trying to explain styles and characters and plots, and as I talked I saw the novels and stories I was discussing as fantastic carving on cherry stones. I did not miss the polite glaze that came over their old-young faces.

The novelist with one arm, who had been deported to Russia as a child for slave labour and had spent his adolescence in DP camps in India and Africa, said that he did not think such works could be published in Poland. 'People would not really understand them. You see, we perhaps don't care so much for purely personal problems. I mean, things you can get over by yourself.'

The young, they said, have learned no ideology; they have learned something else: an interior censorship. There is not only the official censor, but the watchdog inside who tells you in advance what you can get by with. They rebel against this rationed freedom, yet everyone I saw agreed that there is no thought of overthrowing Communism as such. 'No one thinks of capitalism again—that's a past dream—they only think of how to make this better.'

Capitalism is another word that has to be redefined. To the Poles, I think it means lavishness, an unimaginable and even undesirable glut of things not needed. I did not find anyone who coveted our two-toned cars. What they wanted was a room—no matter how small, how bare—of one's own; and two suits, not just one; and two weeks' vacation outside of Poland. They envy us what we value too lightly: our intellectual freedom. Our real richness, in their eyes, is that we can have personal convictions and act on them.

I talked often to a man who seemed to me an encyclopaedia of human experience. He was born rich and lived a princeling life until he was deported, as a boy in his early teens, to Russia for slave labour. He stayed on, freely, after the war because he wanted to see Russia. ('It's a fascinating country.') Still in his teens, he was put in charge of eighty displaced Polish families somewhere at the end of the world, in the hinterland of Russia. When he came back to Europe, he managed to collect what he could of his money and went off to blow it, dazzlingly, in Italy and France. Then he returned to this Polish life which is at once buried and wildly alive. He spends all the money he cannot spare on books, and he knows far more than I do about Western literature.

Above all, I think he wants the West to understand Poland, and he knows how hard that task is. He said, 'You Americans don't understand us. We don't envy you. We are glad that there's something young and beautiful and gay and happy in the world. Only we are often disappointed in you. Because you have so much, and you are not *à votre hauteur*. Not all the time, as you should be. You know, sometimes when I am very sad, I think to myself about English law, and it makes me happy. Just thinking about it. The way they go on, so careful about their law, so respectful of it.'

The Poles love to laugh, and do, and I felt ashamed, for their sakes, because I could not laugh enough. The spectacle of constant bravery does not lead, I find, to laughter; it induces many intense emotions, the simplest of which is awe. But I found one man with whom I laughed at once and steadily, as if some electrical connection of gaiety had been set up between us. He looked irresistibly jolly, for a start, being shortish and roundish, with merry eyes and a face full of loving, laughing kindness. He worked in a small office for a newspaper, and the presses on the floor below shook the building, and the telephone rang all the time, and young people sauntered in and smiled at him and chatted, and you could see he was a benign guardian angel for them. I asked what a girl with enormous dark eyes and a scruffy Sagan haircut had wanted of him, and was told with merriment that she came in to discuss *Doctor Zhivago*.

He said he had a copy, which was a nice surprise, and we agreed that Pasternak's colleagues, yelping like jackals, were a scandal. 'Here,' he said, 'we are no longer under the necessity to pronounce ourselves on what we do not understand. It is not much; but it *is* much,' and he twinkled at me.

He was anxious about the young. 'Perhaps they use up all

their fantasy in trying to get better living conditions. It is their main great preoccupation. And there have been so many plans and rules, people forget a little how to make their own plans and dreams. Besides, we have not your tradition of private freedom. You are ready to make any sacrifices to do what you want.'

If he liked to believe that, it was not up to me to disillusion him.

'I came here to find out about private freedom,' I said 'I wondered whether the young would talk and think alike. I wondered whether a system, any system, if it's the only one you know, could make minds operate to order or on a pattern. Now I think we could take lessons from Poland on how to be rugged individualists. But I'm repelled by Communist economics. Do you remember that wonderful line in *Doctor Zhivago*: "Man was born to live and not to prepare to live?" That's what I've got against Communist economics. One damned steel mill after another, and no joy for the living. I don't understand economics. Does it have to be so ruthless?'

'We were very poor, and the war made us poorer. It is not all as bad as you think. Some people are better off than before. Perhaps seventy per cent of the people. Not those like us, but others.'

'I don't want to argue this with you,' I said. 'I want to get the proper Communist point of view on it. It's too absurd the way I can't seem to find a proper Communist.'

He found this very funny. 'But I am a Communist.'

'You!' I said, shouting with laughter.

'No, no,' he insisted, laughing now at both of us. 'I am, really. Honestly, I am.'

This confirmed my one certainty about Poland: no labels fit.

The Fifties

For a year and a half, Italy was my fifth foreign country of residence. That was well before the population explosion, the travel explosion, the motor car explosion, the hideous cement building explosion had done their dirty work on Europe. I produced enough serious fiction to keep myself excited, enough bilgers to keep afloat, and saw the glory that was Italy when there was room to see it. My relation to countries seems to be like love affairs, leaving tender memories, no disillusion or regrets and no reason to end except the beckoning next love affair. If that is so, my relation to the United Kingdom of England, Scotland and Wales (excluding Northern Ireland) is like an open marriage; I roam freely and return—to London again, in 1953.

London had revived. The remaining bomb sites no longer looked raw and many had bloomed into squatters' gardens. Houses were being painted and repaired: no amputated halves showed wallpaper on a last exposed inner wall. There were few cars, uncrowded unhurried quietness, the streets were clean and the air smelled like air. Weather permitting, to walk idly around the city and the parks, by day and night, was a constant pleasure. Perhaps it was a time of convalescence, a lull, when the Brits seemed glad to be alive, comfortable enough and taking it easy.

I had a loose deal with the *New Republic* which gave me press credentials to poke about whenever I felt inquisitive, and a good understanding with the editor of the *Atlantic Monthly* that allowed me to travel farther afield and look longer and deeper. And I always had my own work: fiction. The *Sunday Times* offer to go to Washington and report the Senate Hearing on Joseph McCarthy was a flattering surprise, the first assignment from an English paper. The trouble with writing for any newspaper is lack of space: I feel as if I am talking at top speed in one breath, as I did in 'The Most Unheard-of Thing.'

Joseph McCarthy, the Junior Republican Senator from Wisconsin, ruled America like a devil king for four years. In March 1954, Ed Murrow, the most respected American broadcaster, had the lonely courage to risk a frontal attack on network TV. Nobody else had dared say anything like, 'No man can terrorize a whole nation unless we are all his accomplices.' A Gallup Poll in January 1954 found that fifty per cent of the country supported and applauded McCarthy. The remaining fifty per cent may have been formed by the usual sludge don't-knows and by people who hated and despised McCarthy; in any case, it was a silenced fifty per cent. McCarthy discovered imaginary communists everywhere or, as an extra frill, homosexuals, *ipso facto* security risks. Red termites were chewing at the foundations of the state and society. He had only to hold up a piece of paper for the TV cameras and announce in his flat nasal voice, 'I have a list here,' and lives were truly destroyed. Hundreds of lives. The details of this period are sickening. Reckless with his long easy triumph, McCarthy finally overreached himself when he set out to bully the Army as he had bullied everyone else.

McCarthy's purges were an American mirror image of Stalin's purges, an unnoticed similarity. But Stalin had the full power of the state police to enforce his suspicions and accusations. McCarthy was merely the chairman of a Senate subcommittee, nothing. He derived his power from the American fear neurosis. McCarthyism did not begin or end with the malignant Senator nor the House Un-American Activities Committee. McCarthyism is rooted in this national neurosis.

Here is a fresh example of that neurosis, neo-McCarthyism, written by a former official in the Reagan White House: 'Indeed with its Clark amendment cutting off aid to the pro-Western guerrillas in Angola, and its Boland amendment cutting off aid to the pro-American guerrillas in Nicaragua, the *liberal wing of the Democratic Party has made itself the silent partner—the indispensable ally—of revolutionary communism in the Third World.* [1] [My italics]

Americans did not acquire their fear neurosis as the result of a traumatic experience—war devastating their country, pestilence sweeping the land, famine wiping out helpless millions. Americans had to be taught to hate and fear an unseen enemy. The teachers were men in official positions, in government, men whom Americans normally trust without question. Politics is their profession, they must know what is happening and what to do about it; the average citizen is busy enough managing his own life. Americans are more apolitical than most people. About half the electorate does not bother to vote in Presidential elections. And America is the biggest island in the world, and the safest. It was always abnormal for people so protected to imagine, with terror, Reds under their beds.

The teaching has been brilliantly successful and now Americans and their leaders are trapped in it. I think, guessing, that this fear neurosis started with the Russian Revolution. Americans, glad to be finished with the 1914–18 war in quarrelsome old Europe, could not possibly work themselves into a frenzy about Bolsheviks, all by themselves. Most of them would not be sure where Russia was, nor care. They were taught. The earliest form of the fear neurosis that I noticed, in the thirties, was called the Red Menace and focused largely on labour organizers and union members. It will not be forgotten that Sacco and Vanzetti were poor working men, of foreign origin, put to death as anarchists.

I think the Truman Doctrine, enunciated by the President as if he had been handed it directly by the Founding Fathers, is the seed from which the post-World War Two fear neurosis has grown. The seed was watered, manured, encouraged to take root and spread over the country by propaganda so hysterical, so

[1]Patrick J. Buchanan, *Newsweek,* July 13, 1987

ridiculous that it casts doubt on the intelligence of America. It defies belief that, in the heyday of McCarthy, Americans lived with the fear that perhaps the neighbour was a secret communist. Communists among us are out to destroy our freedoms, trumpeted the propaganda. How? Never explained. The fear neurosis was mythical, mysterious; it might as well have been fear of dragons or the evil eye; it bore no relation to real danger.

After 1949, the fear neurosis immediately clamped on to China. There was now a whole new set of American communists to fear and hate because they, by God, wanted to let China destroy our freedoms. How was China going to do it? The taught fear neurosis was untaught, promptly, when Nixon went to China and brought back word that the Chinese did not have three heads and cut their children and we could live in the same world with them. Turn it on, turn it off; a fear neurosis for every season.

The hate fear of communism, communists, went upmarket after the war, to feed on the educated class. *Intellectual* and *liberal* became nasty words. Neurotic fear of an unseen and unknown enemy translated into fear of private opinion, of the unconforming conscience, fear of the stranger—and the stranger was anyone who differed from the surrounding majority. True Americans, clearly, would not do something so unpatriotic as think for themselves. America, in this neurotic vision, is always imperilled by enemies, within and without. The leaders of America have a lot to answer for; it was wicked to instill a fear neurosis into people who, by nature, prefer being amiable and open and had, as Franklin Roosevelt memorably said, 'nothing to fear but fear itself.'

McCarthyism was the most acute manifestation of the fear neurosis and it made America nightmarish, sick in the head. Nowadays fear neurosis is institutionalized in the US Government, in the Moral Majority, in countless right-wing organizations, in Fundamentalist Christianity; it claims to represent true patriotism and true Americanism, with God's approval to boot. Everybody, outside that circle of fearing fanatic prejudice, is a potential threat to the safety of the Republic and the American way of life. The neurosis people are miraculously well-financed and united. The 'liberals,' a suspect category since the Second World War, are not. Of course fear neurosis prohibits sane political argument; honest dissent is easily branded 'soft on communism.' If the media and politicians cannot discuss the issues of the time objectively, using common sense, fact, understanding of the complicated real world, without slurs on their patriotism, the country gets a wacky lead. America, the giant power, blindfolded by the fear neurosis, staggers all over the globe meddling, not necessarily with success or in its own interests. No real enemy could damage America as badly as it damages itself by its innate McCarthyism. How I long for someone in public life with the moral and mental stature to free America of the fear neurosis. Fear is bad for people. I am absolutely sure of that.

From the hysteria that poisoned America to the pleasantness of England was like escaping out of a fever ward to the companionship of healthy adults. The two 1955 articles, 'It Don't Matter Who Gets in, Dear' and 'Spies and Starlings,' read like fairy tales but were true of the atmosphere in England then. Imagine a lazy relaxed general election now. Imagine laughter in the House of Commons. I note, as readers will, that Harold Macmillan was factually wrong about Philby, the spy, but morally right; a man is innocent until proved guilty.

At the end of an all too usual rainy London summer, I wanted a heat stroke and went to Greece, Israel and Italy in August 1956. 'The tension' I had heard of, during 'Weekend in Israel,' led to 29 October, 1956, when ten Israeli Brigades moved across the Sinai frontier, routed the Egyptian forces, reached and halted at the Suez Canal, while on 5 and 6 November, English and French forces began to occupy the Canal Zone. The Suez Crisis erupted in Britain. I have never before or since seen the British in such a fury, violently pro- and anti-Suez. Nobody liked Nasser. The argument was about the rightness or wrongness of attacking Egypt, aggression as a crime or a necessity. President Eisenhower pronounced American censure and the whole operation crumbled. I understood the Israelis' motives and actions and shared their view of Nasser as an incipient Pan-Arab Hitler. The Israelis should have gone it alone, thus warding off the third Arab-Israel war in 1967, and saving thousands of soldiers' lives on both sides. Instead the futile Suez episode made Nasser a starry hero to the Arab young. The British and French had been ludicrously inept as conspirators and as a military force and would have done well to stay at home. British internecine anger disappeared, no worse than a sneezing fit, when Macmillan became Prime Minister. We settled back into good humour with relief.

For my first visit to a communist country in the late winter of 1958, I prepared by buying gifts for the natives, a big jar of Nescafé and *Doctor Zhivago*, then famous and forbidden behind the Iron Curtain, and felt quite daring when my suitcase was prodded at Warsaw airport. I had no introductions, could not speak a word of Polish, and stood on the street in front of my Warsaw hotel wondering whether I was a certifiable nutcase. How did I expect to do this job I had assigned myself? For want of a better idea, I walked down the street and saw an art gallery with a window display of paintings like sweet derivations of Chagall. The young painfully thin artist, who happened to be in the gallery at the time, had never heard of Chagall. We talked, he invited me to his attic home. I met everyone like that; one handed me on to another. This chain reaction produced 'Home of the Brave.' All these young people became instant old friends, I doted on them, there was no strangeness between us and no feeling of age difference perhaps because their experience of life was much harder than mine. A mixture of languages—French, German, English—sufficed. We used to call that 'Brigade English' during the Spanish war.

Julek had said that the young were without hope but his vitality, their vitality, disproved his opinion. They gave me enormous hope. These funny, underfed, inadequately clothed, fine-looking kids were a magnificent generation, free and lively in their minds, unafraid. Like all the truly brave, they had no sense of their bravery; bravery was their normal state. I always want to believe in the goodness and courage of the human spirit but rarely, outside war, see its quality tested and passing with high marks. I abominate war and do not deny its reverse side: personal nobility. This haphazard group of Poles afforded me the luxury of admiring. If a generation could grow up as they had, through the cruelty of war and the oppression of government, and be unbroken, generous, tolerant and merry, there was hope for our questionable species.

A few miles from civilized Krakow, Auschwitz stood as a monument to evil, cause to despair for our species. Auschwitz, empty except for a few other silent visitors, horrifed me even more than Dachau when Dachau was full of dazed skeletal figures in striped prison clothes, and corpses lay in a stinking yellow outraged pile. It must have been the size of Auschwitz and the aura of that mammoth efficient murder factory. I could not handle my emotions: I wanted to scream and run and I was frozen by shock; I felt that I was going out of my mind. Only by looking. Evil is not banal, as Hannah Arendt suggested. Evil is fierce, stone cold, ruthless and when unchained but organized, as here, it is all-powerful. I will never forget Auschwitz; the world should never allow itself to forget Auschwitz. For though it is unique in history and was the handiwork of vilely degraded men and women in one nation, evil has no frontiers.

I wish that those good brave kids in Poland were the norm and the majority of our breed, but they are not. I wish that kindness were a universal human quality, but it is not. And I have no solutions.

THE SIXTIES

Return to Poland

As for me, to go to Poland is to step through the Looking Glass. The people are superb, but there's also the Red Queen, dressed up as the State now, and I have simple Alice reactions to the State Queen: barking mad and beastly, is what I say to myself. The Polish people are used to the Red Queen, and besides are indestructible. They stay sane and make jokes. On my second visit to Poland I thought I learned more, but in the end I was only sure of what I felt. This would be of supreme unimportance except that I imagine that emotions are standard, typical, those of anyone of low-average stamina brought up in the Western world and accustomed to such amenities as the lifelong habit of calling your soul your own.

We sat in a charming candlelit cellar in the beautifully rebuilt old town of Warsaw, and it might have been a glamorous restaurant anywhere. The other tables were filled, although this is an expensive place, even on the black-market rate of exchange, let alone on the thieving official rate. I marvelled at the girls—fragile pretty creatures, soft-voiced, fair, wearing the new beehive hairdos, modern products of modern hardship who retain a gentleness and grace seldom seen amongst us. The young men looked chipper. The older couples were neat, dark-clad, middle-class bourgeoisie, you would think, dining out on the cook's night off. My companions might have been a tweedy English professor and his delicate wife.

My professorial friend has been in prison sometime or other, for one of the new reasons: these have to do with economics and are pure other-side-of-the-Looking-Glass. I listened to a trial in Krakow where eight men were being judged, under the criminal code, for incompetence in their State-owned co-operative. They could easily have been stupid or inexperienced, but that sort of common-sense interpretation of life is not the way the law works. Whether you lose money or make money, you can always go to jail, if the State wishes. Listening to Poles, you would imagine that to go to jail, to have been in jail, is about on a par with our reaction to a bad case of influenza. Nasty, rotten luck, can happen to anyone, nothing to shout about, something to avoid if possible, and obviously no stigma attaches to it.

Self-pity seems unknown among Poles, and this lack imparts a fine astringent tone to their thinking and conversation. They talk about themselves and the life of their country as if they stood several miles away. I was therefore not surprised to hear my friend point out, with detachment, some valuable accomplishments of the State. He said, 'This regime gets no credit, even for the good things it does; the people are so against it because it was imposed from the outside.'

At the end of this journey I tried, within my limited knowledge, to draw up a balance sheet in the only terms I understand—which have to do with happiness, decency, dignity—on the good and the bad in Polish life today. Perhaps no Pole would agree with me. They know what I do not: they know what existence is like in the other satellite countries and in Russia. Compared with what others have got, the Poles think they have something resembling real life.

The State giveth and the State taketh away, and the State gives an amazing amount of what it calls culture. True, the tone of this culture has been so brilliant only since 1956, when the Poles made their national revolution against Stalinism. And true, the State is clamping down again on the rationed freedom and range of the arts. A wise journalist explained this gradually renewed but strongly resented death grip on expression: 'I think there are three reasons. The first is economic. We are even poorer than we were a year and a half ago; since there must be saving, some of it must be made on the arts. As to books, we now export more wood because coal didn't turn out well, so there is simply less paper. The second reason is that Poles have been too successful in the arts. Polish films, Polish painting, Polish books have been too much praised in the West. East Germans and Czechs tattle to the Russians; it is very embarrassing for our government, this unorthodox, un-Communist success. Finally, the regime believes that intellectuals of every kind always have to be kept in their place.'

Throughout Poland, there is an enormous attentive audience for the best work that can be done in the theatre, in films, in music, in painting, and in writing. Every little provincial town has its theatre and orchestra; companies go on tour regularly to the smaller villages; editions of the classics and of good foreign and Polish writers are sold out in a matter of days; picture galleries are jammed. I would be amazed to find that Alton, Illinois, had a permanent stock company, with a range from Shakespeare to Arthur Miller (and no bilge in between), and played all week, every week, to a crowded theatre. But the theatre in Katowice, which is a grisly mining town in Silesia, was putting on Arthur Miller's *A View from the Bridge* while I was there, and on a sunny Thursday afternoon you could not get a seat in the hushed house. 'Why do they like it, Julek?' I asked. 'The public adores it,' he said. 'They adore such complicated fantastical problems. It is a nice rest. I think Miller talks too much. Very heavy. The provinces love him.'

And is there any town in America of half a million people, the size of Krakow, which has ten legitimate theatres, one puppet theatre, one operetta company, and a philharmonic? While in Krakow, I noticed advertisements for three current plays by Aeschylus, Shakespeare, and Shaw. A young friend just graduated from the Krakow Beaux Arts, where he studied stage designing, has his first job as one of the designers for the largest Krakow theatre, a whopping place with a huge auditorium. He showed me his sketches for the costumes and sets of the next production, *Troilus and Cressida:* imposing and imaginative warriors' costumes, which will be made of silvered cardboard, cheesecloth, dyed horse-hair plumes; movable panels to suggest the camp of the Greek army, the battlements of Troy, nothing but painted beaverboard giving a heroic impression of space and power. 'It is a very interesting play to the people,' he said, 'because of the political allusions.'

This boy earns the equivalent of twenty dollars a month, which means that he lives on scraps, but he is happy because he has the greatest possible luxury, a room of his own. It is a real attic, with a small skylight for air and light, a chair, a table, a cot, a bookcase; and one part of the room is high enough to stand up in. The washing facilities are distant and lamentable. Young Poles have never known even rudimentary ease; for twenty years the main problem has been to eat. They do not think in material terms; our Beatniks would seem luxurious pampered babies to them. The result of never having had money, nor the prospect of having it, is to cherish more fiercely the values of the mind.

So this boy, who does not dream of a better physical existence, dreams of ballet, and notably of American ballet. He eats even less and saves to buy ballet books that are published in New York. They cost a terrible lot, by his starvation standards; he owns four of them. The Poles do not ask favours, they prefer to offer them; pride is part of their bravery. My young friend knotted himself in apologies before he could bring out his one vital request. 'Could you ask Mr Jerome Robbins if he would have me do a set and costumes? I do not want money; I would be happy to give. I wish only to work for him.' Sadly, I had to point out that life did not function exactly like this in America, and also I did not know Mr Robbins. Privately, I doubted whether at his age, straight from school, he would have the chance anywhere in America to do the work he does in Krakow.

No one believes that the State—in its concrete form, the high Communist bureaucracy—is a devoted lover of the arts. The State merely refuses to waste its money on what it considers junk; the

Poles won't endure being bored; the result of these two different viewpoints is exciting, good art. I think the Polish public is better trained and more eager than we are and wants more from art than we do; and it is nobly served by its artists. In my opinion, the culture—odious word—in its quality, quantity, and availability, is the most laudable aspect of this regime. The Poles would probably say they have wrested their culture from the State, they have made it because it is in them, and that would be true; but the culture is there, and although the State pays misery wages for it, as for all else, still it pays.

Culture rests on, stems from education, and education in Poland is a fascinating mystery. There are twice as many universities as before the war. I have no statistics on student population, but the small city of Krakow alone has 40,000 students of university level. Entrance examinations are the same throughout the country and very stiff; no laggards are allowed to remain in classrooms. And beyond all the formal schooling, the sense of a whole people clamouring for and gulping down education is something you feel as a fact, like the weather. I sought enlightenment; when you want a thoughtful point of view you go to the opposition, the Catholic liberal élite. I put my questions to a man of generally recognized fairness and intelligence. 'Why isn't Communism sowing dragon's teeth with all this education? If education does nothing else, it teaches people to ask, "Why?" And not only does the State provide so much education, but apparently it permits real education, not the teaching of dogma to parrots. Isn't this a crazy risk? They're not going to get a nation of Communists here, anyway. They're going to get a nation of free, liberal intellectuals.'

It should be noted that this man is an honourable anti-Communist and bears no relation to the horrible world-wide crew of professional anti-Communists once headed by Hitler, ably abetted by the late Senator McCarthy, now recently joined by Dr Verwoerd. Many and very nasty people are anti-Communist because they are natural Fascists who see in Communism a power threat to their own repulsive dreams of power, or use

Communism as a handy word for smearing all dissenters. This man is pure in his rejection of Communism, and for my part, I stand with people like him who hate Communism because they believe in humanity, one by one, the only way it comes. Peace and dignity, responsibility and freedom are what we want for ourselves, and so for all other men. The genuine anti-Communists know that the end never justifies the means, in terms of human life. We are accountable for the means; the end is always lost or changed in time: the means of Communism, as of Fascism, are inhuman.

His answer astonished me: 'Of all the bad things anyone can say about Communism, I do not think you can say that they want to keep people stupid so as to control them.' I asked him to repeat this, I found it so startling, both as coming from him and as an unexpected revelation of hope for the world. 'The Communists may have believed that a middle intelligentsia, half educated but thinking itself educated, would be better prepared to swallow their ideology whole. But of course, so far, this does not work.'

There is little or no material advantage, for a Pole, in being educated, yet educated people are the aristocracy of the classless society. There is also no such thing, and never can be any such thing, as a classless society; men, luckily, are not equal. The Poles are equal enough in poverty, but any bright young Pole would rather be an underpaid intellectual than a better-paid worker.

One rainy afternoon we picked up a young man in a café in Nowa Huta, which is the modern steel town the State has built outside Krakow. This eighteen-year-old was enrolled in the law faculty of Krakow University; his father was a steelworker. He announced that after he had finished law he would like to study philosophy, and after that he would like to become a journalist. I was thinking how cross a normal capitalist father would be, having to pay for all this education, and, besides, quite unnecessary education, as we journalists would be the first to testify. How much does it cost? I wondered. Tuition is fourteen dollars a year. Adding up, generously, we figured that with books, carfare, lunches, some clothes, some spending money, he cost his father sixty dollars a year, which is a lot, a very good month's wage in Poland.

The young man—delightful soft voice, open face, the usual manners of all classes in this 'classless society,' which is to say, perfect courtesy in speech, hand-kissing, innate politeness—seemed unworried by his father's financial problems. He loves sports, jazz, movies: the international freemasonry of youth. He reads classical drama for pleasure. He wanted to know whether America was as beautiful as he had heard. Then he wanted to know whether people lived very nervous lives there; he had also heard this. (Few Americans would deny that life is needlessly nervous in God's Own Country; but few of us could take what Polish nerves do, and have to.) Change this boy's clothes, teach him English, and he would be one of the better-bred, more intellectually alert freshman at Princeton.

Someone said, 'Do you want to see a peasants' university?' and indeed I did, so off we went, I and three Poles who had never heard of such an institution, although they lived twenty miles from it. We arrived at an old shabby country manor and found that this house sheltered sixty students who come for seven months, farm boys and girls who have already finished their high schools. Throughout Poland there are ten such peasants' universities, based, we were told, on the Danish model. The couple who ran this school reminded me of the best type of Quakers; in fifteen years they have graduated 2200 students. They have many more applications than they can accept: young men, back home in their villages, send their fiancées to this school, wishing their future wives to have the same advantages they had; alumni bring their children for visits; the local peasants pour in on Sunday afternoons for coffee and cake and discussion with the undergraduates.

The school has no other aim than to set the mind free. It wants to make whole people. It believes, evidently, that truth is beauty, beauty truth, and in a modest way it tries to show students something of the wide world of the mind. After which, the students return to their small poor villages and share this new knowledge, this vision; and they are gladly welcomed by their own kind, as bringers of light. It seems too happily good to be real, but it is real.

For seven months, these boys and girls study dancing, painting, singing, acting; they take courses in geography and history. But above all, they are encouraged to read. Sometimes a student will read fifty books during his stay, sometimes seven; no pressure is exerted. The library is a good one. The students organize almost nightly book evenings, at which one of them reviews what he has read. The schedule of these literary gatherings was tacked on the principal's wall: Balzac, Dickens, Dostoyevsky, Conrad, Hemingway are the foreign authors I remember. One night a student had reviewed a life of Lenin; there was no other indication of politics.

We were treated to a heavenly show of old Polish folk dancing and singing, in costume. When we left, a small group of students were preparing a play for that night; they had dramatized Goethe's *Sorrows of Werther* and were about to stage it, with a homemade set, a spotlight, and whatever costumes they had invented and sewed. No one had told them to do this or helped them; the teachers arrive at the evening entertainment as visitors. There it is. I cannot explain it or fit it into any preconceived notions; I only know it exists. My three Polish chums were as amazed and impressed as I was.

A gentle bourgeois housewife teaches English in a Krakow public school, to earn some extra money. She has twelve students, aged eleven to thirteen, and for two hours twice a week they slug away at the job with rapt attention. Within three months they can take simple English dictation without making mistakes. She says it is wonderful to teach them, they are so clever, so eager to learn. What she reports seems to me a sort of miracle; try thinking of it in reverse, our children learning Polish.

The professor from the medical school at Krakow is, as they always politely say in Poland, 'over sixty.' He is a pre-war professor, and professors were and are very great people in Europe, and he was accustomed to quite an elegant standard of life. His university will celebrate its six hundredth anniversary in 1964;

it is Ivy League in Poland, a famous centre of learning. He doesn't so much talk as explode with energy; he shouted joyfully that, in his work, it is a thousand times better than before the war. There are now ten medical faculties instead of five, no trouble with politics for the last five years, all the money you want for research, every scientific publication from all over the world, colleagues coming from the West to visit; he himself does not want money, he has time only for work; what is bad is that the young assistants are not paid enough, very bad; and they lack foreign exchange to buy equipment in the West; but there are more students with more chances, and young doctors can go to the country, where they are needed, and make a good living. 'We get on with the work,' he roared—marvellous man.

I thought it fine Polish-funny that if you wanted a miner's point of view in Katowice you searched out your man in a night club. In a vast, ill-lit dingy hall (standard for popular night clubs), the younger mining set was doing frantic rock'n'roll and did not look suitable for serious conversation. We found a very correct, nice, pudgy middle-aged man who turned out to be in the engineering section of the mine. He reads technical material in English, German, and Russian, but he is not a university graduate; he is a plain worker.

Perhaps the final comment on education in Poland was made by an old peasant woman who lived in a meadow by a brook, in a log and plaster cottage painted pale blue, with a thatched roof. I loved the looks of this place and the inside of her house, with its big yellow tile stove for heating and cooking, its oil lamps. I thought this was the nearest I'd ever get to nineteenth-century peasants in Russian literature. She was as jolly as a grig; everything was right, her kerchief, her heavy boots, her large wool skirts, her lined face, her small gay blue eyes, her voice like a cackling giggling croak. We brought vodka with us, as a help to knocking on doors and asking personal questions of strangers, and this worked like a charm—not that any private person would refuse to let you in and to answer anything you asked. She wanted mainly and disconnectedly to talk of her sister, who had been in Auschwitz and was always ill, sick with the concentration-camp sickness--terrible changes in the body induced by starvation, which end, by some metabolic twist, as disabling obesity; her sister could not take a job where she had to stay in one room. This old woman's life can never have been anything but stony hardship, and it is the same now; she would not think it worthwhile to complain. But suddenly she said, 'I can only scratch my name like a hen. Now the children go to school.'

I love and admire the Poles, and for their sake I wish I could report that life is better in Poland, more room to breathe, more hope, and more money. In 1958, there seemed little enough of those commodities, and now it is worse.

'Everyone is sick of politics,' said Antoni. 'All they care about is making money.'

'And do they?'

'Oh, no, of course not. There is always less money. And prices go up and wages stay the same, or else, plop, they go down. And many people have no jobs. But there is no unemployment relief, because in a Communist State there can be no unemployment. And the labour exchanges do not find people work. It is a joke, no?'

'Since I'm not Polish, the answer is No.'

'Many people are becoming Communists now, just for the sake of a job. That seems to me a big mistake. I think Communists should at least be sincere, don't you agree?'

A year and a half ago, we talked a great deal about the past war, about Russia, about fear of another war, even occasionally about the Polish government. This time, topic number one was economics, which is the nagging desperate preoccupation of the Poles. When they say they are interested in making money, they mean they are interested in staying alive.

People exist who can write intelligently about Marxist economics. To the ignorant outside observer, Marxist economics in Poland seems like a mad doctrinaire system, unrelated to human life or human nature, which is designed to keep people miserably poor. The state, the overall paymaster, does not pay a living wage.

And meantime, it hounds the pitiful relics of private enterprise that have somehow survived. (A miller by a stream: since the last of the Polish Kings, over two hundred years ago, his family has owned and operated an ancient wooden water wheel and ground grain for the neighbours. He is hardly a threat to any economic system. A wiser state—we will skip the idea of a kinder state—would even consider this man and his mill wheel as art objects to be preserved. He is being chivvied out of existence by taxes; one small man lost in the countryside, one man with a handsome mourning face who sees the end of his line.)

Communist economics in Poland apparently work like Prohibition in America. Prohibition made the United States a nation of illegal drinkers; Communist economics force the Poles to be finaglers, cheats, little or big crooks. If a charwoman is paid ten dollars a month for full-time work, she must obviously have several jobs or starve. So she checks in at two or more jobs, works a little, and badly, at each, and lives. If a janitor who shovels coal into boilers all night in the ravaging Polish climate earns sixteen dollars a month, he must obviously steal some of the coal to sell it on the black market, or starve. If you are higher up in the scale of employment, you can rob more from the State, and be caught and go to jail: a visit to the law courts any day will confirm this. 'The most honest woman you could ever know,' I heard, 'she is in prison for embezzling. She did it for everyone else where she worked, too; she had to help them.' 'We are all honest here,' said the peasant woman who rents rooms in her house for vacationing city people; she could not make a living off the farm. 'But in the next village, someone robbed the co-op.' 'Oh, well,' said the driver of our hired car, 'they were only stealing from the State, not from real people.'

Terror changes its face; for the past few years, there have been no political trials. In fact, what use is political rebellion of any kind? The Poles know their catastrophic geography and their ruthless neighbour. Now the State concentrates on money and snoops after any signs of well-being, for legally there should be none. Lawyers, organized into co-operatives, have private practices, with a fixed scale of fees; but they must not earn more than sixty dollars a month. A peasant remarked, 'If you wear a pair of good trousers, they follow you to see where you got the money.' A year later, a man is ominously questioned as to how he managed to buy a car for his work. The ever-present, ever-menacing State, which taps telephones, opens mail, searches rooms, follows people, seems turned into a suspicious cash register with an X-ray eye. Those who have nothing must go on having nothing.

I don't pretend to understand what purpose or excuse there can be for such economics; I only know the atmosphere—anxiety, disgust, hopelessness—and the visible results. Dirt and neglect: oh, the bad food and scruffy rooms, the broken plumbing, the filthy, slow, overloaded trains, the antique planes with the heating out of order, freeze or boil, the shoddy goods at the absurd prices; and why not, why not? I also think that the pitiful drunkenness of the poor—half the ragged cotton-clad farmers in a squalid village pub dead drunk at two o'clock on a Monday afternoon, shabby men reeling dangerously in the dark streets—is due to this antihuman economics. If you cannot earn enough for a decent life and can no longer hope, you can at least get drunk. The State's solution is to raise the price of vodka, not wages.

When, by some miracle of good sense, a living wage is paid, the effect is of light flooding into darkness. One day we were following the usual custom of knocking on strangers' doors and were thus let into a flat in Nowa Huta. It was a clean one-room dwelling for a young man, his wife, and baby (plus kitchen and bath; rent $1.72 a month). The young man was a mason; starting here as an unskilled worker at the age of fifteen, he had been employed for ten years in building these vast complexes of grey cement sardine tins and was now earning fifty-six dollars a month. That is more than a judge earns in Poland. He had medals for good workmanship, of which he was shyly proud. He reads six or seven newspapers a day and saves them. He loves the movies (favourites: Hitchcock's *Rear Window, Francis*, the 'talking mule,' and anything with Eartha Kitt). He had two books out from the lending library: Feuerbach's *Essence of Religion* and *The Count of Monte Cristo*.

Once a month he goes to the theatre—there is an especially fine one at Nowa Huta; to the movies three or four times a week; he watches and plays soccer. He is a contented man and a hard, competent worker. The State should arrive, in pilgrimage, and study this man and try to learn from him the basic truths about human needs, human hopes, human nature.

The Communist Founding Fathers and their latter-day disciples either have never heard about human nature or regard it as weak, contemptible, not here to stay. The result is a perpetual war between the State, which does not care for individuals, and the people, who continue to be individuals since they cannot deny their nature and become sheep. The most obvious battlefront in this war is religion. You cannot push your way into any church in Poland on Sunday morning; overflow crowds stand outside the doors listening to distant liturgy and music. Anyone, except the State, would realize what the Catholic Church means to the majority of Poles, to each one alone, in his heart. But the State does not learn about people; it only interferes with them. The last stupidity of the State produced a riot. This happened at Nowa Huta, and none of us saw it because the police arrested all journalists who appeared on the scene. About eight hours in the clink for foreigners; no news of what became of foolhardy Poles.

We heard about it within fifteen minutes of its start; all Poland heard about it presently, although nothing was printed in the papers for three days, and finally only a dotty paragraph which spoke of 'irresponsible elements.' Nowa Huta is the State's favourite showpiece; the steelworks are reputed to be first class, and though the housing is hideous, it is habitable, and there are special advantages—the theatre, movies, a cabaret, cafés, library, sports grounds, and so on. The peasantry was then uprooted, brought here, taught skilled work, and paid well. Nowa Huta was meant to be an example of the brave new Communist world. The State did not, of course, build a church.

There are 110,000 people living in Nowa Huta, and they collected money amongst themselves to build a church, which must have depressed the State. They had a plot next to the theatre; a cross was raised and foundations partly dug. One morning three workers arrived and began to dismantle the cross. Workers' wives, in nearby flats, saw this and rushed out to ask why. The State, the workers said, had decided to build a school here, which was more necessary. The housewives hurled themselves on the unlucky workmen and beat them with bits of the cross; in no time there were 30,000 people rioting. They burned the Nowa Huta city hall, which is standard operational procedure when rioting; the object is to burn all the dossiers. They fought the police and some contingents of the army who were called in. There wasn't a policeman left in Krakow. Reports from Krakow residents who lived near the military hospital said that there was a heavy traffic of ambulances. Truckloads of workers were seen driving off to jail. Curfew was declared at Nowa Huta. There were excited rumours of a partial strike at the steelworks. After four days, the cross was back in its place. The workers would have their church. People laughed and congratulated each other in the streets of Krakow; this was a victory for human nature.

Communist countries are prisons in the simplest sense; people are not allowed freedom of movement, to leave and to return when they want to. Since 1956, Poland has been a prison with small doors opening to the West; much better than the doorless prison lands. But the Communist rulers' attitude toward travel in the open world is not only a total admission of failure—contented people need not be denied the right to roam; it also proves their contempt for human needs, or indifference to them. People cannot bear to be locked up. Maybe they would not be able to travel if they were free to do so; money is a problem everywhere. What eats into the soul is the sense of being trapped.

If a Pole can arrange to be invited by someone, preferably a relative, living in the West who will pay for his round-trip ticket in hard currency and guarantee to support him while he is away, he can, with luck, and after both his and his host's massive struggles against red tape, get a passport. This may take anywhere from three months to a year and a half. The passport costs from ten to sixty dollars (I have no idea why there is this price range) and is valid for a short period, a few months. And the Poles long to travel in our world; not to leave Poland forever, but only to breathe another air for a while, see another life, learn. They have been jailed for twenty years.

A young painter asked me where I had been since last he saw me. I tried to remember the countries: various visits to France, Italy, Spain, Switzerland, all over America. He laughed as if I had told him a magical tale, something between the *Arabian Nights* and the best joke of the year. He laughed with joy to think that all the countries were there and that someone he knew could actually go to them. He no longer talks of travelling himself.

I heard of a man who had been coping for over a year with the maddening, wearing obstacles put in the way of travel: at last he had his passport, at last he was to leave for Paris, whereupon the police advised him that it would be better not to go. Why? No reason. At this point, sane people go almost insane from the stupid, oppressive frustration of it all. My informant said, 'It is not now like eyes burned out or somezing like zat; it is only ze tedium, ze tedium, it sacks ze nerves.'

Every day these people are forced into contact with the deadly, cheap, E. Phillips Oppenheim spy-story mentality of the State. Every day they have to swallow sickening doses of illogical bureaucracy, a bureaucracy which is Kafka mixed with Asiatic deviousness. And what for, what for? What does the State want? Clearly, everyone is guilty until proved innocent (crime not specified). Is the sole intention of all this hateful, invisible controlling to intimidate the Poles? It intimidates me all right; it does not intimidate the Poles.

The enslaving State is itself a slave of the Russian master; and Russian government has relied for centuries on the degrading practices of a secret police. The only long-term hope of the Poles is that the Russian people will demand more and more personal freedom, more human dignity, and so, by contagion, government in Poland might eventually become an open, daylight business.

*

One night, four of us were having a feast in a room like a stage set: it was an abject-poverty room, a tiny cell in a dark, dirty, overcrowded flat on an ugly street. There was an iron cot, three folding chairs, a table, an unshaded light bulb, and we were gloriously happy. I haven't been to such a good party since the last time I was in Poland. Our host, the youngest of the three young Poles, had spent his money, to my anxiety, on lots of bread and butter, some salami, a tin of sardines, withered apples, and vodka. We sat in the cold room, on the hard chairs and harder bed, for five perfect hours, eating, drinking, and laughing.

I almost wrecked the party with an outburst against the State, and I learned much of great importance to me. 'The worst hotel rooms are supposed to be those with numbers ending in 2,' I said. 'It's so revolting and so pointless; and where are the mikes? And coming back to a hotel in the north and asking for your key, and the brute of a police agent at the desk says you must have taken it with you; but you couldn't take any room key anywhere in Poland—either it has a wooden turnip attached to it or a ring like a handcuff. Then the second police desk clerk arrives with your key in his hand and says blandly he was just checking to see if the room was still occupied. And never daring to speak anyone's name on the telephone, not that you have anything to say except "Where shall we meet?" but you're afraid someday they'll get in trouble because they've talked to you.' I was breathless; I had been at it on a large scale for some time. I saw that they looked uncomfortable. Julek patted my hand and offered me more vodka and another withered apple.

'Police, spying, terror, all that, we are so used to it; no one pays attention to it any more. It becomes a form of entertainment for us. It is much more irritating if you can never get the sort of shoe polish you want.'

The others laughed, the conversation changed, and I stood deeply corrected. I had behaved like someone who comes, for a few hours, to the front, where others live in constant peril, and babbles fear, spreading panic or dismay. This is not acceptable behaviour at any front, nor in Poland. What the Poles' private secret feelings may be I do not know; singly and collectively they are sardonic about the hazards of their lives, always a little more weary, unyielding.

I listened to my friends and thought of all the Poles I knew or had met in passing. I thought of the extreme individualism of this people, which twenty years of different forms of tyranny has not chipped away. Each person owns his mind, and they are original, interesting minds, too.

Bits of conversation, pictures of places float about in my memory: the entrancing barmaid, who looked like a Bryn Mawr Brigitte Bardot, teaching historical facts to a long, lean, foolish young American. He was saying, 'It's better to get any story over with. In a week, who is going to remember Chessman?' 'I disagree,' she said, 'Don't you remember the Rosenbergs? People will remember Chessman.' The taxi driver who spoke perfect Italian; his father had been killed by the Germans as a Communist; he himself hates all politics. He wished he could have met in his life Jack London and Hemingway; he had all their books in Polish and Italian. He admired America—'all Poles do'—but he deplored 'the war against the Negroes in America. That is not good; that is racialism. America would rise very much in our eyes if they stopped that war.' The students' cabaret, in a small, vaulted, grimy cellar: I could not understand a word and grasped at snippets of translation, but even with such a handicap it seemed to me wildly, irreverently funny and professional, better than any expensive night-club show I could remember. In the middle, the young performers sang 'in honour of our American friend' *Tipperary* in Russian, to the howling delight of the audience, which continues to regard anything in Russian as automatically, killingly comical.

'Antoni,' I said 'could you ever live outside Poland?'

'No, I would not even try.'

The evils that befall their country have no effect on the love of the Poles for their country, which is unique in the line of passionate patriotism. I think, at last, I know why. The very evils that befall them, and have through the centuries, and most cruelly these last twenty years, feed the love: one loves what is hurt and needs help. History treats Poles almost as specially and nearly as badly as it treats Jews. In another, very different room, a Pole, whom history had flung about from Manchuria to Lithuania to Brazil, said, 'If our country were rich and happy, we could all go away. But, as it is not, we will never leave it.'

'Julek,' I asked, 'have you ever been bored?'

'I don't know. Perhaps I have been bored all my life without knowing it. But what are you to do if you are kept waiting for half an hour in a restaurant? Hang yourself?'

Great backhanded compliments can be paid to poverty, suffering, and oppression: if they don't kill, they sharpen the mind and strengthen the spirit. The sharpened mind is lively, hungry, daring, and singularly free. The strengthened spirit is generous, loyal, grateful for life and for any small chance blessing. A visit to Poland is like stepping through the Looking Glass, but it is a highly therapeutic step. You remember again the splendour of human courage, and you learn humility.

I wonder if this is any sort of balance sheet on what is good and what is bad in Polish life today.

The Arabs of Palestine

According to Arab politicians and apologists, this is what happened, this is the authentic view, these are the facts. Doubt is treasonous. There can be only the truth, according to Arab politicans and apologists, and it belongs to them:

In 1948, war took place between five Arab nations of the Middle East and the Jews in Palestine. This war was caused by the United Nations, whose General Assembly resolved to partition Palestine into two states, one for the Palestinian Arabs, the other for the Jews. The Arab nations and the Palestinian Arabs would not accept this monstrous decision. They were obliged to protect themselves against it, with force. The United Nations operated as the tool of the Western Imperialists, notably Great Britain and the United States. The United Nations wanted the Jews to proclaim the upstart state of Israel. Because of the Western Imperialists, who favoured Israel, the Arabs lost the war. By massacre, threatening broadcasts, pointed bayonets, and the murderous siege of cities, the Jews drove hundreds of thousands of Arabs out of their homeland. For thirteen years, these Arab refugees have languished in misery around the borders of Israel. The United Nations (Western branch) bears the blame for these events and must repair the damage. The condition of the refugees is a sore on the conscience of honourable men. The Israeli government refuses to welcome back to their homeland the refugees, now swollen to more than a million in number. This refusal demonstrates the brutality and dishonesty of Israel, an abnormal nation of aliens who not only forced innocent people into exile but also stole their property. There is no solution to this injustice, the greatest the world has ever seen, except to repatriate all Palestinian refugees in Palestine. Palestine is an Arab country, now infamously called Israel. Israel has no right to exist, and the Arab nations will not sign peace treaties with it but will, by every means possible, maintain the state of war.

The details of the Arab case vary, depending on the political climate of the moment and the audience. However, the Palestinian refugees always remain the invaluable, central theme. The case is painted the colour of blood in the Arab countries: Revenge and Return. For the Western public, tears replace blood; the Arab case rests on the plight of the refugees and is a call to conscience rather than to arms. But no Arab statesman has ever promised final peace with Israel if only the million Palestinian refugees may return to their former homes.

The best way to consider this case is close up, by looking at the Palestinian refugees themselves, not as a 'problem', not as statistics, but as people. The Palestinian refugees, battered by thirteen years in the arena of international politics, have lost their shape; they appear as a lump and are spoken of as one object. They are individuals, like everyone else.

Despite the unique care and concern they have received, despite the unique publicity which rages around them, the Arab refugees, alas, are not unique. Although no one knows exactly how many refugees are scattered everywhere over the globe, it is estimated that since World War II, and only since then, at least thirty-nine million *non-Arab* men, women, and children have become homeless refugees, through no choice of their own. Their numbers grow every year; Angolans are the latest addition to the long list. The causes for this uprooting are always different, but the result is the same: the uprooted have lost what they had and where they came from and must start life again as handicapped strangers wherever they are allowed to live.

The world could be far more generous to these unwilling wanderers, but at least the world has never thought of exploiting them. They are recognized as people, not pawns. By their own efforts, and with help from those devoted to their service, all but some six million of the thirty-nine million have made a place for themselves, found work and another chance for the future. To be a refugee is not necessarily a life sentence.

The unique misfortune of the Palestinian refugees is that they are a weapon in what seems to be a permanent war. Alarming signs, from Egypt, warn us that the Palestinian refugees may develop into more than a justification for cold war against Israel. We ignored *Mein Kampf* in its day, as the ravings of a lunatic, written for limited home consumption. We ought to have learned never to ignore dictators or their books. *Egypt's Liberation*, by Gamal Abdel Nasser, deserves careful notice. It is short, low-keyed, and tells us once again that a nation has been ordained by fate to lead—this time, to lead the Arab nations, all Africa, all Islam. The Palestinian refugees are not mentioned, and today, in the Middle East, you get a repeated sinking sensation about the Palestinian refugees: they are only a beginning, not an end. Their function is to hang around and be constantly useful as a goad. The ultimate aim is not such humane small potatoes as repatriating refugees.

The word *refugee* is drenched in memories which stretch back over too many years and too many landscapes: Spain, Czechoslovakia, China, Finland, England, Italy, Holland, Germany. In Madrid, between artillery bombardments, children were stuffed into trucks to be taken somewhere, out of that roulette death, while their mothers clung to the tailboards of the trucks and were dragged weeping after the bewildered, weeping children. In Germany, at war's end, the whole country seemed alive with the roaming mad—slave labourers, concentration camp survivors—who spoke the many tongues of Babel, dressed in whatever scraps they had looted, and searched for food in stalled freight cars though the very rail-yards were being bombed. From China to Finland, people like these defined the meaning of *refugee*.

No one could wish to see even a pale imitation of such anguish again. In the Middle East, there would be no high explosive, no concentration camps, but the imagined, expected scene was bad enough; lice and rickets and tuberculosis, bodies rotting in the heat, the apathy of despair. Why, in 1961, did I have such a picture of the Palestinian refugees? Obviously from what I had read, as one of the average absorbent reading public; notions float in the air exactly as dust does. Nothing that I had read or heard prepared me for what I found.

What do they look like, the undifferentiated mass known as the 'Palestine Refugee Problem'? What do they think, feel, say? What do they want? How do they live, where do they live, what do they do? Who takes care of them? What future can they hope for, in terms of reality, not in terms of slogans, which are meaningless if not actually fatal, as we know.

The children are as fast as birds, irreverent as monkeys, large-eyed, ready to laugh. The young girls, trained by carrying water jars or other heavy household bundles on their heads, move like ballerinas and are shrouded in modesty and silence as if in cocoons. The young men, crudely or finely formed, have in common the hopefulness and swagger of their new manhood. The middle years seem nondescript, in both sexes. After this the women, who age quickly but not as quickly as the men, wear unpainted experience on their faces; they look patient, humorous, and strong. When the men have grown visibly old, they turn into a race of grandees. Their colour, infant to patriarch, ranges from golden fair to mahogany dark, all warmed by the glaze of sun. The instinct for hospitality, the elegance of manner have not been exaggerated.

UNRWA (the United Nations Relief and Works Agency for Palestine Refugees in the Near East), inheriting its role from previous caretakers, has been the splendid mother-and-father of these people for eleven years. In the course of its parenthood UNRWA has spent about $360 million on the Arab refugees, this money having been contributed by members of the United Nations, with smaller but loving donations from private charitable organizations as well. Of the total the United States provided more than $238 million, Great Britain over $65 million—but spread across the years and in varying amounts, sixty-one states, including Israel and the Holy See, have helped with cash. The

Soviet Union has never paid one cent. This is a tiny note of malice: Arab refugees often express tender emotions for the Soviet Union, whereas most of the village orators blame the United States and England, or that bogey, 'Western Imperialism,' for their exile.

In the so-called 'host countries,' Lebanon, Jordan, Syria, and Egypt, UNRWA runs fifty-eight refugee camps. The camps in Egypt are not in Egypt but in the Gaza Strip, which is Palestine; Egypt is the *de facto* mandatory power, the land and the government of the Gaza Strip are Palestinian. The majority of camps in Jordan are also on what was the territory of Palestine, now annexed to Jordan.

UNRWA has never yet been allowed to make a total proper census of its refugee population, so statistics about the number of ex-Palestinians are nothing except the best estimate possible; UNRWA itself says this. Over half of the registered Palestinian refugees do not live in camps, but have made more or less comfortable private arrangements varying from first-class houses, at the top, to hand-built Hooverville shacks, at the bottom. UNRWA calculates that, at the end of June, 1960, 421,500 refugees were living in their camps, almost double their camp population. ten years ago. The advantage of living in a camp is that life there is rent free; and for the poor, the standard of housing and sanitation in an UNRWA camp is better than that of the native population.

The international personnel of UNRWA, Americans and Western Europeans, is small; 128 men and women work in four countries. The mass of those who serve the Palestinian refugees are Palestinian refugees themselves, something over 10,000 of them. UNRWA is running a world, simply, a little welfare state. It makes villages, called camps, and keeps them clean and free of disease, feeds, educates, trains teachers and technicians and craftsmen, operates clinics and maternity centres, sends out visiting nurses, encourages small private enterprises with small loans, distributes clothing, soap, kerosene, blankets, provides hospitalization, footballs, youth clubs, mosques.

UNRWA is a kind, impartial parent; it has no favourites.

201

However, people are all different, luckily; and though one man will arrive in exile as a destitute refugee and in time own a whopping Chevrolet and be a self-employed taxi driver, with a cosy home and a smiling wife in a flowered print dress and a gleaming refrigerator in the dining room, another will remain in whatever shelter UNRWA gave him, sitting either on his own floor, or at a café table, waiting for nothing, or for divine intervention, or for the mailed, promised, delivering fist of Nasser. UNRWA did not invent the human condition.

Of UNRWA's fifty-eight camps, I visited eight—in Lebanon, the Gaza Strip, and Jordan. The plan and facilities of every UNRWA camp are alike; they differ only in size and are better or worse depending on whether they are newer or older and on the character of the people who live in them. Each camp has its clinic and school (or schools), warehouse centre for distributing rations, 'supplementary feeding station', where hot meals are served to those who need them, village bazaar street with small shops, market booths, cafés. The bigger the camp, the bigger the bazaar. I also went round two hospitals, two vocational training schools, and was received in two private homes, having been invited by refugees.

My guide and chaperone was an UNRWA employee, a Palestinian Arab, who served as translator when needed. My system was to say: please show me your best and your worst camp, and if time permits, let us also look at the in-between. In the camps, I knocked on any door and many. Nothing was planned. We chatted at random and went wherever I liked. In the Gaza Strip, I was accompanied for a day by a young Palestinian in a pin-striped suit; he or someone like him is a cross every foreigner has to bear. He is local Secret Service, and the refugees know this; he is an ardent Nasserite, as apparently all Palestinian government officials in Gaza are, or must appear to be; and he is by avocation a propagandist and demagogue. At one Gaza camp, besides this young gent, I had an escort of three Palestinian cops who lent an even heavier note to the proceedings. Otherwise, my visits were uncensored. I may have seen a true cross-section of the

Palestinian refugee population, and I may not have. I only know that I saw real people in the flesh, and a large number of them, and I know what they said. When the word *they* appears on these pages, it means those Arabs whom I saw; it means nothing more.

Beirut is a lovely boom town, an entrancing mixture of Asia Minor and France, with scenery to lift the heart and glamour hotels all over the lot and more abuilding. We set off, my Palestinian guide and I, in a shiny car for an UNRWA camp in the Lebanese hills. My guide, like his colleagues who accompanied me elsewhere, was an executive, responsible for an UNRWA department, dressed in a Western business suit, a self-assured, middle-class Organization Man. The refugees are not only individuals, but they come from widely different social backgrounds. Men of the class of my guides would not be living in refugee camps; they might work in them as doctors or teachers.

This camp was inhabited exclusively by Christian Arabs. I wondered aloud at a separation by creed. My guide was a Muslim and said that Christian camps were always cleaner and superior to Muslim ones, and besides, very few Christians lived in camps; they arranged their lives better on their own.

The camp consisted of little cement or frame houses rambling over the hillside, a village of poor people, disorderly and beflowered and cheerful. School was letting out for lunch; troops of children, dressed in the pinafore uniform that small boys and girls wear in Italian schools, meandered home, shouting bye-bye at friendly, giggling length. They are Roman Catholics here, but the young teachers are refugees, not priests. They have to teach the children about Palestine, since most of them have never seen the country and even the oldest cannot remember it. The children are taught hate, the Garden of Eden stolen from them by murderers; their duty is to live for Return and Revenge.

The miniature white clinic had only one customer, a nice-looking girl of twenty-one who had brought her fourth baby for a checkup. Her husband works in Libya; she too lived there for a few years but returned. Libya is very expensive; she can live here with his parents and thus save money for the future. The resident nurse, a buxom elderly woman, said they had no real sickness; in summer, the children got a bit of conjunctivitis and diarrhoea; oh, no, trachoma is very rare, and besides, we cure it; there's some chicken-pox now. My guide announced that if any refugee needed an operation he was taken in an ambulance to a hospital in Beirut where UNRWA reserved beds and paid for everything; you would have to be a rich man in Lebanon to get such good and speedy treatment. Her fourth baby, I mused, and she only twenty-one. Yes, yes, said my guide, the refugees have a higher birth rate than any other Arabs, and healthier children.

Refugees receive a monthly basic food ration of flour, pulse (dried peas, beans, lentils), sugar, rice, oils, and fats; this amounts to 1500 calories a day per person, increased in winter to 1600 calories a day, and it is not enough. The refugee must find some way to earn money to increase his diet, or keep poultry or rabbits, or grow vegetables. Many had planted tiny gardens here, but charmingly and with more enthusiasm, they also grow flowers for the joy of the thing. There is a daily milk ration for children and pregnant and nursing mothers; and hot meals are served in the 'supplementary feeding station', to those who need them, on the doctor's order. In this camp, said my guide, 85 per cent of the people have work. If there are hardship cases, when no one can bring money to the family, UNRWA's Welfare Section steps in. This pattern is universal.

If you think it your duty, I said, to make everything seem better than it is, don't. I'm not on an inspection tour, I only want to get some idea of what life is really like. He stopped, offended, in the middle of the stony path and explained: here, in Lebanon, 80 per cent of the refugees are better off than they were in Palestine. Twenty per cent are not. The 20 per cent were small capitalists, and there is much rivalry with the Lebanese in business, they make obstacles. Also it is political; they do not give the refugees citizenship, you understand, because the main part of the refugees are Muslims and that would upset the balance here, where the Christians rule. I do not speak to you of the rich Palestinian refugees; they are richer than before, they are very happy.

We went to pay the required *visite de politesse* to the camp leader. Every camp leader acts as an appointed village mayor; he has to keep the place running, serve as liaison officer with UNRWA local headquarters, and handle the complaints of his own people. Sitting in his neat office, with my guide, the principal of the school (a former member of the Palestinian police), and the camp leader, I listened to the first of what became an almost daily Mad Hatter conversation.

It went like this:

'The Arab countries invaded Israel in 1948 to save the Palestine Arabs from being massacred by the Jews.'

'Were there massacres? Where?'

'Oh, yes, everywhere. Terrible, terrible.'

'Then you must have lost many relatives and friends.'

This, being a tiresome deduction from a previous statement, is brushed aside without comment.

'Israel overran the truce lines and stole our country. We left from fear. We have a right to our property, which brings in forty-seven million pounds a year in income. If we had our own money, we would need nothing from UNRWA. Our own money is much more. We do not have to be grateful for the little money spent on us. We should have our own.'

'Then, of course, you want to return to your property and to Israel?'

'*Not* to Israel. Never to Israel. To our own country, to our own part.'

'But didn't the Jews accept Partition, while the Palestine Arabs and the Arab governments refused?'

'Yes, yes. And England protected the Jews. An Arab was arrested if he carried a pistol only to defend himself, but Jews could go through the streets in tanks and nothing happened to them. Also, England told the Arab states to attack Israel.'

The principal of the school then spoke up. 'In our school, we teach the children from their first year about their country and how it was stolen from them. I tell my son of seven. You will see: one day a man of eighty and a child so high, all, all will go home with arms in their hands and take back their country by force.'

On this warlike note, we left. My guide had seemed a sober contented fellow until our little meeting, whereupon he sounded like a politician running recklessly for office. He then astonished me again.

'It can all be solved with money,' he said. 'Now the people have nothing in their mouths but words, so they talk. Money fills the mouth too. If every man got a thousand dollars for each member of his family, for compensation to have lost his country, and he could be a citizen in any Arab country he likes, he would not think of Palestine any more. Then he could start a new life and be rich and happy. And those who really do own something in Palestine must be paid for what they had there. But those are not many. Most had nothing, only work.'

High on a mountain top, with a down-sweeping view of orange groves and the satin blue of the Mediterranean, is a small Muslim camp named Mia Mia. Here one whole Palestinian village, amongst others, had landed; they came from a mountain top in Galilee, a place called Meron. Their headman, or village leader, the Muktar, plied us with Coca-Cola and Turkish coffee in his exile's parlour. He is a beautiful man, perhaps sixty-five years old, lean, with exquisite manners. He wore the handsome white Arab head-dress, held in place by the usual black double-corded crown; he was dressed in a well-preserved cream silk jacket, a white silk shirt, pressed grey flannel trousers, polished Italianate black shoes.

Whilst we sucked Coca-Cola through straws and studied his son's pitifully bad but lovingly executed paintings—a portrait of Nasser; Christ and the Virgin—the Muktar talked. Seventeen people of his village were massacred, which was why they fled, but an old blind woman of 104 was left behind and the Jews poured kerosene over her and burned her alive. How did they know, if they had all fled? Well, then the Jews went away and some villagers crept back and found her, and besides, the United Nations Truce Commission also found her.

My guide looked embarrassed. The Truce Commission was a shaky point. It was a strain to believe that the UN military observers, occupied with armies and frontiers, would have had time to investigate each atrocity story in the country. I wondered where the families of the massacred and the cremated were; everyone knows everyone else in a village, surely the surviving relatives were the best witnesses.

'I could tell you many such stories,' said the Muktar.

'I am sure of it,' said I. 'But please tell me about Meron.'

So I heard of Meron, their beautiful stone houses, their lovely groves, their spacious and happy life in Eden; all lost now. I could readily imagine this aristocrat living in a palace on a mountain top and decided that I would later go and see his home; but for the moment I accepted a rose from him, and we set off to pay calls in the camp.

A woman of forty or so, with a face like the best and juiciest apple, and lively eyes, seized me and hauled me into her house. She began, with gestures, to deliver an oration. She touched the ceiling with contempt, pulling bits away; she called upon heaven to witness her misery. Her voice soared and fell in glorious rhythms. She loved doing it and I loved watching it. In mutual delight, we smiled more and more as the tale of woe unfolded, until she could keep it up no longer, burst into roars of laughter, and kissed me copiously. My guide seemed unduly glum about all this, perhaps because this day we were three; a European UNRWA official had joined us.

'She is a big liar,' said my guide, when we had left her house. 'She lies as she breathes. We gave her all the material for a new roof. She sold it. She is so poor that she is going to make a pilgrimage to Mecca this year. She does not have to make a pilgrimage. Do you know what that costs? One thousand pounds.'

In Lebanese money, this amounts to about $350—a fortune.

'Oh, she is a terrible bad one.'

'I loved her,' I said. 'She's one of my favourite types of people in the world. A really jolly open crook. I hope she has a wonderful time at Mecca.'

'But we have to fix her roof anyhow,' said the UNRWA official.

In our suite of followers, I had noticed a tall boy of sixteen or seventeen, with fine intelligent eyes, a happy face, and a fresh white shirt. I spoke to him in English, and he understood; I asked whether we could visit his family. His house was no larger than any other, but clean, peaceful, and touching, with orderly furniture and picture postcards tacked to the walls. His mother was blind from cataracts, and his grandmother seemed older than time, of a generation so old that she had tattoo marks on her cheeks.

The boy had graduated from high school and now worked as manager of the food distribution centre in the big camp (14,000 inhabitants) on the plain below. He must have been very competent and very reliable to merit this job. He hoped to become a TV-radio engineer. He did not speak of Palestine. There was work he wanted to do, wherever a man could do such work. UNRWA is now building a vocational training school in Lebanon; it should be open in the autumn. With any luck, this boy will learn the technical skill he so desires and make his own life independent of anyone's charity.

We heard shrill painful child's crying and went toward the sound. A child of about two was tied by the ankle to a chair, howling the same word over and over. A younger child was silently trying to hold its body up, clinging to the arm of another chair. On a clean mat, on a clean little sheet, a baby twisted its body restlessly, but its legs lay still. All three were remarkably good-looking, all seemingly husky and well formed.

The camp leader carried on a short barking exchange with their young mother and reported: 'She is twenty-five. None of the children can move their legs; the legs will not hold them. The child is tied because he can pull himself out of the house and get hurt. She says, please, will you help her?'

Speaking French to the UNRWA official, because no one else there knew the language, I said, 'She can easily have five or six more children like this. It is terrible for her. The visiting nurse ought to explain about birth control.'

'You don't know what you're saying. UNRWA could not touch such a thing, not even mention it. Here are these people, and the name of their country does not exist on the map any more. If we start teaching them birth control, we will be accused of trying to wipe out the people too. Besides, the men would never allow it. They want to have a lot of sons; it is a matter of pride with them. And politics enters too, as into everything; I've heard them say it. We need to have many children and grow and increase so that the world will never forget us.'

'They're doing well, from what I've seen.'

'About 30,000 babies a year.'

The camp leader, escorting us to our car, remarked that no one here had any work. He delivered a short speech in English; he was a very nice, gentle man. 'All the men do is sit in café and suffer, suffer. A young man sees time running, running, and he gets old with no years. If I did not get my land to hope for, I lose my brains.'

On our way to Beirut, the UNRWA official said, 'Eighty per cent of the men in that camp work. It's quite a prosperous little camp.'

'Do they lie just for the fun of it?' It had been a long day.

'Well, it's natural in front of us. If they earn too much, they are taken off the ration lists. If they earn above a certain amount, they aren't eligible for the services. Free medicine and doctoring and schooling. So, obviously they don't want us to know.'

'Like non-refugees with the income-tax collectors?'

'That's it.'

'Do you know what they are earning?'

'Not really. How could we? Of course, if anyone has regular employment, we eventually learn of it and cut down the rolls.'

The refugees, in camps as well as outside of camps, do find work of some sort; otherwise, on 1500 calories a day, they would soon become and look like a severely undernourished, sickly group. UNRWA's health statistics can be relied on; they know how many refugees use their medical services and for what reason and with what results. The standard of health is unusually high and is one of UNRWA's finest achievements.

On the plain below Mia Mia, the land is green with citrus groves, banana plantations, where nothing grew before. This is the work of refugees; someone should be very grateful to them. Refugees who were city dwellers in Palestine gravitate to city work: taxi drivers, employees, merchants. No matter what official attitudes are, all of these people tend to seek their own previous level, under the universal refugee handicap of starting from scratch, of being exploitable, and in competition with established locals. Besides, they are living in a part of the world where poverty is an endemic disease and it is hard for anyone to make a good living, unless you are born into a silver-spoon family.

Out of the blue, my guide announced: 'There is no crime in the camps. No thefts, no fires, no blood feuds. It is much better than it was in Palestine. They know they are all brothers in refuge. There were a few murders some time ago; someone raping, something like that. It is natural. But no crime.'

And this is true. In all the camps. Exile has taught one valuable lesson: how to live peacefully and lawfully together.

To enter the Gaza Strip you require a military visa from the Egyptian government in Cairo. I had arrived in Cairo expecting to proceed like the wind directly from there to Gaza but was informed, by the local UNRWA press officer, that this permit took two or three weeks to get, and sometimes you never got it. Besides, there was only one UNEF army plane to Gaza each Saturday, and they didn't like carrying anyone except their own personnel; besides, it was now Thursday, and tomorrow was the Muslim Sunday, and indeed all looked hopeless. I foresaw bumming a jeep ride over the sandstorming desert and infiltrating into the Strip somehow; but meantime I called on the Egyptian authorities.

Because of the Muslim holy day, and the number of passport photos I needed and the number of offices I had to run between, it took about four days to get the visa, and every minute was enjoyable. The Egyptian officials could not have been kinder, and I loved seeing them, the new ruling class, who remind me, in their cheerful, inchoate, important busyness, of many new ruling classes I have observed round and about, over the years. It is difficult to believe that these pleasant young men, in shirt sleeves or uniforms, with their numerous callers, their telephones, their mounds of mimeographed forms, their empty Turkish coffee cups, have any connection with the vainglory, the xenophobia, the anti-Semitic hatred that smear the press and pour over the air of their fascinating city.

The Gaza Strip, from all accounts, would be a real hell hole. It is a roughly rectangular slice of land, on the southernmost Mediterranean frontier of Israel, some forty kilometres long by five to ten kilometres wide, and 365,000 people, refugees and residents, live on it. I imagined it as a sand dune, packed solid with human flesh, blazing hot, hideous, and filthy. It is none of these. The weather was so idyllic—a china-blue sky and a constant cool breeze—that I assumed this was special luck and at once asked my charming landlady about it. No, the weather in Gaza was always delightful. She had lived here for thirty years; there were two 'sticky' weeks in the summer, otherwise you could not find a more benign climate. Flying over the Strip, I had noted plenty of sand, but also plenty of green. There were always citrus groves in Gaza, my landlady reported, Gaza was famous for them, but since the refugees came these had greatly increased, as had the general cultivation. Anything grows here, she said, exhibiting her blossoming garden.

Then I remarked that Gaza town was a beehive of activity, with all the UNEF soldiers, Danes, Norwegians, Indians, Canadians, Yugoslavs, who patrol the Israeli-Gaza border and spend money in the town in their free time, and the Egyptian upper crust which oversees the Palestinian officials, and UNRWA and visitors and the local residents and, indeed, the refugees. The refugees seemed to bring prosperity with them; it was most mysterious.

Not at all, said my landlady, we do not know why we are not completely bankrupt; but she was adding a third floor to her already roomy house, so great is the demand for lodgings.

Sizeable villas are being built in what must be the fashionable section of Gaza. The main square boasts an array of parked Mercedes, finned pastel American cars, and humbler Volkswagens. The taxis in Gaza are new. There is an imposing movie theatre, in the ugly world-wide chromium-and-junk style; there are abundant cafés and numerous ill-lit dingy shops, typical of the region. An economist could surely answer this riddle: if no one has any money, what are these eccentric merchants and purveyors of services doing?

The refugee camps are much larger than those in Lebanon, small towns by Middle Eastern standards. They are by no means luxury establishments, but many people live in a nastier state in American and European slums. The poor villagers of Gaza are not as well housed or cared for as the refugees. The Gaza Strip is not a hell hole, not a visible disaster. It is worse; it is a jail—with a magical long white sand beach, and a breeze, and devoted welfare workers (UNRWA) to look after the prisoners.

The Egyptian government is the jailer. For reasons of its own, it does not allow the refugees to move from this narrow strip of land. The refugees might not want to leave at all, or they might not want to leave for good; but anyone would become claustrophobic if penned, for thirteen years, inside 248 square kilometres. A trickle of refugees, who can prove they have jobs elsewhere, are granted exit visas. The only official number of the departed is less than three hundred, out of 255,000 registered refugees. It seems incredible. Rumour says that more refugees do manage to go away illegally, by unknown methods.

These locked-in people—far too many in far too little space—cannot find adequate work. Naturally, there is less chance of employment than in the other 'host countries.' Meantime, they are exposed to the full and constant blast of Egyptian propaganda. No wonder that Gaza was the home base of the trained paramilitary bands called commandos by the Egyptians and Palestinians, and gangsters by the Israelis—the *fedayin*, whose job was to cross unnoticed into Israel and commit acts of patriotic sabotage and murder. And having been so devastatingly beaten by Israel again, in 1956, has not improved the trapped, bitter Gaza mentality; it only makes the orators more bloodthirsty.

Another Mad Hatter conversation, practically a public meeting, took place in the office of the leader of two adjacent camps, a man in charge of some 29,000 people. The camp leader, the self-appointed orator, sat behind his desk. The Secret Service youth, mentioned earlier, the quiet UNRWA Palestinian, my regular chaperone, and the three uniformed cops of highish rank completed the company.

First the camp leader told me how rich they had all been in Palestine and how miserable they were now and how much land they had all owned. I do not doubt for one minute how much land some of them owned, nor how rich some of them were, and I did not point out this subtle distinction: if *everyone* owned the land claimed, Palestine would be the size of Texas; if *everyone* had been so rich, it would have been largely populated by millionaires. To gild the past is only human, we all do it; and to gild it with solid gold is even more human if you are a refugee. This part of his address was already so familiar that I could have recited it for him.

Then he spoke of Jaffa, his native town. The Jews surrounded the city, firing on all sides; they left one little way out, by the sea, so the Arabs would go away. Only the very old and the very poor stayed, and they were killed. Arab refugees tell many dissimilar versions of the Jaffa story, but the puzzler is: where are the relatives of those who must have perished in the fury of high explosive— the infallible witnesses? No one says he was loaded on a truck (or a boat) at gun point; no one describes being forced from his home by armed Jews; no one recalls the extra menace of enemy attacks, while in flight. The sight of the dead, the horrors of escape are exact, detailed memories never forgotten by those who had them. Surely Arabs would not forget or suppress such memories if they, too, had them.

As for those Arabs who remained behind, they are still in Jaffa—3000 of them—living in peace, prosperity, and discontent, with their heirs and descendants.

'The Jews are criminals,' the camp leader continued in a rising voice. 'Murderers! They are the worst criminals in the whole world.'

Had he ever heard of Hitler?

He banged his table and said, 'Hitler was far better than the Jews!'

'Far better murderer? He killed six million Jews as a start,' I observed.

'Oh, that is all exaggerated. He did not. Besides, the Jews bluffed Hitler. They arranged in secret that he should kill a few of them—old ones, weak ones—to make the others emigrate to Palestine.'

'Thirty-six thousand of them,' said the Secret Service man, proving the point, 'came here, before the war, from Central Europe.'

'It's amazing,' I said. 'I have never before heard anywhere that the Jews arranged with Hitler for him to kill them.'

'It was a secret!' the camp leader shouted. 'The documents have been found. Everyone knows. It was published. The Jews arranged it all with Hitler.'

There is a limit to the amount of Mad Hattery one can endure, so I suggested that we visit the camp. I knocked on a door at random, before the camp leader had a chance to steer me anywhere. Two young married couples lived here. In a corner by the courtyard wall stood a group of visitors, silent Arab women, in their graceful long blue dresses, slightly hiding their faces behind their white head veils. The older women wore silver coins on chains across their foreheads; this is very pretty and is also guaranteed to prevent sickness of the eyes. It was useless to try to lure the women into talk, but one of the husbands talked freely. The Secret Service youth translated.

'It is the blame of America that this happened, because they help the Jews. We only want America to help us to get back to our land.'

'How?' I asked. 'By war?'

'When the Arabs are united, we will make the war.'

'What do you want from us then? Arms to make this war with?'

214

'No, we want you to stop giving arms and money to Israel. Just now Kennedy has given Israel $25 million for arms.'

'I do not believe that the US government has ever given or sold arms to Israel. What about the arms Nasser gets from Russia and Czechoslovakia?'

'That is all right. That is different. They are peace-loving nations. They only want to help the undeveloped countries.'

The Secret Service man put in: 'America offered us arms, but with conditions. We will not accept conditions. So we take from the Eastern countries, who give without conditions.'

'What do you do?' I asked the fat young husband.

'Nothing.'

'What would you like to do?'

'Be a soldier and fight Jews.'

This oratory pleased the public very much.

'Do you all like Nasser?' I asked, politely.

Wide smiles. General joy.

'We do. Certainly. Oh, of course. He will unite us and make us strong. He is our leader.'

For rest and relaxation, together with thousands of locals, I went to the School Sports Day. Fifty thousand refugee children attend school on the Gaza Strip, ninety-eight per cent of the possible school population. In Gaza's spacious stadium, 2,000 school children were gathered. They ranged from tiny tots, the Brownies, in berets and ballet-skirted orange uniforms, to boys in running shorts and muscles. They paraded past the governor of the Gaza Strip in the viewing stand, led by girls in coloured outfits who formed the Palestine flag. The human flag was followed by the Brownie babies, Girl Scouts, Boy Scouts, girl gymnasts, and boy gymnasts. 'We dressed every one of them,' an English UNRWA official said. 'This show costs us about two thousand dollars, but it's worth it. It gives them something to look forward to. They all love it.' They loved it and their admiring families loved it and the public loved it.

The children had marched in earnest stiff-legged style. ('Like the British Army,' I said. 'Like the Egyptian Army,' he said.) They then lined up in formation, and a loudspeaker blared out Arabic. Three times the children shouted a unanimous, squeaky but enthusiastic reply to the loudspeaker's commanding male voice.

'What are the cheers for?'

'The first is: "Long Live a Free Palestine." The second is: "Long Live the United Arab Republic." The third is: "Long Live Gamal Abdel Nasser." '

I stayed to see the white-clad girl gymnasts, as graceful as a field of Isadora Duncans, doing lovely swaying motions with blue gauze handkerchiefs.

The Vocational Training School at Gaza is a freshly painted group of buildings, with well-kept lawns, flower borders, scrubbed Spartan self-respecting dormitories, and impressive workshops equipped with the complex machinery that modern life seems to depend on. The boys were on their playing field that afternoon, a holiday, marking white lines for various sporting events to come. A few of them drifted back and wanted to show off every inch of their school. Did they like it here, did they enjoy their work, were they happy? Needless to ask; the answer glowed and shone on them. The graduates of this school find good jobs for which they are trained; amongst its many other parental functions UNRWA operates a placement bureau throughout the Middle East. This is the new generation, the UNRWA graduates, and you find them everywhere in the Arab refugee world. They have not yet been crippled by exile, regret, or hate, and they may well be the brightest citizens of the Arab future. They are the source of all hope.

Two accidental conversations stick in my memory. Once, lost in the UNRWA compound of offices, I chanced on a pretty, dark secretary, who told me the kind of inside human angle of history which is more interesting than any other. In 1956, when the Israelis took the Gaza Strip, during what they call the Sinai campaign and we call Suez, for short, telephone communication was restored between the Strip and Israel, which is, after all, just across the fields. In the midst of enemy occupation, the secretary's sister-in-law rang up from the small town where she lived in Israel, to have a chat. How was everyone? The sister-in-law reported that they were fine, her husband was doing very well, they had a nice house and no trouble of any kind. The secretary, recalling this family news, said, 'I think if we had all stayed where we were, nothing would have happened to us. All this would not have come about. And what is it for? My children have never seen Palestine. I tell them; and in every school, every minute, they are always told. But when they are grown? The people who knew Palestine will die, and the young ones—will they be interested?'

The second memorable talk took place at the Sewing Centre. The Sewing Centre is another of UNRWA's camp inventions, and it is self-supporting. UNRWA Sewing Centres teach dressmaking and new uses for traditional Palestinian embroidery—vast tablecoths and sets of napkins, blouses, skirts, which sell at good prices to local customers and to city speciality shops. Hundreds of refugee girls earn small wages and stave off boredom, while learning a trade. The Gaza centre was managed by a bustling cheerful plump Palestinian refugee, who would be taken for a bustling cheerful plump young Jewess in any Western country; but, of course, Arabs and Jews are the same race, Semites. The young manageress showed me massive tablecloths (which none of us would be grand enough to own or get washed), and she praised her girls, who sat on a long porch, embroidering, flattered, giggling.

It was as clear as if she wore a sign, but I asked anyhow: 'You're happy, aren't you?'

'I have a nice husband, and two children, and a comfortable house. I like my work very much; it is very interesting. Yes. We are happy.' And she smiled. Such a smile. The world isn't lost, not even on the Gaza Strip.

Most of the Christian Arab refugees live scattered around Gaza in rented private houses. A few Christian families asked for free government land at the edge of a Muslim camp, the usual free allotment of building materials form UNRWA, borrowed extra money, and built their own houses with small well-tended gardens. My UNRWA guide, himself a Greek Orthodox Arab, took me to visit one of these trim, respectable self-made homes, belonging to a family he had known before in Jaffa.

The old mother was half blind; the recurrence of eye disease is a Middle Eastern, not a refugee affliction. My guide and this family had not seen each other for some time, and immediately after their first greeting, the old woman wept with incurable grief and was consoled, gently, but as if he had done so often before, by my guide. He explained: this family had suffered a great tragedy. One of the sons was killed by shellfire, in Jaffa.

I report this because it was the only family I met where an actual human being was known to be dead. Here, at last, the infallible witness testified; and here this death, thirteen years old, was mourned as if it had come upon them yesterday. My UNRWA guide behaved as if this case were unique and deserved the aching pity which everyone feels for those who have lost a loved member of the family in war.

I left Gaza, wishing that I could take all the young people with me, and not to Palestine, but out into a wider world. Their destiny should not be to go back, but to go forth. They need exactly the opposite of what the Jews need. There is plenty of room for both needs.

Officially, over 600,000 Palestinian refugees live in Jordan, more than in the other three 'host countries' put together. But legally there is no such thing as a refugee in Jordan. The refugees are full citizens of Jordan; they have every right and privilege and opportunity that a born Jordanian has. Many of the Palestine Jordanians are contented and have made good lives, despite the limitations that a hot, barren, undeveloped country places on all its inhabitants.

Much of the barrenness and poverty could have been corrected by a scheme for the use of the waters of the Jordan River, to irrigate land now wasted. Eric Johnston, who was President Eisenhower's special representative to implement this life-giving plan, finally reported: 'After two years of discussion, technical experts of Israel, Jordan, Lebanon and Syria agreed upon every important detail of a unified Jordan plan. But in October 1955 it was rejected for political reasons at a meeting of the Arab League.'

Judging by the refugees I saw in Jericho, in camps outside Jerusalem, in Jerusalem itself, the boon of citizenship fosters sanity. The emotional climate in Jordan is noticeably different from that of the Gaza Strip. A school principal stated that children are taught the history of Palestine, 'without politics.' Exactly what this means, I cannot say. In Jordan, a refugee's education and self-reliance showed at once in his politics. The better educated, the more able do not waste their time on thoughts of violent revenge, and give their loyalty to King Hussein. The more ignorant and less competent nourish themselves with a passion for Nasser, war, and Return.

Two men, living next door to each other in a camp outside Jerusalem, aptly illustrate this difference in personality and politics. The camp watchman, who lived in a new little UNRWA house which was already a pigsty, with empty sardine tins on the floor, a filthy yard, rags for bedding, announced, 'We were evicted by force, and so we will return. Led by Nasser and Hussein and all the Arab leaders.' His neighbour, an old man, had cleared the stony ground around his house and made a flourishing vegetable garden. Inside his courtyard you could hardly move for the rows of drying laundry. He did not have a word to say about war or force or Arab leaders. He said that he would rather starve to death than not give his grandchildren education. 'As long as I live and can work, my grandson will go to the university.'

The largest Jericho camp is run by an objectionable tyrant, yet its cleanliness was nearly Swiss. 'I gave them six thousand trees,' said the refugee-tyrant, speaking in his capacity of God. 'Five years ago, the Muktars [the village leaders] would not let me give the people trees; they said if they plant trees, the people will never want to go home.' Now trees rise over the walls that separate the little houses, and more trees are to be distributed. An inexhaustible supply of clean water flows from twenty-one water points. Forty thousand people live here in solid dwellings, under the stern eye of their tyrant; bird-fast children play in the streets.

'How is your name? Are you well? Goodbye! Good night! Hello, leddy!' The children chirped and circled; the tyrant tried roughly to shout them off. One boy, determined to have his say, presented me with a whole English sentence.

He took me to his home, four airy rooms (one lined with chairs for visiting), a neat yard, presided over by a smiling serene-faced mother, very proud of her son who could speak alone in a foreign language to a foreign guest. He told me, slowly, of his life, his family, and his ambitions. He was thirteen and had studied English here for two years, in school. He had never talked English with anyone before, except his teacher. After this encounter, I visited some English classes in another camp, to watch the miracle in the making. The boy wants to become a teacher.

'In this country?' I asked, waiting for the expected cry, 'No! In my country! Palestine!'

'No, not in this country, in Jerusalem or Amman.'

So finally I realized, as I should have all along, that 'country' means town or village; when the Arab peasant refugees talk of their country—even if they happen to be in it, as they are here— they are talking about their own village, their birthplace. The boy's mind had gone no farther than the big cities of the only country he knows; his mind may travel much farther than that. The highest ambition of all the best students is to become a teacher or a doctor. Teachers and doctors are needed throughout the world, and the Arab world needs them intensely.

Jordan has a Vocational Training School also, as happy and hopeful as the school in Gaza. Here I forgathered with a class of budding plumbers, another set of citizens the world can well use. They were very merry in their blue work clothes and greasy hands, and full of plans for the future. One wished to go to Kuwait, one to America. One boy said he wanted to plumb in Palestine. The youngest and smallest of them, in a curiously wise voice—both bored and dismissive—said, 'Oh, all that will take a long time.' None of them was interested enough to go on with it.

The only place that looked as I originally expected refugee life to look was in the Jordanian part of divided Jerusalem in the old Ghetto. Jews had festered in those lightless rat holes, jammed among the ancient stones, for longer than one can imagine; for thirteen years, Arab refugees have endured the same hideous life. This is medieval misery and squalor; nothing like it exists in the modern world.

From a fetid passageway, a straight-backed, cleanly dressed, handsome boy bounded into the cobbled alley street. He took the arm of his teacher, who happened to be my guide that day; they were good friends. He was the star pupil of his class. Where could he possibly study? In the street, the boy said, anywhere outside. He has known no other home than a single damp room, a dungeon, where he lives with his bed-ridden grandfather, his parents, and a brother.

'All the boys from here are good boys,' the teacher said, and his amazement showed in his voice. 'And very witty.' He meant 'intelligent', I later discovered.

Did the UNRWA Director know of this vile slum? No, said the camp leader. I hurried off to ask why UNRWA allowed human beings to live in such revolting squalor. Whereupon I was informed that the Director had visited the Jerusalem Ghetto within two weeks of taking on his job. UNRWA had tried, at various times, to move these refugees, who refused to go because they preferred living inside the city. But now, since their birth rate had risen at such lightning speed, they were more than ready to leave, and within the year they would be settled in a new camp outside Jerusalem. There were two more dreadful refugee slums in the 'host countries'—I did not see either; these were the only subhuman living conditions, and it was not UNRWA's fault they continued. They would, in time, be eradicated.

Despite all difficulties, UNRWA runs a welfare state; no other exists in the Arab Middle East. 'The refugee has a net under him; the local population has none.' Quote from an UNRWA official. It should be stated that the UNRWA personnel loves its Arab charges, which is not only right but essential. You cannot help those you do not cherish.

*

With my suitcases packed, and my mind overpacked with 'treasonous' doubts, I set off for Israel, across the street. I had not dared tell anyone, including the Western UNRWA officials, of this intention: to have been in Israel, to go to Israel, is enough to brand you as an enemy and, more possibly, a spy. The Arab psychosis (an ornate word but not too strong) about Israel is official, and infectious. There may be many reasonable people in the Arab countries who are able to think calmly about Israel and about Arab-Israel relations; if so, they choose safety and keep their mouths shut.

When it comes to moving from one side of Jerusalem which is Jordan, to the other side of Jerusalem which is Israel, the world of dream sets in. You take a taxi, through normal streets, and suddenly you arrive at a small Jordanian frontier post, also in a city street. You wait, in this little shack, while your passport is checked against the exit list. After this formality, a charming courteous young porter carries your suitcases half a block. You tip him, and he deposits them on the porch of a house which is no longer there. Artillery fire removed it, years ago. Around you are shelled houses; one side of the street is Jordan, with laughing soldiers in the shelled houses; one side of the street is Israel, with washing hung out on lines. You walk half a block further, leaving your bags behind. You are now at the Israel frontier post, another shack. Like crossing the river Styx, this is a one-way journey. When you have left Jordan for Israel, you cannot return by this road. The Arab blockade of Israel thus extends to foreign visitors. You would have to fly from Israel to neutral territory and start all over, provided the Arabs still like you, after a visit to Israel.

Since you will not be admitted to any Arab country if you have an Israeli visa on your passport, you carry your Israeli visa on a separate sheet of paper. Other nations than ours present their travelling citizens with two passports. After the Israeli border police have checked your visa, an equally charming courteous young porter, an Israeli, collects your bags from the porch of the nonexistent house in no man's land. You tip him and put the luggage in a taxi and drive a few blocks to your hotel. From your hotel in Israel you have a fine view of the beautiful wall and the Old City of Jerusalem, where you were residing three quarters of an hour ago.

There is not a war on, not by any terms we know. The object of this non-peace – non-war exercise is to destroy Israel, which remains undestroyed. I cannot see how it helps the Arab countries, but perhaps it does. Perhaps they need one enemy they can agree on, as a unifying force, as cement for their nationalism.

I wanted to visit Palestinian Arabs in Israel, the ones who stayed behind, the non-refugees. Seeing them at home, I thought I might better understand the mentality of their brothers in exile. Some important clue was lacking, but I could not name it or define it.

The driver of my car, on the journey in Israel, was an Israeli Jew, born there, who speaks Arabic as his second mother tongue and looks so like Nasser that it is a joke. I said I wanted to visit the village of Meron, on a mountain top in Galilee. He said that at Meron there was an ancient temple of the Jews, the grave of a famous rabbi, a synagogue, a Yeshiva (the Orthodox Jewish equivalent of a Catholic seminary), but nothing else to his knowledge. Let us go and find out, I said. So we drove north through this country, which is a monument to the obstinate, tireless will of man. In 1949, the new immigrants, like ants on the hillsides, were planting trees: their first job. It looked as if they were planting blades of grass and seemed a pitiful act of faith. Now the trees have grown.

There are countless changes in Israel, but the Arab villages along the road to Nazareth have not changed. The old adobe or field-stone houses cling to and grow from each other. They are charming, picturesque, primitive, and wretched; but not to Arab peasants. This is the way it always was; this is the way they like it and want to keep it.

We drove up the mountain. Between the synagogue and the heroic ruins of the two-thousand-year-old temple, we did indeed find Meron, the home of the aristocrat who had offered me a rose on a mountain top in Lebanon. There were not more than twelve houses in the village. The Muktar's palace is a long narrow stone shed, with an ugly narrow porch along the front. Instead of beams, bits of rusted railway track hold up the porch. The other small houses were built of the honey-coloured, rough field stone, with traditional graceful doors and windows. Inside, the houses were like stables unfit for decent animals. The rich fields and groves the Meron refugees had described were the steep slopes of the mountain behind, where the villagers cultivated tobacco and some fruit and fig trees. In their day, the village had no electric light or water; the women carried water on their heads from the wadi at the foot of the mountain. The view is a dream of beauty. Hardship for hardship, Meron is no better than their refugee camp, Mia Mia, perhaps not as good; but memory is magical, and Meron was home.

Beside these pretty stone hovels tower the remains of a great temple. The blocks of granite in the fragmented wall are as massive as those in the wall of Solomon's Temple in Jerusalem. The broken pillars are enormous, unadorned, and suddenly Samson is real and pulled down real pillars as heavy as these. Here, two thousand years ago, the Jews were praying in a new temple, for two thousand years is not all that much in the history of the Jews or of this land. And here, with weeds around their low walls, stand the abandoned houses of the descendants of warrior strangers, the Arabs who came to this country and conquered it when the temple was some six hundred years old, doubtless already a ruin. Were the villagers of Meron happy when they lived on this mountain; did they think it Eden then? And why did they run away? The war never touched this place.

On 1 January, 1960, according to Israeli statistics, 159,236 Muslims, 48,277 Christian Arabs, and 22,351 Druses lived in Israel. These people will have increased, but that is a good enough basis to work on; roughly a quarter of a million Arabs by now. The Jewish population, coming together here from the four corners of the earth, was 1,858,841. These dissimilar people live on eight thousand square miles of quite beautiful, laboriously and lovingly reclaimed rock heap and sand dune—of which one third is irreducible desert. The Druses, a separate and secret sect, are a phenomenon; they are content. They trust and approve of the Jews; they are loyal citizens of Israel. The remaining Arabs are something else again.

On this tour, I visited a Christian Arab village near the Lebanese frontier; a Muslim Arab village on the coastal plain near Acre; two Muslim villages near the Jordanian frontier; a new Muslim settlement near Tel Aviv—the exact copy of a new Jewish settlement, built by the government; and a Roman Catholic priest, in the beautiful Crusader city of Acre.

My idea was to search out Arab school-teachers, on the grounds that they would probably speak English, were educated men, would know the feelings of their communities, and would have thought about Arab problems. Arabs, living in their own communities, have their own schools, by their own wish, where the children are taught in Arabic, according to Arab principles. Nissim, my driver, was to serve as translator until I had found someone I could talk to; he was then to disappear. I did not want anyone to feel hampered by his alien presence. I might have spared myself anxiety. The candour of the Arabs is proof of their freedom inside the state of Israel; they are not in the least cowed.

In the Christian Arab village, the school-teacher was an attractive lean young man, with prematurely grey hair, working in his garden in the cool of the evening. He had a good modern house, a young modern wife, and after six years of marriage, a first baby, a six-month-old girl named Mary, whom he and his wife so adored that neither of them took their eyes off the child at the same moment. He was healthy, prosperous, respected, freely doing his chosen work, loved and loving; by any standards, a fortunate man. After hours of listening to him, I had grasped the lacking clue, and felt hopeless.

'Great Britain helped the Jews,' he said. 'The English gave weapons to the Arab countries, and they gave weapons to us. In this village we were all armed; we all fired at the Jews, every one of us. But our bullets were no good; the English gave bad bullets to the Arabs. Four out of five of the bullets were no good. When we saw this, we ran away to Lebanon for two weeks and then we came back.'

'Were any of you killed in these battles?'

'No, no one. Yes, we refused Partition. We did not want the Jews here; we wanted the whole country for ourselves, as is right. We only lost because of the United Nations and the Western powers.

'The Ottoman Empire crushed the pride of the Arabs. The Western powers divided the Arabs into many nations, after the First World War, to keep them weak. In the 1948 war, the next village was bombed by the Jews; when we saw that, we knew we had no hope.'

(Pause for breath: the Jewish Air Force at the time consisted of nineteen Piper Cubs, a nice little plane, not a bomber; the next village was a good seven or eight miles away.)

'Now we have military zones, all along the frontiers. We must ask for permission to travel or work in different places. They have taken our land which is in the military zones. Yes, they pay for it, but very cheaply.'

'At the price it used to be worth in the Mandate? Before it was improved by the Jews?'

'Something like that. No, even cheaper. Just now two boys from this village were caught on the Lebanese frontier; the Lebanese police sent them back. The Israelis are holding them for interrogation. How could such boys be spies?'

'I don't know. But you do remember that the Arab countries are at war with Israel? I should think it might be hard for the Jews to know what Arabs they could trust.'

'They are right not to trust fifty per cent of the Arabs in this country.'

'How can they know *which* fifty per cent?'

'Oh, they know everything. They have a C.I.D. agent in every Arab village. He is a Jew, and everyone knows him.'

'What's the use of having a secret policeman if everyone knows he's a secret policeman?'

'There are plenty of informers. I don't know what it is that has taught all Arabs to be spies.' He said this with real despair.

'There is compulsory education in this country up to the age of fourteen. That is a very good thing. We did not have such a thing before. But the Muslims do not send their girls to school half the time and do not send the boys if they can earn. Then what? The fine for the father is only five pounds. What is five pounds to the father?'

'Do you really mean that you want the Jews to supply the schools and the law which makes education compulsory, and also to force the Arabs and Druses to send their children to school and take advantage of this education? Wouldn't that make the Jews even more unpopular?'

He admitted, with a smile, that this might be the case and went on: 'Nasser buys arms from Russia because he could not get them from the West. Egypt has twenty-two million people, so it needs many more arms than the Israelis, who are only two million. But Nasser is not crazy; he will not make war. He spends as much on social reform as on arms. All children now go to school in the Arab countries.'

'Have you ever visited the Arab countries? Have you been to Egypt?'

'No.'

We drank more coffee, we lit more cigarettes. I braced myself for further enlightenment.

'The Arab Kings were not the true representatives of the Arab peoples when they made war against Israel. Now all the refugees should come back and we should have Partition.'

At this point, I decided to make one long, determined stand to see whether there was any meeting ground of minds on a basis of mutually accepted facts and reasoning.

'Please bear with me and help me,' said I. 'I am a simple American, and I am trying to understand how the Arab mind works, and I am finding it very difficult. I want to put some things in order; if I have everything wrong, you will correct me. In 1947, the United Nations recommended the Partition of Palestine.

I have seen the Partition map and studied it. I cannot tell, but it does not look to me as if the Arabs were being cheated of their share of good land. The idea was that this division would work, if both Jews and Arabs accepted it and lived under an Economic Union. And, of course, the Arab countries around the borders would have to be peaceful and co-operative or else nothing would work at all. The Jews accepted this Partition plan; I suppose because they felt they had to. They were outnumbered about two to one inside the country, and there were the neighbouring Arab states with five regular armies and forty million or more citizens, not feeling friendly. Are we agreed so far?'

'It is right.'

'The Arab governments and the Palestinian Arabs rejected Partition absolutely. You wanted the whole country. There is no secret about this. The statements of the Arab representatives in the UN are on record. The Arab governments never hid the fact that they started the war against Israel. But you, the Palestinian Arabs, agreed to this, you wanted it. And you thought, it seems to me very reasonably, that you would win and win quickly. It hardly seemed a gamble; it seemed a sure bet. You took the gamble and you lost. I can understand why you have all been searching for explanations of that defeat ever since, because it does seem incredible. I don't happen to accept your explanations, but that is beside the point. The point is that you lost.'

'Yes.' It was too astonishing; at long last, East and West were in accord on the meaning of words.

'Now you say that you want to return to the past; you want Partition. So, in fact you say, let us forget that war we started, and the defeat, and, after all, we think Partition is a good, sensible idea. Please answer me this, which is what I must know. If the position were reversed, if the Jews had started the war and lost it, if you had *won* the war, would you now accept Partition? Would you give up part of the country and allow the 650,000 Jewish residents of Palestine—who had fled from the war—to come back?'

'Certainly not,' he said, without an instant's hesitation. 'But there would have been no Jewish refugees. They had no place to go.

They would all be dead or in the sea.'

He had given me the missing clue. The fancy word we use nowadays is *empathy*—entering into the emotions of others. I had appreciated and admired individual refugees but realized I had felt no blanket empathy for the Palestinian refugees, and finally I knew why—owing to this nice, grey-haired school-teacher. It is hard to sorrow for those who only sorrow over themselves. It is difficult to pity the pitiless. To wring the heart past all doubt, those who cry aloud for justice must be innocent. They cannot have wished for a victorious rewarding war, blame everyone else for their defeat, and remain guiltless. Some of them may be unfortunate human beings, and civilization would collapse (as it notoriously did in Nazi Germany) if most people did not naturally move to help their hurt fellow men. But a profound difference exists between victims of misfortune (there, but for the grace of God, go I) and victims of injustice. My empathy knew where it stood, thanks to the school-teacher.

'Do you follow the Eichmann trial?' I asked. An Arabic daily paper, weeklies, and radio stations thrive in Israel.

'Yes. Every day.' He wrinkled his nose with disgust.

'Do you not imagine that all the Jews in Israel believe this massacre of their people could have been prevented if the Jews had had a homeland to escape to? Don't you think that they knew, also, what you just said: there would have been no Jewish refugees from here—they would be dead or in the sea? Doesn't that perhaps explain them to you a little?'

He shrugged, he smiled; with these gestures he tacitly admitted the point, but it was of minor importance. 'In 1948, the Arabs were not united; that is why we lost. In 1956 the Jews beat Nasser. He will never make war. But when there are five million Jews here in Israel, the Jews will make war, because they will need more land.'

'Israel is about the size of New Jersey, a state in America. Some six million people live quite comfortably in New Jersey. Israel could become an industrial state, a very useful one.'

'No, it cannot. The Arab nations will not allow it. They will not trade with Israel. They will not let Israeli ships go through the

Canal. They do not wish Israel to do these things. They will not accept Israel.'

'It is hopeless,' I said. 'In my lifetime, those who threatened war sooner or later produced it. If Arab-Israel politics keep up like this, my friend, perhaps all of us, everywhere—you and your wife and Mary, and my child and my husband and I—will have the privilege of dying in the same stupid final war.'

He thought I was making a rich foreign joke. He has never seen even a corner of a real big war; he cannot imagine it. He thinks war is something that lasts a few weeks, during which you shoot off bad bullets at a remote enemy, no one is killed, you run away for a bit and then come home to your undamaged houses and lead a good life, indeed a better material life than before. None of these Arabs has suffered anything comparable to what survivors of modern war know; none can imagine such catastrophe.

The Christian school-teacher sent me on to a friend of his, a Muslim school-teacher, in a village called Masra on the plain near Acre. The Muslim school-teacher was a young black-eyed beauty, who received me in a bleak cement-walled room, scantily furnished with an ugly desk, wardrobe, straight chairs, and day bed. He wore striped pyjamas, traces of shaving cream, and a princely ease of manner. We got right down to business.

'Before 1948, the population of Masra was 350; now it is 200. They owned little land, they had worked on neighbouring *kibbutzim* and in Acre factories. They always had good relations with the Jews. 'No one here shot at Jews; and no Jews shot at us.' (Note the order of the sentence.) But now Masra had grown and swollen; 900 refugees lived here.

'Refugees?'

'Yes, people from those villages.'

He gestured out the door, across the fields.

'What? From villages nearby?'

'Yes, yes. Those villages. They are maybe seven kilometres away.'

'And you consider them refugees?'

'Of course. There was no fighting near here, but the people

are frightened, so they fled to the Druse villages, where they know they will be safe, because the Druses were always friendly with the Jews, and after, they came here. The Israeli government will not let them go back to their villages. The government offered them other land, but they will not take it. Before the war, only my father sent his sons to school from this village. Now we have a school and 240 children in it, 100 girls and 140 boys. We have a water tap at every house and electric light; never such things before. No one owned a radio; now there are 100 radios and frigidaires too. The people earn good wages.'

'Then everyone must be happy.'

'No. The people are not glad. They want to go back to their old houses, even if there is no light or water or money.'

They knew the refugees were 'living under good conditions'; he had brothers in Lebanon and Syria who were doing well. How did he know? They wrote messages to the Israel radio, which broadcast them, and the Lebanon radio sent messages back; that way they heard news of their families.

But all the refugees should return and Israel should be partitioned. I put the same proposition to him as to his Christian colleague; if the Arabs had won the war, would they accept Partition?

'No, never, of course not. We would let some few Jews live here as immigrants but not be master, not in any part of Palestine.'

'Why do you think these refugees left in the first place?'

Well, there was much fear. Then, they all knew about Dir Yassin and expected the same to happen to them. Inside Israel, the Arabs do not need or use the refugees' stories of massacres; they do not have to account for flight, since they are still at home. They know what happened around them, and their neighbours know, and such stories would be pointless. But they do speak of Dir Yassin, which was a genuine massacre and took place in the village of that name, near Jerusalem, on 9 April, 1948.

Before the official Arab-Israel war started (on 15 May, 1948) there had been months and months of 'incidents.' ('From the first week of December 1947, disorder in Palestine had begun to mount. The Arabs repeatedly asserted that they would resist Partition by force.

231

They seemed to be determined to drive that point home by assaults upon the Jewish community in Palestine.'—Trygve Lie, *In the Cause of Peace*, Macmillan, 1954.) By February 1948, aside from scattered Arab attacks on scattered Jews, and reprisals for same, the 'Arab Liberation Army' had moved into Palestine from the north, and Jerusalem was bombarded, besieged, and cut off. The Jews were trying to run food to the beleaguered Jewish population of Jerusalem. A lot of Jews were getting killed in that effort, in Jerusalem and elsewhere, and in the eyes of some Jews not enough was being done to prevent or avenge this. The state of Israel did not exist; no functioning Jewish government could control this anarchic, deadly phase of undeclared war.

Two famous illegal groups of militant Jews, the Stern Gang and the Irgun Zvai Leumi, had their own ideas on how to fight fire with fire. The British regarded them both as terrorists. The Jewish Agency and their underground army, the Haganah, which were the official Jewish authorities in Palestine, also rejected the Stern Gang and the Irgun Zvai Leumi, because of their ruthlessness. Under the circumstances that created them, these two outlawed bands do not seem very different from Resistance groups, Partisans, or Commandos, all of whom were admired as patriots, and none of whom obeyed the Queensberry rules.

The Irgun Zvai Leumi, in any case, behaved like desperate men at war, not like the millenial inheritors of a high moral code. The village of Dir Yassin lay close to besieged Jerusalem and its life-line road. According to the Irgun, Dir Yassin was a nest of snipers and armed Arabs; an effective enemy concentration. On their own, the Irgun decided to attack Dir Yassin. Their leader was killed by Arab fire from the village; the Irgun fighters then went brutally mad and shot everyone in sight. Two hundred and fifty Arabs were killed.

To this day, Israelis cannot get over their shame for Dir Yassin while failing to remind themselves, the Arabs, and the world that murder, horribly, begets murder; and they could present a long casualty list of Jews killed by Arabs, before and after Dir Yassin, during the twilight period of terror that preceded open war.

The news of Dir Yassin spread like the tolling of a funeral bell throughout Arab Palestine. According to their own ethical code and practice of war, Dir Yassin must have seemd a natural portent of the future to the Arabs. They intended to massacre the Jews; if the Jews were victorious, obviously they would massacre the Arabs. As the beautiful school-teacher pointed out, Dir Yassin threw the fear of death into vast numbers of the Arab population. In panic, they fled from Palestine.

Since we were talking about war, we came easily to the subject of Nasser.

'Here they love Nasser. All love him. He is Arab person. They do not believe what he says on the radio—kill the Jews, kick them into the sea. So long he says it, and nothing happens. It will not be war. Something else will arrange, but not soon.'

The Christian Arab school-teacher had told me of a priest in Acre whom I should see, but I could not find him. Instead, I directed myself toward the nearest church steeple, rang a doorbell beneath, and was admitted by an enormous, rotund priest in a brown cassock. He looked like an Arab but was an Italian. He had lived in this country for nearly thirty years and had learned how to survive: by laughter. He laughed at everything, and it was an awesome sight, as if a hippopotamus broke into silent mirth.

We settled on his stiff upholstered visitors' chairs, and he ruminated on the problem of the refugees. If there was the choice between a big financial compensation or return, only fifty per cent of the refugees would wish to return, and most of those who came back would not stay. 'They could not endure how this country is run. The discipline. The work.' The refugees are kept thinking of Palestine by the Arab leaders, by propaganda. Why not build factories and arrange land resettlement in the Arab countries? (The Arab governments do not wish this, Father.) Give the money to the Arab governments and tell them to get on with the job and control it. (How?) By force. (But what force, Father?)

He often told Arab priests about the thirteen million refugees who came from East Germany to West Germany; they were all absorbed into West Germany and enriched the country. Why would not 800,000 Arab refugees enrich the Arab countries, which were big and underpopulated? But it is no use; Arabs have never heard of any other refugees or any other problem than their own, and they cannot think about that, in a practical way.

The whole problem is between the East and the West; the Arabs are very happy in the middle, using blackmail. This would stop if the East and the West came to terms, or if the West was united and strong and could impose its will. (But how, Father?)

Ah well, the Jews might as well let the refugees come back; the Arabs here are loyal to the state. ('The ones I've seen detest the Jews and the state, Father, and you know it.' I expected his laughter to make a sound, it was so violent.) Yes, yes, that is true, but they do nothing. There is no resistance, no underground. Think what they could do if they really wanted to, with the Arab countries all around as a base. (Some Arabs did for a long time, Father—until 1956, in fact; look at the countless incidents with the UN police force called out to investigate murders, thefts, sabotage.) Oh, that was nothing, nothing to what they could do if they really wanted to.

With another mute roar, he told me that the Arabs said, First we will finish with the Shabbaths, and then with the Sundays. They never changed their ideas. They went around looking at the women and the houses they would take when they managed to get rid of the Jews and the Christians. He laughed himself into a good shake over this one.

I asked about the Eichmann trial and the reaction of his Roman Catholic parishioners. Well, his Christian Arabs thought Eichmann was right, because the Jews were the enemy of the German state. They were always the enemy of the state; the Pharaohs had to drive them out of Egypt, the Persian King tried to clear them out, Ferdinand and Isabella kicked them out of Spain. No one could live on good terms with them, so Eichmann was right. (Horrified, really horrified, I said, 'Surely that is not a Christian attitude to the most appalling murders we know about?' He found it terribly funny that I should expect a Christian attitude from Arabs.)

'I do not like either Arabs or Jews,' the priest announced with great good humour, 'But I serve them with my whole heart, as I must.'

He asked me at the door whether there are any Christian Arabs in refugee camps. Yes, I had seen a camp of Christians in Lebanon.

'I am surprised. There must be very few. I would have expected them to manage better. They do not dream all the time. They have more contact with reality than the Muslims.'

By now I could foretell one local Arab account of reality. First they explain that they did *not* lose the war against the Jews; various others are responsible for the defeat. Then they boast cheerfully of their present material well-being, as if they had invented prosperity. At this stage, the Israeli Jews might be wisps of smoke; they had nothing to do with building the country. However, Arabs are miserable; although they never had it so good, it is not good enough, owing, of course, to the Jews. Usually these Arabs say how much they love Nasser and in their devotion are curiously remindful of Nazi Austrians, twenty five years ago, when they praised the handsome distant leader, Adolf, from whose hand all blessings would flow. What they believe they now want is to bring the refugees home and partition the state. They have not considered this as a practical matter, nor imagined its effects on their new-found prosperity.

I visited a school in a village where prosperity had broken out like a rash—new houses, shops, hospital, high school, bigger elementary schools—and the teachers harangued me as foreseen. After telling me how well off everyone was, and bragging of their growth, they told me they were unhappy and poor because they had owned 40,000 *dunams* of land (10,000 acres) and now only owned 10,000 *dunams*. But another Arab, who had not overheard this conversation and was employed as an agricultural inspector, explained that the 10,000 *dunams* were irrigated, which was new, and also they were scientifically farmed, and therefore produced far more than the 40,000 *dunams* had. To listen to these conversations is work for a psychiatrist, not a journalist.

I yearned for my silent hotel room in Jerusalem, but Nissim had two heart's-desires, and Nissim was such a nice man that I could not refuse him. There was a 'great lady' he wanted me to meet, a Muslim. 'She began a Muslim women's club all alone, she,' Nissim said. 'Such a thing has never been. What a brave woman. The Muslims go to a place and learn together, and hear lectures, the women. Is it not wonderful?' I could see that Nissim was by nature a suffragette. He also wanted me to visit a new village of government-built houses, which the Arab citizens buy on the installment plan by paying a low rent. Not everyone has a chance to own such fine, inexpensive houses, and Nissim—like all Jewish Israelis—is ardently proud of every improvement in his country.

First we called on the lady, who lived in a modern villa, luxurious by middle-class standards anywhere and palatial by Middle Eastern standards, very shiny and tasteless. Nissim thought it wonderful; so did she, with well-bred restraint. She was young, charming, just returned from her school-teacher's job, bathed and dressed for the afternoon in a sleeveless red dress. She spoke of her Muslim women's club, whose members ranged in age from fifteen to sixty, and learned sewing, cooking, child care, listened to lectures, and were enthusiastic over their new venture. I am a suffragette like Nissim and was delighted. Then the predictable complaints began. The peasants, she said, have work and money and don't care about anything else. But the educated people suffer; they have all this education, and after they finish their studies, what can they do? Only the professions, and business, and a few are elected to Parliament; but they cannot get positions in the army. Her husband, a pharmacist, has to take four buses to reach his place of work, but here is this village of eight thousand people without a pharmacy; why don't the Jews open a pharmacy?

'If there is such a crying need for a pharmacy here, why doesn't your husband start one himself? This is not a Communist state; there are no laws against private enterprise. You are well-known people, full and free citizens. You could certainly raise a loan, if you need it.'

You are not supposed to argue about complaints; it is abominable manners. Her face closed like a lovely olive-coloured trap.

'The Israelis say that they do not conscript Arabs—except the Druses, who insisted on it themselves—because the only people the Israeli Army would ever have to fight are Arabs. It seems decent to me, and it seems like reasonable military security. How would your men feel if called upon to fight fellow Arabs, who might be their blood relatives and intended to be their liberators? Do you think it is a good job for a man to join an army he cannot serve with his heart, and would sell out if the time came? That may be excellent work for spies, but not for soldiers.'

She opened her closed face to say, 'Yes, I see. But it *is* our country.'

It was too hot, and too futile. Besides, I was tired of the convention which apparently requires non-Arabs to treat Arabs as if they were neurotic children, subject either to tantrums or to internal bleeding from spiritual wounds. This girl did not strike me as a pathetic weakling.

'Only by right of conquest,' I said. 'In the seventh century. The Jews got here first, about two thousand years ahead of you. You haven't lived as masters in your own house for a long time. Aside from the Crusaders, the Ottoman Turks bossed you for a steady four hundred years, before the British took over. Now the Jews have won back their land by right of conquest. Turn and turn about,' I said, feeling as beastly minded as an Arab myself. 'Fair's fair.'

'How was it?' asked Nissim, who had been waiting in the car. 'She is fine, isn't she? Think that she starts to teach the Muslim women. No other one did.'

Israelis are the first to explain (and who can know better?) that it is painful to be a minority: the Arabs in Palestine became a minority suddenly. It is grievous (as who knows better than Israelis?) to be separated from the numerous, needed members of your family. Israelis will also explain that the Arabs in Israel are torn in two: their racial loyalty belongs to the enemies of Israel, and they are afraid; if the Arab nations make war against Israel, as is regularly promised on the radio from Cairo, Damascus,

Beirut, what will be their fate? Would the outside Arabs regard them, the Arabs inside Israel, as collaborators, traitors?

The emotional position of the Israeli Arabs is tormenting (and is held in that torment by the Arab radio stations), though they are materially secure, protected by equal justice under law, and by an almost exaggerated respect for their feelings. If the Arab nations made peace with Israel, it is possible that all Israeli Arabs would relax, be happy, and wholehearted supporters of Israel. If not, not. No one, after listening to Israeli Arabs, could believe that Palestinian refugees would be either contented or loyal citizens of Israel.

The new village, that so pleased Nissim, was rows of small plastered houses painted in pastel shades, or white with pastel-coloured woodwork. They have a porch-veranda, two fairly large rooms, a kitchen, a shower-washroom, and small gardens. No working-class Arabs I saw anywhere in the Middle East possess houses like these, but the owners were not satisfied, as I knew they would not be. One boy of about fourteen could speak English; boys of this age are valuable informants—they parrot their elders without reflection.

'We are very poor,' he said.

'How can you be very poor and live in these houses? You have to pay for them.'

'We must to work very hard. More harder than before. Terrible work. We have no land.'

'Wasn't farming hard work?'

'No. That was easy. Not like now.'

'How does your family manage?'

'My brother works. In Tel Aviv. In a gasoline station. That is terrible hard work.'

When we left, the pretty, healthy children ran beside the car, shouting. I waved. Nissim looked queer, something was wrong. that chronic optimist seemed sad.

'What's the matter, Nissim?'

'Nothing. What the children say.'

'You mean just now, shouting?'

'Yes. They say: "Where you going, bastard! I spit on you." '
What for, I thought, what for, and will it never stop?
'Do you hate the Arabs, Nissim?'
'No. Of course no.'
'Why not?'
'What is the good of hate?'

What indeed? Arabs gorge on hate, they roll in it, they breathe it. Jews top the hate list, but any foreigners are hateful enough. Arabs also hate each other, separately and en masse. Their politicians change the direction of their hate as they would change their shirts. Their press is vulgarly base with hate-filled cartoons; their reporting describes whatever hate is now uppermost and convenient. Their radio is a long scream of hate, a call to hate. They teach their children hate in school. They must love the taste of hate; it is their daily bread. And what good has it done them?

There is no future in spending UN money to breed hate. There is no future in nagging or bullying Israel to commit suicide by the admission of a fatal locust swarm of enemies. There is no future in Nasser's solution, the Holy War against Israel; and we had better make this very clear, very quickly. Long bleak memories will recall the Sudentendeutsch and Czechoslovakia. In a new setting, Palestinian refugees assume the role of the Sudentendeutsch. Israel becomes Czechoslovakia. Propaganda prepares the war for liberation of 'our brothers.' Victory over a minor near enemy is planned as the essential first step on a long triumphant road of conquest. A thousand-year Muslim Reich, the African continent ruled by Egypt, may be a mad dream, but we have experience of mad dreams and mad dreamers. We cannot be too careful. The echo of Hitler's voice is heard again in the land, now speaking Arabic.

Unfortunately for us all, including the Arabs, the Middle Eastern Arab nations have been hit by independence and the twentieth century at the same time. It is a lot to handle, and they are not handling it safely or sanely. The Cold War does not help them; it encourages folly. East and West both treat the Arabs with

239

nervous anxiety; placatory and bribing, East and West keep their eyes fixed on the geographical location of the Arab states and the immense amount of oil under their deserts. No one does or can talk practical facts about Israel to the Arabs; it would be useless. Even the soundest Arab leaders have tied their own hands tight in an official hate policy. At present, any Arab government which urged a quick, peaceful, advantageous settlement of the Palestine Refugee Problem would be mobbed. The mobs have been indoctrinated for thirteen years, as have the Arab refugees.

The Palestinian refugees could have been absorbed into the economic life of the Arab countries long ago, despite the remark of UNRWA's Director—in his 1960 report—that jobs do not exist for the refugees in the Arab countries. Of course they do not exist; if they did, the Arab standard of life would be a finer and a better thing than it is now. The jobs must be made; but the Arab countries need to have the jobs done as much as the refugees need to do them. The Director of UNRWA states, in the same report, that the majority of Palestinian refugees are unskilled peasants and there are enough or too many of those in the Arab countries already. No doubt. But unskilled peasants, all over the world, have learned to become skilled factory workers or scientific farmers, at very short notice; that ability to learn is what makes our modern industrial civilization tick. The Yemenite Jews who moved in a week from the Middle Ages to Israel, the unskilled Polish peasants operating the Nowa Huta steel mills are obvious examples of this transformation. Neighbouring Arabs regard the Palestinian Arabs as outstandingly intelligent. I would think this reputation deserved. There is no reason to believe that they cannot learn as others have.

Where there's a will—and as much unused land and wasted water, mineral and oil resources, underpopulation and undeveloped industries as in the vast Arab territories—there's a way. 'Western Imperialists' would have to contribute most of the cash for the way, and it would be cheap at the price. It is more expensive to maintain paupers forever than to establish free, self-supporting citizens. One outlay of capital is futile and never ends;

the other is a capital investment, humane and profitable, and pays for itself. It pays in buying peace, and we don't have to argue which is the better bargain, peace or war. 'Western Imperialists' should provide the way; the Arab governments would have to provide the will.

Economics are not all, and the tragedy of most refugees is not that they starve in their countries of adoption, but that their hearts and minds and souls starve. They are lonely strangers who do not speak the language of the new land, or know its customs; they are aliens. But the Palestinian refugees look, think, feel, and organize themselves socially as the Arabs of the 'host countries' do. They speak the same language, they practise the same religion. The Christian minority would find fellow minority Christians in every Arab country except Lebanon, where they are on top. The Palestinian Arabs are not foreigners in the Arab world; they are members of their own family.

According to Arab politicians and apologists, the Palestinian refugees refuse to become integrated in the Arab world; it is Palestine or nothing for them. Everyone shouts for the Palestinian refugees, and at them, and about them, but no one has ever asked the refugees what they themselves want: where do you want to live; what do you want to do? My tiny personal Gallup poll unearthed plenty of refugees who were happy where they were and had no desire to return to Palestine, no matter what; and plenty of refugees who longed to emigrate to the richer Arab countries, where the future looks brighter, or out into the great non-Arab world. Except for one Christian Arab from Jaffa, who thinks Jews more honest than Arab Muslims and better people to do business with, none of them wanted to return to Israel, as Israeli citizens, and dwell in peace with their Jewish neighbours. We need a secret poll of both sexes, from the age of twelve onward, to discover the refugees' own wishes for their own lives. The poll would have to be secret because it is impossible, even perilous, for an Arab refugee openly to disclaim interest in Palestine. Such a freethinker would be marked as a traitor to the Arab cause. Man is a political animal, but he also wants to live. Politics have offered a very dry crust to these refugees for a very long time.

Yet the Arab governments insist that the Palestinian refugees are a political problem. Once a year, formally, they brandish these waiting lives at the UN Assembly. The rest of the year, with different degrees of intensity, depending on their domestic politics, they wield these waiting lives to stir up Arab hate at home. The Arab governments say they will not accept the existence of the state of Israel, now or ever. The logical conclusion is that, when ready, they intend to burst from their cold belligerent status into hot armed conflict and terminate Israel's existence. We cannot force the Arab nations to make peace with Israel, but we have to prevent them from making actual war—for the sake of all human life, their own included. A vital preventive act would be to remove the Palestinian refugees as a justification of war.

Is it fruitless to offer terms to the Arab governments? We cannot hurry them, or threaten them. Their pride has been scarred; they are uncertain noisy adolescents in a tricky clever adult world; their nationalism is new, and they suspect insults or attacks on it, from every side; they do not live easily with themselves or with each other; and they have not yet understood that a nation is only as strong as its people—arms laid on top of disease, illiteracy, and poverty are a useless burden. But if we know our own minds, are patient, firm, and generous, in time the Arab governments might allow us to enrich their countries.

Our Western offer should be clear: UNRWA is to continue as a bridge to the future; we will pay for the bridge and the future—Palestinian refugees are gradually to become Arab citizens, earning their own livelihood on land, in industries, which our money and technical help will make available. All of this, but not another penny for a political problem. The Palestinian refugees must be taken out of politics forever and given the same chance that millions of refugees have had before them: a chance for work, private peace, and private life.

Would the Arab government reject such an offer flatly, in pique, and turn UNRWA over to the Russians? The Arab leaders do not care for Communism at home. Russia, as parent and teacher of hundreds of thousands of young Arab refugees, would not charm them. In the ugly East-West rivalry for Arab affection (and oil and geography), we might for once risk taking a reasonable, compassionate line. We are not likely to be outbid in this field. The Arab governments do not love us, but they fear the proselytizing Communists more.

UNRWA has been a splendid mother-and-father and can serve these refugees as a guide to the future. UNRWA's greatest gift to the refugees, to the Arab world, and, indirectly, to us all is the education and health of its charges. UNRWA should receive more money and be considered primarily an educational institution. In my opinion, UNRWA will be with us for some time, an admirable training school for young Palestinians and a kindly old people's home for aged Palestinians. But UNRWA too must be taken out of politics. Its work should not be subject to Arab political supervision; none of its activities should be used for Arab propaganda purposes; and its Western personnel must keep themselves rigorously detached from the Arab-Israel controversy.

The Palestinian refugees are a chain reaction. Arab politicians and apologists would have us believe that the explosion began with the Balfour Declaration to 'view with favour the establishment in Palestine of a home for the Jewish people.' More likely, the explosion started in the depths of time when the Romans drove the Jews from their one and only homeland, the soil that grew their history, the Bible. Nearly two thousand years later, Hitler and his followers committed such barbarous crimes against the Jews as all Christendom and all Islam, barbarous too, had never inflicted in the centuries of the Jewish dispersion. The Nazis and the gas chambers made the state of Israel inevitable: the Palestinian Arabs and the five invading Arab armies determined the boundaries of Israel.

The Palestinian refugees are unfortunate victims of a brief moment in history. It is forgotten that Jews are also victims in the same manner, of the same moment. The Arab-Israel war and its continuous aftermath produced a two-way flight of peoples.

Nearly half a million Jews, leaving behind everything they owned, escaped from the Arab countries where they lived to start life again as refugees in Israel. Within one generation, if civilization lasts, Palestinian refugees will merge into the Arab nations, because the young will insist on real lives instead of endless waiting. If we can keep the peace, however troubled, the children of Palesinian refugees will make themselves at home among their own kind, in their ancestral lands. For the Jews there is no other ancestral land than Israel.

Eichmann and the Private Conscience

In the bulletproof glass dock, shaped like the prow of a ship, sits a little man with a thin neck, high shoulders, curiously reptilian eyes, a sharp face, balding dark hair. He changes his glasses frequently, for no explicable reason. He tightens his narrow mouth, purses it. Sometimes there is a slight tic under his left eye. He runs his tongue around his teeth, he seems to suck his gums. The only sound ever heard from his glass cage is when—with a large white handkerchief—he blows his nose. People, coming fresh to this courtroom, stare at him. We have all stared; from time to time we stare again. We are trying, in vain, to answer the same question: how is it possible? He looks like a human being, which is to say he is formed as other men. He breathes, eats, sleeps, reads, hears, sees. What goes on inside him? Who is he; who on God's earth is he? How can he have been what he was, done what he did? How is it possible?

The normal reaction to a man alone, in trouble, is pity. One man, caught, held to account for his crime, one small creature, however odious his wrongdoing, becomes pitiful when faced by society in all its power. His loneliness compels pity. Yet this man in the dock arouses no such feeling, not once, not for an instant. Day after day he leans back in his chair, impassive, and listens to the testimony of men and women he tormented. Usually their words seem to weary him; sometimes there is a flicker of irritation, a frown. He comes awake only when documents are submitted in evidence, when he can shift the piles of folders on his desk, sort, search for a paper, make notes: the organization man at his chosen task. No single gesture, no passing expression of his face lays claim to our sympathy—an emotion men feel for each other because they need it, they could not live together without it, they recognize themselves in each other. This man is exempt from our pity, as he was pitiless beyond the reaches of imagination. We cannot understand him because of this; and we fear him.

We have cause for fear, and what we fear is deeper and stronger than the tangible terrors we live with: menacing struggles between rival states, weapons which pre-empt nature's own rights. We fear him because we know that he is sane. It would be a great comfort to us if he were insane; we could then dismiss him, with horror, no doubt, but reassuring ourselves that he is not like us, his machinery went criminally wrong, our machinery is in good order. There is no comfort.

This is a sane man, and a sane man is capable of unrepentant, unlimited, planned evil. He was the genius bureaucrat, he was the powerful frozen mind which directed a gigantic organization; he is the perfect model of inhumanness; but he was not alone. Eager thousands obeyed him. Everyone could not have his special talents; many people were needed to smash a baby's head against the pavement before the mother's eyes, to urge a sick old man to rest and shoot him in the back of the head, there was endless work for willing hands. How many more like these exist everywhere? What produced them—all sane, all inhuman?

We consider this man, and everything he stands for, with justified fear. We belong to the same species. Is the human race able—at any time, anywhere—to spew up others like him? Why not? Adolf Eichmann is the most dire warning to us all. He is a warning to guard our souls; to refuse utterly and forever to give allegiance without question, to obey orders silently, to scream slogans. He is a warning that the private conscience is the last and only protection of the civilized world.

For three months, documents and living witnesses, all tested and checked every inch of the way, have bound this man to the crimes he is accused of: murder in a manner and on a scale unknown in history, and murder for gain. The Jews of Europe were robbed of everything they owned before they were killed; after death, there was still more to be wrested from their bodies—gold from their mouths, and occasionally in the slashed stomachs of corpses precious stones could be found, the pathetic last hope of buying safety somewhere. This vast plunder greatly enriched the Reich. Aside from the patriotic and spiritual uplift attendant upon murdering defenceless people, to kill Jews was profitable big business. The exact bookkeeping which accompanied the murders is the final loathsomeness. A man should be hanged only for stealing the shoes of children sent barefoot to their death in gas chambers. Their shoes had value, would be noted in a ledger, and shipped to Germany, to keep non Jewish feet warm.

Eichmann, devotedly and tirelessly organizing the murders, stopping every bolt-hole, never too busy to say no to a plea for mercy, meticulously accounting for the plunder, is now recognized to be what he was: the man in charge of 'Jewish Affairs,' the executive responsible for destroying European Jewry. Since he was not unleashed on the rest of us, since we are safe in our bodies, surrounded by our possessions, we tend to forget that Eichmann despoiled us all. He robbed humanity of six million lives. Who were they? We know of some—their names, light as leaves, float through the days of testimony: artists, scientists, teachers, musicians, jurists, saints. The innumerable others, members of a most gifted race, had no time to mould their raw material of brain and heart and spirit. The world needed what they had to give, as a shield against darkness; to avoid becoming the world this man tried to build. He stole lives, from us all. The world will never know how much it lost, but will always be poorer.

The indictment of the Trial—unique in history, as the crime is also unique—is dated: Jerusalem, this fifth day of Adar, 5721. In the state of Israel, that is the usual way to date documents or official correspondence. More than two thousand years before Christ, the patriarchs of this ancient people were writing the history of their nation. Calculating the creation of the world, from

Biblical data, they hit upon a year which coincides with 3760 BC as the basis for their chronology. In the year 5721, a Jewish Attorney General in the District Court of Jerusalem in the modern state of Israel rose and said: 'When I stand before you here, O Judges of Israel, I do not stand alone. With me are six million accusers.' Thus began the Trial of Adolf Eichmann.

At the beginning of this grave, scrupulous, heartbreaking Trial, the world's press attended: for a brief time the Trial was the brightest sensation the newspapers had to offer. Then a man, in a silver capsule, hurtled around the earth through outer space; there was other news; the Trial went on and on; people groaned in weariness; protested that the whole thing was uselss—how could one man pay for six million deaths, perhaps having a trial at all was a mistake; most likely it would only start up a wave of anti-Semitism.

I think this so shocking that I cannot find words for my indignation. The Trial was essential, to every human being now alive, and to all who follow us; and, despite its length, its carefulness, the Trial furnishes only a partial record—for the scene of the crime was a whole continent, the victims were a whole nation, the methodical savages who committed the crimes were as clever as they were evil, ingenious, brilliant organizers, addicts to paperwork. This is the best record we and our descendants will ever have; and we owe the state of Israel an immeasurable debt for providing it. No one who tries to understand our times, now or in the future, can overlook this documentation of a way of life and death which will stain our century forever. No one will see the complete dimensions of twentieth-century man—and that includes all of us, I insist—without studying the Eichmann Trial.

Does it by any chance bore us to hear of the agony of a people? Deadness of imagination, deadness of heart are fatal diseases. Or are we afraid to know because we are afraid to examine our own consciences, our own responsibilities, and our immense selfishness? Do we possibly think that this Trial does not concern us—it concerns European Jews and Germans; and in our blessed land, running over with milk shakes and jars of honey, no such thing could ever happen? The Jews are not a separate breed from the human race, and, alas, neither are the Germans. We are desperately involved, all of us, everywhere.

The massive destruction of innocent people, only because they were born Jews, happened in our lifetime. We must know everything about it; we must be able to recognize every symptom, every sign, to ensure that it never happens again—under any other disguise—to any people, anywhere. To turn away is as mad as turning away from cancer, saying that cancer is cruel, painful, unjust, and results in death. Anti-Semitism is cancer, and afflicts the weaker members of the human race. We have seen what Germany became, when the cancer cells multiplied, organized, gained control of the entire body politic. Not only Jews die; everything we believe in—decency, justice, truth, mercy—dies too. This Trial is meant for our education, and we are obliged to learn from it, for the safety and honour of our species.

Admiration for the court grew, daily. The crimes covered twelve years in time. Some 2000 documents—as thick as sheaves, or a single sheet—were submitted, verified, numbered, accepted or rejected. Witnesses spoke Hebrew, Yiddish, German, Polish, English, more languages. It was visible torture for all the witnesses to speak; one wandered in his head, screamed something wordless but terrifying to hear, fainted, remembering Auschwitz. The audience was tense, still, straining forward to listen, until now and again a voice would cry out in despair; then the police silently led the disturber from the hall. The glaring light—for the security of the prisoner, for the hidden television—hurt the eyes. The air conditioning was too cold, and yet one sweated. Every day was more than the mind and heart could bear; and the Trial was kept running, always on time, always under quiet control. No lawyers or judges anywhere else have been presented with such a task or so dominated it. This is not intended as denigration of the Nuremberg Trials, which I also watched; but is intended, humbly, as praise of the coherence, the order, the absolute respect for rules of evidence, the courtesy, the shining justness of the Trial in Jerusalem.

An American educational foundation could render an immediate sevice by collecting the stenographic Hebrew reports of the Trial—a paper mountain—and translating them into accurate, clean English. The conduct of the Trial was in every way above criticism, but the Israelis could not invent translators who had an equal grasp of Hebrew and English. The English transcripts of the day's proceedings are often opaque if not incomprehensible. We need the volumes of the Trial, in good English, in all our libraries; and we need them now.

For two thirds of the Trial, the Prosecution piled up evidence of the black hell which stretched from the Urals to the Pyrenees, from the Baltic to the Mediterranean, and was ruled by Adolf Eichmann. Random excerpts from the testimony may give some slight sense of the climate of a life we never knew. The Trial proceeded chronologically, country by country; two months after taking power in 1933, the Nazis were already hunting down the Jews in Germany.

Everywhere, the Jews were first deprived of all their rights as citizens, then of all their worldly goods, then marked with a yellow star and herded together in Ghettos, to starve and die of the diseases of hunger and filth, and finally, since none of this was quick enough, they were slaughtered in tens of thousands daily. Those who could work were used as slave labour; their death was delayed until they became useless from exhaustion. On the way, all along the way, they were beaten, maimed, and murdered at will. Their bodies were broken quickly and with skill; their spirit seems to have endured even inside the gas chambers. People, being asphyxiated by cyanide gas, no easy way to die, apparently still kept their humanity: for corpses of women were found crouched over their children, trying to the last to protect them, and men and women were found with their hands clasped in love.

Most of the witnesses were middle-aged; some looked older than they can have been; a few were young. There were men in business suits, with gold-rimmed glasses and tiepins, and men in short-sleeved open-necked shirts; women in tailored clothes, women in housecoats. Every one of them, in war, would have received medals for valour. Middle-aged and old men and women had represented the Jews and worked for their safety, stubbornly treating with the Germans, with Eichmann, and so had exposed themselves to special notice and wrath. Younger ones, bereft of their families, used and treated as animals with calculated cruelty, waiting their turn to die, nevertheless had risen against their murderers in doomed revolts. All of the witnesses were humble; none had anything much to say about his own life or acts. They were only reporting what they knew because they had seen and heard it, lived through it. They spoke of others.

An old lawyer, a German Jew, a Zionist leader who had been in prison 'for insulting the Gestapo,' tried to explain to the Court what life had been like for the Jews in Germany before the war. This was the first phase, when the Nazis were learning their trade, even Eichmann was learning. There was the ban against Jews as humanity—no work with or for gentiles, no cafés, no transport, no theatres, no shops; Jewish musicians must not play the music of Bach and Brahms, though Mendelssohn was permitted; the books of great Jewish writers were burned, while mobs gloated loudly around the bonfires. Keep the Jew vermin away from the pure Aryan supermen. Boxes of ashes were returned from Dachau on payment of a fee. Synagogues were destroyed. Many of the hunted killed themselves while the rest searched frantically for a country to escape to. At this time, the Germans were merely driving these now penniless people to emigrate. The 'Final' Solution' is in part the fault of the Western world; the Germans saw the blank casualness of the democracies and decided that no one wanted Jews; Jews were a drug on the market; it did not matter what was done to Jews.

The old man cried out suddenly, 'A planet without a visa!'

Here is the guilt of the free democracies. We ought never to forget it. In this, the United States must bear the heaviest share of blame. From 1933 to 1943, we opened our golden doors a miserly crack to admit 190,000 of the millions of doomed Jews. Great

Britain, even harder hit by the Depression, small, so soon to be at war, bombed, rationed, quartering its Allies' soldiers on its overcrowded land, took in 65,000 refugee Jews. The comparison speaks for itself, though none of us has cause for self-congratulation.

Later on, a brave old man, a German Christian, Pastor Grueber, spoke again in the same way. He had earned the right to speak; he helped the Jews in Germany openly; he believed the teachings of his Lord; and he paid for his faith by imprisonment in Dachau. After the pogroms organized by the Nazis throughout Germany in 1938, Pastor Grueber went to Switzerland to beg for more foreign visas for Jews: 'All the official institutions, embassies, they did not reveal any understanding or interest in the lot of these Jews. Very often we came out of those places full of anger, not only full of shame at the lack of readiness to help . . . May I be permitted to say that had these foreign countries at the time shown only a small percentage of the responsibility and interest being revealed now in the lot of refugees and displaced persons and immigrants, it would have been possible to save millions of souls?'

But he would not tell the court the name of a compatriot, now living in Germany, who had *helped* Jews during the Nazi regime. 'I could bring to the Court a whole file of threats and derision which I received, especially in connection with my trip to Israel . . . To me these things do not mean much . . . but I would not like to cause this suffering to others.'

What is the sickness of Germany?

Pastor Grueber knew Eichmann well; he was often in Eichmann's office, pleading uselessly. 'The impression he [Eichmann] made on me was that of a block of ice or marble, completely devoid of human feelings.'

In hundreds, the Israelis wrote letters to thank and bless Pastor Grueber. For them, one good man redeemed a nation.

A Jew from Greece, a poor merchant, described what had happened in Salonika; he spoke in a wondering voice, as though hardly able to believe this story himself. Their fellow citizens, the Greeks of Salonika, were given carte blanche to take anything they wanted from Jewish shops, paying with a cynical IOU. And, alas, they did so, like locusts. The Jews, dispossessed of all they owned, were crowded into Ghettos, where typhus immediately raged; the Germans feared typhus. This man probably survived because the Germans were loath to winkle him out as he lay sick in his hole. The Germans, following their usual practice of deceit, told the Salonika Jews that now they were going to leave all this misery and be happily settled in Poland and live together in peace. With their last hoarded savings, the people bought worthless zlotys (the disgusting theme of robbery recurs again and again); moreover, they bought umbrellas, for surely it rained in Krakow, unlike the sunny land of Greece. Doubt as to their future must have come quickly when they found they were seventy-eight people packed into sealed freight cars meant to hold forty. This was the regulation number of 'transport material,' as the Germans called the Jews, to each goods wagon. The journey was very long; no freight car ever arrived without its load of dead. One can barely imagine the days and nights in those suffocating boxes, the thirst, the filth, the sickness, the fear, and the faces of the children. There had been 56,000 Jews in Salonika; afterwards there were 1,950. This man had a mother, a father, a wife, four brothers, four sisters. 'I remain alone,' he said, and looked about him as if he did not know where he was.

Now there is a young man who grew up in the death camp of Treblinka. At the age of fourteen, separated from his mother, as was the custom at the entry to the concentration camp, he shouted to her where to write to him in Warsaw; his mother, of course, was sent straight to the gas chamber along what the Germans humorously called the 'Himmelstrasse,' the barbed-wire path to heaven. By his first night, the boy had understood this place and he tried to kill himself but an old Jew saved him, telling him it was his duty to live and help others and, since he was young, he might have the strength to survive, and then it was his duty to tell the world.

The young man explained Treblinka in the voice we became used to: you could almost see muscles straining in the effort to speak clearly and calmly. Before 1943, the bodies from the gas chambers were pitchforked into ditches or dumped by a crane; after a visit from Himmler, the pyre system was adopted as more efficient. There were thirteen separate gas chambers, and once, in thirty-five minutes, 10,000 people were killed in them. He had many jobs, this child, from cutting off women's hair for mattress stuffing to pulling out the gold teeth of corpses. Then, one day he found his sister's corpse on the pile. (He took a very deep breath; he held himself rigid.) From these teeth, eight to ten kilos of gold were collected each week and shipped in suitcases to Berlin.

Behind me, in the public section of the courtroom, an old woman with a worn fine face, wearing a kerchief on her head and a newspaper around her shoulder, against the unaccustomed air cooling, wept—without movement, without sound, and without stopping.

Another Polish Jew, an older workman, described Chelmno, a more primitive extermination camp, as it operated before the experiments in mass murder had reached Cyclon B, the cyanide crystals filtered into gas chambers disguised to look like shower rooms. At Chelmno, they still used trucks; gave the people a towel and a piece of soap, told them they were on their way to get a bath, see the doctor, receive fresh clothes, and start their new life. Then the sealed trucks were driven into a forest, and carbon monoxide was pumped into them. It was a slow death, wasted precious SS time, and killed too few people per truckload. Some Jews, of whom this man was one, were kept alive to dig the great trenches in which the corpses were buried; but this work gang was killed too, for sport, since the labour supply was not only unlimited but meant to be expended.

'Yes, forty of us were left—forty-one. The others killed. On Sundays there was no work, and we were placed in a row; each man had a bottle on his head, and they amused themselves by shooting at the bottles. When the bottle was hit, the man survived, but if the bullet landed below the target, he had had it. The others stayed behind to work.'

An attractive dark-haired woman, who had been deported to the women's section of Auschwitz at the age of twenty-one, spoke of a man whose name we all know by now, and revile: Dr Mengele. He is alive in the world still, hidden somewhere. He was the chief doctor at Auschwitz. The Germans practiced subhuman experiments on living flesh, in various camps: Dr Mengele, of Auschwitz, seems to have been the most debased sadist of them all, an abomination among men.

The young woman was a block leader; in this capacity she had some freedom of movement, and thus could visit the gypsies in the camp. (It should be noted that the Israelis were also trying Adolf Eichmann for the planned racial murder of gypsies, whom the Germans had decided to exterminate because they were an 'asocial element.' The dead gypsies have no one else to speak for them.) The young woman was beaten—and lucky not to be killed by the whip, as so many were—for warning the gypsy women never to say they were ill, never to complain, never to ask for missing members of their families: the German answer to all such remarks was immediate death in the gas chamber. One day, in the gypsy camp, she saw newly born gypsy twins, returned to their mother; but Dr Mengele had sewed them back to back, being interested apparently in creating Siamese twins. And again, since birth was not allowed to Jews, a baby was taken from its mother and thrown on a handy fire: the mother walked into the electrified fence to kill herself. But, said the girl, women were always doing that; it was the quickest way.

Behind me, like soft surf, I could hear women in the audience, an indrawn sob of horror and grief. Horror and grief were the common daily emotions in that courtroom.

It is impossible to convey the anguish felt only by hearing of the anguish suffered. Despair for mankind, a real darkening of the mind, would have drowned us, had it not been for the few, beautiful examples of human solidarity against human evil.

The Danes, led by their King Christian X, saved their Jews— to the furious rage of Eichmann. The Jews in Denmark never wore a yellow star, because the king said he would be the first to wear one, if such an order was imposed on any of his people; nor were they herded into Ghettos. The Nazis tried, as usual, to inflame the Danes into anti-Semitism by publishing obscene lies about Jews. The Danes, without hesitation, ferried their Jews across the water to Sweden. They hid old Jews in their hospitals, under Danish gentile names; they saved the sacred objects of the synagogue in the crypt of a Lutheran church. No Dane disgraced himself or his nation by betraying a Jew to the Gestapo. Many Danes paid for their humanity with their lives.

Those few hundred Danish Jews—out of some seven thousand—whom the Gestapo managed to capture while escaping were deported to Theresienstadt, the least murderous of the German concentration camps. When the Danes learned of the hunger there, everyone from King to cobbler contributed money and sent to their people in captivity the food they needed to remain alive. The Danes see nothing extraordinary in their record.

The Swedes, though neutral in war, were not neutral in their humanity. They gave asylum to any Jew who could reach their shores; they were so freehanded in creating sudden Jewish Swedish citizens that Eichmann issued special orders against them—any Jew known to be obtaining neutral citizenship must be deported to the East, to the gas chambers, immediately. And the Swedes produced a saint, named Raoul Wallenberg, the Counsellor of the Swedish Legation in Budapest. At the rate of 12,000 a day, Eichmann was sending Hungarian Jewry to its death—this was when the war was clearly lost, in the summer and autumn of 1944. Raoul Wallenberg rented houses in Budapest, flew the Swedish flag over them, and filled them with Jews who were now called Swedes. When, at last, freight cars were unobtainable and Auschwitz was closed down before the approach of the Russian armies, Eichmann—still determined to eradicate surviving Jews—ordered the atrocious winter death march of Jews from Hungary to Austria. This was such open and appalling murder, for everyone to see, that Himmler finally commanded Eichmann to stop it. Wallenberg drove beside the stumbling column of people and distributed food, blankets, medicines. He was a fanatic too, on the side of the angels. The Russians captured Wallenberg in Hungary, and he is dead. It passes understanding how the Russians, who had themselves suffered so fearfully from the Germans, could have harmed this noble man.

The Nazis swooped fast in Norway, but even so, the Norwegian underground managed to lead half of Norway's Jews to safety in Sweden, over terrible mountain country in sub-zero weather, past a dangerously patrolled frontier. The Dutch staged general strikes, in protest against the treatment of Jews; the strikes were repressed by the usual German firing squads. The Nazis raised the bribe for betraying Jews; the Dutch continued to hide Jews; always more Jews were found. Grumbling documents from Eichmann's office discussed this maddening attitude of the Dutch, who refused to 'sympathize' with the German policy. There are countless examples of Italian humaneness which neither a Fascist government, nor war, nor defeat (twice defeated, by the Germans, by the Allies), nor the incomprehensible official silence of the Pope could weaken.

An Italian Jewess, the daughter of a university professor, found herself alone (the rest of her family lost, caught) with five small children, her own and her missing brother's: 'I wish to add that I saved my chidren by handing them over to Christian families whom I did not know before—different strata of life of the gentile population . . . Each child with another family. My children and my brother's children . . . I was helped by the clergy and also the lay population—labourers and others, in the city of Rome, the intellectuals . . . The goodness, the kindheartedness I met with on my way. Every Italian Jew owes his life to the Italian population.'

The gates of Luxembourg were open to all fleeing Jews. There, in that tiny defenceless country, they could rest, hide, remember—in the kindness of the Luxembourg people—that they were human beings, not hunted animals; and with time and luck, some could obtain visas to safety in neutral territory. Under the moral leadership of Elizabeth, Queen Mother of the Belgians, and with the support of the Primate of Belgium, the Belgian underground aided groups of Jews to escape and managed to derail several death trains.

There were these brave, isolated acts of humanity, and for them we must be eternally grateful.

There were more, in all the German-occupied countries, nameless individuals who protected their fellow men against the savages. The penalty for helping Jews was death. Everyone who took the risk, rather than aid barbarism or watch from a safe distance or close his eyes, bought back a piece of the honour of mankind. And they were effective; they did save lives; they did cheat Eichmann and his servants of their prey. If there had been many many more, millions more, could Eichmann have succeeded as he did?

The Jews themselves were not sheep led to the slaughter. They were too civilized to believe that Germans, a reputedly civilized nation, could behave as these Germans did. The Germans tricked the Jews, lied, raised hope and destroyed it, mocked, lied again: the soap in the Auschwitz gas chambers, where the people expected a shower bath, was made of stone; on death trains the people were given picture postcards of an imaginary place, 'Waldsee,' and forced to write cheerful news back to the Ghetto. No ruse was too mean if it served to lull the Jews and keep them from acts of desperation. There were not so many troops to allot to Jew-killing, despite the bureaucratic mania of Eichmann.

And yet, broken in health, starving, and helpless, the Jews revolted, even in Auschwitz and Treblinka and Sobibor. The revolts could not be more than acts of undaunted defiance; few people survived. The uprising of the Warsaw Ghetto remains a monument to courage; and twenty people live to tell the tale, out of half a million. Jewish partisans, escaped from the massacre, fought in the woods of Poland, in Hungary, in France.

The little man sits in the dock and listens, day after day; and he alone is unmoved; he alone is not burdened by the weight of grief and shame and outrage which we all carry. He proved this, without knowing what he did, on the first day of his testimony in his own defence.

On the morning when we would finally hear the silent man in the glass dock, the courtroom was packed. Dr Servatius, Eichmann's German lawyer, presented his client and his case. Dr Servatius' voice had changed, he became a quavering elderly gentleman, beseeching these honourable strong judges of Israel to pity an insignificant underling. All during the Trial, the Court treated Dr Servatius with the most benign courtesy: one had the impression that everyone in the streetcar was rising to give his seat to an old lady. Dr Servatius is the good, fat, honest German—a pre-war figure of affection or caricature, depending on taste. He could come here (fee of $25,000 paid by the Israeli government) to defend Eichmann because his own record is clean: he was lucky enough to be in a Wehrmacht regiment all during the war, and so had no hand in the horrors committed by and in the name of Germans.

Eichmann looked different, yellowish-grey, afraid at last. His voice was low when he began to speak, telling us the story of his life and times. A modest young man, he saw an opening in a little-known field—the problem of the Jews. He chose this career, but he was nobody important; he just happened to have taken up Jews as his speciality. Nazism was against Versailles, against the democracies. He was far too obscure to forsee where all this would lead; though, for himself, he went straight as an arrow into the SS.

Recounting his early struggles to get ahead in life and the SS, Eichmann said that he desired to learn Hebrew and this provoked the ridicule and even the suspicion of his superiors. But he had seen a Hebrew newspaper published in Riga, and he thought if he could learn the language, he would get much useful information. He wanted to take lessons from a rabbi; his superiors feared that in close contact with a rabbi he might be influenced and talk of other things than the Hebrew language. Finally he overcame their doubts: 'It would have been easy to say, let's grab a rabbi and lock him up and he'll have to teach me; but no, I paid three marks per hour, the usual price.'

Eichmann was so startled by the low wave of sound this statement evoked from the courtroom that, for the first and only time, he turned his head, and stared in an instant's bewilderment at the public. How could he know, this hollow man, that what seemed to him a natural phrase exposed wastelands of feeling to people who, under no circumstances on earth, would have imagined that you could 'grab' an innocent scholar and jail him in order to get lessons for nothing. After all the years in hiding, the weeks in this court, Eichmann was the same SS officer: he regarded Jews as objects, still. Being an honest man, he had treated an object correctly, though under no obligation to do so. He paid the object three marks: he refrained from seizing and locking up the object. The reaction in the courtroom was spontaneous and complex: disbelief, revelation, disgust—a groaning murmur. As time went on, we realized that Eichmann would never know why or how ordinary people reacted to him or his crimes.

Hourly, Eichmann grew more sure of himself. His grasp of the complexities of Nazi bureaucracy was dazzling. He never faltered when explaining a machinery which seems too involved to have been workable: but it was, it was. The workings of his own department—RSHA IV B of the Gestapo charged with the 'Final Solution'—were so efficient that Eichmann stands out as the greatest organization man of all time. One branch of the Nazi government, dedicated to the extinction of one branch of the population of Europe, killed six million civilians, of whom one million were children, in six years. In World War II, spread over the entire globe, the total of the dead combatants of twenty-four nations was 14,700,000.

Eichmann's memory was fabulous, when he so desired. It gave out, when expedient. And even replying to his own lawyer, he would not speak to the point. It took him five minutes of double-talk not to answer a simple question as to whether he had, or had not, been in Berlin on a certain date.

Dr Servatius bumbled; he mixed documents; he could not find the paper he wanted. Eichmann, in control of all papers always, sent the required document from his glass dock to his attorney's desk. Very soon, he was conducting his own defence, saying, 'The assertions I am making will be proved in later documents.'

His voice is ugly, with a hard *R*, a sound that makes one think of a hammer and a knife. Neither by voice, accent, nor vocabulary is he an educated man. As Dr Servatius fumbled, Eichmann's voice sharpened: the cold snarl, the bark that many of the witnesses remembered was there, one tone beneath what we heard. From the first day of this testimony, we could imagine Eichmann clearly as an old Hungarian Jewish aristocrat had described him: 'an officer in boots, with one hand on his pistol, in all the pride of his race.'

On the second day, Eichmann established his line of defence and stuck to it until the end. 'I had no special positions or privileges—they gave me instructions.' Furthermore, he was exclusively concerned 'with matters of pure transport.' This is the reverse of Goebbels' Big Lie; this is the Little Lie. He was not unnerved by the testimony of witnesses who knew him and dealt with him in his years of power, or saw him on his concentration camp visits, nor by the avalanche of documents showing that he commanded the fate of the Jews as no general was able to command a whole theatre of war. He wriggled, he talked a great deal; he returned again and again to the same lies. He was only a minor bureaucrat. It is possible that the outside world—lazy, busy with other things, glancing briefly at headlines—will believe him. Should the State of Israel execute this man, there may well be an outcry in the unharmed, spectator countries, and the adjective *vengeful* will be applied to the Jews. I am not inventing this peculiar if not perverse line of thought: I have already heard it bruited about. People who are forever opposed to the death penalty, anywhere for any crime, have the right to this opinion. Others should study the entire trial, as a moral obligation, before they dare to condemn the punishment meted out to Eichmann. In that courtroom in Jerusalem, there could be no doubt as to Eichmann's guilt, nor the immensity of this guilt. We were not impressed by the Little Lie.

It was no small railway clerk who dealt directly on the highest level with foreign governments. Again and again, through diplomatic channels, Eichmann was requested to locate and spare one Jew, or two or three, by name. For some reason, these individuals troubled the conscience of Germany's allies. Again and again, Eichmann replied icily that these Jews could not be found; his local representatives were instructed to discourage 'on principle' such time-wasting demands for mercy. If the named Jew or Jews were not already dead, Eichmann ordered immediate deportation to the gas chambers, thus closing the file against future intrusion on his work.

The Laval government tried to save one Jew—a man whose gallantry in the French Army could not be forgotten. Eichmann answered officially that the whereabouts of this hero was unknown, but arranged for his instant, secret removal to Auschwitz and Cyclon B. Admiral Horthy, the Fascist dictator of Hungary, directed his police to stop a death train of 1,200 Jews and return the Jews to their camp near Budapest. That night Eichmann sent buses to collect these reprieved people and drive them to rejoin the train far from the capital. Horthy's interference annoyed and hampered Eichmann; soon Horthy was deposed and a thoroughly co-operative puppet was installed.

The duties, the authority of a minor bureaucrat? A new emotion spread and became common to us all: flat contempt for the man who had valued no other lives but so shamelessly cherished his own.

Eichmann knew what was happening; he states this himself in his deposition—a four-volume document, covering months of questioning during which the Israeli police superintendent acted as a gently prodding psychiatrist and Eichmann talked and talked. He deplored what he saw: he found the screams of people strangling in the gas trucks in Poland unbearable; a fountain of blood, which gurgled up through the ground of a mass grave, revolted him. Specifically, somewhere near Minsk, he saw naked Jews moving forward to the edge of a pit where the SS riflemen shot them; some shots were sloppy, the half-dead squirmed, so they fired into the heaped bodies as well. Eichmann reported this scene to an SS leader in Lemberg. ' "Yes, that is horrible," I said to him. "There the young people are being educated to become sadists . . . How can you just bang into a pile of people, women and children, how is that possible!" I said. "This can't be. The people must either turn crazy or become sadists. Our own people." ' Everything about this man is the stuff of nightmare: he never thought of the murdered; he thought of the effect they made on him, and the probable bad effect on the nerves of the young SS.

He said he was too squeamish for this sort of thing; 'People have told me I could never have been a doctor.' So, instead of watching exterminations, he increased the range of the operation, speeded it up, wove a net meant to catch every living Jew, and sent them to what he knew but really could not bear to look at.

In a single sentence, Eichmann divided the world into the powers of light and darkness. He chose the doctrine of darkness, as did the majority of his countrymen, as did thousands throughout Europe—men with slave minds, pig-greedy for power: the Vichy police, the Iron Guard, big and little Quislings everywhere. He stated their creed in one line: 'The question of conscience is a matter for the head of the state, the sovereign.'

Absolved of thought, of responsibility, of guilt, and finally of humanity, all is well: the head of the state thinks for us, we need only obey. If the head of the state happens to be criminally insane, that is not our affair.

The purpose of all education and all religion is to fight that creed, by every act of life and until death. The private conscience is not only the last protection of the civilized world, it is the one guarantee of the dignity of man. And if we have failed to learn this, even now, Eichmann is before us, a fact and a symbol, to teach the lesson.

Is There a New Germany?

To criticize, to doubt, to probe the Germans is by now not only anti-German but apparently un-American. In eighteen years, we have turned an astonishing emotional and intellectual somersault. Have the Germans done anything of the sort? Is there a 'New Germany,' or is there simply another Germany? My acquaintance with Germany began in 1924 and continued until the end of the Nürnberg Trials, though from the summer of 1936 until American troops entered Germany during the war, I watched from a distance and listened to those who had escaped the fatherland. In these post-war years, while the United States has become officially more loving every minute toward its former enemy, I have been reading of this New Germany, and wondering. Last winter I returned to West Germany to try to find what must be New Germans, those who were children or newly born at the end of the Second World War, so young then as to be untouched by the poison their people fed on for twelve years.

I had one introduction, to a Hungarian journalist established in Germany after the Hungarian revolution of 1956. My plan was to visit universities; I meant to meet Germany's future rulers. Hitler was a freak in German history in the sense that he was semi-literate; Germany is normally directed by university graduates, and the academic title Doctor has always abounded in German governmental circles. From the University of Hamburg, through those of Free Berlin, Frankfurt, Bonn, and

Munich, I was passed along by students, either casually met or introduced by the student self-government in each university. We were strangers, they having no ideas about me and I no ideas about them. There was nothing official in this tour. I would wander into a student government office and chat with anyone I could find, and in turn they whistled up anyone they could find with spare time and a wish to talk; though I did try to meet all kinds, ranging from socialist to nationalist to don't-know. These boys and girls were in their twenties; they had known no other form of government than 'democracy.' They had also grown up in an affluent society, though few of them were rich, but none was miserably poor as were the European students of my youth. I liked some of them very much, and thought some almost as detestable as their fathers had been in their brand new brown uniforms in the pre-war universities.

In my opinion there is no New Germany, only another Germany. Germany needs a revolution which it has not had and shows no signs of having; not a bloody, old-fashioned revolution, with firing squads and prisons, ending in one more dictatorship, but an interior revolution of the mind, the conscience. Obedience is a German sin. Possibly the greatest German sin. Cruelty and bullying are the reverse side of this disciplined obedience. And Germans have been taught obedience systematically, as if it were the highest virtue, for as long as they have been taught anything. They are still so taught, beginning at Mom's knee and continuing through the universities. Twice their victors have imposed 'democracy' on a people who never fought for it themselves. Democracy may not be the most perfect form of government (E.M. Forster was right in saying 'Two Cheers for Democracy'), but it is the best we have yet found, because it implies that the citizen has private duties of conscience, judgement, and action. The citizen who says Yes to the state, no matter what, is a traitor to his country; but citizens have to learn how to say No and why to say No. Germans are still trained as before in their old authoritarian way; the young are not rebels either. At their best they are deeply troubled by their state and suspicious of it; at their worst they are indistinguishable from their ancestors—the interests of the state come first—and they are potentially dangerous sheep.

The adults of Germany, who knew Nazism and in their millions cheered and adored Hitler until he started losing, have performed a nationwide act of amnesia; no one individually had a thing to do with the Hitlerian regime and its horrors. (This amnesia began as soon as the conquering Allies entered Germany; not a soul could be found who had approved Hitler or harmed a fly.) The young realize this cannot be true, yet one by one, each explains how guiltless his father was; somebody else's father must have been doing the dirty work. Santayana observed that if a man forgets his past he is condemned to relive it. Germans trained in obedience and dedicated to moral whitewashing are not a new people, nor are they reliable partners for anyone else.

There has always been a small minority of Germans who thought of themselves as members of the human race first, and Germans afterwards; there still is such a minority, and they are exiles-at-home. For the sake of humanity, it is to be hoped that their numbers will grow until, for the first time, they wield power in Germany. Buf if what makes Germans the way they are—the home, the churches, the schools, the universities—does not change, Germany will continue to be itself. It is fat, rich, and happy now, and no German wants a war; life is good. What happens if life becomes less good? And no one seems to notice that peaceful Germany is, nevertheless, the one great obstacle to peace in Europe. We quarrel with Russia over the divided Germans as over a festering bone; and no one considers that the fear of our former allies, now enemies in the Soviet bloc, are not hysterical fantasies but are based on a long memory.

It is worth remembering that the German national anthem is, as before, 'Deutschland über Alles,' and that the second and third verses, deleted by the Allies as too aggressive, were restored immediately Germany became independent, and are sung with enthusiasm. There *is* a German problem, and it will not be solved

266

by denying it or acting as if the problem were a geographical one; let Germany be united, and all will be dandy. The problem is moral, and only the Germans themselves can handle it. They talk ceaselessly about democracy, but 'democracy' is a virtuous slogan, without meaning. Until Germans really believe that the state is the servant of the people, and each man is responsible for his acts and his conscience, and that orders are not their own justification, Germany merely changes its leaders, not its character.

The forms of teaching in German universities are the exercise (a small study group of twelve to twenty-four students), the seminar (up to two hundred students), and the lecture in the large amphitheatre (about six hundred students). The students learn by dictation from above, the unquestioned professorial word, the assigned books: they listen for thirty hours a week or more. Many students said bitterly that the only sure way to pass examinations and get the essential degree was to repeat to your professor what the professor had told you. Young Germans, throughout their schooling, are taught to memorize facts but are not guided to relate facts, experience, observation, and emotion to produce their own personal thought.

High school teachers and professors (like judges) have tenure of office; regimes may come, regimes may go, but the opportunist pedagogue or jurist can remain at his post. Denazification courts (which Adenauer objected to as early as 1949) deal only with physical brutality; there is no penalty for having misled and lied to young minds. The old boys are still around, and the young assistant professors, if they hope to advance, must be very tactful with them. German professors are hierarchical figures. It is not surprising that, up to 1957, modern German history, as taught in high schools, stopped at the end of the First World War. Now the Nazi era is rushed over lightly in the last year of high school, and a knowledge of the Nazi period is not required for a university degree; it is an optional subject. German educational methods and a lot of German educators seem to me worse than useless in preparing citizens for life in a free society.

German universities are the size of small towns: ten to twenty-two thousand students. All the young complain of the loneliness of these institutions. The universities are factories for learning by heart; it is no part of their job to provide more than teaching. Dormitories are scarce and for the lucky few. Though the students, for human and economical reasons, would love to live in dormitories, the German government is opposed to housing students as we do. Students are considered radical, and it is perilous to concentrate them together. This is an ironical joke; sixty per cent of the students at Munich University voted for the ruling reactionary Bavarian party, while the Socialist Students Club has exactly forty members out of a student population of 22,000. Furthermore, the only students who always live together in houses are members of the Korps (the duelling societies) and their allied fraternities, the Burschenschaften (nonduelling societies). Roughly, these groups may be compared to American fraternities, as membership is by invitation and the houses are not supported by the state or university but by the 'elders,' former members. Thirty per cent of all German students belong to the Korps and the Burschenschaften and are the largest homogeneous group in the universities; these fraternities are also strongholds of traditionalism and nationalism and have been throughout their history. The German government makes a small financial contribution to any student organization which undertakes political education. Government money is given to the Korps and the Burschenschaften, which are completely right wing, but no money is given to the tiny left-wing Socialist German Students League. Even more than in America, German governmental circles find it convenient to confuse socialism with Communism. From observation, I would say that the only people in Germany who believe wholeheartedly in the democratic process as a form of government are socialists.

The students, lost in these giant universities, and in their separate homes or solitary lodgings, join groups: some for fun (jazz, photography), some for politics (Young Christian Democrats, Young Socialists), some for study or argument (English literature, current events), some for sports. In every university they also have compulsory student government called ASTA: 'compulsory' because all students must pay dues. ASTA manages the student restaurants, gets out a newspaper, arranges meetings, and discusses student problems with the academic authorities, but less than half the students vote in their own elections or bother with ASTA in any way. ASTA is immensely organized and bureaucratic. I mentioned this, seeing the mountains of mimeographed paper and the charts and the proliferating departments and officers in the headquarters of Berlin University's ASTA. 'After all, we are German,' said the young president, a charmer wearing a Russian-style astrakhan cap, large specs, and clearly endowed with a saving scepticism. Then there is a president of all German students, elected by the ASTA presidents of each German university. This gives you a hint of the organization-man aspect of German life.

I attended various seminars and lectures and found them more than depressing. Here is an example: a session of the Advanced English Seminar at Frankfurt University. One hundred and thirty students sat in tiers in a fine modern lecture room while their instructor talked to them about the works of John Steinbeck. The course was an analysis of the 'characterization, structure, plot and language' of *Tortilla Flat*, *The Grapes of Wrath*, *East of Eden*, and *Of Mice and Men*. This two-hour session was taken up with a discussion of the difference between 'plot' and 'story.' Eager students raised their hands and, speaking excellent English, babbled on about this matter, which seemed pointless to me, both as a writer and reader. No one mentioned the meaning of Steinbeck's novels. No one was concerned with Steinbeck's picture of the human condition, with understanding and sharing experience. No one commented on the furious moral indignation which drove Steinbeck to write his earlier books. At the end of the term, the students would know the names of all Steinbeck's characters and every detail of his plots and stories better than Steinbeck does, and that is all. The instructor looked like an American, with bow tie, crew cut, horn-rims; he behaved like an actor playing the part of a young American teacher. After class I asked him where he had learned to speak American. 'I learned in Germany,' he said. 'All I needed was the accent. So I went to the University of Chicago for a year and I got it.'

It was not my impression that the majority of students resented this intellectual sterility and doubted the value of their education. In any case, they cannot afford to dissent; a university degree is not a status symbol in Germany; it is essential to middle-class getting ahead. A postgraduate degree, which allows the lifelong title of Doctor, is better still. Observe that the Chancellor of Germany is called Doctor, and so is the manager of the Kempinski Hotel in Berlin. Young Germans want to get ahead. Power, nowadays, is wealth. A pretentious and patriotic young woman, rising fast in a Frankfurt publishing house, put it neatly: 'We must work hard, for ourselves and for Germany.' The university degree is a big step up on the ladder of success. In the universities, only five per cent of the students come from working-class homes: perhaps the working class is fortunate not to have its young shaped for so long in such old, tight, unhealthy moulds.

The cities were all different in atmosphere. Hamburg, the most different of all, is a port, and the outside world is somewhere near. The government of Hamburg is socialist, and so is the government of the province; perhaps because of this Hamburg is the home of that *Time*-like weekly, *Der Spiegel*, which for long has been the only effective opposition in Germany. It is odd that a weekly magazine, patterned on the gadfly side of *Time*, should take over the role of a political opposition.

By accident I met three students in Hamburg who fascinated me; they seemed like symbolic characters in a morality play. Johann was studying medicine, Hans was studying political science, and Trudi was studying law. Johann was very good-looking, fair-haired, blue-eyed, dressed in an English duffle coat and speaking slightly cockney English. He was so gay, outspoken, and unlike a German that I could not decipher him until he explained that his mother was Jewish, had fled Germany after a short prison term in the early Hitler days, and he had therefore been brought up in England until the age of twelve. We agreed, he and I, as the days passed, that the very best thing that could happen to Germans would be an early transplanting into some less authoritarian country, so that they got their first ideas in an open climate. Hans was a giant, looking rather like a Teutonic boy Abe Lincoln. He was also an oddball; he could not endure his father for good personal reasons and extended this dislike to the entire older generation, which severed his connection with traditional Germany and with traditional obedience. Moreover, he had had an enlightened history teacher in high school, and had thus really studied the Nazi era, ending by going to Belsen with some thousands of other young Germans, who went, he thought, largely out of curiosity, though some made the journey as an act of mourning. Hans was deeply impressed by what he had studied and by Belsen itself; he had learned to be a liberal on his own and meant to become a journalist when he finished his studies 'to tell people the truth so it can never happen again.'

Trudi, the law student, was a natural Hitler maiden.

We drank bad coffee in a cheap café in the red-light district. Horse steak was advertised on the wall, a jukebox played, the other customers occasionally erupted into drunken shouting. The boys and I found the place funny; Trudi thought it disgusting. The boys felt little esteem for the Adenauer government and all its works, and said so in detail. Trudi objected angrily; she did not consider it right to run down Germany, especially in front of a foreigner. Her reaction was typically German. I heard it often and could not understand it until a bright young journalist in Munich explained: Germans identify their government with their country; therefore any attack on the established political authority is unpatriotic. I believe this, and I think it weird and deadly. When Republicans used to foam at the mouth, if speaking of Franklin D. Roosevelt, neither they nor anybody else thought them traitors to America; they were recognized as Republicans.

Johann dismissed the girl's burst of nationalism by saying, 'She's old-fashioned.' He concluded all our remarks on Germany:

'In comparison with other democracies, Germany is still learning to crawl.'

Trudi fidgeted so much that we decided to move on. The boys suggested an espresso bar where we could get decent cappuccino coffee. Trudi did not want to go, saying, 'I hate to see German girls catching those oily Italians.'

'Would it be all right if they were catching Germans?'

'That is different,' said she.

To humour her, we stopped at the only student café in Hamburg, but there was no room to sit, and most of the benches were crowded with dark-skinned students, Arabs, Orientals, Africans. Trudi wrinkled her nose and said, 'You see, it is not a very nice place.'

West Berlin was a stunning surprise. I had not seen the city since the first winter after the war, when Berlin was a wilderness of jagged grey stone. From my reading, I imagined something like a fortified medieval town, cramped, crowded, stoical, hemmed in by the Wall. West Berlin has three airports and is a displeasingly spread-out city, ruinous in taxi fares. It is as garish as if the people had just struck oil, jammed with expensive cars and expensive shops, and the Berliners are not heroes of the front line: they love their hometown, make good money, like being newsworthy and important; and so they stay. There are material inducements as well: an automatic reduction of five per cent in income tax, a 'welcome gift' of $75 for moving to the city, a marriage grant of $750, repayable in ten years, with twenty-five per cent off for every child born in Berlin. And young men in Berlin are exempt from military conscription. These are all perfectly sound reasons for living in West Berlin, and it is high time we stopped being sentimental about the place. For political reasons it may be expedient or vital to keep free Berlin ticking busily, but to act as if it were the stronghold of our faith and the new Jerusalem is absolute rot. We should also stop calling it, in our idiotic slogan, 'the showroom of the West.' The West, whatever it is, is a lot better than this over-dramatized city.

Germans should not be so outraged by the Wall; they built similar walls everywhere in Europe not too long ago. It is a concentration-camp wall with thugs in guard towers ready to shoot their own people as they used to shoot others. The bus hostess, who was either declaiming on the brutality of the Communist East Germans or selling us postcards and colour slides, neglected to point out that for nearly seventeen years East Germans could escape quite easily to West Germany, and did so in millions. They had to come without portable possessions, but they did not arrive in a foreign land where they were unwanted and lonely. They emerged from the West Berlin undergound into the arms of their compatriots and within a short time were better off, materially, than they had ever been before. West Germany needs so many workers that it imports labour; refugees from East Germany get special consideration. They are not refugees, in the tragic meaning of that word; they are German citizens at home in another part of their country.

You see plenty of uniforms about the place: Russian soldiers in East Berlin, American soldiers in West Berlin; French and English troops are inconspicuous. *We* think the East Germans are puppets of Russia. *They* think the West Germans are puppets of America. What if the two German regimes are puppet masters themselves, and shrewdly run their own separate shows, profiting from the cold war and from two opposed gigantic sugar daddies?

Those West German young who do not regard Germany as the centre of the universe take a pretty detached view of the Wall and East Germany. They don't see how Germany can be reunited without war, and they do not want war. There has been one splendid change of heart in Germany. The great majority of the younger generation abhors militarism, armies, and uniforms. A pretentious young woman in Frankfurt amazed me by saying, 'Losing the war means losing East Germany and East Berlin. It is terrible. This is something our elders did without asking us. But we must accept. And make here fine.' It would have been a nobler sentiment if she had said 'starting the war,' but one should be grateful for small favours, such as recognition of cause and effect. A young sociologist at Frankfurt University who had studied in America on a Fulbright grant was blessed with the clearest mind I met. He was just and penetrating about America and used the same eyes on his own country. 'Ulbricht and Adenauer are the ones who prevent a solution. They need this quarrel to stay in power. We must recognize East Germany and the Polish frontier; you'll have to guarantee West Berlin. Eighteen years is long enough for a dangerous tug-of-war.'

East German refugee students, who get scholarships and are favoured sons, have emotional reasons for following the Christian Democrat party line. In West Berlin, the pink-cheeked president of the local chapter of Refugee Students from East Germany said that they didn't want an H-bomb war to reunify Germany. They realized this would be no use to them. But he foresaw a swap with Poland—give back East Poland and get back East Germany. He hadn't figured out why the Russians would part with their slice of Poland.

He wanted Germany to be proud, 'like America.' After the war, America (few speak of the Allies) held the Nürnberg Trials and created democracy here; 'they treated the Germans like children.' I hear this often, in various terms from a variety of students. We should apparently have shot the war criminals but not embarrassed the Germans with recorded trials. As for democracy, we ought somehow to have imposed it and not have imposed it. There must be a *German* democracy, he said, made by Germans and honouring German ways, traditions, and customs. *German* democracy is the battle cry of the serious fascists. Only crackpots paint swastikas on synagogues or meet in noisy Nazi style.

In Munich, the Prussian-born president of another student refugee organization said that 'a young German looks behind and sees fifty years of mistakes and atrocities. Better forget it and become a European. But De Gaulle says it will be a Europe of nations, so I have to remain a German. This *isn't* Germany—the other part is gone. We must get it back to be whole.' He is pro-military, Prussian still. He wants the H-bomb given to NATO, where German officers hold high rank. He believes that the government should have emergency powers to dismiss parliament and rule by decree. 'All our symbols were discredited by Hitler—our flag and our country. What is there for us to do? Most young people think of work and their own careers. The Hitler regime had a spiritual side; people were actively engaged. Now there is apathy. No one knows what democracy means; no one knows what Germany means.'

It is safe to generalize here: the conservative, the traditionalist, the authoritarian young want Germany to be reunited and powerful. The socialists, the democratically minded want to accept the present frontiers for the sake of peace on earth. That leaves the usual bulk of the uncommitted, the young who care about living their own lives quietly. The Federal Republic is the only homeland they know; they are not 'hurting for anything,' as American GIs used to say. The unification of Germany is not a subject that torments them.

Frankfurt is hideous, rebuilt, prosperous, and more bearable than Berlin. It is not pretending to be other than it is: business is better than usual, and a socialist regime is in power. I liked this city only because of a tiny seed, planted long ago by an inspired officer in the US Military Government. This seed is called 'Seminar für Politik,' and as far as I can see, it is the best legacy we left to Germany. The Germans copy all our materialism; here in a small clean building we left behind something of what we ought to mean. The seminar is free, in every way. Young people, most of whom earn their living by day, come here from six to eight o'clock in the evening and are encouraged, led, lured into thinking for themselves and asking the basic question of free men: *Why?* A woman who is wise, loving, and intellectually honest runs this school; she is a Catholic and a socialist, an interesting combination in Germany, where the government has been dominated by clerical reactionaries.

After listening to the young and their young teacher argue, question, learn about Nietzsche and determinism, we went off to a café, where I tried to get at something that puzzles me: the role of German women. There were six girls and two boys who invited themselves; it was a mistake to let the boys join us. Even these girls reacted largely in the traditional German way; they secede before the male. I suggested to them that there was something very wrong about German women, who, in my opinion, are the Arab women of the West. Since they bring up the children and manage the home, they must fatally instil into their offspring their own unquestioning respect for authority, beginning with father and going on inexorably to a ruler. How can there be hope for the inquiring mind and the free spirit if the women are such abject intellectual and moral slaves? The girls did not get too far with this question, disappointingly. The boys suggested it was fine for women to study and work until they had children; after that, their place was in the home. But one boy, on leave from military service, finally said, 'The worst thing for the young women is their old mothers'—their old mothers who forever teach blind obedience, handing on this sin from generation to generation.

A bit of that evening's conversation is revealing and worth reporting; and it must be emphasized that these young people were as near to our sort of free-wheeling young as one can find in Germany.

I asked, because I wanted to know, whether Germans had ever fought foreign or domestic tyrants for their own freedom. Or did they only fight non-Germans, on orders from above?

The second boy, an open-faced shipping clerk, explained. 'Germans think carefully before revolting. What is on this side, what is on that side? So they do not.'

'Do they think carefully before following a dictator?'

'But then they cannot protest for they would be killed.'

'They're killed fighting others, too.'

'There was 1848,' the clerk said hopefully. They all trot out 1848, hopefully. It is pitiful the way they cling to the most inept, inadequate, spineless, and brief revolution in Europe as their passport into democratic society. 'And at the time of the Peasants' Revolt, Martin Luther told them not. So they could not because the Catholic Church was against them.'

'If you mean,' said the girl medical student, with large spectacles and dimples, 'can it happen again in Germany, obeying the bad orders, then the answer is Yes.'

'But what is so wrong with us?' the clerk asked. 'Ten years after the war, we were already best friends with England and America. But if we want to be more left and freer, America will not like it.'

The university in Bonn is housed in a baroque palace, and the town is pretty, snug, and old between the hills and the Rhine. All travellers know the desperate feeling that one must quickly get out of a place, a country, and the irrational fear that one won't. Many people have this reaction to Germany; in Bonn, the capital of a great power, the sensation of being closed away became very strong. Yet Germans have an enviable free currency, and they journey in hordes all over Europe. Foreign newspapers arrive. Still the Germans, more than any other people I know, seem isolated in their country and in their Germanness. During Nazism, this was actually true; the claustrophobia persists.

Everywhere in Germany I had been asking the young about Jews; how did German students feel now, how did their elders feel? Few of them knew any Jews (there are some 25,000 left in Germany); and the subject is delicate: it becomes at once an attack on their nation and their parents. As for the elders, none would admit to having ever approved the murderous Nazi anti-Semitism, and practically everyone claimed to have helped Jews to escape to Brazil. A professor in Berlin said that there was no racial feeling whatsoever in Germany; on the contrary, the Germans fell over backwards to avoid all discrimination. He himself had just passed a Pakistani when he would have failed a German. 'But I said to myself, oh well, he is going back to his own country.'

Anti-Semitism has gone undergound; it is an illegal emotion. Anything that is disliked can be safely called Communist; Jewish, as a term of abuse, is reserved for private conversation or letters to the newspapers. Yet if you pry too hard, you get sharp reactions from Germans. The treatment of Negroes in the United States is cited to prove that we are no better than they were. And once I was told an instructive story by a Berlin editor; a group of hand-picked, simon-pure, democratic young Germans were sent on a trip to the United States. On every Greyhound bus, in every train, they heard anti-Semitic talk. They returned scandalized. Such talk can be answered by pointing out that the United States is not an ideal democracy, but there are plenty of unsleeping people who will never give up trying to improve it.

I held a private seminar in my hotel room in Bonn—four young people who talked all day. They were the editor of the Christian Democrat student newspaper; a medical student, son of a Lutheran pastor who had been jailed by the Nazis; a girl member of the Liberal Club; and the girl secretary of the German-Israel club, which has branches in every university. The German combination of excessive factual knowledge and illogic was never more wondrously displayed, but they were nice young people, muddled in heart and mind.

The medical student said, 'If you protest against authority here they say you are a fool or a Communist. My parents don't like it that I am so mixed in politics in the university because they have bad experiences of politics.'

This appears to be a universal rule: all the young are warned by their parents not to think or act politically—in short, to be sheep as their elders were, though of a different passive nature. 'We were punished once,' the elders say.

'We must discuss with Russia,' the medical student went on. 'We cannot keep this cold war up forever. But we have a problem here. Any boy who is Catholic must vote for the Christian Democrat party because the priest tells him to. We cannot have a democracy if priests tell people how to vote.'

This did not go down well with the editor, a member of that party. The argument meandered off into another one about birth control, which is against the law in Germany, the editor being in favour of forbidding birth-control information and the girl liberal protesting against this interference by the state in private life.

Most interesting was their talk of anti-Semitism. The medical student was impressed by the girl secretary of the German-Israel club. 'It is wonderful for a German to be doing this work,' he said, while the girl stiffened. He could not quite believe it though, and finally asked her if she had Jewish ancestors, which she did not; she is studying theology, to enter the Lutheran Church as a pastor. She said that she had noticed an increase in anti-Semitism among the older generation, though young people were pro-Israel or indifferent. However, a few weeks ago in the student restaurant, anti-Semitic tracts were distributed on all the tables; the culprits had not been found. She had visited Israel twice, before and after the Eichmann trial; she was studying Hebrew for her theology degree. 'We reach out the hand of friendship to the young Israelis but there is difficulty that they take it. The Herut party, which is anti-German, called us Germans enemies of humanity. And also one Israeli has one mind; you talk to another and he has another mind. It is very difficult if there is no general way.'

The editor had gone to Israel to report the Eichmann trial for his student magazine. He had 'a very interesting discussion with an Israeli girl. She suggested that Germany had become a ghetto for Germans.'

None of them knew how to take that, and they were startled by my laughter.

The girl theologian said, 'Ben Gurion told that he made the Eichmann trial to educate the young Israelis. They were different after it.'

'You mean they learned to be pro-German?' the medical student asked.

Probably the reason for the sensation of claustrophobia in Germany derives from just this: the incurable egocentricity of German thinking. Their inability to put themselves in the place of others, even briefly, is like being blind and deaf. It really is *Deutschland über Alles*; everything returns to them. There was a peculiar lack of curiosity among these young about other people outside Germany. And yet they talked to me with righteous indignation about bad treatment they had received in foreign countries: in a shop in Finland a woman had refused to serve one of them, in Denmark a waiter had been hostile, on and on. It was useless to explain that these countries had suffered abominably at the hands of Germans; these small slights were a trifling penalty for the history of their country. 'But we did nothing,' they would cry. 'We are innocent.' True, and yet, where is the imagination? This same line of reasoning applies to post-war Germany; what Germany endured during two years after the war was terrible. They never remind themselves of what others endured not only for two years after the war but during six and a half years of war. The very notion that a large part of the world has unhealed and unhealable wounds inflicted by Germany, and that there must be some punishment for crime, is an outrage to them. 'What have we to pay?' asked a budding young politican, president of the Munich Students Christian Democrat League. 'We are innocent.'

All Germany looks rebuilt and spotless, but much of this no doubt comfortable new construction is ugly; Munich is restored and lovely. You do find yourself observing that the best architecture seems to derive from the genius of others: pseudo-Greek, pseudo-French; the overall effect is prosperity and charm. Most Germans are overweight and dressed against the cold; in Munich they are more affable than in the other German cities.

Here I met a group of happy students, happy because they lived in a dormitory, boys and girls together, which they managed themselves. It was a tangible proof that the dormitory system is good; the students were not only pleased with their living conditions, but they had a chance to develop normal human relations and did not, as do almost all German students, solemnly call each other Herr and Fräulein, or treat each other with the caution that marked communal talk among other young people. These laughed freely, were frankly critical of their university and government, were not afraid to think and to speak, and had the habit of doing both. They are not taken in by the whitewashing of the past, but they are not interested in the past; the present concerns them. As one of them said, 'The only safe, approved subject for discussion now, in Germany, is anti-Communism.' They said that any dissent, any hostility to the powers that be was immediately branded as Communism; a German form of McCarthyism is growing, if not already here. They fear this, as a limit on their ability to make a really free country and be responsible citizens. Some students had predicted, with despair, that a Salazar-type dictatorship would be the next step in German history. These Munich students did not believe Germany would have an official dictator but do believe that their state is moving more and more to the right, with less liberty for the individual and increased censorship of the mind. They pointed out that America is envied for its wealth and power, nothing more.

Germany has certainly gobbled up the forms of our material-ism, but our two most valuable articles of export—the Declaration of Independence and the Bill of Rights—are unknown. Perhaps we no longer know much about them ourselves. In Bonn, the student editor had said, 'The young need somebody to show the way. There is no one. We have no elders.' That is a genuine cry of distress. Few German elders are fit to answer it. The new generation needs a New Germany; they can hardly expect the older generation to build democracy for them. But have they themselves the imagination and guts required to do the job?

Monkeys on the Roof

The moral of this tale is: look before you leap. On the other hand, people miss a great deal by being sensible. If *he'd* been sensible, Columbus would certainly not have sailed the ocean blue in fourteen hundred and ninety-two. Astronauts would stay on the ground instead of whizzing off in space capsules. As for me, I would be waking to the music of the telephone, in the damp, dark air of London; whereas I am woken by Vervet monkeys romping over the roof as the sun rises out of the Indian Ocean in a gold sky.

Disheartened by the cold, rainy English summer and by memories of too many cold winters, I rented a house, sight unseen, on the Kenya coast just north of Mombasa and just south of the Equator. That 'sight unseen' is not as reckless as it sounds. I knew this beach, a long wide strip of flour-white sand fringed with royal palms, and I had visited a few houses in the neighbourhood. These homes were comfortable and pretty, equipped with all modern conveniences; a charming suburb, I thought, which happens to be in Africa.

For myself, I'd have liked something more authentically African, on the slopes of Kilimanjaro or the highlands around Mount Kenya, but Carmen and Milagro were coming with me, since we cannot be parted, and they would not take readily to the untamed outdoors. The agent described this house as being on a slight rise above the Indian Ocean, a white bungalow surrounded by trees, covered in bougainvillaea, with a swimming pool. It seemed almost too civilized, but Carmen and Milagro would love it, and as soon as I got them settled I could journey into the greater excitements of the interior. Carmen and Milagro are officially my cook and maid, but actually they are a cross between maiden aunts and middle-aged daughters. Unlike me, they hold a steady, factual, low-keyed view of reality.

They were to travel out by ship while I flew to the United States and back in time to meet them when they docked at Mombasa. We parted at Tilbury in rain and joined again three weeks later under the fierce African sun. They were delighted to be here; and eager to get to our new home, where we could eat decently and lead a clean, well-regulated life. I explained that the outgoing tenant was still using our house, but never mind, we had plenty of shopping to do. The agent had informed me that I must provide crockery, cutlery, linen and kitchen utensils; all else that I required, he said, would be supplied.

We shopped ourselves blind. It is never heart-lifting to concentrate on garbage cans, pillow slips, knives, forks, etc., but there were compensations. Between the bath-towel store and the frying-pan emporium, one passed on the Mombasa streets a whole exotic world: Sikhs with their beards in hair nets; Indian ladies wearing saris, caste marks, and octagonal glasses; Muslim African women, enormous and coy, hidden except for their eyes in black rayon sheets; tattooed tribesmen loading vegetable trucks; memsahibs driving neat cars filled with groceries and blond children; bwanas in white shirts and shorts and long white socks, hurrying to their offices. Hand cars held up Mercedes-Benzes. Bicycles zoomed like flies. Little African girls, with proper black mantillas and clutched rosaries, jived gently outside the cathedral gate. And it is less dispiriting to hunt for an electric iron if you discover surprise mosques and Hindu temples on the way.

'What a tin can,' said Carmen—this being a Spanish expression which means bore, mess, imbecility—'to spend so much money on things the Señora will only want for a year!'

'It's worth it,' I said, 'to live in Africa. Besides, we've finished. No more shopping. All we have to do now is unpack.'

'Will these people be out there at our house?' Milagro asked.

'What people?'

'These people with black skins. Who are they?'

'They are Africans. This is their country.'

'You never told me they had black skins.'

'I find them noble,' Carmen said. 'They are poor but polite.'

'Consider that they may think your white skin as strange as you think their black skin, Milagro.'

'Really?'

'Really.'

Followed by a truck bearing thirteen pieces of luggage and a mountain of bundles and boxes, we drove four miles north of the city to our new residence. The agent, the departing tenant and I were to check the inventory, and then at last we would be at home in Africa.

The air was soft as feathers; the sky went up forever, water-blue and bright. The northern hemisphere would be entering autumn with the threat of winter to come. We revelled in late spring, and summer lay ahead. We were soaked with sun and hope; dreams were about to come true.

We left the paved road, bumped through a patch of high brush and saw our gateway, worn stone pillars with bougainvillaea arching over them. The drive rapidly turned into a dry creek bed, rutted and strewn with boulders. A romantic wilderness spread around us; purple, scarlet and pink blossoms, tropical trees— doum palm, wild almond, Mbambakafi, Uganda flame, cork— and high tawny grass. The drive ended at a cluster of white buildings: a shed garage with a corrugated tin roof, a guesthouse like a child's overgrown playhouse; the main bungalow, small, with odd pillars, a wide stone-paved porch, a red-tiled roof; and an oblong box of a house for African servants. Surrounding this congeries was what had once been a lawn, now a desert of sand and weed, ornamented with an old bicycle tyre and rusted cans.

The two Englishmen and I attacked the inventory. The outgoing tenant watched my face with amusement; I was past speech. 'Four wrought-iron bedsteads,' the agent read from his list. The previous tenant indicated four ancient black army cots. 'Eight feather pillows,' said the agent, and eight mildewed dirty lumpy objects were produced. 'One silk dressing-table cover'; after some search and discussion we unearthed a faded, stained piece of rayon, formerly blue and patterned with revolting birds. 'Six rugs,' said the agent, and we examined a weird assortment of unrelated but equally nasty old spotted carpets and mats.

The furniture was scarred dull-brown wood of a style suitable to country railroad stations or abandoned government offices. The walls had been painted long ago in pastel shades, different on every wall. Lamp brackets and chandeliers of dingy iron lent an extra touch of squalor. And over all there was a fur of dirt, or a faint gloss, as of grease.

The agent read briskly through his list, behaving as if this were a normal house to rent for a high price to an innocent stranger. In explanation or excuse, the outgoing tenant remarked that he was on his last post in Africa, and had lived here for only a few months. 'The swimming pool?' I asked. We walked across the non-lawn and looked down at a scabrous cement pit from which green water was slowly oozing. Several frogs were contented there, but many crabs had died in it.

The men said goodbye and drove away. Carmen and Milagro and I stood silent on the porch, three Ruths in ghastly alien corn.

'The view is lovely,' I said, though I could not raise my voice above a whisper. And it is, more South Seas than African, the shining sea, layered sapphire and aquamarine, the pencil line of surf over the reef, the white sand glimpsed through palms.

'Yes, Señora.'

'The weather is lovely.'

'Yes, Señora.'

'We'll have to fix it up,' I said desperately. 'There isn't anything else to do.'

'It is *not* a serpent,' I said. 'It is a sort of caterpillar.' To prove the point, I picked the thing up and threw it out the window. It was caterpillar shape, about ten inches long, covered in gleaming black armour, with a thousand soft coral pink feet that waved as if moved by wind.

'The Señora is brave,' said Milagro.

'Nonsense,' I said, highly pleased with myself. By now I was somewhat confused in mind and not at all sure who I was. I was playing a mixed role, part pioneer woman in a covered wagon, part the boy who stood on the burning deck, and part Simon Legree. The Simon Legree angle came out during the day when I harried the seven painters, the four citizens with pickaxes who were churning up the non-lawn, the Indian carpenters, and any other stray experts who arrived to repair our house. The pioneer woman took over when it was a question of local wildlife, notably the creeping, crawling, flying varieties. As for the boy who stood on the burning deck, I feared I would soon get a bulldog jaw from that heroic pretence. It occurred to me that I might add Pharaoh, building his pyramid, to my other fake personalities.

Milagro and Carmen were not acting at all; they were plainly overcome with horror at our establishment and Africa in general. They looked the way they did nowadays, haggard, never seen without a broom or mop or scrubbing brush or dust cloth. I looked the way I did, wild-eyed, wearing an expression of semi-controlled hysteria, grasping a shopping list and a tape measure, with a pencil and glasses somehow latched in my hair.

'There is no stove,' Carmen announced. 'It belonged to those who have left. They sent for it.'

'I'll get one tomorrow. Milagro, do hold the end of the tape.' I was measuring the scruffy black floor. It seemed too optimistic to believe that we would ever have clean white walls and something to cover this foul cement.

'There is no hot water in the kitchen. Has the Señora noticed?'

'Nor in the laundry either,' Milagro said, kneeling over the tape measure. 'Shoo!' she suddenly shouted.

Carmen and I jumped; we were all fairly jumpy anyhow. I was prepared for a black mamba, but it appeared Milagro was addressing two lizards who were hunting on the wall beside her.

'Filthy beasts,' she said with hatred. 'Have you ever before lived in a house without ceilings, Señora? What sort of country is this? Those filthy beasts and their vile little oily sausages everywhere.'

'They are good beasts, they eat insects,' I said distractedly. 'Did the plumber come?'

'No.'

'The electrician?'

'No.'

'If only we had a telephone,' I said. 'It might go faster.'

'If only we had ceilings,' Milagro said. 'If only we had a stove,' Carmen said.

'Cheer up. Let's eat sandwiches on the porch and look at the stars.'

So we sat in a row on the steps because the chipped porch furniture was being repainted. And munched and contemplated the heavens, which are of an inconceivable size, brilliance and grandeur. I began to feel no bigger than an ant, and happy. Though life definitely reached a nadir about every forty-five minutes, if we could survive each day, the night sky was reward and consolation.

'That's Jupiter,' I said, on the off-chance. 'And that's Orion's Belt and that's the Southern Cross.'

What did it matter? There they were in all their glory, millions of blazing lights in the smooth black night. It was bliss to have eyes to see them.

'But *where* is Mr Shaafi?' And who is he? I thought. The Scarlet Pimpernel amongst Africans. Every day I drove to this gasoline station to find Mr Shaafi. In vain.

'He come early, he going now. You want petrol, Memsahib?'

'No, no. I want Mr Shaafi. Did you tell him I needed twenty tons of black earth to make my lawn?'

'I tell him.'

'What did he say?'

'He no say nothing.'

'This place is infested with monkeys,' Carmen said.

'Really? Where? I love monkeys.'

'Everywhere. They sit and watch. They are very dangerous.'

'Oh, no, they're not. You couldn't catch one if you tried. Besides, I haven't seen any.'

But Carmen was right. They must have been off on a visit; in any case they returned at dawn and leaped and gambolled over the roofs. They sound like elephants on the tiles. They swing merrily from the trees and sit on top of the garage, as on a grandstand, to enjoy the sights. We have rented a monkey playground, and that is the finest feature of our estate.

'But Mr Johnson promised he'd have six bags of Portuguese grass here for me today.'

'He forgot maybe.'

'When will he be back?'

'I doan know. Tomorrow. Yesterday.'

'Oh *Lord*. Will you remind him about that grass? *Please*. I must get it planted before the rains.'

'I tell him if he coming. Maybe he forget some more.'

'Señora, Joseph has cut off his finger with his big knife!'

Joseph is the gardener; we are learning his trade together, the blind leading the blind. He had been whacking at the jungle around us (an anti-snake drive) with a panga, the huge knife that is an African's tool and weapon. Now Joseph appeared, tall, with a bony, sad, unmoving face. Blood dripped from his hand. He had cut his forefinger deeply, but not cut it off. I got iodine and bandages.

'Does it hurt, Joseph?'

Without batting an eyelid as I doused iodine on the wound, Joseph said, 'Yes.'

I had a new role: the settler in the bush, practicing medicine on the trustful natives. Before breakfast every morning I changed Joseph's bandage, and the cut healed nicely, and Joseph treats me with the respect due a qualified doctor.

*

The noise that waked me in the night sounded like all the souls in hell, and I knew Carmen and Milagro would be in a panic. I was too tired for panic and also too stunned by these deafening wails. Lights flashed on in the main bungalow; I had moved to the guesthouse. The dreadful screaming sounds went on and on until I realized that we were now infested with bush babies. These big-eyed, nocturnal creatures are the size of a newborn kitten and have voices that would fit a rhino in pain. Using their monkeyish tails for security, they sit in the trees, drunk or neurotic, and howl their heads off harmlessly. Our cup was really running over. The delightful monkeys woke us at dawn and the delightful bush babies would keep us awake all night. If my hair had not been turning orange in the sun, it would have turned white.

'I am sick of them!' I shouted at the top of my lungs. 'Sick of them all! What do they think they're doing!'

'The Señora never had such a bad temper in London,' Milagro said disapprovingly.

I was staring at my sumptuous new mosquito net, the size of a tent. It hung gracefully two feet off the floor.

'Three trips to Mombasa to order and collect these nets,' I thundered at Milagro. 'And twice to get the frames. And once to bring the accursed carpenter here to hang them. Are they insane?'

'Mine lies all over the floor,' Milagro observed. 'And Carmen's hangs half on the floor and half in the air.'

'Can't any African or any Indian or any European ever get one thing right, just once?'

'No,' said Milagro.

'I'm going swimming,' I announced, as one might say I am going to get sozzled. The sea is just down the steps past the non-pool and along a short sandy path. Sometimes there are fishermen on this part of the beach; usually it is empty. I waded into the satin sea and swam out where the water was cooler and floated with my eyes closed, and mosquito nets did not matter.

None of it mattered. I would take the afternoon off and at low tide go goggling on the hotel boat, a shabby flat-bottomed affair which put-puts out towards the reef and anchors over the coral cities. The hotel, large, comfy, completely English in style, is ten minutes' walk down the beach from us; and one of its tourist attractions is this ancient tub which carries swimmers out to see the underwater world.

Yussuf, a wiry little African in a fez, knows the ocean floor as I now know all the hardware stores in Mombasa. We communicate by signs because my Swahili is limited to valuable phrases such as, 'Burn that rubbish,' 'No, no, plant the grass here,' 'Do not paint that, paint this.' Yussuf swims like a barracuda and takes me always to my favourite mountain range of brain coral. I do not shoot fish nor dive down and muck about in their private territory. Live and let live is the rule. I swim quietly and watch the enthralling mysterious marine society, and the great landscapes of the sea; and for two hours there is no other life, and the mind is cleaned of the follies of every day.

'The Señora is very rare,' Milagro remarked. 'Imagine being made so cheerful by fish.'

Then the rains came. The air did not move all day and we gasped inside a hot steel box. When the skies opened, water poured through our roofs where the joyful monkeys had cracked the tiles. Insects spawned in their millions, different loathsome breeds each night. Carmen and Milagro would never switch on a lamp. After endurance had been stretched like a rubber band, and I thought we had best drift out to sea and drown or catch the next plane for Alaska, bats invaded us. We hardly spoke, but went grimly on with the endless job of housemaking, though none of us had any idea why we were doing it, and who cared whether there were curtains or whether they were the same length, or whether the new stove worked or exploded, or whether we lived or died. I kept saying, though with doubt, that this could not last, it was all a mistake, and would pass. Shining with sweat, for one streamed sweat like tears if one moved, Carmen and Milagro looked at me in silent accusation. I felt like a monster; I had led them here and we would obviously leave our whitened bones in this suburb.

Driven beyond herself by the weather and the swarming insects, Milagro cried out, 'Where are we? We are alone in the middle of Africa!'

'We are not in the middle,' I said, in a furiously reasonable voice. 'We are at the edge. There is the ocean. And if you would take courage and walk twenty yards from this house you would see lights through the trees. People live here. People have lived here for years.'

'They are mad,' Milagro said.

'Carmen! Milagro! The wind has come back!' I rushed for the compass which stays in my safari kit along with the tyre gauge. We stood on the green beginnings of our lawn while I got the bearings of the wind. 'Northeast,' I said. 'It's the good monsoon. We'll be able to breathe again.'

And indeed we can. This beautiful unlikely country has now reverted to Eden. A cool breeze blows, it is hot in the sun, fresh in the shade, and the nights are like velvet if you wear the velvet side next to your skin. And the interminable idiot task is finished: out of a shambles we have made a home. It is comfortable and astonishingly pretty, all white with clear-coloured cottons—lime green, yellow, cherry red—in the different rooms. We are sufficiently acclimatized to take defects in our stride; as people here never tire of saying, if you are a perfectionist in Africa you go crazy. Milagro has come to terms (hostile) with the lizards; Carmen still fights the wasps who build their nests even in curtains, but she fights them confidently as though wrestling with inferiors; and Joseph and I are launched on tree pruning, a new passion. I am no great shakes with a panga as yet, but mean to get there. Suburb for suburb, I would not change this African one for any other. Milagro smiles, and Carmen has bought a bathing suit.

Spiral to a Gun

The St Louis Municipal Courts Building was finished in 1911 and must have seemed the last word in Palaces of Justice at the time. Made of grey stone, it is three very high storeys high, adorned with carved wreaths around impressive windows, a sweeping front stairway, slabs of Corinthian columns, and two large, handsome granite ladies, in 1900 hairdos and draperies, lounging on the roof beside an outsize flowerpot which sprouts granite flames. Except for Juvenile offenders and Federal offences, all the law violation of the city—from parking tickets to murder—is brought to judgement inside this one building.

On weekday mornings, the wide corridors of the first floor resemble a bus station, strewn with candy wrappers, paper cups, and cigarette butts, and crowded with restless people. These are the clientele of the Police Courts (maximum punishment, three months in the workhouse and $500 fine) and the Courts of Criminal Correction (maximum punishment, one year in the City jail and $1,000 fine). On the third floor, in suitable quiet and decorum, the Circuit Courts handle felonies (punishment, from two years in the state penitentiary to death).

The personnel of the courts is an intimate, practically permanent group; Judges are addressed as Judge, everyone else by first names. It is pleasing to hear a Judge call a Special Assistant Circuit Attorney 'Buster,' during a trial recess. No one can make a fortune here; driving ambition would be pointless; no one is worked to ulcers in this unhurried atmosphere; and no one is bored with his job. If you are on the right side of the law, the Municipal Courts Building is singularly agreeable. To an outsider, constant dealing with crime and punishment would seem melancholy and finally disgusting. It is not. Crime, here, has a face and a story, and human behaviour is still the most fascinating subject on earth. Crime, like war, strips off everyday camouflage. In these courtrooms you get a full view of the basement of our society and the basement life that produces criminals. No one could be bored with that, though attitudes to the work vary.

The majority of officials see their function and duty as punishment: catch and convict, and the heavier the punishment the better; keep the misfits out of circulation as long as possible and protect the law-abiding. The minority cling to a concern for individuals and the tired but humane belief in a second chance. Nobody talks of justice, a condition not to be obtained here below. The best that men of goodwill and sensitive conscience can aim for is the limiting of injustice.

St Louis is the tenth-largest city in the United States and a steady, settled sort of place. The law-abiding population is much flaunted and poverty stays largely out of sight, on side streets. Crime seems not only dangerous in this solid middle-class setting, but abnormal. Crime may be expected in flashy cities like New York or Chicago or Los Angeles but it is a shock, here, to feel nervous about walking in the parks or on the streets after dark. St Louisans read in their papers that major crimes—murder, rape, robbery, assault—have increased in their town by eight per cent in 1965; and they are alarmed and indignant. Like all other urban Americans.

The Deputy Sheriffs are old men with a tendency to wear their stomachs over their belts. One of these shouts a name. A door to the left of the Judge's dais opens and a man, watching his feet, walks down a few steps and is nudged into place, before and below the Judge. The man is dressed however he was when arrested. These are the criminals who have pleaded guilty; none of them are advertisements for the affluent society. Too poor to pay a bondsman's fee and buy liberty until the Judge decides their fate, too poor to hire a lawyer, they have been locked in the City Jail until this moment. The sentencing. If it please Your Honour, says an Assistant Circuit Attorney, and recites the man's crime and vital statistics, including any previous convictions. The man waits; he has already waited for two months in the cells down the street. He is a Negro, the poorest of the poor. Crime is a failure too, beginning with the first one, which leads inevitably to the others. Who wants to employ an unskilled Negro with a prison record? There are more than enough unskilled and unblemished Negroes.

It goes briskly now; these confessed criminals are the delight of the police, the ease of the Circuit Attorney's Office. This Judge is a kind man; a local newspaper, when it has nothing better to do, howls at him for being too generous with paroles. The criminal is twenty-three years old, thin, of medium height, shabby, his skin a lifeless soot colour. He has been in the penitentiary almost steadily since he was eighteen; he is a hopelessly incompetent, small-time burglar. He never tried for a big haul and he got nothing except two different prison terms and, in between, ninety days in the workhouse for carrying a concealed weapon. He has been caught for the third time. He pleaded guilty and asked to be sent to the Federal Hospital for Narcotic Addicts. The Federal Hospital, however, is full and, besides, not eager for felons.

The Judge says regretfully that his request has been turned down and he will, instead, be sentenced to seven years in the penitentiary. The man cries out, 'Seven years!' The cry becomes a choking sort of gasp; then he is sobbing, 'Seven years, seven years.' The Judge says he is sorry and the Deputy Sheriff hustles the man back the way he came. He was the only man, in a month, who showed emotion when the final words of the sentence were pronounced. Most of them seem too dazed to understand. All courtrooms have a curious air of unreality; the very rules of law prevent people from speaking out about real life.

An elderly white man, a rarity because he is white, shuffles in; he is fifty-two and was arrested after an accident caused by his drunken driving. Searching his car, the police found two guns and a knife. The man has been arrested five times before, for drunkenness, gambling, and disturbing the peace; but never jailed. He is a steady worker and keeps saying this: years and years at the same job, married, with one child. Why did he have that collection of weapons? He mumbles incoherently about taking them to a friend, didn't know they were in the car. He is given fifty days in the workhouse, but the sentence is suspended, and he goes free on probation.

Now it is the Court of Criminal Correction: a Negro is in the witness chair, accused of stealing three shirts from a shop in a slum street. His face is ravaged, cut in black stone; his body is not as old as his face. The prosecuting Attorney says this man has 'numerous convictions.' The Judge asks, 'Did you threaten to kill him?' indicating the shop owner, a small, puffy white man with glasses. 'I didn't have no weapon,' the Negro says. Who would threaten to kill without a gun? He needs a new shirt badly.

Three Negro boys are on trial in a Circuit Court for attempted burglary. The police say they were trying to tunnel their way through a brick wall into a supermarket. The crimes often sound dotty, being the handiwork of pea-brains. These boys had enough money to pay a bondsman so they came into court free, neat, and clean; they could also hire a lawyer. The police on the beat keep a mistrustful eye on Negroes. They arrest fast, but they are not adequately trained to collect the sort of evidence that stands up infallibly in court. The defence lawyer is a Negro and very talented. The jury is not convinced by the police evidence and returns a verdict of Not Guilty. If nothing else is clear, it is clear that money makes a big difference. All men are equal before the law but some are more equal than others. A man is a lot more equal if he walks into court from the street, not the City Jail, wearing a clean shirt and a pressed suit, with a good lawyer by his side.

Behind the scenes, the Parole Office is more revealing than the courts, where desperation and muddle and humanity are smoothed out into fancy questions and incomplete answers: 'Were you in close proximity to the accused at the time of the incident?' 'Prior to this incident, were any words spoken to you by the accused?' In the Parole Office a cheerful young Negro is reporting to a new, sympathetic, young white Parole Officer. They chat inside a glass cubicle; it was rather like a friendly consultation between patient and family physician. The Negro had been convicted of burglary, nothing much; another case of stealing from need. Now, free on parole, he has miraculously found a job at $40 a week, for a thirty-hour week, and can spend $20 of his wages on fun, and it is gilded heaven after Alabama, his home state. He goes bowling, has a few beers, takes in the movie shows, knows a girl: bliss. 'There's very little sign of the criminal mentality around here,' I suggest. 'Oh no,' says the young Parole Officer. 'They're just uneducated and dumb and unlucky, most of them. They're pretty nice people.'

A white boy checks in now, accompanied by his mother, recently widowed, and beside herself with anxiety—the boy has had another run-in with the police. The boy is nineteen, with rimless glasses and a weak chin, a dull boy, 'a good boy,' his mother insists. But he drinks beer in a tavern and 'somebody says something' and he gets fighting mad. He is on parole from a conviction for assault; he attacked another boy with a tyre tool. To look at him, you would not think he would attempt to beat up a rabbit. 'The police see us sitting around and they just pick us up,' the boy says, without rancour. This happens steadily to Negroes, apparently also to poor whites. 'There's nothing to do in our neighbourhood,' the boy says, trying to explain himself and the emptiness of his life. He worked as a printer's apprentice but was fired after his conviction; only two boys in his set have jobs. He dropped out of high school after two years: 'I just never could get interested in books.' The boy is suffering from boredom as if from infantile paralysis. 'What do you *want* to do?' I ask. He'll only have to get beery drunk once more and assault someone else and he's off to the penitentiary. 'I've never really thought about it,' the boy says.

That month, the children were rapists, not the adults. In the Juvenile Court, the Judge was hearing the case of a thirteen-year-old girl raped by five boys, two of whom were under sixteen and three of whom had just passed seventeen and were therefore beyond the jurisdiction of this court. The girl was skinny, shamed, wearing ill-assorted, outgrown clothes; the boys were resplendent in their uniforms of black felt hats, three-quarter-length black leather coats, black trousers, and shoes. She knew all these boys. The story was odious but puzzling; it was as if kids' street games had turned into this. Like their elders, the children are nocturnal and nomadic. The girl had been twenty blocks from her home at ten at night, presumably to meet one of the boys, her steady. She was not a virgin before the mass assault.

The scene of this orgy for babies was the tenth-floor corridor of a giant apartment block which the state built, as slum clearance. A housing project. This one is a cold, inhuman congeries of buildings that look like factories, where the poor are packed together to form the densest population of the city. The crime rate there is also the highest. It must have been a fairly noisy event but no one opened a door into that corridor, no one looked out or called the police. The poor live in these apartments as if barricaded inside separate caves, hiding from wild animals. Slum clearance, which simply produced bigger slums, is a hideous joke; everyone knows this, yet the great slums of the future are still planned and erected.

The juvenile rapists were sentenced to reform school; the older ones went free because the girl's mother could not bear to prosecute them in public at the Municipal Courts. The two boys, led off to the detention wing, asked about their leather coats: could they send them home, would they be safe, were they going to lose them? The coats were all their status in the world. Later, waiting in a little room for a different sort of uniform, they put their heads down on a table and looked like scared children.

The Juvenile Court is a heartbreak place, for here the pitiful, usually fatherless families start to crack up, and the children are marked with their first official brand as failures. A Negro woman, helplessly weeping, agrees that her son must be sent away to reform school; he isn't a criminal yet, he is a rebel; she cannot control him. The boy, aged fourteen, gets up from his chair, kisses her quickly and gently on the cheek, pats her shoulder, and goes through the door which is a door to jail, head high. Another woman, screaming with tears, follows her daughter to that door which shuts in her face. *'No! No!* You ain't gonna take my daughter! I wants my daughter! I needs my daughter! What you tryin' to do, take all my chillrun away from me! I loves my chillrun! I needs my chillrun!' This is the worst; there is no gleam of light here, it is pure tragedy.

'Yes, these people got a lot of love,' says the young Negro Juvenile Officer. He has left that messy, passionate, menaced basement life far behind. He is well integrated into the American Way of Life. 'But love isn't enough.'

In the adult courts, even in murder cases, one has glimpses of the basement life which are not all folly and misery, mistakes and hardship. There are hints of indomitable gaiety; people living on the bottom of the world are still so alive that they make joy for themselves, out of nothing, on the spur of the moment. There are hints, too, of a prevailing generosity; the impoverished are always lending money, regardless of risk. And in these families, amputated by poverty, brothers and sisters are loyal to each other, and the mother loves unquestioningly. Their friendships are astounding too, as if each man had a private little country made up of his friends. Their lives are nightmares of insecurity, and yet they have saved some human qualities which are not so readily found on the comfortable upper storeys of our society; enviable human qualities. You catch sight of these, briefly, even in murder trials.

A quite beautiful Negro woman, with small, elegant features and a Nefertiti neck, had been giving a party. Her brother-in-law dropped in, bringing a friend of his; a woman neighbour came along bringing a chum of hers. It was open-house hospitality, one of the most endearing aspects of basement life; strangers are welcome. There was music from the radio to dance to; the men went out and borrowed money to buy whiskey and beer; the unplanned party breezed on happily into the small hours. The beautiful woman, a widow, had an ex-lover, a bad type who had molested her daughter. She denounced him to the police for that, but he was now out of jail and had threatened her. She bought a rifle and told her troubles to her brother-in-law, a handsome bus driver studying to become a preacher. At 2.30 in the morning, the ex-lover arived, drunk, to crash the impromptu party.

'He talked in a rough tone like he was ready to take on anybody,' said the bus driver, on the witness stand. Presently, the ex-lover put his hand in his pocket, a fatal gesture; it means reaching for a gun. The bus driver jumped him; they fought in the kitchen; the bus driver was winning, the ex-lover was flat on the floor, his shoulders held down. Suddenly there were three shots, the ex-lover was dead, and panic set in. If guns were not as available as transistor radios, there would have been no death that night. There would have been a fight, and an unwanted drunk would have been kicked out of the house.

Now, in a Circuit Court, the bus driver's companion is accused of this murder and has signed a confession but retracted it. He had never seen the beautiful woman and the ex-lover before that night; he came to the party with the bus driver, his best friend, his hero. The accused was a slow, simple fellow, a dutiful wage earner, with not so much as a parking ticket against his name. At the last minute his family hired a lawyer, but the lawyer could get no sensible story from his client. Bewildered and outraged by this sheep led to the slaughter, the lawyer asked, 'Why did you sign that confession?' It was indeed baffling. The beautiful woman had confessed too, but the police made no record of her confession and she later denied it. Yet she was the obvious suspect; she alone had cause to hate and fear her ex-lover. 'The police tell me she was having a heart attack so I better sign up and stop all the trouble.' He was sentenced to two years in the penitentiary for manslaughter; the jury was uneasy about the case, and allotted the minimum punishment. It turned out that the murdered ex-lover had no gun in his pocket anyhow, but who was to know?

This murder was even more meaningless. A very thin small

young Negro sits in the chair of the accused; he is shrunken inside a cheap suit. The light and space and voices of the courtroom dazzle him. He has been sitting in a cell in the City Jail for eleven long months, waiting for his trial. An essential witness vanished, so the trial was delayed. The accused of course could not pay a bondsman's fee and thus buy his last months of freedom. Nearly a year ago, in a slum coffee shop at four in the morning, he shot and killed another young man; after which he ran to his girl friend's house and wept. She hid the gun under her bed and they took a taxi to his sister's house. The sister and a neighbour advised that he call the police; it was not a hard case for the cops. The law is not obliged to make sense of a crime, nor does it try.

The first witness for the state was the girl friend, now nineteen years old. At sixteen she and the youth James became something, it is not clear what, because the accused is a homosexual. In the opinion of the detectives and lawyers, this was a crime of passion but the wrong way round. The murdered man was James's lover, jealous of the girl and more jealous of a new boy who was about to replace him. The victim, properly, should have done the shooting. If there is a grain of reason in it, one must assume that James feared this and shot first.

The girl friend, pot-faced, homely, wearing a bandana and a grimy coat, took the oath and settled in the witness chair. She had not seen James since the night of the murder. For a moment, the lawyers huddled in consultation with the Judge; everyone forgot these two. Unnoticed by the white grown-ups, they smiled at each other across the well of the court, smiled with such warmth and gentleness and love as one rarely sees anywhere. Then the white grown-ups took over again. The girl's face went blank; she answered in monosyllables; she seemed nearly half-witted in her stupidity; she didn't want to send this frail idiotic boy to prison.

The missing witness had been found; he was apparently the new love and the cause of the tragedy. He was an impish coffee-coloured boy, whom the police located at last because, in a gay mood, tight as a tick, he stole a Greyhound bus in Arkansas and drove it straight into a wall. The Arkansas police extradited him.

When the news of this subsidiary crime came out, everyone in court laughed; so did he. 'Are you a homosexual?' the State's Attorney asked. 'Not that I know of.'

Without a gun, this grotesque story would have finished in a tiff, insults, pique, a general change of partners, and they would have forgotten there was anything to tiff about, and gone on their obscure, harmless way. Instead one young man is dead and James was sentenced to twenty years in the penitentiary which, for all practical purposes, is the end of that mixed-up life.

These are samples of the major crimes: murder, rape, robbery, assault. And samples of the criminals. They do not look very impressive, supposing that a criminal has some ability in his work. They look like people whose lives have been a downward spiral since childhood. 'We never get any clever people in here,' said the Circuit Attorney. Statistics appear to bear out the observation of eye and ear, for in 1965 only 36.8 per cent of all crimes in St Louis were solved; and this is approximately the national average. The uncaught 63.2 per cent of criminals must be the more competent and deadly: the psychotic killers; the vandals whose lust is to destroy rather than steal, or destroy what they cannot steal; the sadists who beat their victims as much for that pleasure as for the stolen wallet; the rapists; the successful robbers.

The basement of our society is unfit for human habitation, a disgrace to the world's richest nation, and moreover it is victimized. The criminals who are spawned there prey first on their neighbours, the law-abiding poor. Aside from being unlivable, a disgrace and a menace, our national basement is also an armoury. It begins to seem that everyone in it is armed with a gun and fear of the other man's gun.

Missouri is one of the seven states in the Union that forbid the purchase of handguns without a police permit. But anyone can buy a gun across the river in Illinois, or order a dozen by mail, or pick up a secondhand weapon on a dingy street corner for $5 if he is known in the neighbourhood. Testifying on a proposed (but shelved) Federal Firearms Act before a Senate Subcommittee, the chief law-enforcement officers from every crime-ridden city in America stated that the growing volume and violence of crime are *directly* related to our free-for-all system of obtaining weapons. No other civilized Western democracy indulges in such insanity; nowhere else can lethal weapons be acquired as easily as tennis rackets. But we've always been hipped on being biggest and best, so perhaps it is not surprising that we also have the biggest and best slums, the biggest and best private armaments, and the biggest and best crime.

A Tale of Two Wars

The United States Government is waging two wars at once: the war on communism in Vietnam and the war on poverty in the US.

In the summer and autumn of 1964, when Mr Johnson was campaigning for election as President in his own right, he spoke loudly and clearly about the war in Vietnam. On 29 August, 1964, he said: 'I have had advice to load our planes with bombs and to drop them on certain areas that I think would enlarge the war and result in committing a good many American boys to fighting a war that I think ought to be fought by the boys of Asia to help protect their own land. And for that reason I haven't chosen to enlarge the war.'

On 25 September, 1964, he said: 'There are those that say you ought to go north and drop bombs, to try to wipe out the supply lines, and they think that would escalate the war. We don't want our American boys to do the fighting for Asian boys. We don't want to get involved in a nation with 700 million people and get tied down in a land war in Asia.'

Again on 21 October, 1964, President Johnson said: 'We are not going to send American boys nine or ten thousand miles away from home to do what Asian boys ought to be doing for themselves.'

The American electorate had reason to believe that Mr Johnson would disentangle us from a remote Asian conflict which we slid into, almost secretively, not knowing why or caring, until it started to eat American lives. The Republican candidate, Senator Goldwater, terrified the electorate by proposing to 'defoliate the trees' in Vietnam. President Johnson was overwhelmingly the nation's choice, as a man of peace.

But he was also enthusiastically chosen as commander-in-chief for an entirely different war: the war on American poverty. Even before his presidential campaign, Mr Johnson spoke ringingly of his intention to fight that good war to a victorious end: 'For the first time in our history it is possible to conquer poverty.' In his first State of the Union message, as the newly elected President, he said, 'But we are only at the beginning of the road to the Great Society. Ahead now is the summit where freedom from the wants of the body can help fulfil the needs of the spirit.'

Splendid words, in spite of some embarrassed unease about the code name for this Administration. President Kennedy's 'New Frontier' was a signpost title, showing where we might try to go. 'The Great Society' sounded a bit like a premature boast. Still, you cannot build a great society on top of a crushed, impoverished minority, and everyone would like to live in a great society. Declaring war on American poverty and declaring distaste for war in Vietnam was a brilliant vote-getting combination.

We hear less and less ringingly about the war on poverty and ever more fervently about the war on communism. Patriotic 'nu-speak' and 'double-think' trumpet us on to stand fast or defend the US or honour our commitments or save the world from communism in Vietnam. The young dead Americans, whom we believed were never going to Vietnam, are used to justify sending more young draftees to this abominable war. When the President has time to remember the war on poverty, he talks of it in sorrowing tones. Evidently, the President and his advisers have decided that it is more vital to our national interests to destroy communism in a poverty-ridden country 10,000 miles from our shores than to destroy poverty within the US.

*

We lisp in numbers, in the US. We are deluged by ample, often mysterious statistics. A few comparative statistics on the two wars are enlightening. Like many in this country, I have come to regard statistics with doubt and merely as a hint of the probable shape of fact. For instance: the estimated population of South Vietnam is 16,000,000, and we are supposedly saving them from communism. According to President Johnson, the estimated number of Americans living 'below the poverty line' is 34,000,000 and we are supposedly saving them from another form of slavery.

It is easy to define the South Vietnamese: they are the unfortunate people who live there. The poverty line in the US is defined as follows: a family of four living on $3,015 per year or less. Bureaucracy cannot function without such arbitrary rules. Poverty goes up or down at the rate of $500 per member of family. A single adult with an annual income of $1,515 should then be a poverty statistic. But if such a person has $20 more a year, bureaucracy would not consider him poor, though he would rightly know he was. In any case, these figures have a dream quality; the poor are much poorer than the law allows.

No one has explained how the census of the poverty line was taken. The eye can receive impressions but not concoct statistics: 34,000,000 would seem a minimum figure. This number paints no picture for the imagination. Then try to imagine the entire combined populations of Tokyo, New York, London and Moscow, living in want—and you begin to realize what 34,000,000 people 'below the poverty line' means.

The war on communism in Vietnam has not been fully, frankly 'cost analysed' since it started in 1955, when John Foster Dulles led the way into this quagmire. We know that US military expenses are at least $2 billion now *each month*. There has been no denial of the carefully documented statistic (Sherrod: *Life* magazine) that it costs $400,000 to kill a *single* enemy, Vietcong or North Vietnamese, which includes the expense of seventy-five bombs and 150 artillery shells for each corpse. One does not know whether the cost of killing uncounted thousands of Vietnamese civilians unintentionally is lumped into that sum.

In 1966, USAID spent $600 million 'to keep the South Vietnamese economy viable' and in direct gifts, such as corrugated tin roofs for refugees. The total of known USAID for Vietnam adds up to $3,005,600,000. No one can suggest that the US Government has been niggardly of funds for the war on communism.

The war on poverty in the US began two years and three months ago, with noble words, grandiose aims and limited cash. The total appropriation for winning this just war is $3,900,000,000 to date. Somehow that minor sum was meant to improve the lives of thirty-four million people in a country fifty-seven times larger than South Vietnam. How could thirty-four million lives be noticeably improved when the funds have provided less than $100 to bring help to each of these poor? The war on poverty is unique: money could win it without a single casualty.

The President has asked for an increase in funds, during the next fiscal year, in order to fight the war on poverty a tiny bit better. He wants $2.06 billion to slow the steady destruction of human life inside the US; it isn't a wildly extravagant sum, considering the $2 billion used monthly for destruction inside Vietnam. The betting is that Congress will not agree to this request and will vote a smaller budget for the war on poverty. This January, in spite of objections from an admirable few, Congress granted an additional $12.3 billion to finance a mere half year of the war on communism.

The Office of Economic Opportunity (OEO) is the Pentagon of the war on poverty. OEO has overall command of strategy and finances, but each separate state, county and city sets up its own anti-poverty operation. The resulting bureaucracy is, of course, large and complicated, though it is peanuts compared to the bureaucracy of USAID and the Defence Department. It is beyond my competence and this space to describe how the war on poverty is waged throughout the US, so I shall try to give a limited view of the battle in one large Midwestern city and its adjacent county.

The population of the area is about 1,500,000 and someone has decided that 250,000 of the residents (mostly Negroes) are living below the legal poverty line. OEO, this year, allocated $11 million to raise a quarter of a million people above that dark line into the upper air. The figure of $11 million compares interestingly with these: $25 million to build a Pentagon in Vietnam for the use of sixty-eight American generals; $18 million to construct two dairies in Vietnam for supplying reconstituted milk, cottage cheese and ice cream to US troops; $39,500,000 for a year's stock of chemicals to defoliate trees in Vietnam.

This Midwestern branch of OEO spends forty-six per cent of its budget on bureaucracy: staff, office rents, supplies, staff travel, and the maddening voluminous paper work that is bureaucracy's main product. Forty-five per cent provides salaries for the poor, on learning jobs or as assistants to the professional staff. Seven per cent goes for services to the poor, such as medical examinations, educational materials, carfare to seek employment. Some day there will have to be a war on bureaucracy, which is a worldwide crippling disease. The US is gravely infected. But the young OEO bureaucrats whom I saw in this Midwestern city were fine people, fired by a sense of justice and gentled by affection for their clients, the poor. One can only hope they will preserve their souls, as well as their jobs.

There is nothing revolutionary about the war on poverty here—and here is a typical American city. The local OEO office gives money, advice, and supervisory staff to forty-five existing public and private charities that have been dealing with the poor since time began. These forty-five charities continue their usual work.

They teach illiterate adults to read, operate birth-control clinics, train the young and the unskilled for jobs, run pre-kindergarten kindergartens, offer limited legal aid to the penniless, provide free tutoring in and out of school. The money is inadequate and so are the programmes. Most of the 250,000 poor remain in their slum homes, unaware of the special benefits of the Great Society.

But OEO, to its credit, has invented one new war tactic, called 'Neighbourhood Action.' For the first time, in their derelict streets, the poor have places to meet and a concerned, respectful staff to explain their role and rights as citizens. This is the most valuable and controversial of all the war-on-poverty operations.

An evening meeting of a Negro Neighbourhood Action Group, in a ramshackle OEO slum office, lifts the heart. The war on poverty fails for lack of money and vision and leadership. But hopefully, excitingly, little by little, the poor are training their own noncommissioned officers.

The same Americans who detest and protest the war in Vietnam are staunch partisans of the war on poverty. These are the doves. A true hawk sees no need to waste money on the poor, to pamper the lazy, thieving lot; but would like more and bigger and better bombs to crash all over Vietnam. *Dove* and *hawk* are terms which entered our curious political vocabulary at the time of the Cuban missile crisis. President Johnson seems to have joined the present-day Vietnam hawks. But the doves are misnamed; they have bulldog blood.

Our leaders tell us, again and again, that we are the richest and most powerful nation on earth; in fact, the richest and most powerful the world has ever known. None of them tells us that we are the happiest nation. How can a nation be happy when it has two wars on its hands and its people can't agree on either of them? Riches and power are not enough; we are short on wisdom and compassion.

The Vietcong's Peacemaker

In November, this woman was unknown to the outside world. Then she appeared in Paris and the picture of a grave rather beautiful Asian face appeared in newspapers everywhere. Her name, we were told, was Madame Nguyen Thi Binh, and she was acting chief of the National Liberation Front delegation at the Vietnamese Peace Conference.

The peace conference had involved only Hanoi and the United States, and was stale and bitter news. It had dragged on and off, mostly off, since May, while every week thousands of Vietnamese and hundreds of young Americans were killed and mourned, and this despairful, senseless war continued without change. In America, opinion grew that the Paris meetings were a fake, intended to soothe vast public disgust for the war, but not to bring peace.

Madame Binh's arrival was news and sensational. The N.L.F. had been recognized as a power and this unknown woman was equal in rank to the American negotiator, Mr Cyrus Vance, a far from unknown figure.

The National Liberation Front of South Vietnam is the brain, the guiding force, the government, while the Vietcong is the army. Madame Binh does not bother with these definitions and distinctions. She speaks of all the South Vietnamese on her side, simply, as 'patriots.' The Johnson Administration did not bother with definitions and distinctions either: those on Madame Binh's side were, simply, 'the enemy.'

The press has found an easy adjective to describe Madame Binh: she is 'austere.' *Austere*, according to my dictionary, means 'harsh, stern', this she is not at all. She wears the long Vietnamese tunic and trousers with a European woollen jacket for warmth. She uses neither make-up nor a hairdresser. She is small, very thin, pitifully and heroically tired, undaunted, probably shy and certainly modest. She has great dignity, her eyes are sad. Yet she laughed in the delicious way of her people, like a child crumpling into giggles, when I said with wonder that she has no lines on her face, not a single one, after such a life. Madame Binh does not think her life is special; it is how Vietnamese 'patriots' live.

When Madame Binh was a girl of eighteen, the Second World War ended and the Japanese were defeated and expelled from her country. Since older 'patriots', led by Ho Chi Minh, had been largely responsible for this result (and in those days Ho was honoured by the American Government), the Vietnamese expected to be free and independent, rulers in their own land.

Madame Binh had just finished her education in a lycée: 'I learned French, and French history. Not our history. Our ancestors were the Gauls.' Her smile was brief, ironic, like a shrug of the shoulders. 'I had vague patriotic ideas. We were despised by the colonialists; I was often indignant, humiliated. I saw how poor my people were. I wanted then to be a doctor, to help my people. I saw how they went to doctors and were asked first how much money they had.'

Her grandfather had been a famous patriot, imprisoned in his day by the French, but he died before she was born. Her father was a civil servant, 'a small *fonctionnaire*, neither rich nor poor.' She was the oldest of six children, her mother was dead. In 1945, they were full of hope, the war was over, now they would live in peace, at home among themselves.

But the French returned; the 'patriots' were cheated of their nationhood, again to become second-class citizens in a colony. So the 'patriots' took up arms a second time in September 1945, and Madame Binh's father joined them: Vietnam for the Vietnamese.

'From 1945, we had no money. After he was arrested two or three times by the French, my father had to escape to the maquis. I stayed; there were five children to look after.'

She was in Saigon alone at eighteen, teaching 'little classes of children' to earn money, taking courses to qualify for a proper lycée post, and 'participating.' 'I could not have done it without help from my friends.' First she worked with students, then with women's organizations, then with the 'intellectuals.' 'The great majority of intellectuals in our country have always been patriots.'

How did she know what to do? 'Me, I never received any political education'—again that brief smile. 'I learned from experience. We organized protest marches against the arrest of patriots, we distributed leaflets, we met and discussed.' For six years she kept her family of brothers and sisters together and 'participated.' Then, at the age of twenty-four, she was arrested by the French. She spent four years in prison.

'And I was tortured too, you know, to make me confess to subversive activities and to say I was a communist. I did not speak, but they wrote anything they liked in anyone's dossier.'

I asked who tortured her.

'Vietnamese, with the French directing. Just as now it is Vietnamese who torture, with Americans directing. There are people like that in every country. Mercenaries, who torture their own for money.' She says the word *mercenaries* with loathing. But she would not speak of what had been done to her; she dislikes talking about herself as if the subject was without importance. Her memory is full of the endurance of others.

'When I was in prison,' Madame Binh went on, 'there were hundreds and hundreds of women with me who did not even know why they were there. They asked, what have we done? They did not know when they came but when they left, they knew. They left as patriots.'

Her brothers and sisters were dispersed among friends, it was really the end of the family. Four locked-up years, and finally the 'patriots' won and the French were defeated. The prison doors opened. The agreement reached at Geneva looked forward to elections that would eventually unify the country. 'We were so happy,' Madame Binh said, 'so happy to have peace at last and to be free. My father came back, and the children.'

In that short spell of hope, she married 'someone I had known for a long time. For a few months, we were all together.' This is the best memory; her eyes shone. For a few months in 1954 is the only time they have been 'all together.' Madame Binh is now forty-one years old and the mother of two and she has never had a home with her husband and children.

When the people poured into the streets of Saigon to celebrate the Geneva Agreement and their freedom, Diem's police fired into the crowd. Madame Binh was there that day, when rejoicing instantly changed to fear and a girl friend of hers was killed by a bullet in the stomach. The 'intellectuals' understood quickly that the Geneva Agreement would not be respected, and Diem's 'repression' grew.

'There would be a police raid, closing both ends of the street, and the police would look at identity cards and collect the young men and take them away to the army; it happened like that even in cinemas. And patriots were arrested and shot. Later even whole villages would be decimated with machine guns. They pulled the guillotine through the streets of towns and villages to intimidate the people. They executed people openly in market squares and made their families watch.'

'And that division of our country, it was to last only two years until we could vote, and instead it lasted for always. Children do not remember ever seeing their fathers who went north with our army as the treaty planned. We have a profound tradition of the family in Vietnam; men and women remain faithful, all these years, without ever knowing happiness.'

Madame Binh taught mathematics in a Saigon Lycée and helped to organize 'peaceful protests.' But her husband had been forced to flee to the country in 1955, her father was gone too; their meetings after that were rare, secret and perilous. Peaceful protests meant marches and petitions and they became a guarantee of arrest.

In 1957 Madame Binh left Saigon to hide in the country, 'moving from one place to another, always moving. Sometimes we would arrive and be told no, you must go on at once. We lived underground often, never coming out into the air except at night. 1957 through 1959: those were the black years. By 1960, the people could not bear it any longer. They demanded the right to fight and protect themselves.'

'We organized village by village. Those who knew how to fight taught the others. It was the third time we fought, you know. The Geneva Agreement was torn up by Diem; we knew we would never have the vote to decide how our country should live. And then the Americans came. I think the whole world knows that our patriots are brave.'

During her first year of hiding and flight, Madame Binh bore a son, and four years later a daughter. These children, now aged twelve and eight, have always lived with friends in what has so far remained a safe place. 'I can count the days—not weeks, not months—in all these years that I have seen my husband. My children count the time they have seen me or their father in days. People say we are accustomed to this life. But we have the same desires and wants as everyone else. The same. It is diffiult to live as we do.'

Obviously, Madame Binh will not give details about this difficult life: in how many places does she live; in what sort of places—a village house with thatched roof, a concrete-lined underground shelter; how does she travel; does she ever rest; is there any amusement in her days? She says of her husband only that he is a patriot too and constantly occupied; they are never able to visit their children together. Nor can one know her exact position in the N.L.F.—but clearly she must have risen to this great responsibility through intelligence, work and courage. All one can tell, for sure, by her voice and eyes, is that she loves and misses her husband and her children. A 'difficult' life: she seemed little and lonely and not even very well.

A young man brought in tea and Vietnamese sweets; there was a pause in the story and a chance to examine this small salon in a small villa in an undistinguished Parisian suburb. Madame Binh's delegation is not rich. Large photographs hung on the shiny reddish brown walls. One showed a young American with fair hair and a quiet, gentle face, burning his draft card. Another showed five radiantly gay young Vietnamese, two boys with accordions, two girls and a boy with rifles. Madame Binh explained that the accordian players were a village entertainment team; in the 'liberated zones,' all villages had them. The laughing youngsters with rifles were members of the militia who protected the village.

They cared a great deal about songs and music, as also about schools and hospitals. Sometimes the schools were underground, sometimes above ground, depending. Education was a hunger with the people, the schools continued despite bombing. Their medical teams were at least devoted in their care of the wounded and had learned more skill, improving their traditional medicine. They could do nothing for those burned by napalm or white phosphorus unless the burns were slight. Otherwise the people died. Which led us to the bombing. How did her children survive the rain of fire and steel?

'The little girl is more sensitive,' Madame Binh said, and smiled as if to excuse the child. 'When she hears planes she runs quickly to the shelter. The boy is harder; he waits a minute and looks at the sky before he goes. But we tell our children that the bombs cannot kill everyone; they must not be afraid.' Her head was bowed, her voice very low.

'We know that our sacrifice is necessary. If the bombs do not fall on you, they fall on friends. We accept fate. We are calm. It is useless to be a pessimist. One day, we will win a beautiful life, if not for ourselves then for our children.'

But there will be a whole army of children in Vietnam who will never have a beautiful life: the amputees, the blind, the mutilated, the orphans, the tuberculous, the small ones who have gone insane.

Madame Binh continued, 'They bomb even our work animals, the oxen. As they spray poison on the fields so the people will starve or become refugees in the cities. To ravage the countryside is another form of pacification.'

I asked, would not her people hate Americans forever?

'No!' Madame Binh said. 'No, you must not believe that. My people are touched by all the acts—the small as well as the large—that the American people make against this war. We are really moved. We do distinguish between people of goodwill everywhere and governments. We feel that the public opinion of the world has understood us. You see, I was imprisoned by a French government and yet I have French friends, best friends, and my people keep a good relationship with the French people to this day. We do not want hate and war. We want only peace and the right to be independent in our own land.'

In his Inaugural Address, President Nixon said: 'The peace we seek to win is not victory over any other people, but the peace that comes "with healing in its wings" . . . with opportunity for all peoples of this earth to choose their own destiny.'

The Sixties

At this late date, I perceive a muddle. Newspapers are brisk and publish at once but magazines have their different delayed unpredictable schedules. Now in the sixties, I see that the time when I collected information and wrote the article is completely out of sync with the time of its publication. The way to surmount this muddle is to ignore it; I will stick to my personal timetable.

The second visit to Poland in the spring of 1960 was self-indulgence: hard life in Poland interested me more than comfortable life in London. The hard life, described in 'Return to Poland,' continuing since the end of World War Two, with hiccoughs of improvement, led to Solidarity, martial law and whatever comes next. Apart from the pleasure of their company, I wanted to organize the Polish Fun Fellowship. I would give money—peanuts, but young Poles were used to living on less than peanuts—and the Professor of Art History at Krakow University would choose a Fellow each year. Said Fellow could then satisfy his heart's hunger in the museums of France and/or Italy as long as the money and his passport permitted.

I cannot imagine why I expected this private plan by a private foreigner to get past the rigid communist authorities but finally it did, and Julek was the first Fun Fellow. He had a whale of a time, sleeping under the bridges in Paris to save money, and no doubt bringing home from France and Italy a rucksack full of museum postcards and fascinating news for his friends. The second Fellow was something else; the State had moved in and chosen its own. My Polish chums advised that the Fun Fellowship cease. No point in subsidizing clots.

As soon as the Eichmann Trial was announced, I knew I would report it and might also use the journey to enquire into the unending Palestinian Problem, since I mistrusted the clichés of politics and statistics: I wanted to find out about the people. The information for the articles on the Palestinians and the Eichmann Trial was collected in May and June 1961, and both were written before the end of that summer.

Camp is an emotive misnomer, applied to the Palestinian refugees, but camp people are the poor Palestinians and doomed because they will never be treated as people. For almost twenty years, they served as a war-cry, a slogan for Arab governments. Since 1967 they have been wickedly misled by their self-appointed leader, that squat ugly little man, with his cultivated two-day stubble, his spooky smile and theatrical guerrilla clothes, Yassir Arafat. Nobody elected Arafat and no Palestinians dare defy his PLO; you get murdered for dissent.

Arafat has had enough protection money from the oil Arabs to finance the education of two generations of young Palestinians, a chance to rise beyond the poverty of the camps into a good self-reliant life. Instead he has recruited two generations for training only in the use of guns and plastique, and insisted on a futile goal: Palestine for the Palestinians. Israel is not going to commit suicide and will not be conquered by force. Terrorism has been the PLO's contribution to history. The PLO might be considered the Harvard Business School of terrorism, with an international student enrollment. The camp Palestinians are worse off now than they were twenty-six years ago. Under Arafat's leadership, Palestinians roused the civil war that has finished Lebanon. No Arab government wants to give house room to Palestinian gunmen whose sole trade is creating chaos.

I pity the Palestinian women, the only people in the camps who seemed to me sane and admirable. The Muslim Arab attitude toward women is one of the reasons that Arabs remain so drearily retarded. The chief reason is hate. These people really love to hate, as I observed long ago, and as everyone must have observed by now. Hate diseases the mind.

By the time I reached the icy air-conditioned courtoom in Jerusalem, the world's press had departed. I was waiting for that; I wanted to hear the Eichmann Trial with Israelis who were now the audience. At night, I listened to Israelis. The trial was more intimate than the Nuremberg Trials; the witnesses knew Eichmann and were telling their own life stories. I could not describe then or now the feeling in Israel. Something like anguished mourning at a family death-bed; something like nervous breakdown from the news of a cruel family death. Israel cannot be understood without fully understanding the Holocaust, a collective memory that will never be erased. The ceaseless ratbites of the PLO, the stubborn hostility of Arab countries, augmented now by non-Arab Iran, strengthen that memory and lock Israel into its harsh military self-protection. No other country has been forced to live in a permanent state of siege for two generations. This puts iron in the soul and it is a great pity. Israel desperately needs what it cannot get: acceptance by the Muslim world, and peace. Israel needs to rest.

I was so grateful to the Danes for preserving some honour in the gentile world that I went to Denmark, after the Eichmann Trial, to lay a wreath on the grave of King Christian X. And could not find it. Nobody seemed to know where this noble man had been buried, but I hunted it down; as I remember it was an inconspicuous plaque on a wall between two inconspicuous buildings. I laid a wreath alongside a bunch of dried flowers. The janitor at the Synagogue gave me the address of a Theresienstadt survivor, a respected woman writer who was still in weak health. I asked her why the Danes alone, as a nation, had behaved so beautifully when Eichmann was at the height of his power. She thought that the Danes were naturally good but also, 'They are not very Christian.' Why? They did not have figures of the bleeding dying Christ nailed to crosses in their churches. My loving respect for the Danes has been renewed by their acts over the years. The Danes are not haters, they are saviours.

Perhaps the Eichmann Trial gave me the idea, in the winter of 1962, that it would be interesting to meet young Germans, a guiltless generation. The Germans (West) were by then the darlings of the US government, favourite allies in the Cold War. I think my trouble with the young Germans was that they bored me, even those few that I liked. The absence of jokes and jolly laughter was painful. The Green Party and the mammoth anti-war and anti-nuclear weapons demos in Germany indicate a far livelier lot of young Germans nowadays. The students whom I met are now the élite class, in their mid-forties; I wonder if the present young Germans approve of them.

I was ready for a new love affair with a foreign country and had found the love object, at the end of a dotty journey across Africa along the equator from the west to the east coast. I left Kenya in March 1962, besotted by the land, the sky, the animals, the birds, the reef fish and the weather. I thought this impractical infatuation would wear itself out but the lure of a rugged untried thrilling African future was too strong. I imagined myself as a pioneer women in Kenya though prudently keeping a toehold in London, a flat slightly larger than a broom cupboard.

'Monkeys on the Roof' is a sample of journalism-for-money, light cheerful stuff, and an accurate account of the start of my Africa era, in September 1963. That house was not your everyday suburban residence since you don't usually find a black mamba entering through the rear French doors, gliding along the wall under the bookshelves and out the front French doors. Milagro was standing at the bookshelves, fiddling with the useless radio, and luckily too paralyzed by fear to move as the snake slid past her feet. It curled up on a big cement flowerpot on the verandah, where I was trying to grow vines as cover for the verandah's lamentable pole pillars. The gardener and I, armed with sticks, then began an eerie ballet, leaping in to strike the snake, leaping back. I was as terrified as the Spaniards but dared not show it, for the sake of morale. Nor is it every suburban house which requires you to kill a huge tarantula under the dining table with a rolled up magazine. The house offered plenty of pioneer-woman type activitity.

I had a marvellous time in Africa, those first years, free of newspapers, radio, television, out of touch with the man-made world. I wrote a novel and put it in a drawer, unseen by any other eye, my second stillborn novel; I travelled all over East Africa in my heroic yellow VW beetle; I wrote a few serious articles about Africa; and I snorkelled to my heart's content in the cool clear silky water of the Indian Ocean. My mother was by then too old for the strenuous plane trip from St Louis to Mombasa. Instead I went to St Louis every year.

By intention, I lived remote from news. But in St Louis, in the autumn of 1965, the Vietnam war—nightly on TV—overwhelmed me with its horror and its wrongness. I had been slow to become aware but immediate in becoming opposed. War was not new to me. This war was altogether new. Napalm. My country was dumping napalm on thin poor people who lived in thatched huts? My country was sending young inexperienced boys to South East Asia and obliging them to act like mindless heartless oppressors, and get killed doing it? I loathed the men in Washington, safe in their elegant offices, making war on paper, intoning geopolitical rubbish, giving the orders, taking none of the pain.

The months in St Louis were longer and harder each year: hometown claustrophobia, watching the last of my magnificent mother's life, and now the unbearable pictures from Vietnam. From October 1965 to February 1966, the Vietnam news was disturbing the balance of my mind. '*Travail, opium unique.*' At the age of eighteen, I tacked that quotation from Mauriac on the wall of my college room. A certain daftness attaches to an eighteen-year-old who felt she needed the opium solace of work, but it has served me ever since. I took refuge in the St Louis Criminal Courts and was saved by work. Journalism is education for me; the readers, if any, may get some education too but the big profit is mine. Writing is payment for the chance to look and learn.

The weeks spent in the basement life of St Louis were a valuable education. It was surely no worse than in any other American city and may have been better, due to the placidity of St Louis. The basement life was pitifully sad, not frightening. Any rational person can see that the freedom to buy and own guns in America is irrational, not to say insane. The gun lobby is sacrosanct; Americans have the God-given right of free men to own weapons. And to shoot each other more freely and crazily than any other people. Twenty years on, there is more poverty, more and more violent crime, hard drugs have been added as a special catastrophe for the workless hopeless young; the cities are dangerous and the basement of society is a dungeon.

In the common tradition, the St Louis cops were racists, niggers being their version of commies. A detective, who was a new pal, a likeable fellow, told me about the cops arresting two Black Liberators, two young men identified as belonging to a group of some thirteen rebels, hauling them into the station house because of a faulty rear light on their car, and beating them up so that they had broken hands, stitches on their heads and internal injuries. The two young blacks were arraigned for assaulting the police and convicted. When I observed with heat that the police were fools as well as bastards, he asked pleasantly, 'Whose side are you on, Martha?' On the side of the downtrodden. Even, risking pomposity, on the side of justice.

America disgusted me, killing poor people called commies in Vietnam, maltreating poor people called niggers at home. I wrote to a friend that I felt like a displaced person and all I wanted to do was get out. In February 1966, I fled the US and landed on the Dutch island of Bonaire, in the Caribbean. This was my usual form of expeditionary travel; I had read that Bonaire was frequented by flamingoes which sounded strange and attractive. I wrote 'Spiral to a Gun'; then put on a mask, clamped my teeth on a snorkel and washed off the world's wrongs in the turquoise sea.

I could escape from the world by moving from one unspoiled off-the-track Caribbean island to another but could only escape my Vietnam obsession by replacing it with another obsession. I withdrew in my mind to memories of Mexico and in five solitary months wrote a happy novel, living entirely in an invented village among enjoyable odd characters. As always, 'travail, opium unique' worked. It was the only fiction I wrote for the next nine years. When the novel was finished, I was back at square one, obsessed by the distant war.

All I really wanted to do was get to Vietnam. Where were the unmentioned people of South Vietnam, our luckless allies, while being saved from communism by bombs? Newspapers had their staffs of young war correspondents on site, reporting as if Vietnam were a sports event; I was overage for active service and without connections. I flopped around, not knowing what to do, until I persuaded the *Guardian* in London that Vietnamese civilians were valid news. The *Guardian* accepted my proposal to give me credentials and pay my airfare, the heaviest expense, if I paid everything else with the writing thrown in. That brief stay in Vietnam, in August-September 1966, churned up my life until 30 April, 1975, when the war finally ended.

After my reports appeared in the *Guardian*, the South Vietnamese government marked my name with a black X and forever refused a visa to return. The last information that the South Vietnamese and American overlords wanted to have spread abroad was what I had written, the massacre of the innocents. There was no censorship of the media in Vietnam but excluding a reporter is the tightest censorship, nothing can beat it. I was cut off from the only useful work I could have done to discredit the war, a minor act yet any act however small had value if it helped to end the war. And it was the only work that had any value for me. I never doubted that the Vietnamese people would win, but every day of that vicious war meant more and worse of everything I had seen.

I did not think that the stars would veer in their courses because I had lost a sense of purpose, felt shelved, redundant, as if I had lived too long. I was haunted by Vietnam even when I took care not to read about the war and lived out of reach of TV. My inner climate was overcast by shame and grief and rage with, as the British weather reports say, sunny intervals.

In the spring of 1967, again in St Louis, I filled time by studying the basement life from a different angle. The magazine *Ave Maria* is a mystery to me. The few copies I have seen look very waif-like, printed on cheap paper. Obviously it is Catholic from its name but what extraordinary Catholics they must be. They reprinted some of my Vietnam war reports, when Cardinal Spellman of New York was blessing the Vietnam war as a Christian crusade against communism. Probably I sent them 'A Tale of Two Wars' thinking that they alone would want it.

As sunny intervals go, another war seems bizarre, but Israel's Six Day War was in every way unlike the Vietnam War: necessary, brilliantly executed and unique in the Israelis' resolution to spare civilians. Reporting what that war had really been, as opposed to what Arab propaganda said it had been, and writing three later articles on Israel kept me occupied from June until September 1967, and temporarily released from Vietnam. After that, nothing until January 1969.

The London papers carried stereotype snippets about Madame Binh. I wanted to see her, I wanted to see someone from Vietnam, very queer, almost like homesickness. The *Times* gave me credentials readily enough; I was a discount price journalist and Madame Binh was enough of a rarity to be worth some space. Madame Binh was adorable. It sounds silly, and *adorable* is not an adjective that pops up every week in my vocabulary. I expected to admire her but not to feel instant devotion. In Vietnam I had been repelled by us, the big white Americans, an awkward crude people with unfinished faces, and moved by the elegance of form and bearing and the dignity of the Vietnamese. I towered over Madame Binh and felt all of us outsize Americans, with our accursed power and money, to be pygmies beside the strength of this tired tiny woman.

The Paris Peace Talks smelled rotten from the beginning.

Offhand, there were not two men living I would trust less than President Nixon and Dr Kissinger. The Swedes must have been asleep at the wheel to award Dr Kissinger half the Nobel Peace Prize. The man of peace who counselled the bombing of Hanoi and Haiphong, as soon as the 1972 US Presidential election was safely won; who counselled the secret saturation bombing of Cambodia. The Paris Peace Talks, an on-and-off show from 1968 until 1973, were another American public relations job; lying, hypocrisy, window dressing. I never believed a word Nixon said except his remark that he did not mean to be the first American President to lose a war. No matter how many people died. The vanity of the man, the vanity of the whole stupid inhuman lot of them in Washington, from first to last.

If I had been twenty years younger, I bet I would not have wasted almost a decade of my life in sterile torment of spirit. I would have got myself to Vietnam somehow and joined the Vietcong, though handicapped by my height. Not much use digging tunnels. Vietnam for the Vietnamese. Afghanistan for the Afghans. El Salvador for the Salvadorans. Nicaragua for the Nicaraguans. The inherent right of all peoples to self-determination. If they need civil war to determine how they shall be governed, that is their business and nobody else's. Down with intruding bullies. How would Americans like it if a foreign power decided it wanted a US government by Republicans only, or by Democrats only, and sent its armed might on American soil to enforce its choice, all the while spraying napalm and talking of freedom and democracy?

There is no way that I will ever forgive the American governments—from Eisenhower through Nixon—who led America, first sneakily then arrogantly, into the Vietnam war. They are responsible for disgracing America in history. Changes in the fashion of judging the Vietnam war, now, are irrelevant. History keeps the record.

THE SEVENTIES

Beautiful Day of Dissent

They move like migrations of birds and like a nation of gypsies, roaming. They are always walking and unencumbered. Where do they sleep, where do they eat? How did they arrive? Suddenly the young were in Washington, convoked as mysteriously and swiftly as birds, only four days after four of them, protesting the Cambodia attack, had been shot dead by Authority in the uniform of the National Guard. They began to gather in tens of thousands on Friday, a warm spring day, the horse chestnuts and azaleas blooming, tulips ranged on all official lawns, the grass blindingly emerald. The young floated and drifted through the spring and on into the great stony office buildings of the Senate and the House, which had never before seen such an invasion, quiet, unimpressed by the pomp of the State, mostly wearing blue jeans and lots of exuberant hair.

The young were calling on their elected representatives, who received them with marked attention and courtesy. The marble corridors of the Senate Office Building and the luxurious committee rooms were full of them, an entirely new constituency armed with persistent questions and demands for congressional action. On the steps of the Senate Building, in the noonday sun, there was an astounding rally: Federal Employees Against the Vietnam War, servants of the government protesting their government's action, all of them young. The youngest was a baby in a small pram, whose sides bore hand-painted signs: SPEAK

FOR THE PEOPLE. On the steps of the Capitol, an overflow crowd of the young listened to Senator Kennedy and applauded him warmly. Not the words but the special sound of the Kennedy voice carried across the lawn where more young were talking little, as seems their style, but resting with that delightful ease of body they have, unselfconscious, barefooted if that's best and no possessions to mar their look of freedom.

By late afternoon, the migration appeared to flow toward the Washington Monument, a huge stone spear on a hill top. Kids, this time real kids, small ones, accompanied by nuns who now wear habits like old-fashioned English nannies, walked round and round the Monument. They gave the impression of making a vigil. Broad lawns sloped down to a small stage on which a rock band was performing electronically. The young sprawled, sat, sauntered on the hillside: the music beat against *l'heure bleue* sky. There were announcements. A clear assured male voice over the microphone, 'Hey, the sun is going down.' And it was, a huge burning orange ball. 'This may be the last day the sun goes down on this kind of world. Tomorrow it will rise on a new one!' Warm, friendly cheers, laughter, applause. Then the same voice, 'Now something serious. People, please don't step over the fence to come up here. All the wires are on the ground, about a foot over the ground, for the lights and stuff. All right?' More music. Then 'When it gets dark, people will be collecting bail money. Give whatever you can, anything, whatever you can. The money you give may be used to free you.' And presently, as the lights went on in the park and the city, long-haired girls wandered through the crowd with brown paper bags, calling softly 'Bail Money! Bail Money!'

On the street corners, young people had been giving out cheaply printed handbills all day. Kent State Memorial Service. Nixon sends GIs into Cambodia, Mass Meeting, Rip Off Armed Forces Day, Manpower Makes War Power, Repeal the Draft. Now, in the cool evening light, the young made paper airplanes of these sheets. Having read them, they became useful for fun. Like large butterflies, the air was full of paper planes sailing from group to group.

Next to me on the grass sat a very young mother, perhaps nineteen or twenty years old, pale, serious, tired, dressed as the young are, in clothes which would be the very uniform of poverty and hardship in America, were it not that all the young choose these clothes; the ragged jeans, the shapeless faded top, bare feet with sandals carelessly to the side. Her baby was a silent cheerful busy creature of about fourteen months, spotlessly clean, with the Peace logo sewn to the arm of a tiny yellow windbreaker. The baby was living a happy life in this throng, in this wildly loud music, crawling, trying to chew Mummy's sandals, pulling over a collapsible pram. Without fuss, Mummy spread an underground newspaper on the grass and changed diapers and gave the baby a plastic bottle of orange juice which it gulped at speed. A young black, saying 'Hiya baby,' danced down the hillside, feet light, shoulders loose; three young men, bare to the waist, clumped past. These people never step on each other nor on babies. Two girls appeared from nowhere, long haired, blue jeaned, and took over the baby, playing with it, chatting to the mother: instant comradeship between members of the same tribe.

Higher up the hill, near the Monument, oblivious to the rock music, four young Americans, dressed in what I take to be the robes of Tibetan priests (this guess based on the hair arrangement of the men) chanted and slowly danced around a small mound of incense. People stopped to watch: the words were a language unknown to us. Just stopped, listened, watched: without comment. There was a very great sense, all the time, that everyone did his thing, and the tolerance this implies is wonderful.

The White House is the only beautiful official building in Washington, and in the sudden spring, its gardens were a lovely flowering softness. The gates were all closed with signs saying NO VISITORS ALLOWED. There were few police about. On the street side, on Pennsylvania Avenue, four silvery white coffins stood upended against the White House fence. Each one bore a single large black-lettered word: 'THOU SHALT NOT KILL.' Close to the coffins, wearing skull caps, a group of young Jews intoned what sounded like a prayer. People again stopped to look and

and listen. A boy handed out paper armbands: KSU (for Kent State University where the four young people were killed) / Peace. But he didn't know who the praying people were, nor who put up the coffins, he was from another university, giving out armbands to those who wanted them.

Then there was the President on television, no longer that beaming man who always seemed radiant with delight to be at last where he had so long and tirelessly struggled to be. He looked nervous tonight; his smile was a mechanical twitch. The papers described him next day as 'conciliatory.' Too late, I think, for these young: he will never understand them; they will never trust him or forgive him. The TV face everyone remembers and believes is that of the father, himself so young, of a nineteen-year-old girl killed at Kent State University. He stood before his home in bright sunlight, he looked like the image of decent Middle America, he was fighting against tears and no one could forget that voice saying slowly, with anguish and anger, 'She resented being called a bum because she disagreed with someone else's opinion. She felt the war in Cambodia was wrong. Is this dissent a crime? Is this a reason for killing her? Have we come to such a state in this country that a young girl has to be shot because she disagrees deeply with the government?'

The sun did not rise on a new world as the rock singer predicted, but rose on a day unlike any other seen before in the American capital. Only eight days ago, the President had stunned the nation by announcing that troops were moving into Cambodia. Protests exploded throughout the country. A few days later, four students were killed on an American campus. National Guard and tear gas and fighting cops seemed to be on campuses everywhere. That same morning, though we did not know it, construction workers, faced by almost no police, were brutally beating student war protesters and bystanders in Wall Street, while singing the Star Spangled Banner and forcing the flag to be raised from half-mast mourning for the student dead. Hundreds of colleges and universities were on strike. Every sort and kind of organization in the country was condemning murder of students at home and murder in Indochina. The country felt *polarized*, a new favourite word, meaning simply that America is dividing fiercely and dangerously into two camps. The President and his administration are anathema to one side, Defenders of the Flag to another.

It was an electric day and the sun shone mercilessly. This reporter, trying in vain to affix the paper armband, asked for help from an old Negro maid in the hotel corridor.

'You be careful, honey,' she said. 'Don't get yourself hurt. You seen the father of that girl got killed on TV? I'm black, you white, but we's the same ain't we, that don't make no difference. What they trying to do honey, what they trying to do?'

'I'll protest for you too.'

'God bless you,' she said, moving on with the clean towels.

This demonstration was never organized; it was the most giant happening yet seen. People came who had never protested before, and they came from everywhere. It is useless to estimate crowds; this reporter has not seen so many people at once since VE Day in Paris, but they say that the Moratorium Days collected greater crowds. The wonder of this was how fast it happened, and how instantly the young took over responsibility: they provided medics and their own marshals, in one day. Again, by their mysterious system of vibrations or emanations, they got to each other the tone they wanted for this day, they understood each other.

For once, Authority used its head and kept the troops out of sight and evidently gave orders to the police to play it cool. Buses were parked, end to end, a solid barrier, around blocks of the city, closing off the White House, the park before it, the Treasury and State Department; an enormous barrier of aluminium. The police stood two feet apart along the streets to channel the migration but none came onto the Ellipse, a great oval like a giant cricket field, below and in sight of the White House.

Now the morning streets were filled with drifting troops of the young, strangers to this city. One keeps wondering how on earth they travel and how they live. No girl carries so much as a shoulder bag. One girl was funny and odd because, nearly concealed under a battered floppy brown felt hat, she trailed a flowered quilt. Some people had army canteens; some veterans of college battles wore crash helmet and gas masks, some carried paper bags with food. But mostly, in tens and thousands, this vast tribe of the young floated together, empty-handed, easy with each other, down the streets of Washington to the Ellipse.

'Hey, where we going?' a boy asked.

'Follow the people,' a girl said.

That is how they talk of themselves and to themselves: the people. We, the old, call them the kids: I did not hear any of them using that word, but they are in every way remarkable, and one of their unusual aspects is how little they talk. The symbol of this day was a stencilled closed fist: the Strike fist. On the backs of sweat-shirts and sweaters and shirts, on buttons and stickers, the stencilled fist was new and impressive. They tied strips of red rags or black rags around their thighs, over the jeans; many wore the names of their colleges and universities which are now like regimental badges. Most of the girls are without bras or make-up, with long straight hair; the boys are often bearded and hair length varies: all hair was too hot. The sun blazed on the now naked torsos of boys, the girls with shirts rolled up into improvised bikinis, shoes and sandals came off. There were few blacks and they seemed melded with the white young, part of integrated groups.

A priest lay on the grass on the Ellipse, already filling at ten-thirty in the morning; very white bare feet below his clerical black, a large red button beneath his dog collar: STOP REPRESSION/STOP GENOCIDE. There were nuns, only to be recognized by a brown veil like a nursing sister, and priests in brown robes. White-haired men wore the blue overseas cap of the American Legion, but with the riveting sign: VETS AGAINST THE VIETNAM WAR.

Another group of middle-aged people bore a home-made sign declaring 'We are All Bums.' But the old, the over-forties, were few and far between; and though solidly with the young they were outsiders. There should have been more of us and grouped together, simply to show the young that the generation gap, which one feels sadly as if one belonged to an outdated species, need not mean alienation of the spirit.

Meanwhile the crowd flowed and moved, and everywhere on the ground were bare hands and feet, and it was startling to see the extreme care and politeness of these young, who are often presented to us as mad hooligans. I cannot imagine how they wove, like Mignon amongst the eggs, through their seated and sprawling peers, without trampling on each other, but they did, and the words 'Excuse me' were constantly heard. That is not a phrase you hear much in America. Their voices are quiet. In that huge gathering, all day and everywhere, people could talk to each other in low conversational tones. Nearer the unseen speaker's platform, a young man with beard and long hair held back in a rubber band, announced to two girls with earnest faces and eyeglasses, 'I'm trying to free myself of the shackles the Establishment has forced on me, get it?'

Farther along in a group reading one of the innumerable student papers and handbills, given and sold all day, a girl said, 'You think Nixon wants us to use violence, I don't, I don't agree.'

A girl clapped a shapeless man's felt hat on her head: a sign on the back said, FIRST AID. Young men in white with Red Cross armbands were everywhere. There were MOBE stands, selling black buttons for mourning and blue buttons saying PEACE NOW and stickers saying STRIKE THE WAR MACHINE, STRIKE OUT NIXON, and a girl calling, 'People, we need your money, give us whatever you can, buy stuff, we're $12,000 in debt. Money to free the Panthers.' For steadily, joined to the protest against the war and the killing of students, there was always the cry 'Free Bobby Seale,' and the Panthers are linked in the young collective mind with the Vietnamese as oppressed people.

More hand-made signs everywhere: WILL THERE REALLY BE AN ELECTION IN 1972? FUCK THE MOON, FIX THE EARTH. ASIANS AGAINST VIETNAM WAR. LOSE BODIES TO SAVE FACE? and on and on. Everyone doing his thing, spontaneously. Meanwhile the heat grew murderous; Washington is like the Sahara; there was one small, park-type drinking fountain at the far end of that huge field. From the speakers' stage came announcements about salt tablets, heat stroke, please people sit down, if anyone faints near you, stand up so the medics can see, make room for the medics. I was watching a bearded young man folding a paper hat from a news sheet called *The Student Mobilizer.* He felt me staring, and looked up. 'I wanted to see how to do it.' 'Be my guest,' he said, and gave me the hat. A few yards farther along, a blonde long-haired bare-legged girl said, 'Excuse me, can you show me how to make a paper hat?' Thirst was really painful; heads bare to that sun bad enough.

Behind us three young men were standing. 'Anybody hungry?' They had sandwiches; they threw them out to people who answered yes. Later it was the same with water; the same everywhere.

Is this the place for a declaration of love, a declaration of faith? Having been long away, I had never seen these young, nor ever imagined such a multitude of them, nor expected them to be as they are, and a revelation. Consider that there were at least one hundred thousand of them, and no discord, not even the sort of small snarling that any crowd might work up when literally fainting from heat. Their quiet, their politeness, their generosity were unlike anything I have ever witnessed in America. There was also a strong sense of their seriousness, and their intelligence. Their appearance offends millions of their countrymen, as well it might, for their appearance is a statement that they choose freedom, they are not going to be bothered with the advertising, buying-selling lunacy that keeps America so frantically busy. Perhaps this generation has even settled the ancient battle of the sexes for they seem perfectly natural together, these young, as partners. They are surely rebels and rebels with a complex of causes, but they are not violent by choice, by nature, by principle. Their basic demand is simple: *stop killing anybody anywhere.* No wonder they don't get on with the government.

From noon until after three o'clock, speaker after speaker made the point that this mass rally was a beginning: spread the student strike until the whole country is striking against this hated war, go home and work out from the campuses, involve everyone, talk to everyone, work, work, work. Sentences like these brought applause: 'It isn't *their* system, it's *ours*, and we're going to take it back.' 'We salute a million Vietnamese who died patriotically to defend their country against a foreign invasion.' 'The President knows what we're saying. We're saying: Stop the War, Stop Repression, Stop War Research on our Campuses.' 'The people should run the country. Let Congress stay here and do its job.' 'Spend money on life.' 'The only way to bring peace is to bring the GIs home now.' 'Nixon is a liar, always has been and always will be a liar.' In between the speeches, they clapped in time, shouted 'Peace Now,' welcomed Dr Spock by standing with the raised strike fist; loudly applauded the arrival of the Federal Employees Against the War, who bore three black-robed death's-heads, marked Vietnam, Laos, Cambodia. 'Right on,' they shouted in agreement. 'Free Bobby Seale,' they chanted intermittently. From the speakers' stand, repeatedly, came a voice saying, 'Lost people meet at the glass information booth to the right of this stand.' One young man, having finished his speech, said in a tone of pure exasperation, 'Oh fuck Nixon!' This was greeted by joyful laughter, cheers, applause and presently, happily, all together with large smiles, the crowd was chanting 'Fuck Nixon,' until someone had the splendid idea of starting 'Fuck you Agnew,' which charmed everybody since it also rhymed so nicely.

Now it was over. Symbolic coffins, hastily improvised, black cloth over wood frames, appeared, to be borne by the crowd, urged not to push or hurry, to the White House. The coffins represented the dead GIs, the dead Vietnamese and Laotians and Cambodians and the Panthers, and the Kent students.

Finally, over the loudspeaker, 'People, please pick up your litter. Do your kitchen yoga.' No trash baskets, no water: Washington is an incredible place. But the young had found large paper cartons and deposited them around the field, and suddenly the mess of papers near me had vanished, as if by magic; and indeed they were picking up litter, for these are the same young who came out less than a month ago on Earth Day to arouse their elders to the doom of the American environment.

Wide and slow as a river, we flowed away from the Ellipse and up the long street in the direction of the White House, which no one could reach. The cops stood two feet apart, stiff-faced. Authority made a small cheap gesture; obvious plainclothes cops trying to look like demonstrators and taking pictures madly. Who cared?

Behind me a cop said to a girl, 'Thank you for that smile, that was very pleasant.'

We stared at each other, laughing, and the girl said, 'Wasn't that surprising? What got into him?'

The boy with her said, 'If we're going to be hit by the cops, let's get him.'

Farther along, leaning out of high windows in the Washington Hotel, two children were shouting their heads off, a boy of perhaps fourteen clearly heard because this great crowd was so quiet. 'Peace Now,' the child shouted, 'Free Bobby Seale! Right on!' Everyone laughed and gave the child strike salutes. A large bearded student observed, mildly, 'In a minute his mamma's going to catch him and spank him.' And so the makeshift coffins were borne on and the crowd began breaking up. When last seen, again like migrating birds, a mass of the people had drifted over the bridge to Arlington National Cemetery, to leave the coffins among the dead, killed in the wars, near a President who might have understood these young and valued them.

When Franco Died

On the day Franco died, I returned to Madrid, the city I lived in and loved during the Spanish Civil War, and stayed at the Palace Hotel for memory's sake. The Palace looks and feels like all old grand European hotels; marble and gilt and plush and expensive quiet. The clientele was always the same seen in such places—a timeless lot, lacquered ladies, well-dressed, well-fed elderly gents. When last I visited the Palace it smelled of ether and cabbage and there was often blood on the marble steps. The Palace had been the largest military hospital in Madrid.

The clientele was very young then, though pain ages the face, and wore shabby pyjamas, scraps of uniform. In the corridors, now deeply carpeted and discreetly lit, piles of used bandages collected on the bare floors. Sleazy cotton blackout curtains hung at the windows and there was no furniture except iron cots. Food was scarce, and medicines, especially morphine. I don't remember sheets and pillowcases, only grey army blankets.

Recognizing nothing, I nerved myself to ask an old concierge whether it was true that the Palace had been a military hospital in the Civil War. *Sí, señora*, all of it; but he didn't offer more information and I didn't dare to go on questioning. I wandered around the pompous rotunda where ladies sustained themselves on morning coffee and pastries; I was trying to find the operating room.

The surgeons used to work by the light of two cut-glass

chandeliers. Fancy Edwardian show cabinets, for displaying jewellery and crocodile handbags, held their tools. The room seemed to have vanished. Then, while watching Franco's funeral in the walnut-panelled TV room, I stretched back to rest from that curious TV spectacular, and saw above me the chandeliers and the stained glass skylight and knew this was it. In this room, filled with Franco's devoted followers—old men wiping their eyes at the sight of the coffin, ladies sniffling into delicate handkerchiefs—soldiers of the Spanish Republic had pieces of steel cut from their bodies, had their legs and arms amputated.

By the first winter of the war, in 1937, Madrid was half destroyed, open to ranging artillery fire day and night. A sample score: '275 shells today, 32 killed, over 200 gravely wounded. What we thought the safe pavement of the Gran Via full of new shell holes.' The city was encircled on three sides; you could walk to the trenches, or watch an attack in the Casa de Campo from the upper storey of a gutted house. People scrounged wood from the smashed abandoned buildings or burned their furniture to keep off the cold. Despite the danger in the streets, women queued everywhere, following a stray pushcart of oranges, waiting for rations of chick peas and milk.

It was always a poor man's war in the Republic, desperately poor. Though he had the valuable allies, Germany and Italy, to provide all he needed, Franco took nearly three years to starve out the Republic and he hated the conquered and called them all, with hatred, *los Rojos*—the Reds. Spain is a young country now, seventy per cent of its population born since the Civil War. But Franco never let the newcomers forget that old war; in every speech he reminded them that he had defeated *los Rojos*.

The startling news is that there are more Reds in Spain today than there were during the Republic. I use 'Red' as Franco did, meaning everyone who opposed him. New generations and categories have grown up to become Rojos, to form with workers and peasants the Opposition: priests, students, professors, lawyers, architects, journalists, movie directors, actors, bank clerks, businessmen, bankers, housewives, even Army officers. Political opinion polls are illegal in Spain but *L'Express* ran an opinion poll, I can't imagine how, and discovered that only twenty-seven per cent of Spaniards favour some kind of authoritarian government. That leaves a lot of Reds. The new varied Reds share one common aim: to live as free citizens in a democracy. Not a 'cosmetic democracy,' as they say, a paint job for the EEC, the European Economic Community. They mean to end Franco's police state for good.

There was 'much tension,' as they later explained, during the three days between Franco's death and burial. People were not sleeping at home or had left town suddenly. Rumours had spread of 4,000 arrests in Madrid to follow Franco's death, rumours of police allowing the armed bully-boys who call themselves Guerrillas of Christ the King to run wild. None of this happened, it is said by order of the army. But the city was leaden, silent, and the atmosphere very strange, uneasy, dark. After Franco was finally laid to rest, the air became breathable, the city started to live.

In Madrid on the night of Franco's burial, an illegal meeting of wives of political prisoners was held in the small back room of a flat, with their children playing in the kitchen behind us. Seven women, four young, three in their late fifties, nice looking, dowdy—they could be housewives you'd see in any supermarket. 'I've been married for ten years and my husband has been in prison for seven years. Our only child only knows his father in prison.' Among them, their husbands have already spent a total of 76 years in prison. None is accused of crimes of violence. Their crime is very common: illegal association, in this case being members of the Workers' Committees, the only genuine, though forbidden, trade unions. Their present sentence is seven years, but prison has not stopped them before. They come out of jail, go on with trade union work, and are rearrested.

The State has used all its police power against the Workers' Committees and failed, as the present wave of strikes proves. Spain's famous prosperity made the rich richer while the poor stayed poor due to 'tyrannical capitalism,' in the words of a Basque priest, 'based on cheap oppressed labour.'

Like all other wives of political prisoners, these women must support themselves and their children as best they can; life is lonely and hard. They seemed calm and undaunted, even able to laugh. They had met to discuss amnesty. Unlike pardon, amnesty declares that no crime had been committed and thus in effect abrogates Franco's vicious political laws. The wives were heartbreakingly optimistic; they expected the jails to empty in a fortnight. The opposition needed to hope for quick liberating change once the dictator was dead. They know better now.

From that night on, amnesty has been the boiling issue. It is the key to the future. Changes in Spain will be merely 'cosmetic' until there is total amnesty for all political prisoners, some 2,000 men and women, and for all political exiles and for all political offences. I was told that 100,000 offenders, now at liberty, are awaiting trial. This sounds improbable until you realize that handing out a leaflet, putting up a poster, even private talk, are crimes.

Everywhere, slowly, people began to risk talking though no one forgot that only Franco had died: the police were still alive and well.

A woman, a shopkeeper in a Basque village, crying her anguish and hatred: her only son, age nineteen, coming home from his graduation party, was shot dead for no reason by a Civil Guard, one of the loathed rural police. The guard remains in the village, unpunished. 'Is that justice?' A rock-steady worker in Barcelona telling about his years in Mauthausen, a Nazi extermination prison, where 7,500 out of 8,500 Spanish Republicans died, but not even that has changed his will for a free Spain. A delightful Catalan scholar explaining how he was imprisoned and his career ruined for refusing to answer the Spanish police in Spanish; he is a patriot, he speaks only Catalan.

In Catalonia and Euzqadi, the Basque country, Franco's regime is universally detested. There are no Basques or Catalans in the state police. They were self-governing regions in the Republic and are passionately determined to be so again. Barcelona felt free and gentle compared with Madrid, though that is not how the Catalans see it. They feel themselves occupied and exploited by a foreign power. In Bilbao and the Basque country, the population lives under a reign of naked terror, the city falling to pieces, the countryside filthy and polluted, the alien Spanish police trigger-happy and addicted to torture. A line in my notebook: 'The police shot another boy today, eighteen years old.'

Not unnaturally, the ferocity of the Spanish police to the Basque people has produced counter-terror in ETA, a small, secret band of Basque Nationalists. ETA is altogether different from the IRA or the Palestinian guerrillas, terrorists who murder innocents at random. ETA executes specific police torturers and police informers. These young ETA men come from the Basque villages and the people admire and support them. Another small group of executioners, called FRAP, is not exclusively Basque; it is said to have Marxist leanings but no wide popular base. Three young men from FRAP and two from ETA were shot in Franco's final burst of death sentences in September.

A Xeroxed, intensely illegal pamphlet gives full details of the tortures used to extract confessions from these men, which were denied in court and followed by more torture. The lack of proof and the dishonesty tolerated in the military courts are documented at length. The members of Solidaridad, an apolitical organization throughout Spain, chance at least long imprisonment to publish such pamphlets. Their aim is to spread information, through this secret Xerox machine, that the censored public press can never give. Anyone reading that pamphlet would only be surprised that there is not more counter-terror, horribly justified by police terror.

The barbarous police and the injustice and oppression of Franco's laws have also produced a whole new breed, the young civil rights lawyers, men and women. They are a glory to Spain. Their offices are jammed like doctors' waiting rooms. They keep the true record of detentions without charge and arrests and torture during interrogations. They are faithful prison visitors, and lawyers like these stayed through their last night with the last five political prisoners Franco executed.

An enchanting Jesuit priest received me in his cupboard-size Madrid office: baby blue wallpaper and a print of Picasso's *Guernica* behind his desk. He wore a leather jacket and brown polo shirt; I didn't meet any priests dressed as priests. These are a new species in Spain, an active ingredient in what the priest calls 'the other Spain—a majority of the working class, the youth, the intellectuals, the professisonals, the majority of the clergy and the church.' I had been sent to him by a Communist who told me he was 'a fine man and a good friend.' 'How can I explain that a Jesuit is good friends with Communists?' That made him laugh. 'I think there are Communists and Communists, as there are Catholics and Catholics. For instance, the Portuguese church is fascist but that's no longer true here. The Spanish Communists I know are stupendous people and we want the same things: an end to this Franco regime, amnesty, human rights. Whether the Communists would be so fine if they were in power, I don't know.'

'Do you think they ever will be?'

'No.'

The Spanish Communists are about ten per cent of the population, as they were long ago in the Republic. They opposed Franco for 36 years; they are stupendous people on the basis of bravery alone. In Spain, they seem to me exactly like the Russian civil rights dissidents. One day, sitting in his freezing kitchen, I said this to a resolute little Basque, so much guts in such a small body. (The Spanish working class is still undersized, a commentary on the division of wealth and the conditions of labour.) He had come home after three years in prison a few days before; he was in his early thirties but his teeth were rotten and he was half bald; he had made too many hunger strikes in jail.

'Yes, probably,' he said with indifference. 'They need to have a political revolution in Russia.' Russia didn't concern him; he was a member of the Communist party of Spain.

As I couldn't believe there were opponents of the regime on the right, I was directed to a charming upper-class executive in the world of the multinationals. ('The multinationals have no interest in liberalizing Spain.') His office was stylish, his English faultless; in England he'd be a Tory, in America an Establishment Republican. He talked economics: how inflation and growing unemployment would affect workers' actions; how Spain had become the ninth industrial power in the world with a per capita income of $2,200. (This looks great until you break it down: three per cent of the population owns thirty per cent of the wealth; fifty-two per cent owns twenty-one per cent, and they have to work like hell for it.) He said that most businessmen wanted to get into Europe, into the Common Market, but hadn't really thought about the price, such as free trade unions. He believes democracy must come to Spain; he hopes for changes within a year. Suddenly he said, 'I don't know how this whole Franco thing is going to collapse, but it will.'

If the money power in Spain decides it is essential to enter Europe, join the Common Market, the police state would be obliged to reform. People reassure each other earnestly, saying that Holland and Denmark will refuse to admit Spain if there are still political prisoners, torture, no elected parliament, no free trade unions. Holland and Denmark. Nobody in Spain who longs for our ordinary freedoms expects any support, moral or political, from the government of the United States. On the contrary. That's sad and shameful, but that's how it is.

The way news gets around in Spain is a mystery. You do not read it in the censored press, but everyone knew about the 26-year-old student in La Paz, a hospital the size of a small town, where Franco died. He was fighting for his life on the eighth floor. A Spanish journalist observed (not in print, of course) that they were both perfect victims of Franco's regime; the boy beaten nearly to death by the police. Franco's 30 doctors so afraid of future blame and punishment that they subjected him to 'exquisite legal torture' to keep him alive. After the student spent three weeks in La Paz, hanging between life and death, the hospital announced that he would survive. Three days later, Franco finally released himself from torture by dying, like other Spaniards before him.

The boy was remarkably handsome though pale yellow in colour and very weak. His right elbow was bandaged and through his open pyjama jacket you could see a swelling like a huge tumour in the region of the liver. He replied instantly to my sympathetic muttering, 'I am not the only one.' Which is the important point. On 13 October, this boy went to the Students' Room in the College of Engineering at the university to meet friends. He had a daytime job and studied at night. Three plain-clothes police (secret police, the dreaded Social-Political Brigade) seized him and hauled him away in a car.

At their headquarters, from eight that night until six the next morning, they beat the boy with iron bars and the special police truncheons, steel wands encased in heavy rubber and leather. 'They laid me on a table, it was a regular office, and beat me. Or some of them held me up while others beat me or they pushed me around between them and took turns.' They questioned him about the keys in his pocket which he said belonged to business premises of his father. The police went on beating him 'to make me say they were keys to a room full of progaganda or weapons or God knows what.' In the morning, the police checked and found that the keys fitted the address he had given.

He was left alone in a cell for eight days without medical attention. 'I couldn't eat, I only vomited.' Then he was taken before a police judge who sent him to the prison hospital at Carabanchel. The prison doctor said they had no equipment to treat him and he would die. Three days later, now eleven days after the beating, he was taken to La Paz in a coma. The medical report at La Paz stated that he had 'lesions' on eleven zones of his body: the left knee, the left testicle, the right elbow, the base of the spine, the lower stomach above the genitals, the backs of the thighs, the back from the waist down, the buttocks, the left side (that tumour swelling?), the mouth with the lips and tongue cut. His kidneys had been so damaged that they had ceased to function. In the raw meat on his back were marks of cigarette burns.

A judge of the Tribunal of Public Order declared that there was no accusation, the incident had been a mistake, and the boy was at liberty. The police, who make their own laws, fined him $4,000 for 'agitation and progaganda.' He laughed, telling me that. 'When would I have time, with a job and my studies and my wife and child?' The $4,000 was raised in one day at the university by the students and professors.

'They just picked me by chance. They don't need reasons. Three of them were about 30, the other was a man of 40. They wore sports clothes. They looked like anyone else, but they were not normal, they were sadists. When I was in the cell, I wanted to kill them, but afterwards I knew I could never do that.'

There is nothing unusual about this story except that the boy is in a civilian hospital and can be seen. And also, with the help of one of the heroic civil-rights lawyers, he means to prosecute the police, which has never been done. The day police torturers are sentenced for their crimes would be a day of national rejoicing, but it won't be soon.

The first official act of King Juan Carlos was the famous Pardon. The word in Spanish is *indulto*. Within hours the Pardon was called *'indulto-insulto'* and Juan Carlos was bitterly named Franco Junior. Poor Juan Carlos, king by the grace of Franco, not God. Franco left him, as a legacy, the entire structure of a police state and an immense military and civil bureaucracy firmly entrenched. Juan Carlos is a trapped king.

The Pardon infuriated the opposition. It commuted pending death sentences, but Juan Carlos got no credit for that; everyone agreed he had no choice, since Franco's September executions caused such an outcry around the world. Otherwise the Pardon released thousands of common criminals but was so restricted that at this time of writing, a mere 230 political prisoners had gone free. About an equal number were soon arrested, which doesn't necessarily mean prison terms but does mean police detention and intimidation. The cops' conveyor belt operates without pause.

A protest was called, by mysterious underground means as if by invisible tom-toms. It was a cold clear day, nice weather for a demo. Some three thousand people, mainly young, gathered in silence outside the red brick walls and watch towers of Carabanchel, Spain's largest prison, built by the prisoners themselves after the Civil War. It was the first demonstration of its kind in 37 years. We stood as ordered, not stepping off the curb, one group opposite the gates and two groups lining the curved entry road to the gates. More and more police arrived, enough to control a violent crowd of 20,000. We simply stood.

Presently a cop with a bull horn said no one would be released this morning, so go home. A man shouted *'Amnestia'* and the crowd raggedly took up the word. At once, the mounted police started to move and the crowd broke up hurriedly, but still shouting. A middle-aged woman stepped into the roadway, raised her arms, and cried with great authority, *'Silencio!'* I asked a young colleague why, what was the point in being here and not shouting; 'Because they don't want everyone to have their skulls factured and get shoved into jail, that's why.'

Altogether, the young Reds in Spain are dazzling. Those I met were mainly the children of parents who could afford a university education, hence middle class. If they had been willing to conform, the Franco state offers plenty of perks and goodies to such as these. They looked tired, ill nourished, dressed in worn corduroys and jeans. One endearing bunch of law students in Barcelona described their fathers as 'to the right of Franco,' *'nouveau riche,'* 'Fascist,' and took no money from them. Some had badly paid jobs to see them through; some, like the civil rights lawyers, live by chance—the clients pay what they can, if not, not. The girls, the young women, are equals and partners with the men. They do the same work, are committed together. And after all, the police make no distinction as to sex. They are Catholics,

Communists, Basque and Catalan Nationalists, Socialists, humanists. The old *Rojos* of the Republic would be very proud of them.

I was ashamed to be so dejected in a few weeks by what the Opposition is still fighting after more than a generation. Especially when energy and guts are their only weapons against the entrenched power of the State. So I withdrew on a nostalgia trip, asking a grey-haired taxi driver to take me to the Retiro Park where the zoo used to be. We often walked there on quiet days to visit an old keeper who mourned the animals. The people had no food, the animals were shot to spare them starvation, but he had saved some birds. The driver stopped at gates I had forgotten, brick pillars with stone lions on top.

He said, 'The animals are in the Casa de Campo now.'

'I know. Tell me, weren't there trolley cars on the Gran Via and going around the fountain by the Palace Hotel and Cibeles?'

'There were, long ago. How do you know that?'

'I was here in my youth.' Then suddenly I was sick of this Spain where the only 'heroes' are Franco's Falange and the war monuments only commemorate Franco's dead. 'I was here in Madrid on the side of the Republic.'

He turned with a big warm smile and shook hands. He had been here too. 'Look, feel my head,' guiding my hand to a scar under the hairline on the side of his neck. 'I got that at the Puente de los Franceses. You remember it? I was seventeen and in the Fifty-third Transport Brigade and I was driving an ammo truck to the Casa de Campo. I lost consciousness and the truck fell in the river, but I was rescued and cured.'

We had a good old-soldiers' chat; I checked everything against his better memory. Cuatro Caminos and Arguelles are just city streets now but yes, they had been battlefields. And yes, Madrid was pounded all the time by the German artillery on Garabitas Hill. He remembered walking along the Gran Via when a shell hit a trolley car and he and a comrade pulled out a young girl, 'a beautiful girl, about sixteen, and her whole breast was sliced off by a shell fragment. They took her in the ambulance to

Atocha Hospital. I'll never forget it . . .'

He spoke of the years of hunger after the war and how all the young soldiers of the Republic like him had been forced to do three years' military service in Franco's army. 'They looked at us with a funny eye and gave us the dirtiest jobs. Ah man, I tell my children these things and they believe me because I am their father and would not lie to them, but they cannot really believe, they cannot understand. Do you think Juan Carlos will be a king like they have in England? That's what we want, say, four political parties and everyone has the vote and a king like the English. *Madre!* No one wants another war. But you know, if the Germans and Italians hadn't helped him, Franco would never have won our war.'

I felt at home again, and after that I talked to all grey-haired taxi drivers and they had all been in the war and we were instant friends. A taxi is a safe place; they could talk about their thirteen-hour working day, the wife doing piecework on the sewing machine at home, the price of food is a disaster (not that farm labourers are wearing fur coats—we are rich compared to those sons of misery), and what a horrible state Franco had made where a man was afraid to speak his thoughts. 'The newspapers are novels. The only true facts in them are about football.' 'We are supposed to be grateful to him for peace. The way to keep peace in a country is to ring it round with bayonets and anyone who moves—hop! a Communist or ETA, shoot him.' 'This country is the marvel of the world, didn't you know? Here we are all content. Or in jail.'

I wanted to see Garabitas before I left Madrid and took with me a young writer. From that hill, where I had never been before, you saw Madrid spread out below, street by street, with the tower of the Telefonica sticking up like a direction finder. They could aim their heavy guns as if they were rifles. The city was like a shooting gallery for them, with fixed and moving targets. Hundreds of thousands of shells, day and night, year after year, killing the small, brave, hungry people of Madrid, destroying their homes.

I was in a rage and close to tears, so suggested that we eat tremendously and get drunk and forget everything. We went to the oldest restaurant in Madrid and ate a superb expense-account lunch, the only good meal I had in the country and perhaps the only good meal he ever had on a monthly salary of $200. We drank pitchers of the local wine and felt like old, close, loving friends, perfectly united in our views, though we had met that day and with a slight time pinch I could be his grandmother.

He said, 'There has to be something wonderful about my country because all of you loved it so much. I believe it's still alive, and no one is ever going to be able to kill it, despite everything.'

Yes, of course it's alive. If defeat in a long, appalling war and 36 years of Franco couldn't crush the spirit of *Los Rojos*, nothing can. When the losers are indomitable, someday, somehow they must win.

Christmas with the Outcast

The unemployed have become a hated statistic. A political face on TV announces: 'We must expect increased unemployment next year.' As if talking about bad weather, not doomed people. The unemployed, one by one, are human beings in trouble we do not begin to know. They are doing their best to stay alive, for which they can scarcely be blamed; after all, they didn't invent this Depression. Christmas (the Great Spending Spree for others) is the hardest time; they were still gallantly doing their best.

A vicious campaign against the unemployed is growing by word of mouth and in the Press. We are led to believe the unemployed are scroungers, if not straight cheats, who'd rather live on State money than do an honest day's work. You get the picture of layabouts, loafing in comfy homes on fat cheques the State has gladly handed out. No one would dare spread such ugly lies if they knew the truth about the real lives of the unemployed. In fact, a vast, suspicious complex bureaucracy unwillingly doles out just enough money to keep people from starving in the streets.

Officialdom is hostile to inquiring outsiders. Charitable organizations misguidedly protect their clients from what they most need: publicity. A wall of silence is built around the unemployed, and they have no way to speak for themselves. For two weeks, night and day, I have been trying to break through that wall of silence, and simply *see* unemployed people in their homes. It was far easier to meet dissidents in Russia and the underground opposition to Franco. When finally I reached their homes, I found these hidden-away people likeable and admirable, eager to talk, welcoming a listener.

The bureaucracy gave me leaflets which explain the citizen's rights to State aid. These leaflets are a universal black joke; no one understands them, including me. Two friends, with first-class degrees from Oxford, were baffled. Another friend, faced with a bureaucratic form, said she would be happy to answer any questions but could not decipher the form. The brightest and bravest of the young unemployed have formed small groups called Claimants' Unions. They print a guidebook, 'Fight to Live,' to help the helpless through the dread maze of bureaucracy. It's fine if you can read. You'd be surprised by how many people of all ages are illiterate in the Welfare State.

It is too complicated to describe here what the unemployed go through before receiving Giro cheques, their poverty pay. Labour Exchanges and Social Security Offices; interviews and interrogation proving your absolute need; home visits from the Social Security to check on your life; weekly begging for essentials (the children must have shoes), weekly signing on at the Labour Exchange and searching there for a job opening. And all the time, as the unemployed say, you are treated as guilty until proved innocent.

Let's look at the money supposedly lavished on the unemployed. Everyone, except jobless school-leavers, has paid compulsory National Insurance throughout his or her working life. The more you earn, the higher your National Insurance contribution. Think of yourself: say you've earned £3,450 or above in the last tax year: you are then in the *top* class for unemployed benefits. For one year. And you will get weekly: £12.90 for a man, £8 for your wife, £4.05 for your first child, £2.55 each for other children. You will also get a top class bonus: £12.18 a week. A family of four will be rolling in riches on £39.68 a week. But only for six months. Then your high income bonus stops and you revert to the flat rate: £27.50 weekly for a family of four.

After a year of unemployment you drop down to Social

Security—the Dole, which pays somewhat less and is trickily variable. And remember, all the unemployed on the Dole have also paid compulsory National Insurance whenever they had work. Does it sound like the lap of luxury?

I met nobody receiving the full, if puny, Dole assistance except for one, a determined father rearing four children alone. After paying rent, rates and heating on his flat, Mr Hardy is left with £28.40 to keep himself and the children aged four to eleven. But he had a small plastic Christmas tree and a present for each child and a bucket of fruit, which thrilled the children, and a medium turkey. 'We'll be broke next week but we're going to have a good Christmas dinner.'

It was pouring icy rain; the Blackfriars Settlement, that haven of kindness, had given Janice a big carton of tinned food and toys for her sons. She looked stylishly King's Road with her tight head scarf and large black-pencilled eyes. Closer inspection showed that her much washed slacks were thin cotton and her poncho the same. On £19.90 a week to provide for herself and two small boys, the warm clothes are for them. Janice is a gentle soft-spoken girl whose husband vanished long ago. She had battled alone against the entire range of bureaucracy to keep a home for her boys. Janice is a squatter.

Her home is one room, about 10 feet by 10 feet, because she has no furniture for the other room. Every day for a month, she has hauled a heavy coal sack to cook in the tiny fireplace. Her most desperate need is a second-hand cooker.

Her furniture is a prehistoric sofa, a padded bench and a few big square cushions, all of which serve as beds. With scraps of cloth and remnants of paint, Janice has made this room charming, interesting and warm, a place where children can feel happy.

Like two and a half million others in Britain, Janice receives her money from the Dole. The Dole also gives grants for a list of essentials if the S.S. home visitor agrees to the 'need.' A cooker is on the Social Security list of 'essentials.' Janice was stuck with the coal grate until a visitor arrived to make sure she wasn't lying about her 'need.' Maybe he was in a bad temper that day or ill or disapproved of the charm of her home, concocted from nothing. Result: no cooker.

St Agnes Place in Lambeth is a street of little broken-down houses, where 100 people, mostly squatters, mostly unemployed, live in friendship. It's a lovely neighbourhood, whatever its looks.

James shares a five-room house with three other young men, and a girl and her two children. Each house is a cherished commune on a communal street. St Agnes Place deserves to survive for its human value alone. James said: 'Lambeth Council spends £500,000 a year on bed and breakfast accommodation and still they're trying to make the people here homeless too.'

On a derelict street in South London stands the Greens' house, with an outside toilet, a roof that leaks so badly it has ruined the second floor, and mice everywhere. The furniture is dirty, worn junk. Mr and Mrs Green, aged 39 and 40, both illiterate, are at the end of their rope. They have five adorable little boys, aged three to ten all with hair home-cut like close fur caps. They sit on the floor and listen quietly.

Three years ago, this poor, ignorant man, a cleaner in a police station, obliged a mate by pinching a gallon of detergent worth £2.50. Mr Green got a £5 fine and a twelve-month suspended sentence. Job applications ask if you've ever had trouble with the police and Mr Green, who cannot write or explain this single, modest trouble, must print the word *yes*. He's tried everywhere but has had no work since. 'I made one mistake in my life. It's a shadow I can't get away from.'

On £32.95 for all living expenses, the kids' clothes are in rags. No Christmas tree here. The children had gone to the back part of the room where, laughing, they turned somersaults on a broken-down daybed. Helpless and hopeless as they are, the Greens have managed to keep their children healthy and capable of fun. Walking with me through the night streets, to find a taxi, I saw tears on Mrs Green's face.

On Christmas Eve, which was fiercely cold, I toured the town, talking to destitute single homeless. At a hostel for homeless women in north London I was not allowed inside the door. I stood on the steps and was handed the telephone number of the manageress. The walls of official silence positively towered.

By telephone I asked the manageress how she knew the women there wouldn't be pleased to chat on this lonely night? Why was she justified in setting herself up as a censor? I was angry enough to make *her* angry so that finally she said, 'I've signed the Official Secrets Act and so have my staff. There's nothing more to say.' The unemployed, the homeless are *an official secret?*

The first paragraph of a booklet called 'Welfare Rights Guide' states: The Supplementary Benefits Commission is given responsibility for deciding whether a claimant is entitled to benefit and if so how much . . . In practice, of course, a great part of responsibility is delegated to local social security officers who make the day-to-day decisions, having regard to the statutes in force and instructions issued by the Supplementary Benefits Commission. *These instructions are contained mainly in the 'A' code and are covered by the Official Secrets Act.* [My italics.]

What is the 'A' Code? I found some of the answer in the 'Fight to Live' handbook. 'Excerpts from the Secret 'A' code instructions to Employment Review Officers: Para 517: *It is not essential that the applicant should be likely to derive benefit from a re-establishment centre . . . It may be felt acceptable that a particular man might most effectively be dealt with by obtaining a Section 12 order in the confident expectation that he would take employment rather than go to the centre.'*

The concept is horrifying. The unemployed are to be considered as enemies not victims, and repressive or harassing techniques for dealing with them hidden behind the Official Secrets Act?

A graduate from a re-establishment centre, Gerry Cardiff, reported in 'Fight to Live': 'I was at this rehabilitation place for eight weeks.' Gerry describes chiselling a piece of metal into a cube and later making concrete bricks. 'You don't necessarily get any re-training course after that.'

There are happy endings. On Christmas Day I returned to the Greens. This newspaper had been there the day before and taken Mrs Green shopping. I found a radiant family.

Janice got her £14 second-hand cooker for Christmas: the social worker from the council forced the Social Security visitor to relent.

In St Agnes Place tables were borrowed, and 20 people would sit down to Christmas dinner. I was never worried about St Agnes Place. Worry instead for the State which cannot put to use such honourable and intelligent young.

Probably the Government should turn over the whole ramshackle bureaucracy that handles and mishandles the unemployed to the organizational geniuses at Marks and Spencer. Let them devise a humane efficient system, free of suspicion and mistrust and Official Secrets.

The Seventies

From January 1969 to May 1975, 'Beautiful Day of Dissent' was my only completed work. A writer's block made of solid concrete. Those few pages were not published. I suppose that my London agent sent the article to a couple of uninterested London editors. I was neither surprised nor downcast, I expected failure. 'Beautiful Day of Dissent' is really a love letter, but also the record of one fine event in America. By the spring of 1970, hatred of the Vietnam war boiled all over the country. I no longer had to feel derelict in my duty; that duty was assumed by tens of thousands of my young compatriots.

The young had dug a deep wide trench around themselves called the generation gap. I understood it and did not blame them. The leaders in Washington, older generation, invented and prosecuted this war. The majority of older Americans took the docile my-country-right-or-wrong view. For myself, I felt sadly isolated while accepting it as unimportant. I was on the side of the young, I was angrier than they were because I knew more, but barred from joining them by my age. America had become the most foreign country in the world to me. When Richard Nixon was triumphantly re-elected in 1972, I gave up hope. The war went on and on.

I do not think the paralysis that gripped my mind was neurotic. The American war in Vietnam was mass neurosis. When I went to South Vietnam, I had already reported war in ten countries and in ten countries seen how it hurt non-combatants, the people who live on the ground. I was far beyond being shocked by war, but war in South Vietnam was not like any other. A whole nation of poor peasants was sacrificed remorselessly to an American phobia and the cold indifference of the Vietnamese ruling, profiteering class. Our weapons were horrendous and the way they were used was horrendous.

I would have loathed that war under any circumstances, but it was directed by the American government, administered and fought by Americans in Vietnam and all the time I thought: in the name of the American people. This unforgivable evil is committed in the name of the American people, in my name as an American. If I say that I felt responsible for every wounded, napalmed, amputated Vietnamese child I had seen, and all those I knew were suffering each day of the war, I refuse to believe that is neurotic: I think it is just. And it made everything meaningless except an end to the war.

Not that I spent those years in a dark room with my face turned to the wall. I spent them like a Mexican jumping bean, bouncing around for no reason except perpetual motion to Turkey, Greece, Russia, Denmark, Holland, Sweden, Italy, Switzerland, Yugoslavia, France, Costa Rica, Malta, always to Africa, always in and out of London, where I bought a flat with a view, still my one durable base. I dreamed up occupations which ranged from building a two-room house on the slopes of a volcano in the Rift Valley to collecting litter at Kew Gardens. In 1972 I rang doorbells and drove about with a bullhorn in Cambridge, Massachusetts, urging the citizens to register for the vote. A friend who heard me said it sounded like a voice from on high bellowing Prepare to Meet Your God. I even took cooking lessons, rather late in life to face a kitchen stove.

Those years would have done me in if I had not been sustained by dear friends in need, who put up with me and gave me affection and laughter which I needed most. It was the worst time of my life. Compared to the variety of worst times then available, it was a long holiday; and I did not forget that.

Then the last American bombers and the last American diplomats left Indochina; the war in Vietnam was over. As if prison gates had opened, I walked out into a wide world where I could see to the horizon in all directions. I wrote two books one after the other; my life took shape again.

Franco was slow in dying. While he lay in hospital, the editor of *New York* magazine telephoned to London and asked if I wanted to go to Spain. There was no assignment I wanted more; there was nobody I wanted dead more than Franco. I said I would wait until the execrable old tyrant had retired for good. News of his welcome demise came over the radio on the morning of 20 November, 1975; I caught the afternoon plane for Madrid.

I had not been to Spain for fifteen years and decided then that I would not go again. The Franco supporters I met were, as expected, dull mean-spirited people but the young workers also depressed me. They had become sly and dishonest, adapted to fit the regime. I was afraid that I would not find anyone left in Spain who reminded me of the people I loved in the Republic. Finding the wonderful new *Rojos* felt like coming home to familiar friends.

Nobody in Spain, in the nervy climate of fear when Franco died, could have imagined Spain now. Certainly none of us imagined that Juan Carlos would turn out to be the guardian of Spanish democracy, the open-minded model of a constitutional monarch. Nor could anyone imagine that in a few years a young Socialist would be the popular Prime Minister of a country that had been ruled for thirty-six years by the deadening steel hand of Franco. Spain endured the longest Fascist reign; 'tyrannical capitalism,' as the Basque priest said, enforced by torture, executions and prison. That defines Fascism everywhere.

Long overdue, Fascism has at last vanished from Western Europe. I wish to trust that it can never return. The term *Fascism* is out of date but not the fact. In modified forms and under different names, Fascism persists all over the globe. I have been reading with deep gloom Amnesty's report, 'Torture in the

Eighties,' which concentrates on sixty-four from a total of ninety countries where torture is sanctioned by the state. Ten of these states are communist and differ from each other as much as the fifty-four non-communist states. Torture is a political weapon used to suppress or intimidate any sign of dissent. We don't label nations 'fascist' now; they are called Republics. The Republic of South Africa. The Islamic Republic of Iran. The Republic of Chile. The Republic of Turkey. The Republic of Paraguay.

'Christmas with the Outcast' is the product of indignation. I remember everything about unemployment in the thirties and the way it ruined lives, the loneliness, the sense of rejection, the despair of people who had lost what we all need: work, as our place in society. Here again, in England in 1976, I was reading and hearing slander about the unemployed that sounded like an echo from the distant past. Now, in 1987, there are officially half a million more unemployed and unemployment is a fact of life, something like arthritis. Painful and crippling to those who suffer from it, no problem for those who don't. Some treatments and painkillers help, but after all, arthritis has always existed and no one has found a remedy. The government will say it is sorry, though it has more pressing affairs on its mind. I have no idea how the terrible social sickness of unemployment can be cured; I am not an economist. But I do not think that any society will survive in health if millions of its members are destitute and idle; and the young grow up, faced by that empty future.

Riots in British cities should not surprise anyone; they are prison riots. Those millions without hope of work are living in an open jail. Maybe there are more Rolls-Royces per capita than ever before in Britain; mass unemployment makes the boast of growing prosperity suspect and unseemly. Capitalism needs a human face. British capitalism has a sharp hard face now and an ugly tone of voice: sink or swim, never mind who drowns, keep swimming.

I was ordered out of the London Social Security offices where the unemployed collected their weekly cheques, but not before several men had started willingly to talk to me. I only learned, due to a fit of mutual bad temper, that the bureaucracy which administers the unemployed is guarded by the Official Secrets Act. Are we to believe that the KGB is panting for information about unemployment? The Official Secrets Act is a blanket cover-up. All governments claim secrecy as a need and right, to confound enemies, and use it to hide mistakes or misdeeds or plain incompetence. The British government is barricaded behind D-notices to the press—effectively censorship—the Official Secrets Act and the smoke-screen of 'national security.' By now this secrecy looks hysterical and vindictive. What is the British government afraid of? Public opinion?

I cannot remember whether it was my brief encounter with the British Official Secrets Act that inspired me to test the American Freedom of Information Act. I asked about myself. I took my typed request to the American Embassy in London, passport in hand, to prove my identity and get my request authenticated by a consulate officer. To my delight, a roll of red tape was produced, I mean a huge roll of the stuff, like ribbon for Christmas presents, and a seal and a stamp; and my request was forwarded to Washington. Months later, a large manila envelope arrived. I saw at once that, properly, we should call it the Freedom of Partial Information Act. Blacked out lines marked every page. On one page, single spaced, the only words I could read were my name.

My first reaction was what I think I would feel if a peeping Tom lurked outside my bedroom window at night: shivery disgust. How dare these people sneak about, spying on me? Then I fell into a fury: why was the government allowed to collect misinformation trash at taxpayers' expense; collect it anywhere, everywhere and hoard it? By what right and for what reason? Then I found it all so absurd that I laughed; but of course it is no laughing matter.

The FBI is intended to discover crime at home; the CIA is intended to winkle out enemies abroad; neither is empowered to snoop on the open activities of American citizens because the citizens dissent from official policies. We knew that J. Edgar Hoover would command the FBI, until his death delivered the nation, since he had gathered so much tattle about the private lives of politicians that none dared attack him, including Presidents. A sleazy system for the land of the free. Now that J. Edgar is laid to rest, perhaps the system has improved. Unrepentant, the CIA has a remarkable tendency to lurch from one abuse of its legal function to another. We can never really know what governments' secret organizations are up to. Not in the US. Not in Britain. My Freedom of Partial Information file held seven references, clear of black marks, to my long ago *New Republic* article, 'Cry Shame,' about the Un-American Activities Committee. Evidently the *New Republic*'s most devoted readers were the FBI and their informants. One of those spy-notes states, unforgettably, 'She tells the people to rise up and overthrow the government.' Not only snoops but crackpots who don't understand English.

Still, a Freedom of Partial Information Act is better than none. Better yet, stop spying on the lawful citizenry. Democracy and dossiers go ill together. It is all right for God but all wrong for the State to keep its eye on sparrows.

THE EIGHTIES

White into Black

This is a cautionary tale, showing how travel narrows the mind.

I left my happy home in Mexico in February 1952 to spend five or six weeks in Haiti. I knew nothing about Haiti except the splendid name of Toussaint l'Ouverture, but Haiti as such was not the point. The point was scenery, weather, sea to swim in as background for sitting still and solitary and starting a novel. Resident travel. When you can't write at home, go someplace else. I had seen Haiti in passing, years earlier, and remembered high green mountains, cobalt sea and Port-au-Prince, a climbing white city festooned in flowering vines and bougainvillaea. Any Caribbean island would have suited; Haiti was a careless choice.

The years had done Port-au-Prince no good. A taxi-driver recommended the grandest hotel by the sea. The walls were peeling, a juke box deafened, drunks abounded, and the rooms were sticky with old dust. Bar talk whined in discouragement. Tourism was on the skids, people were selling up and leaving, president followed president, all crooks, and in the general chaos no one knew what would happen next. The streets of the city now looked like dust tracks, the black citizens wretchedly poor and glum. I should have left then, after a day. The vibes, which existed before being named, were very bad. Instead, at ten o'clock on the second night, I moved from the loud hotel to a pension higher up the hillside where I was the only guest. Here, too, everything was seedy but at least quiet.

It rained; unheard of. I took against Port-au-Prince and bought a map. South over the mountains, on a bay, was a tiny dot marked Jacmel. The manageress at the pension had never heard of the place. This sort of information cheers me instead of sensibly putting me off. I imagined Jacmel as unspoiled, unexcited, a sleepy fishing village where I would find a simple room with sea view and breezes. Work hard, swim in the bay, amble about, eat, sleep and repeat same. It took two days to make travel arrangements, now forgotten; no one seemed to have any reason to go to Jacmel. The delay allowed time for Voodoo and a sprained ankle.

The waiter invited me to the Voodoo ceremony. I was flattered and interested: exotic mysteries in the Haitian jungle. In those days Voodoo was a secret religion; now it figures in a popular TV serial. Slaves, in the seventeenth century in Haiti, invented Voodoo from confused West African tribal memories. Voodoo remains the true religion of the peasants, the majority of Haitians. That night, in a crumbling shack lit by kerosene lamps, I wondered whether these barefoot ragged people looked much different from their slave ancestors. The priest, a bony fiery-eyed man in a cloak and trousers, crouched and cavorted, tracing magical signs on the dirt floor, but kept a calculating eye on the believers. He seemed a dubious manipulator. A woman, another woman, a man, became possessed by a Voodoo god and thrashed about violently, ran, staggered, shouting in unintelligible unnatural voices. If enough people ended up foaming and fainting, presumably the priest was a success. The result of all the chanting and drumming and hysteria was fear. I could see it on the faces around me. When the priest grabbed a squawking chicken, preparatory to biting off its head in sacrifice, I moved silently out the door.

The bad vibes came back as I groped my way along the path. Uneasy unlivable country. But the night air was soft on my skin and sweet to breathe and the sky was true Caribbean, soft blackness, fur soft, with more diamond starlight than anywhere I know in the world and I told myself to buck up, nothing could be too wrong in such a beautiful place. Next morning the sun shone on sea and mountains and I leapt like a Kudu downhill to finish departure chores. Skidding on a stone, I wrenched my ankle and hopped and limped into town, thinking this was a bruise that would soon cure itself. And so arrived in Jacmel with optimism and a badly swollen ankle.

At first sight, Jacmel charmed. What I saw was an unpaved street running back from the cliff that edged the bay. The far view was glinting blue water; the near view was wooden houses, two storeys high, with balconies and long windows (tropical French) and pillars and fretwork. They were painted strawberry pink, lemon yellow, white with green trimmings, pretty as a picture. Opposite the row of houses, a sort of village green was shaded by big feathery trees, flamboyante and jacaranda, and huge mangoes and others, perhaps Indian laurel. Lovely, I thought, what luck. I presented myself with winning smiles at the Pension Croft, middle house in the row, white with green trim, the only hotel. Madame Croft received me icily in the ground floor dining-room. She was an ornate coal-black lady with a mountainous involved hair-do over mean eyes. She did not bother to answer and I stood there, weight on my operational foot, wondering if this was a bad morning or if she was always rude to guests. How was I to know that my skin colour revolted Madame Croft? Her skin didn't matter a hoot to me, though her manner did.

I had not thought of Haiti in terms of colour. Probably I knew it was a black republic. Good. No concern of mine. Most of the people in this part of the world were black or coppery brown or a mixture; non-white, anyway. Mexican Indians, whom I knew best, were one of the main reasons I loved living in Mexico. I had travelled a lot in the Caribbean and found the islanders specially kind and agreeable. Why should Haiti be different?

A maid, giggling from nerves, showed me my room. A corridor ran the length of the floor, doors opened on both sides to cubicles whose thin wood walls did not meet the ceiling. Primitive air conditioning. A window at either end of the corridor let in scant air and light. My cubicle had no window, a weak bulb on a cord from the ceiling, a bowl and pitcher, an iron cot, wobbly table and chair and a rope nailed to the wall for hanging clothes. I wanted to lie down but the sheets gave off a daunting sour smell, so I sat on the chair, my foot on the cot, listening to a man who yawned and spat, yawned and spat. And listened to the school next door where lessons had resumed. For four hours in the morning and two in the afternoon, little Haitians kneeled on their school benches and shouted in unison whatever they were learning. *'Deux fois deux font quatre, trois fois deux font six.'* In due course I heard geography—*les grands fleuves du monde sont*—French kings and spelling. If it stunned my mind, what did it do to theirs?

Come lunch-time, I limped downstairs to the soiled table-cloths and the flies. The dining-room was a bare white room with seven or eight tables, opening to the street and the village green. I was given a table stuck off in a corner. Nearby tables had been pulled away so that I sat in a *cordon sanitaire* of space. No one looked at me directly; sly glances took me in; no one answered my *bonjour* then, or ever spoke to me. With prickly intuition, I knew that the whispering and bursts of laughter had to do with me. The food was inedible, tasting of garlic and sugar.

At stressful moments in travel, I try to console myself with worse moments elsewhere. Is this as ghastly as The Light of Shaokwan? Not quite, cheer up, it isn't raining, the weather is perfect, you can lie under a tree; for clearly, walking was a thing of the past.

My search for a tree out of sight of the Pension Croft led me close to a small shoebox-shaped building of cream-coloured stucco with a sign: Bibliothèque. A public library in Jacmel seemed a miracle, as did Monsieur Réné the librarian and his assistant Mademoiselle Annette, a girl so silent that she became invisible. Monsieur Réné was small, thin, brown not coal black, with receding greying hair, glasses and a proper dark suit. He smiled at me so that I wanted to kiss him and blubber thanks but instead told him that I was a writer with no place to write and could I work in the library. Monsieur Réné fluttered with enthusiasm; he had never met a writer; he would gladly give me an empty room in the back.

By way of confirming what I guessed, I asked Monsieur Réné if there was any other foreigner here. Such as a foreigner washed ashore from a wreck with permanent brain damage, or a criminal foreigner hiding from the cops of three countries. Monsieur Réné was puzzled by my question. No, he said, we are all Haitians. Foreigners never come here; our village offers no distractions. I saw it, then. I was the only Negro in Jacmel. And, furthermore, a Negro who had gate-crashed an exclusive white club, the Pension Croft. The Pension Croft, I lied, was very nice but a bit noisy; could I rent a quieter room in someone's house? Monsieur Réné was amazed. The houses were filled with large families, nobody would wish to take in a guest. Not surprising. Few white families would welcome an unknown black visitor. I dared not ask, so soon, about transport back to Port-au-Prince, but when I did Monsieur Réné had no ideas; he never went himself; his car was not strong enough and Port-au-Prince seemed too far, too strange; no one from Jacmel went there.

Beyond the main library with its two rows of bookshelves, Monsieur Réné ushered me into an oversized empty closet. They found a table and chair, the window was luxury, the silence blessed. Since I hadn't brought anything with me, might I just sit here? Monsieur Réné hurried to find a writing-pad and two pencils and left on tiptoe so that creation could begin. I wrote on the pad 'Self pity, that way madness lies,' then stretched out on the clean floor, to rest my ankle. Monsieur Réné knocked and entered before I could scramble up. In this position, he saw what ailed me, was full of sympathy and insisted on driving me to the clinic.

The clinic has vanished from memory but I remember the smiling doctor, a slightly larger edition of Monsieur Réné, in a white coat. He produced an enormous syringe, suitable for a horse, and a gigantic thick needle, about six inches long. I was paralyzed by my new role, lonely Negro scared to offend white authority. With terror, I let that kind dangerous doctor plunge the needle into my hot puffed ankle and force in what seemed a pint of liquid. Novocaine, said the doctor, all goes well now. Monsieur Réné drove me back to the Pension Croft.

By four that afternoon, my left foot and ankle resembled elephantiasis and the pain was torture. I clamped the pillow over my face and groaned aloud; through the pillow I heard myself making animal noises. I wept torrents. I couldn't stop and was frightened to be so helpless among enemies: shivering, sweating, snivelling, half crazy. Madame Croft told a maid to inquire why the white-Negro was being a nuisance. Madame Croft appeared in the doorway to check for herself. She stared at me with glacial contempt, but did send up pitcher after pitcher of boiling water. For the next three hours I soaked my elephantine extremity in the washbowl and was finally beyond the howling stage. Madame Croft sent up greasy soup. I slept despite the cot smell and gruelling sounds from other rooms.

Suffering is supposed to ennoble; not me, it stupefies me. I could have saved myself by ordering a bottle of rum and getting sodden drunk, and then another bottle, though first finding a telephone to call the US Consulate in Port-au-Prince and demand evacuation on medical grounds. I thought drink was for pleasure among friends and never turned to consulates in an hour of need. In growing misery, I clung to one plan: survive until I could walk, then dump my suitcase and proceed on foot, hippety-hop over the mountains, to an airplane and flight from this doom island.

When I could return to the library, I did not report that the nice doctor had just about finished me but Monseiur Réné saw that I was barely mobile and brought me a cane. Creeping along with a cane, sneaker on right foot, cut-open bedroom slipper on left foot, added to my repellent skin colour, made me an irresistible target. When classes ended at noon the homing schoolchildren picked up stones and cheerfully stoned me. They were behind me and I didn't know what the yelling and laughing was about until a stone hit me. I thought this an accident and turned to smile forgiveness, only to see a bunch of pretty little kids, dressed in those French-style black school smocks, jumping up and down and aiming more stones. Which hit me. 'Blanc! Blanc!' they shouted, meaning 'Nigger! Nigger!' The stones weren't large, nor were the kids; I wasn't hurt. I was an old lame Negro, chivvied and harassed by white kids, and I burned with outrage. And with hatred for those adults on the street who watched, smiling approval.

There was nothing to do except retreat to the library, where again I suppressed the news of the day. The silent retreat shamed me. Shame was hardest to bear. I could see it would take a while to get used to humiliation. If anyone ever got used to it?

My unborn novel was by now a sad joke. All day, I sat on the hard library chair, resting my foot on an orange crate, and read and brooded. From whenever ideas first reach a child's mind, I had been indoctrinated by my parents' words and deeds never to condemn by race, creed, colour or even nationality. The history of our time gave that early teaching the force of moral law; I refer, above all, to the Nazis. But there was still plenty of repression in the world, by race, creed and colour, and I was wholeheartedly against it. Yet here I sat, in racist Jacmel, grinding my teeth in a fury of counter-racism. I wondered whether I was ruined for life and would become a disgrace to my parents, loathing blacks.

It is hard to believe that, in 1952, there were only two places on earth where blacks could not be insulted or mistreated simply because of their colour: Haiti and Liberia. The Caribbean colonies were intact though certainly benign by 1952, but the African colonies were far from guaranteed humane and insult was automatic: no dogs or natives allowed. The American South practised apartheid, discrimination and segregation, and deprived Negroes of the basic right to vote. Ugly and violent white racism: and the Civil Rights Act, which finally outlawed all this, was twelve years away. South Africa made customary apartheid into the law of the land, in 1948. But Haiti had been a sovereign state for just short of one hundred and fifty years. No living Haitian ever suffered here from white racism.

Hold on. Error. For twenty years, from 1915 until 1934, when Franklin Roosevelt recalled them, the US Marines were overlords of Haiti. They had been sent for allegedly humanitarian reasons, to quell disorder in Haiti; this action was justified by the Monroe

371

Doctrine (the time-honoured precursor of the Brezhnev Doctrine). Ordinary Haitians resented the Marines who treated them like American Negroes. No Negroes were then accepted in the Marine Corps. But surely the Marines hadn't troubled remote little Jacmel? There is a sort of folk knowledge that drifts and stays in the air. Could I have been reaping what the Marines sowed: anger, revenge, insult for injury? Americans tend to forget, or never knew, how often our government through our soldiery has interfered in the domestic affairs of others in the Caribbean area; and certainly we ignore the after-effects, lingering on in collective memory.

Haiti baffled me then and baffles me now, decades later. It is, I think, the most beautiful country in the Caribbean. It has a marvellous healthy climate, fertile soil, plenty of water, some mineral resources, possible hydro-electric power, a surrounding sea full of fish. With responsible government, education, public health care, Haiti could long since have become happy and prosperous. It has never been happy, though; as a slave-owning French colony called Saint Domingue, for well over a hundred years it made French investors and local landowners rich. Saint Domingue was notorious for brutality to slaves, which means something in view of contemporary standards. Slaves were worked to death, with all the attendant punishments and degradations. Ten labouring years was average life expectancy. Saint Domingue was really an eighteenth-century forerunner of Nazi concentration camps. Half a million slaves finally rebelled in the bloodiest uprising of the slave world, fought French soldiers with raging bravery for three years, and won their freedom. It is a colossal story of will and courage. After the United States, Haiti was the second independent nation in the New World. Since 1804, Haiti has been misruled by Haitians.

Misrule is nothing new anywhere at any time. Perhaps Haiti never had a hope, poisoned from the beginning by its terrible past. There is something in this, looking around the world today. The worse the early oppression, the worse oppression continues, like battered babies maturing into baby-batterers. It is rubbish to pretend, as the Reagan administration does, that communism alone assures misrule. Consider capitalist states in Central and South America, Turkey, Pakistan, the Philippines, most of Africa from north to south. Zaire is a model of rapacious corruption; as the Congo, it had a famously nasty rapacious past. Can the relentless siege mentality of the Afrikaners in South Africa be traced back to the Boer War? The rulers in the Kremlin are more understandable as lineal descendants of the Tsars; too bad they weren't all brought up in Sweden. How long does it take a people to outgrow and reject inherited misrule? However long, they have to do it themselves if they can.

Toussaint l'Ouverture, the hero slave leader, might have been the founding father Haiti needed, but he died in a French prison. Two self-styled Emperors, engrossed in their imperial life style, were followed by a turnover of greedy presidents, grabbing power by palace *putsch*, rigged elections, assassinations. The procession of presidents ended fatally in 1957 with Papa Doc Duvalier who locked his people in a sinister police state, ruling by terror through thugs in sunglasses, the Tonton Macoutes, by torture, murder and the ominous use of Voodoo. Now Papa Doc's heir, Baby Doc, upholds the family tradition. Maybe the Duvaliers, Presidents-for-Life, have founded a dynasty and can give Haiti another hundred years of slavery.

After one hundred and seventy-nine years of home-grown misrule to date, Haiti is among the world's least developed countries, economically and socially. Haiti ranks 122. Only thirteen countries, mostly new African states, are more deprived. (The US ranks 7, Britain ranks 16.) These statistics are not a comment on style of government but on the material conditions, within each state, of the mass of the governed. In the western hemisphere, Haiti has the lowest per-capita income; the fewest schools, teachers and literates; the fewest hospitals and doctors; the highest infant mortality; the lowest life expectancy. Misrule is an ongoing (as they say) fact from Haiti south, and can be measured in the same terms. (El Salvador 84, Guatemala 85, etc; but Cuba 36, far ahead of all countries in the Caribbean, in Central and South America with only Argentina, 37, a close rival. What do we make of that?) Haiti's sorry distinction is to be bottom of the bottom class in an area where public welfare is not the most urgent priority of government and poverty ranges from heavy to crushing.

People often say, with pride, 'I'm not interested in politics.' They might as well say, 'I'm not interested in my standard of living, my health, my job, my rights, my freedoms, my future or any future.' Politics is the business of governing and nobody can escape being governed, for better or worse. In the few fortunate societies where voting is free and honest, most people take the weird view that politics is a horse race—you bet on a winner or loser every so often, if you can bestir yourself; but politics is not a personal concern. Politics is *everything*—from clean drinking water through the preservation of forests, whales, British Leyland to nuclear weapons and the disposal thereof. If we mean to keep any control over our world and lives, we must be interested in politics.

The unlucky ignorant people of Haiti never understood that they had to take an interest in politics while they still had the chance. I think their brains were fuddled by three hundred years of Voodoo. They were too busy propitiating a gang of demented malevolent gods to notice that men, not gods, were running their country and themselves into the ground. If they know now, it is late. Once you get a tyranny, you don't easily get rid of it. Much better to remember about eternal vigilance.

While I was brooding on my chair one morning, Monsieur Réné appeared with a book. He said it was the only book in English in the library, where I was always the only customer. No one could read English but perhaps it would interest me. The book was E. M. Forster's *Two Cheers for Democracy*. A miracle of the highest order. Oh, that beautiful book! It shines with reason, mercy, honour, good will and wit; and is written in those water-smooth sentences that one wants to stroke for the pleasure of feeling them. No longer isolated, I had Mr Forster's mind for company. When

I finished the book, I wrote pages to Mr Forster, like a letter in a bottle, telling him that he was a light in the darkness and a moral example to mankind. I resolved to reform. I would not disgrace my parents or Mr Forster; no goddamned black racists were going to make a racist of me.

During these month-long days, I observed the weather but took no joy from it, though it was joyful. The sky went up in pale to darker translucent layers of blue, the air smelled of flowers and sea and sun, so delicious you could taste it. The Caribbean, my favourite sea, stretched out like a great smooth sapphire carpet with wind moving gently under it. I hungered for the sea and one afternoon nerved myself to chance the path down the cliff. With a dress over my bathing-suit, a towel around my neck, the usual footwear and cane, I made my way slowly to the beach. The sand was golden, empty and lovely; no boats, no people and no sign of there having been either.

I chucked my stuff and got into the sea like a crab, using my arms. Freedom returned; I could move. I swam far out in the silky water and floated, rejoicing. Jacmel washed off me, body and soul. Unable to sing, a felt lack, I made shouting noises of delight. Every day, until I had two sound legs, I would bring bread and papaya, the only edible pension food, to the glorious beach and swim and sunbathe. Happiness was possible, even in Jacmel.

When I started to drag myself up the sand to my clothes, I saw the boys. They were playing ball with my dress, footwear, cane, towel. There were eight of them, teenagers, fleet of foot and laughing their heads off. I stood up, with dignity, and informed them that they were too big for this game and please give me my effects. They instantly invented a new game. They ran in close and flicked me with dress and towel, twirled my sneaker against my face, feinted and jabbed with the cane. After lurching once for my dress, I realized that pleased them; also that it was useless. I imagined, with dread, hobbling up the street in my white bathing-suit while all Jacmel came out to jeer. But I could not make it, not without foot covering and cane.

I limped on the comfortable sand toward the path, maintaining cold silence and, I hoped, a calm face. They followed, same game, same taunting laughter. My good resolves left me. I wanted to cause them grievous bodily harm. Failing that, I wanted to curse them at the top of my lungs. But I was afraid to anger these white bully boys. They could do much worse to a defenceless Negro. And who would punish them, who would care? Monsieur Réné, the tolerant educated white, could hardly stand up to the whole nigger-baiting town. I had to conceal rage and alarm, as other Negroes have surely done, and stand and take it. Suddenly, they had had all the fun they needed, threw my things around the beach, and ran up the path. I collected them piece by piece, got organized, and climbed to the street, knowing I would not risk the sea again. Jacmel had defeated me.

Now it was Mardi Gras and Jacmel seethed with excitement because the Carnival Queen of Haiti was arriving by air to preside over the festivities. Everyone was costumed and painted and bouncing around the streets. Alone on the pension balcony, I watched this throng of merry Haitians and thought them grotesque and hideous, just as they thought me. My only interest in the event was the Queen; I had to get a ride back to Port-au-Prince. Neither the Queen nor her plane were available to a white Negro but an ancient limousine had brought the Queen's mother as chaperone and the Magistrate, whatever that meant. I elbowed through the crowd to this gentleman and made him a threatening speech. If I were left here, probably to die of gangrene, the entire world would know and blame Haiti; I was a famous journalist with powerful connections, et cetera. I don't think I have ever behaved worse and I didn't care.

They allowed me to pay for a place in the limousine. I was ordered to the front seat where the chauffeur, a servant, had to put up with me. The grand passengers in the rear did not deign to speak to me. If they thought I wanted to sit near them or talk with them, they were crazy. We were all racists together. And I had the best view of the country, lush and flowered like a Douanier Rousseau jungle, and beautiful every mile of the way.

Air service between the islands was sketchy. I got to St Thomas where I met a man who frolicked about in a Piper Cub, an air bum. He gave me a lift to Philipsburg on the Dutch side of St Martin, an enchanting island that was, and still is by choice, half Dutch, half French. I had been blissfully becalmed on the French side, ten years earlier; why didn't I come here at once and spare myself Haiti? Because Haiti was the unknown, that's all and that's enough. I haven't yet learned to be careful in travel.

Philipsburg had a dear dinky Dutch charm; freshly-painted shutters on little square houses, starched white curtains, neat gardens, swept streets. The houses belonged to friendly composed black people, speaking Caribbean English. Accommodation was in the Government Rest House, four barely furnished but spotless rooms. Here, at last, I would get to work. But I felt tender to myself, I deserved a long convalescence to recover from Jacmel. Beyond the village, I found a cove where I spent my days, swimming naked in aquamarine water, lying on white sand, dreaming a novel instead of writing it.

A handful of white people lived on the Dutch side of the island. We had no reason to foregather and didn't. The two races lived in amity under the guardian eye of a lone black policeman. Since no one despised and maltreated me because of my skin, I stopped being a racist. Much later I began to think, imagine, hope, that maybe, somehow, possibly I understood just the tiniest bit of what it really means to be black in a bad place.

The Women of Greenham Common

Nine miles of fence surround the American base and the Cruise missiles at Greenham Common. The steel mesh outer fence is 10 feet high with out-and-down sloping steel bars draped in barbed wire. A continuous roll of barbed wire, 2 feet in diameter, lies just behind. A patrol path separates the outer from the inner fence, also steel mesh, about 5 feet high, topped by more barbed wire. Small wooden guard towers stand empty on this clear cold day. That fence has a very strong personality. It reminds me of Nazi concentration camps. The fenced-in land is bare, the dispersed building bleak, ugly, prison type. It is a dark place, alien in the countryside. The people who live and work on the base, and the missiles, are further protected by police, soldiers, dogs. They have all the power but seem helplessly trapped. They are under siege by a small group of women who have no power at all except an idea.

At four gates outside the fence, the women of Greenham Common camp in conditions of such startling hardship as would cause mutiny in a peacetime army. Those camps also have very strong personalities but they remind me of nothing because they are new in the world, unique, and amazing.

Over two years ago, 60 British women met at Cardiff and walked to Greenham Common. They had no plan but shared a sense of outrage. Nuclear weapons poison life and the future; children could not grow up sanely, hopefully, with the fear of planetary massacre. Now new needless deadly weapons were to be stationed in their homeland, increasing an already intolerable danger. They believed it was time for ordinary people to say no. Then they decided to stay where they had walked. The camps have grown and never been empty since that day. Any woman from anywhere in the world can come, remain, go, return; and be welcomed. No questions are asked. There is no hierarchy, no 'structure'. There is no distinction by race, creed, colour, money, age, class or nationality. These unpretentious women, in their beat-up warm clothes, have become a world-wide symbol and model for countless ordinary people who also say no.

The women's headquarters is outside the main gate: a campfire circled by junkyard bits, ancient damp sofa, big collapsing chair, old straight chairs, and a makeshift canvas roof over the food supplies. We check in and are taken on a sightseeing tour along a path by the fence. 'See that? It's new, it's razor wire.' Progress even in barbed wire. A shiny roll of the new wire lies behind the second fence; instead of the old fashioned rusty barbs, silvery bits of steel maybe an inch long by half an inch wide. These slash like razors instead of gouging like barbs. 'We were worried about it: we didn't know if it sprang back at you when cut but it doesn't, it springs outwards.' Our guide is the oldest woman there, in years and length of residence: a tall strong grandmother, a war widow, with a wind-and sunburned face, her hair pulled back in a rubber band.

Two mounted police ride along the path and we step off into the bushes. Our guide says good morning pleasantly and is pleasantly answered. 'We were terribly afraid of the horses but we aren't any more. They're lovely. If you stand right up under their heads they won't do anything.' Now we see three policemen inside the fence, huddled by a guardhouse. Again our guide speaks pleasantly but is not answered. 'They're Ministry of Defence police; they're always like that.' The men look curiously shrunken by cold, boredom, sullenness. 'The Americans are forbidden to have eye contact with us.' *What?* 'They're not allowed to look at us; they can't see us. They drive in from their other bases, in their buses, staring straight ahead. But the local police are very nice and friendly. It's when they bring in the police support groups; the Thames Valley ones are very rough. They don't care what they do.'

Back at the fire, the only heat in the camps and the only means of cooking, we find eight women at lunchtime, some casually making sandwiches. They cook one hot meal at night: Who does? 'Anyone who wants to.' I ask what they all were before coming here. A sociologist, a worker in a hostel, a teacher, a forester from Scotland, a psychotherapist from America, a young German kindergarten teacher, a housewife, aged 50-plus, who announced that she was going home for a while next week as it was her son's 17th birthday. Next to me, a pretty brown-haired girl, a researcher by profession, spent seven weeks last summer at seminars and meetings in Japan as a rep from Greenham Common to the Japanese women's peace movement.

The brown-haired researcher was saying, 'It's no good blaming Reagan and Andropov and Thatcher. We all have to take responsibility.' Yes indeed, nuclear weapons are too important to leave to politicians. What have they done, in 39 years, except waste the nation's wealth on more and more of the abominable things, an insane overkill? As you get older, I find, politicians seem increasingly tiresome. There they are, on both sides of the Iron Curtain, solemnly mouthing identical prophecies: without these nuclear weapons, the Communists, the Capitalists, as the case may be, will invade our countries. They never explain why either side should wish or need to invade the other.

I wanted to talk about suffragettes because I am haunted to remember that I never thanked my beautiful mother, a suffragette, but took for granted what those women struggled to provide me: a legal identity, the freedom to choose how I live. Suffragettes were reviled, mocked, maltreated, yet without them, all of us women would still be tyrannized by Mrs Thatcher's beloved Victorian values and Mrs Thatcher would not be in 10 Downing Street, decrying peace women. How proud the suffragettes would be of their descendants in these hardship camps. How impressed Gandhi would be by this non-violent, determined protest. The women attack a fence, much as Gandhi attacked salt.

The women have learned from Gandhi and thought about the suffragettes. 'Why do you think we wear their colours?' asks the researcher, showing me a Greenham badge with streamers of purple, green and white ribbon. I didn't even know the suffragettes had colours. 'But we are going further.'

Now a very small girl in a poodle coat, cheap imitation astrakhan, arrives with a wonderful baby. The baby was born here, aided by 'a radical midwife.' They all love the baby, who is healthy and contented in his unusual extended family. Thinking of the girl mother, I ask about injuries. She says she stays out of actions. But five women have had legs and arms broken, one woman was badly kicked in the stomach, another girl had fingers broken by a deliberate boot, another's hand smashed by a truncheon at the fence, an ear torn, a scalp cut; all know what it feels like to have arms twisted up behind the back, to be dragged along the ground. What happens to the injured? 'We go to the hospital in Newbury.' 'I think the police select us at actions; they must have photos; they know who we are. We're usually the ones who get hurt.' But there are no heroics about this, not even rancour.

The vigilantes are something else, and news to me. At night, unidentifiable men have come and thrown buckets of maggots, animal blood, slurry into their shelters. They say that volunteers for this vile work are recruited in a pub in Newbury. 'But who are they?' I ask, unable to imagine such people. 'Angry men,' says a woman, shrugging.

We cross the road to visit the living quarters, the 'benders,' so named because they are built by bending twigs into an igloo shape and covering them with plastic sheeting. I have no idea who invented this or how they learned survival skills. They carry water from some distant tap; they find firewood in the surrounding forest and chop it to size; they dig latrine pits in the woods. The light in the camps is from candles and a few kerosene lamps. No wonder they don't look like what the fashionable outdoor woman will wear this year.

I ask how many women live here. This camp is big enough to need three fires. Nobody knows. Our guide thinks there are women from France, Germany, Holland, Italy, Japan, but everyone moves freely so you can't keep count and no one wants to.

We crawl into our guide's bender on hands and knees; the opening is small to shut out wind and rain. Leaves are still on the twigs that hold up the plastic hut. 'Isn't it lovely? Much better than tents because you can stand up.' 'But the floor,' I say, with horror. 'It's wet!' An old piece of carpet laid over something else. 'No, it isn't. Come here, sit on the bed, I have boards under the bed.' A thinnish foam mattress. Dear God, the long freezing nights, the freezing morning.

Our guide, who owns a van, has to hurry with two days' mailed cheques to the bank in Newbury. She picks up a sheaf of cheques from the van's seat. Cheques for £5, £10, £65, money orders, dollar bills in an envelope from America. Many cheques signed by men. 'And they say we get our money from Moscow.' On Wednesdays, there is a 'money meeting.' Women from the four camps meet at headquarters to share out money where it is required, beyond what the camp members can contribute.

Cheques also flow to finance another brilliantly original protest. In the US District Court of New York, 13 Greenham Common Women, joined by a few admirable US Congressmen, have sued the US Government, naming as defendants President Reagan, Secretary of Defence Caspar Weinberger, Verne Orr, the Secretary of the Air Force, top boss of the Greenham USAF base for the missiles, and John O. Marsh, Secretary of the Army. Their case is that Cruise missiles breach Human Rights Law, the Law of War, and the American Constitution. They are backed by chilling testimony from an impressive list of experts, and supported by peace movements throughout Europe and the Green Party in Germany. The Federal Judge has ordered the United States Government to produce its defence.

The Greenham women cannot win but they will not give up

easily and I must say I love the nerve of it. Their aim is to arouse more American public opinion against further deployment of the new missiles in Europe. There is plenty of aroused anti-nuclear public opinion in America and it will grow because Americans learned very slowly, from Vietnam, that their government is not always right.

The Green Gate camp, known as the 'eviction camp,' has the most attractive site, down a steep path inside the woods. The girls are gathered around their fire in the fading light. I use the word girls because of their youth. They never do. They are all equally and firmly women. 'On Thursdays, at dusk, a podgy little man, he's the bailiff, appears and says, "Eviction, ladies". ' The speaker is a very pretty student with long red hair and emerald green ski clothes. 'Then two women run out to the road, to the dump truck, and shout "That's mine! That's mine!" before they can throw in any of our chairs to be chewed up. They can't destroy personal property.' Another girl continues, 'The rest of us grab the benders and everything and run down there.' She gestures to the woods beyond. 'A man owns some land in the common and he lets us park our stuff on it, until the bailiff's men go away.' After which, in the dark, they try to sort themselves out and rebuild their shelters. It cannot be fun; they laugh about it.

'They haven't come for seven weeks,' says the oldest woman there, formerly a teacher of weaving, now engaged on a bright piece of crocheting. 'Maybe they're getting tired of it.' 'There are fewer police, too,' someone says. 'We think they're running out of money.' The bailiff is a standing hassle but the vigilantes have been here, burning several benders. Some girls think the vigilantes are National Front, one says perhaps police in plain clothes; they can't tell, in the dark. By good luck, nobody was sleeping in those benders.

'You look so clean,' I say, which causes merriment. 'We have a bathroom.' Another plastic sheet, hung up to hide them from police eyes, and decorated with soggy towels; cans of water; a homemade table for an enamel washbowl, glasses with tooth-brushes. 'Toothpaste freezes,' says a girl cheerfully. Another says,

'You have to wash your hands quickly before ice forms.' Instantly, because they reject the sound of complaint, everyone explains that they can take a hot shower at the swimming baths in Newbury.

I had seen on TV news a woman being dragged by her arms by two policemen; I thought how painful that must be. The red-haired girl says, 'If you sit like this, they can't get at your arms.' She joins her arms under drawn-up knees. A blonde beauty in a Chilean poncho says, laughing hard, 'They've got workshops now, to learn how to handle limp women.' Beside me, a girl says quietly, 'They're all sorts. I've had my arm twisted but then another one has picked me up gently and when he put me down he said, "You all right?" All sorts.'

I said, 'You all seem happy.' I meant much more. I had never seen any women so sure of themselves and each other, so easy together, without any sign of rivalry or tension or hostility. All of them, from the oldest to the youngest. Yet they are very different, probably would not have met in ordinary life. You feel their trusting and respecting friendship; it is an atmosphere of remarkable peace. And freedom. And lightness of spirit. 'We know why we're here,' the blonde girl said gravely. 'We know what we're doing.'

Women from the Main Gate arrived; they visit among the camps. Greetings and laughter. They were joking about my cleanliness remark and describing the surplus of baths and showers they used to have. We drove to the newest camp at the Blue Gate, the 'singing camp.' Wedged between a noisy main road and the fence, the benders are squashed together. They looked abandoned until we saw firelight through a chink; here they have rigged up a communal bender around their fire, for some privacy in this exposed spot. 'Why singing?' I asked. 'Do you have fine voices?' 'No, we have useless voices,' said the girl next to me, formerly a journalist on a provincial paper. 'We just like to sing. And they hate it,' nodding to the nearby police post. 'I heard one of them saying, "Oh God, not again." ' On request, they sing gaily but not very tunefully a song with the refrain, 'Ban the Bomb.'

It is night at 5.30 and they are about to cook supper, a

vegetable curry. This is the youngest age group except for the middle-aged housewife from the Main Gate, who apparently lives here. She says, 'Kirsten, are you on watch tonight?' Kirsten is one of three Dutch girls in residence. We talked of harassment. A helicopter circles at night and beams light on them. 'I don't mind the helicopter,' said the housewife. 'I mind the light when they park their trucks close up. Last time, I began reading a newspaper so they went away.'

Suddenly I understand that all day I have seen an open university. They have bridged the generation gap, obliterated class, surmounted nationality; everyone here is learning. I leave the camps with admiration for their courage, knowing that I haven't the stamina to last one night on Greenham Common. I can only praise these famous women. Though when, at some half-frozen moment by a fire, I announced that they were a fact in history, a jolly girl wearing sweaters and long tin earrings said, 'Yeah, I read things like that and I think why it's just me and Debbie and Jean and all. Just us lot.'

On Torture

The following document was given to me in San Salvador, in the dusty yard behind the offices of the Archdiocese. There are a few shade trees in the yard, a couple of wooden benches, and a green corrugated tin shack, the headquarters of the Commission of Human Rights of El Salvador. The shack is filled with shelves of box files, odd-lot tables for desks, chairs, an old typewriter, an old mimeograph machine and people. Wherever power resides in San Salvador, it is protected by armed guards, high walls and steel doors. This place is open; nobody is afraid to talk; the air is different. In that diseased city, the yard and the shack are beautiful.

The Commission of Human Rights is a company of volunteers determined to record for the world, if the world will listen, ceaseless violations of human rights by Salvadoran Security Forces. The volunteers are young, probably not long ago students at the university which is now closed, looted and occupied by soldiers. They are a band of heroes, nothing less, and their life expectancy is uncertain. Human rights in El Salvador are reduced to one: the right to live. Two people, who originally set up the commission, are dead in their thirties: a woman lawyer, assassinated, which means her body was found; a gifted doctor, universally loved, disappeared, which means his body will never be found. Everyone working for the commission is marked. The witnesses themselves are in danger; it is 'subversive' to testify to the crimes of the state. The Security Forces can do what they like to anyone they choose: none of them has ever been punished for kidnapping, torture and murder. They are invulnerable against the defenceless.

In 1982, the Human Rights Commission recorded the fate of 6,952 Salvadorans, men, women, boys, girls, who were seized (*capturados*), disappeared or assassinated. Torture is not recorded as a separate violation of human rights because it is automatic. The Security Forces and the Death Squads, their unofficial colleagues, do not even kill cleanly with a bullet as proved by the mutilated bodies found at random anywhere in El Salvador. Of 6,952 human beings, only 325 survived to be sent, after torture, to the political prisons.

One of these was the young man whose testimony is printed here. It is a unique document, not because his anguish was exceptional, but because he lived to tell the story from beginning to end. Had it not been for a fluke rescue, he would have died and disappeared, like thousands before and since. 'Torture in El Salvador,' the Human Rights Commission explains, 'has become routine, as a method of work, considered natural and necessary by those who practise it.' For twelve days, this young man was tortured as routine and for his torturers' pleasure. Diseased imaginations invented these tortures, designed to unhinge the mind while ruining the body. They are an abominable advance on Gestapo techniques. After twelve days, he was interrogated briefly and absurdly. Knowing nothing, he confessed nothing. He was tortured again. Near death, he was revived by doctors. After nineteen days he was taken to court, charged by the Security Forces with concocted 'subversion.' He still had the unbroken nerve and clarity of mind to deny the charges, denounce his torturers and insist that the International Red Cross hear his testimony and examine the marks on his body.

Torture has spread from the Gestapo, the disease carrier, worldwide—increasing in virulence over the years. Before the Second World War, for the first time in modern history, torture was integral state policy in Nazi Germany. It was less systematic but no less vicious in Fascist Italy. The Lubianka was a synonym for torture in Stalinist Russia. Torture returned to Spain, like a memory of the Inquisition, in Franco's prisons. If torture was practised elsewhere in the world, then, it was sporadic and secret, not part of the state bureaucracy. Now, Amnesty has evidence of the practise of torture in ninety countries: it is updating its list this year. The earth is covered by one hundred and sixty-four nations, including such minatures as Andorra and St Lucia. In more than half the nations of our world, torture certifies that the form of government is tyranny. Only tyranny, no matter how camouflaged, needs and employs torturers. Torture has no ideology.

Once we thought that Germany was peculiarly diseased since it produced an abundance of torturers. Now we know that torturers appear wherever they're wanted. Shortage of labour is not a problem. Previous experience is helpful but unnecessary, learn on the job, regular eight-hour shifts, good wages from a grateful government. In ninety countries, torturers are on the state payroll, like postmen. What is their work; how do they talk; where do they operate: who are they? It is all here to read, not a fictional horror but a fact of barbarity now. And though the machinery and manner may vary according to nationality—variations from Chile to South Africa to Russia, for instance—the purpose is the same: the purpose is to silence those who disagree.

All member states of the United Nations are obliged to honour the Universal Declaration of Human Rights. El Salvador is a member of the United Nations; so are eighty-five other countries where torture is practised. The majority of the torturers' regimes belong in the Free World, friendly clients or allies. I don't know exactly what 'Free World' means except as a politician's phrase. If it means the total of nations not under communist control, it is a misnomer; we should speak of the Partially Free World, or the Free Enterprise World. Our leaders, especially the present leaders of the two great English-speaking democracies, denounce the Soviet Union for its abuse of human rights. The abuse of human rights, culminating in torture as the final and worst abuse, should always be denounced everywhere. But our freedom-loving leaders condone or—unforgivably—assist the torturers' regimes on our side. El Salvador is only one example. There are too many. Lop-sided morality is not morality at all; it is fraud.

Dr Henry Kissinger is widely regarded by decision-makers and governments as a champion geopolitical thinker. Dr Kissinger believes in power and is believed by the powerful. He talks their language, telling them what they like to hear. He was the natural choice for chairman of President Reagan's advisory committee on Central America. Concluding that task, he said: 'If we cannot manage Central America, it will be impossible to convince threatened nations in the Persian Gulf and other places that we know how to manage the Global Equilibrium.'

The arrogance is matched by the moral idiocy. The people of Central America do not count; they have no individual existence, let alone rights. Nor do the people around the Persian Gulf matter; the oil matters. The Global Equilibrium to which Dr Kissinger refers is a world-wide dread of insane nuclear war coming closer and closer. To balance on a tightrope over an abyss is not the ordinary man's idea of equilibrium.

Geopolitics tend to fail, after causing immeasurable misery. You might say that Hitler was the top geopolitical failure. The bombing of Laos and Cambodia, a geopolitical action guided by Dr Kissinger, did not give the planned results but destroyed two countries and millions of lives. Never mind, if it doesn't work in Southeast Asia, try again in Central America. There must be a Kissinger clone in the Kremlin offices, advising that 'If we cannot manage Afghanistan, it will be impossible to convince threatened nations in Eastern Europe and other places that we know how to manage the Global Equilibrium.'

Governments think big; they think geopolitically. Human rights are irrelevant to geopolitics. This may kill us all in the end.

*

SAN SALVADOR, *4–22 April, 1982*

On 4 April, 1982 at around 4.30 in the afternoon I was waiting at a bus stop, just opposite the petrol station on San Antonio Abad Street. A military convoy appeared, a white Ford van with eight policemen carrying M16 rifles, followed by two radio patrol cars from the National Police and two military jeeps. The men got out and surrounded the area, blocking off traffic. Plainclothes police, without explanation, tied me up. There were witnesses around, so I said, 'What's happening, Señores?' An army officer came up and hit me in the lower stomach with his rifle butt, saying, 'You think I don't know who you are?' His soldiers began to beat me, knocking me to the ground. A sergeant pulled me up and pushed me in a patrol car, the white Ford van followed. We stopped at the Vieytez Cinema; inside, in a sort of bar, they blindfolded and handcuffed me and took me back and threw me on the floor of the van.

When they took me out of the van, they led me up and down stairs for about five minutes, left me in an intensely cold room for another fifteen minutes, then led me out where someone, I assumed the chief, put his hand on my shoulder and said in a friendly way, 'I think I know you. You're from San Miguel, aren't you?'

I said, 'Yes.'

'Do you know why you're here or haven't the boys told you?'

I said, 'No.'

'Take him away and give him the most comfortable bed and the best food.'

Another man said, 'The Guardia are looking for him.'

'No problem,' another said. 'If he doesn't collaborate we'll turn him over to them.'

Another man hit me in the stomach and said, 'Not only the Guardia but the Treasury Police are looking for this son of a whore! Take him away!'

Someone grabbed my hair and like that they led me again up and down stairs and I figured I was in the Barracks of the National Police from what they had said. They stopped and took off my clothes and handcuffs and blindfold and said, 'Don't look back,' and shoved so that I slipped and fell on a floor covered with excrement and urine in a completely black room.

Three or four hours passed before a man, looking like a peasant, opened the door and gave me a blindfold and told me to tie it tightly. In the hall, someone tied a long cord around my testicles and pulled me by this to a room where loud music was playing. Someone said, 'Do you like the Bee Gees or would you prefer something of Mejia Godoy?' I said it was their business and he grabbed my hair and said, 'Answer my question.' 'Then the Bee Gees,' I said. 'You'll see how nice it is to take a beating to musical accompaniment.' They tied the cord around my testicles to something, then tied my feet and hands, and then all of them began to beat me with truncheons. I fell down from being hit in the stomach, they beat me on the back of the neck, the ankles, and the head, someone else punched me under the ribs and in the thorax. Someone clapped his hands repeatedly over my ears. They pulled me to my knees with the cord on my testicles. I don't know how long it lasted but it seemed interminable. I said, 'Stop, don't go on, man,' and one said, 'This is the way to shut up this whore asshole.' He pulled the corners of my mouth to open it and put in something that filled my mouth into the cheeks while another held me up and someone gave me a karate chop behind the knee, he did this six times and the pain in the kneecap was intense. Then a man straddled my shoulders and put two fingers in each nostril, pulling my head back. I thought I was going to choke, my nose bled heavily.

Someone jumped on my tied feet and another hit me in the back; when I fell, they pulled me up again by the cord around my testicles.

They ordered me to sit down. They took out the thing they had put in my mouth and my cheeks had an uncontrollable movement, like a nervous tic, when they placed the hood over my head. This instrument of torture is rubber specially made so that it clings to your nostrils when you breathe. I panicked, I couldn't breathe and my heartbeat went wild. Someone said, 'Now,' which I soon understood meant the order to take off the hood. They gave me just enough time to gulp air then put it on again. On, off; about the ninth time I felt a total faintness of the body and a kind of amnesia so that I wondered *Who am I?* and forgot what was happening. I passed out.

When I came to, someone with big hands was squeezing my neck in the region of the tonsils, I was dizzy, without strength, with difficulty in breathing. A voice said, 'Get up,' and I tried but fell, hitting my head on the concrete floor. I did not feel my body, which alarmed me, but they threw buckets of ice water on me and sensation returned. I was lying on my stomach and pushed up my blindfold a little to see around me. They put two round metal objects on the sole of my left foot, then rolled me over, put a sticky ointment on my forehead and attached another round metal object there. I could see that wires went from these to a black metal industrial box with three coloured buttons, red, green, yellow; the box was placed on a metal table and a man beside it pressed the buttons. Suddenly an electric shock went through my body, my whole body writhed, my eyes rolled around in terrible pain, my hands were stiff, my neck was twisted. I did not lose consciousness but I felt terror of another shock. They threw another bucket of ice water on me and another shock made my whole body arch up and I lost consciousness, my last sensation was agony in the head.

When I came to, I said, 'No more, man, I'm epileptic, you can give me convulsions, if you want to question me at least leave me some consciousness.' As I stopped talking, I felt another shock, equal to the first, of a kind that tears up the whole body. They threw water on me again. The pain in my eyes and forehead was intense and I felt something like needles in my brain.

Some time elapsed. I don't know how much, perhaps ten minutes. I heard a voice.

'Get up,' it said. 'Do you want to have a bath?'

'Yes,' I said.

He took me out of the room. 'I want to help you,' he said.

'No,' I said.

'I'll run the bath for you. And just to prove that I mean to help you, I'll take off the blindfold. No one ever does that here.'

The bathroom in which I found myself was spacious and clean and had one fairly large mirror. It was painted the same colours as the National Police uniform, the lower part a dark coffee-brown and the upper a pale yellow. The policeman left, and I began my bath.

Very little time passed before two men entered. They were both tall and heavily built and had Afro hairstyles. One had a full beard. The other was shaven but with a heavy blue-green shadow on his chin. They were angry to find me without my blindfold, and they immediately put it back on, very tightly. They did not look like they were from El Salvador, and they spoke with Argentine accents.

'Put the bolt on the door,' one of them said.

'What do you say,' I heard next, 'shall we screw him?'

The other began to fondle me and I pushed his hand away. He put his hand over my mouth and asked: 'Haven't you ever sucked cock?' I didn't answer, and I was knocked down and made to kneel. One grabbed me by the hair from behind, while the other forced his erect penis into my mouth.

When I left the bathroom, I heard the sounds of dawn. They gave me my clothes but not shoes. Leading me by holding my right wrist, I got the impression that now we were in the upper part of the building. They put me in a room and closed the door. I took off the blindfold and saw it was a small clean room with a metal desk and two chairs and a polarized mirror, so I put back the blindfold. Not by any fixed plan, an agent would open the door and say, 'Stand up,' then later another would come and say, 'Sit down.' This was the day after my capture, 5 April, and I stayed here the 5th, 6th, and 7th, being given water and a tortilla, sometimes twice, sometimes three times a day. The floors up here were wood and I could hear other prisoners being brought in and out of these rooms.

On the third day here, 7 April, I had to relieve myself and asked the agent when he opened the door to let me go to the toilet. He said, 'You're not in your house here, son of a whore,' and locked the door. My bladder was full and I felt terrible unease and cold sweats from not being able to defecate or urinate. The next day I asked again and he said, 'If you piss here, you'll swallow it. Wait, I'll fix you up.' About ten minutes later, he came back with other men. I was stripped and a strong adhesive tape was bound around my penis, closing it. The pain was bad and got worse. The next morning, they came and made me drink water and splashed water on my stomach, making the need to urinate and the pain always worse. On 10 April, they came and said, 'Don't you want to urinate?' and took me to the toilet where I urinated blood, with pain.

They took me back to the same room where I stayed three days. They cared for my wounds and fed me decently and I thought they were trying to soften me up, but I recuperated some strength. An agent came in and found me without the blindfold. I explained that the blindfold made me see flashing lights and I feared this would bring on an epileptic attack. He locked the door and said I could keep it off with him. He was white, tall, with light brown eyes, reddish hair, aquiline nose, he wore an Arrow shirt and had an Omega watch. He gave me a cigarette and talked amiably, asking if I spoke English, what countries I had visited, what type of woman I liked. I said, 'You're not from here.' By his accent he was somewhere between Guatemalan and Colombian. He smiled and said, 'You're very intelligent and observant and here that's a death penalty, so keep your mouth shut.'

On 12 April, the interrogation began; this was the 'good' man who said he wanted to help me after the electric shocks. By his accent he was Panamanian. He told me to sit on a chair, let me take off the blindfold, gave me a cigarette and said, 'Our ideology is not to kill, we want to make you into a new man. That is what society wants. But to become a new man you must co-operate. We treat well everyone who co-operates.' Then he asked endless questions. I answered all the personal ones about my family, my mother and brother were in the United States, two other brothers lived in Holland; I lived on an allowance from my mother and had come to San Salvador to visit the Psychiatric Clinic. I said my profession was writer, though not published. The name of my unfinished book was *A Comical Word Called Justice*. He had my passport and asked specially about Nicaragua; the dates were all from 1979. I explained that I had gone to Nicaragua with my Nicaraguan girlfriend who had to see her parents but was afraid to go alone because Nicaragua was very disturbed. I was in and out of Nicaragua for a couple of days only. Then he asked about organizations I belonged to and what was my pseudonym in the

Communist Party and he said I was a leader in the CP and had been sent for training to Cuba and Nicaragua. I told him I studied psychology and philosophy at the University of Colombia at Medellin and if he knew anything he would know that Kierkegaard had nothing to do with Marxist-Leninism. I said I am an Existentialist and I don't know anything about organizations or politics and I don't give a damn about them. This went on a long time because he said he had to fill 70 pages with answers on the orders of his chiefs. He kept saying he was the kindest man I would meet and must answer his questions. I said how can I answer things I don't know? He put his papers in a folder, put back my blindfold and said, 'This is the way you've helped me,' and punched me on the back of the neck. He said, 'Stand up' and hit me so hard in the stomach that he knocked out my breath. He called to someone outside and said, 'He thinks he's the boss of San Salvador, he won't collaborate for shit.'

They stripped me and four held me down while another grabbed my hair because I was shouting and trying to resist. They tied my wrists behind me and tied my ankles and then tied both together behind, trussed like a chicken. The pain was terrible. After about 20 minutes I was picked up—by the knot—and carried, suspended in the air, to another room. I heard the groans of someone else there who, like me, was also trussed up. I shuffled closer to him and we managed to work loose our blindfolds. The man was a peasant, about forty-eight or fifty. He had white hair and a bushy beard, and worked at the Suchitoto hospital. He was still wearing his pale green hospital uniform. 'I am here,' he said, 'because I threw a stone to get some mangoes from a tree and broke a street lamp which blacked out the whole block.' Leonidas had been there since eleven o'clock in the morning and they were trying to make him say that the hospital staff was made up of communists. But they weren't—they were good people—and even if they were, Leonidas knew nothing about it.

Some torturers entered. 'Leonidas,' one of them said, 'you're a good man. You don't want to spend your last days like this, but you must co-operate.' Leonidas' reply filled me with courage: 'Don't talk to me. I don't even know who you are. You say you want me to co-operate, but you've done nothing but beat me since I got here.' I was so pleased I laughed out loud and the torturer kicked me in the ribcage. 'I have nothing to say,' Leonidas said. 'I don't know anything. My only comrades are Christ and his Apostles.' But then Leonidas added: 'But I know you're a good person at heart. Can't you untie me for a while? I can't take any more.'

The police agent replied: 'Here, we only treat kindly those people who co-operate. We'll untie you if you'll co-operate.'

'Yes,' Leonidas said at last. 'I will co-operate.' He was then untied, but he was unable to walk and someone had to lift him and help him.

They left me trussed from about midnight to five o'clock on 13 April, but constantly agents came in and touched my body in debasing ways and did things so disgusting that I vomited. I was in such despair that I told them to kill me but they only rubbed my face in the vomit. Then they made me get up and walk to the bath, gave me back my underpants and took me to a room, blindfolded. About eight o'clock, men came in violently shouting, 'Who told the Red Cross about you? This proves you're a leader! If it was one of our agents you will tell us!' They put something like a bulletproof vest on me and hung me up by my wrists and beat me with rubber truncheons on every part of my body for about two hours, until I vomited blood. They kept asking who told the Red Cross and one of them said, 'Get him out of here, the bastards are coming at eleven.'

They took me to the Officers' Club; I could see beneath the blindfold a billiard table, red plastic sofas, a television set and the machine for electric shocks. They played loud music and laughed and clapped, pretending to have a party where no one from the Red Cross would want, or be allowed, to enter. They gave me innumerable electric shocks, I kept losing consciousness, and the party went on.

At about four o'clock, as best I can calculate, a male nurse came and injected something intravenously into my left arm and gave me a pill. Within fifteen minutes, I felt no pain from the beatings or the electric shocks, I felt euphoric, without fear. They left me in the Officers' Club until night when they took me to the stinking room where I was the first day. Two men put on rubber gloves, another grabbed my hair, and against my violent resistance, they forced me to kneel and pushed my face into the latrine filled with excrement. Each time they took me out they asked about safe houses and guns and how many I'd killed and where I got dynamite and who were the doctors who helped and what diplomats or journalists talked to us. I answered always, 'Don't know.' When they let my head up, I tried to get the excrement out of my mouth by rubbing against my shoulders. This lasted all night, until dawn on 14 April.

They took me to the bathroom and gave me soap to wash myself and my clothes and the effect of the injection had not worn off, I felt no fatigue. Then they left me alone, blindfolded on the floor of a cell for two days, giving me tortillas and water three times.

On the night of 16 April, naked and blindfolded, they put me on my back on the floor of a Toyota panel truck, seen under the blindfold. There were five of them. We drove around the city. One said, 'This is your last chance, because we'd like to take revenge on the Red Cross.' I said, 'If you're going to kill me, shoot me in the chest not the face so at least I'll be recognized.' One of the soldiers put the barrel of his gun in my mouth. 'Such a pity,' he said, 'to die so young for nothing.' And then he pulled the trigger. He took the gun out of my mouth, and I heard him loading it. Again, he put the barrel in my mouth, and there was a click of the trigger: but nothing happened. He did this several times. I began to cry. I was returned to the barracks.

Back inside I was given another injection. There was someone else in the room with me, another prisoner. We talked for a short while. The prisoner was Mexican. I had asked him why he had been arrested. 'Because I'm Mexican.' I suggested we sleep. We tried.

But I was not allowed to. Twenty minutes later, I was given something to drink—a thick viscous liquid that tasted of vanilla. I was taken to another cell. My blindfold was removed and there were four men, each wearing a mask, a black balaclava, with openings only for the eyes, nose and mouth. One was wearing nail varnish, and had a case full of magazines with pictures of naked men. I said I wasn't interested, and he produced a copy of *Playboy*. He took off his clothes, as did his friend; the one with nail varnish seemed to be wearing women's knickers. I was told to masturbate, but I couldn't. My blindfold was put back on, and, shortly after, I heard someone masturbating and felt semen ejaculated into my face. I spat and was then hit ten or fifteen times on the side of my head.

My blindfold was removed. One of the men took out a small, thin, coffee-coloured tube about eight centimetres long. He squeezed out some Johnson's lubricant jelly and rubbed it across its length. Someone else was touching and massaging my testicles and, to my alarm, an erection appeared. The small thin tube was then inserted into my urethra—a small bit was left to stick out—while someone else pushed a gun, with an extremely large barrel, up into my anus, rupturing the walls of my rectum and making it bleed.

I was crying with rage. I wanted to kill myself. I wanted to die.

There was something that looked much like a small tub. It rested on thick rubber wheels, and was about a metre deep and half a metre wide. Attached to the lower part was a hose with a nozzle at the end. They started filling the tub with water, adding a large quantity of soap powder.

A sergeant entered. I recognized him from the National Police in San Miguel. He was angry that I was without my blindfold because I could identify him. He checked the tub: he wanted to be certain there was enough foam. 'It's the foam that does it,' he said.

They wheeled in the machine for electric shocks. This time they put the metal objects and the sticky ointment on the soles of my feet, the palms of my hands, the forehead, behind the ears, on the chin and on the back of my head. They gave me electric shocks with about five-minute intervals, pain everywhere, but on the fifth, the shocks from the chin and forehead made my whole body shake uncontrollably and my heart beat so wildly that I was sure I would have an attack. The sergeant said, 'If this shit wants to be like this,' and after about ten minutes they slipped the nozzle from the tub into my mouth and opened the valve. I was forced to swallow the soapy water. My stomach heaved and contracted but still they forced the liquid down until the tub was empty. Then they sealed my mouth with thick adhesive tape. I started to vomit but had to swallow it.

The pain was in my eyes and head, it spread to my nails, I felt as if there were stones in my stomach. The sergeant said, 'Take off the blindfold, look at his eyes, he may be dying. Take the stuff off his mouth, quick!' Also they took out the tube they had put in my penis. I tried to vomit and couldn't. They carried me to the bathroom and called a doctor who said, 'No, there's no danger,' and opened my mouth and tried to put a little funnel in it but I closed my teeth. The doctor said, 'This is for your good, this is a vomitorium so you can get rid of everything.' I drank it and in a few minutes began to vomit and defecate, foamy water came out of my nose and ears; this went on for about twenty minutes, and something the doctor did to my penis made a thick burning liquid come out of the urethra. I could not move. I was like paper, completely destroyed.

They carried me to a room with a wooden bed and treated me with injections and a serum drip and sedatives and gave me food for two days. Then two of them came and held me by the arms so that I could walk with difficulty. When we stopped, one of them said, 'Don't take off his blindfold till we go.' Afterwards, a prison turnkey led me up many stairs to a floor with numbered cells and shut me in cell number 16 with another prisoner. Though I was demolished, this man gave me a feeling of liberty and strength. He helped me to wash and gave me the lower bunk and lit cigarettes and we talked. He had been here 86 days. He said, 'They can't do anything to you now you're here, because the International Red Cross comes every Tuesday, they are Swiss. Forget everything they did to you in CAIN. Don't give it importance for yourself. If I told you all they'd done to me it would make you sick.' I asked what CAIN meant and he said, 'Centro de Analisis e Informacion Nacional, that is the real shit, the big aid the gringos started here a year ago, after they sent groups to the United States to study "psychology". When CAIN come to get you to sign papers, just do it.' 'What papers?' I asked. 'Your confession, don't try to read it, they won't let you, just sign and when you get out, tell everything about what happens here.'

On Tuesday 20 April, the International Red Cross representative came and talked and gave me soap and cigarettes and the Red Cross telephone number, to call as soon as I got out. He asked Luis, my fellow prisoner, if he was getting his food parcels all right. On 21 April, two CAIN agents came with nine pieces of paper to sign, then they took me to another cell in the basement, without beds, stinking, but with no excrement on the floor, and shut me in with a teenage boy, Tomas, for two days. On 21 April, they took Tomas away; he came back after four hours, hysterical, saying, 'They're going to kill us, they told me, on the way to court they're going to kill us.' At six that evening two agents of CAIN took away our clothes and brought no food and I was alarmed too. At one in the morning they came and made us stand against the wall, with our hands up, pointing a revolver at us. Tomas looked crazy, lost, he tore off a tile and threw it at the agent who fired, and hit the wall. Another agent came and ordered me to beat Tomas. I said, 'I am not an assassin, nor a terrorist, nor a torturer, do your own dirty work.'

On 22 April, at six in the morning they took us both, handcuffed, two agents in front, one beside us, and two behind with shotguns, from the main barracks of the National Police to court. They told us that if we didn't agree in court that everything they said was true, they would get us afterwards, they would kill us later.

The prisoner, because of the intercession of the International Red Cross, was taken to a court of law where he was accused of being 'a leader of the Communist Party with daily contact among subversive associations.' He denied these charges and demanded that the CAIN agent leave the court. He informed the Red Cross that he had been released, and then gave the court a complete account of his capture and imprisonment. The judge presiding over the case granted official recognition of the beatings and punishment which the prisoner suffered. The statement was made on 22 April, 1982, and a copy of it can be found in the Court of El Salvador, San Salvador. The statement offered to the Commission of Human Rights in El Salvador (from which the above testimony has for reasons of space been extracted and edited) was made on 18 May, 1982.

Translated for *Granta* from the Spanish by Margaret Whitehead and Margaret Jull Costa, 1984. Revised and expanded by Martha Gellhorn, 1987.

The Enemy Within

The Valleys was a name, a part of Wales full of coal mines, imagined as grimy black, barren and sad. Instead here is the valley of the Ebbw, a mountain stream racing beside the road, and the land is breathtakingly beautiful. Towering hillsides are covered with forest, swathes of gold against green, in a silver light. The land makes a point at once. This is the Welsh miners' own ancestral country. People fight to save their country.

No guide book would recommend the stony village of Newbridge for charm; that, however, is beside the point. The Memorial Hall is the miners' clubhouse, freely open to all. It is huge, eyesore redbrick, built in 1914 when a quarter of a million miners worked in the Valleys and the nation needed coal to win a war. Inside, the Memorial Hall is clean, warm, shabbily comfortable and friendly. TV pontificators of every ilk should come here and listen to miners, three generations of them, and their wives, fine people, good people. They might understand what a 'mining community' means.

I cannot think of any other like it in a society that is upwardly and downwardly mobile and there are barriers of class and money, and loneliness. Much more than jobs is at stake for these miners

The *Times*, 20 July 1984: 'Mrs Thatcher said that at the time of the [Falklands] conflict they had had to fight the enemy without; but the enemy within, much more difficult to fight, was just as dangerous to liberty.' British Miners' Strike: March 1984–March 1985.

and their families: the rock they stand on, their old communal way of life.

Bad trouble is not new here but this time the women are sharing in the action. Upstairs, the wives have taken over a room, set up tables with bright plastic cloths, and daily provide a hot mid-day meal for strikers: 'We run raffles, coffee mornings, collections at churches, beg, you know, anything to get money for food.' This was the stick-thin woman with glasses. 'Today we have shepherd's pie, carrots and potatoes. We asked the wives and children to come but I don't think they will.'

They didn't. Men drift in, greet the women by name, and are served one plate, lots of gravy. They ate very quickly and left, clearly needing but embarrassed by this unusual charity. Behind the counter, five women gathered to talk, small middle-aged women, fierce in their anger. 'If the mines go, the village dies. You ought to see [a Welsh name that escapes me], where the mine closed, nobody on the street, not a shop open, it's a ghost town.'

'This is where we live. We were born here and our parents before us. We're not going to lose our village.'

'*She* says we're the best paid workers. My husband is 46 and he's been in the mines all his life and he's the top grade and his take-home pay is £80. As if we're millionaires! Everybody's sold everything they could here. Everything. We have £19 a week supplementary benefit for my husband and me. It's worse for the young families.'

'And if my husband was half an hour late home from work I stand at the door thinking *accident, accident*; we all do. What does she know about us?'

Some men are sitting at a table with mugs of tea, quietly thinking aloud. A man in his sixties, I'd guess, also stick-thin, cap and suit; the other younger, bulkier, in old sweaters. 'The way I see it, we got manipulated into this strike. First she chose MacGregor. Well, we know him. Then out of the blue in March he comes up with closing mines so the lads in Yorkshire struck on their own and then it spread. But the timing was the worst for us, all wrong, wasn't it? The way I see it, she means to break this union because we're the strongest.

'After us, any union will be easy. She wants to do with coal what she did with steel—cut it in half—and privatize what's left. There's nothing in the Valleys but coal, no other work at all. My father, me, my sons, all miners. There'd be no future in the Valleys.'

Which brings to mind the dubious promise that any miner who wants work is guaranteed work somewhere; anyway it is already being rescinded. Who would buy their little quarry stone houses here? What homes would they go to?

'The fines,' says a younger man, 'that's another way of getting at us. If there was a bash at a pub on Saturday and you actually hit a man you'd get £16. But the lads on the picket lines get £100, £120, £150. The Union pays—we haven't any money at all. I don't know how many they've arrested, maybe 8,000, big money—our dues. Robbery.'

'The miners get blamed for everything. It's the pickets are violent. But can't they see? All summer the lads were out in shirt sleeves and soft shoes and look at the police, that riot gear. Just look at them and who do you think is getting hurt? Oh yes, we put in complaints about the police all the time. Not one of them was answered.'

'The police can do what they want; it's the miners who're violent. We can't send middle-aged men to picket any more; it's too dangerous.'

(An interesting point—the casualty figures. Not the latest, but all I've seen; some miners have died on the picket line; 3,000 hurt badly enough to need medical treatment; 750 police injured, 75 hospitalized. If it was war, you'd know which side was better armed and winning.)

We are off in a beaten-up van to Abertillery, to the food depot. I tell the charming grey-haired miner who is driving that I am thrilled by the land. 'Oh yes, it is very beautiful,' he says. 'We have a scenic drive back there, six miles, you should see it. It is most beautiful here in the spring.'

Three store rooms, loaned by the council, and two women, a man and his daughter are preparing the weekly free food ration, a carrier bag with flour, tea, half-a-dozen eggs, bread, a tin of meat, tins of fruit, soup, veg, baby food, whatever. Five thousand of these go to the neediest in a community of 8,000 miners across this valley.

'Our people go around the villages with a trolley and ring doorbells. "Something for the miners," they say, and it's wonderful how people help.'

'Pensioners give a few tins of soup, everybody tries to give something. And of course we've raised money however we could. It's about £5 worth in each bag. No, it's not enough to eat, that's the truth of it, people are going hungry.'

The van will deposit 300 bags in a garage to be collected on foot in that neighbourhood; more bags are taken elsewhere.

I said I'd like to see a young miner's family with children. An attractive bearded man said. 'I've got two kids.' I had not thought he was young. The kids are five and seven.

'His wife gets £23 supplementary benefit,' said a square, busy, little woman, the boss here. 'He'd get £54 on the dole. The electric is about £5 a week, 50p in the meter you know, and the milkman is £2.'

How can they manage?

'You have to,' says the young-old man. 'This helps,' pointing to a carrier bag. 'But the children,' I said—£16 a week for a family of four. 'They get free dinner at school now.'

Upstairs is a room crammed with free old clothes, which probably help too; it must be painful for those self-reliant people to accept them. The clothes were sent from France, Belgium, Sweden.

Money for the food bags is running out; so is the free coal, a miner's perk. 'I've got three hundredweight left for the winter,' says the young father and no one says anything. It is the same for them all.

It would be useless to beseech Mrs Thatcher in the bowels of Christ to think it possible that she might be mistaken. Politicians do not err and repent; sometimes they U-turn, though not Mrs Thatcher. But what if she has been grievously mistaken? Was it right to select that elderly gentleman, who knows nothing of mining communities, and give him the sole directive—profitability?

The miners did not provoke this strike; they reacted at a hopeless time to a direct threat. Apart from the gigantic cost to the taxpayers of breaking the strike, something far worse has happened: the emergence of a national, almost paramilitary riot police, looking as ugly as any in the world, and of a new hatred between police and working men.

Has anyone thought out coal and the future? The next generation may regard as madness the stockpiling of indestructible deadly nuclear waste, and demand coal—but where will miners be found, a vanishing species.

If, through hunger, the spirit of the bravest of the working class has been crushed, that will indeed be a famous victory. And a most grievous mistake.

Newness of Life

I am about to tell you an historical tale of travel in 1931, in the spring, when the world was young and gay. Of course the world was not young and gay, it was already spiralling down the Great Depression towards war. But I didn't know that, I didn't know anything much and all things are relative: the world was undeniably younger and I truly believe gayer than it is now. As for me, I was twenty-two and never more alight with gaiety.

The purpose of the journey then and forever after was to see the world and everything happening and everyone in it. The means were a triumph. I persuaded the St Louis *Post Dispatch* that I would write dazzling feature stories for their Sunday magazine at $25 each, and persuaded the Missouri Pacific Railway that these stories would publicize their fine trains and the captivating sights along their routes, if they would give me a Pullman pass. At last I had become, in my own eyes only, a roving correspondent, heart's desire. I set out in my regular warm weather clothes, blue cotton shirt, matching full cotton skirt and sneakers, but carried a small suitcase since the knapsack of previous European journeys was not suitable to my new estate.

Trains were lovely. (No one in his right mind can say the same of airplanes.) You were flung about as on the high seas while cinders from the engine blew through the open windows like a black hail storm. Only the porters, who served as kind nannies, and the waiters could walk upright in a straight line. The passengers grew very chummy as they banged into each other and fell on strangers' laps. The meals in the dining car were delicious though tricky with plates and cups and glasses leaping around the table. At night, behind the swaying green curtains of the Pullman berth, I listened with excitement to the train. When it stopped to take on water or coal, the train made animal noises, puffing, groaning; the whistle sounded like a fierce bird cry. The wheels clanged their special beat, dragging us through the miles and the dark. By day I listened to others and was entertained and instructed. People travelled on business and to visit relatives, usually to help in illness or childbirth. Holiday travel was a summer event for the privileged few.

Trains were leisurely. You had time to see the modest little towns and isolated farmhouses, both built of wood with shade trees; mules and wagons on the roads; old trucks collecting goods or family at the stations. Not a shiny rich scene, from the train window, but peaceful. Perhaps it was a hard life; I have an ancient memory of stern faces on those station platforms and obesity was certainly not a national problem. But places and people were nothing compared to the land. You had time to watch it change, to feel the differences and the great distance. You knew you were travelling.

I bounced across the continent to the Pacific coast and back, on that journey, and America looked vast, beautiful and empty. A year earlier, at the 1930 census, the population of the USA was 122,775,046, roughly two thirds of it east of the Mississippi. Texas and California, the largest states, had the largest population in the west, but people were still thin on the ground. In California, just over five and a half million people lived uncrowded lives in the sun. By 1980, three million people lived in the Los Angeles smog; who knows how many more are now frazzling their nerves on the freeways.

The first stop, my first feature story, was an oil boom. The name of that town in East Texas is long gone; besides it wasn't a town, it was a straggle of weatherbeaten frame houses on dirt roads in the middle of a dead flat landscape. Home for 200 impoverished citizens. Within sixty days, oil having spouted from their front yards, 30,000 crazy joyous men were churning up dust among a forest of oil wells, towers eighty feet high. The gaunt new millionaires sat in rocking chairs on their crumbling porches, bemused. The ladies wore faded flowered calico garments, the gents wore old jeans and collarless shirts; both sexes sparkling with diamonds. Hordes of people besieged the only store, waving fistfuls of greenbacks, and an iron cot sold for $200. Peddlers swarmed. A suitcase of new shoe-laces was worth a fast small fortune, and no one could buy enough diamonds.

Everybody seemed to be drunk despite Prohibition, still officially in force. The noise was colossal: trains of tank cars, four hundred every day, clanking in and out, machinery scraping, chugging, pounding, and overall human bedlam. Law and order problems, arising from theft, assault and battery, extreme drunkenness, were handled by three Texas Rangers with enormous hats and enormous pearl-handled pistols. There was no jail so the Rangers pegged a chain in a large circle in the dust and chained their prisoners to it by the leg. The prisoners were as cheerful as everyone else. Their friends brought them booze and they managed to huddle for crap games, papering the dust with dollar bills, singing uproariously when the spirit moved them. To impress me, the Rangers stuck matches upright in the ground, pulled out their pistols like gunfighters in the movies, and shot the heads off.

At night, I retired to luxury quarters, a de-railed Pullman car which I shared with the élite, oil men who had arrived to make this gold rush work. Like the rest of the population, they drank and gambled all night, leaning from their berths, while greenbacks fluttered down like falling leaves. They addressed me as little lady and whenever excitement or rage caused anyone to shout four-letter words the others hushed him, no bad language in front of the little lady. We lived on cold baked beans, eaten from the can.

The Mayor, having heard that the Press was in town, came to call with diamonds on eight fingers. He apologized for being hurried but he had laid on a private train and was taking his townfolk, in their jewels and worn-out clothes, to New York for a spree at the Waldorf. I laughed from dawn to dawn and loved every minute of it.

Nowadays if you don't want to risk sleeping in the airport or in any fleabag hotel with a spare room, you are well advised to make reservations when you travel. I believe this sorry state of affairs began about twenty-five years ago and has been getting steadily worse and worse. Before, you never had to make reservations for anything anywhere. You moved by whim, when you pleased. To my mind that is the only good way to travel. By whim, I came to Ciudad Juarez in Mexico, across the border from El Paso, where I intended to interview the only woman bullfighter in the world, another dazzling feature story. Ciudad Juarez had an attractive bad reputation. All the pleasure domes—saloons, brothels, gambling joints—forbidden in the US were wide open and cheap in this picturesque dump of a town. Sin had not paid, judging by the unpainted false-front buildings, derelict cars and scurf of garbage on unpaved streets, and the general lassitude of the citizenry. I walked from my sleazy hotel to a sleazy cabaret-brothel where a group of ladies invited me to their table.

They were the resident prostitutes, keeping a colleague company; she was temporarily unemployed due to advanced pregnancy. She looked dowdy and middle-aged to me, a very nice French woman who was reading Alexandre Dumas and André Gide as a good pre-natal influence on her child. Her friends, heavily painted in low-cut gowns with lashings of sequins, were charming and soft-spoken in French. French, not English, was then the lingua franca, fortunate for me as I knew no Spanish. They complained that business was bad and I suggested helpfully that they buy a tent and move to East Texas where business was sure to be splendid.

A scarecrow figure in dinner jacket, Maurice Chevalier straw hat and monocle began to sing gibberish and jerk dance steps in the middle of the dirty room. That was the cabaret. He joined us, kissed my hand and told me he was a Bavarian Baron, a passionate monarchist who fled the detestable Republic of Germany in 1919. His talk and eyes grew wilder. Never having met a junkie before, I knew by instinct that he was on the needle, poor fellow. What a fine evening, I thought, you didn't meet such interesting people every day.

The only woman bullfighter in the world turned out to be Juanita, a pretty gentle shy seventeen-year-old. Her mother and brothers kept her locked in a squalid hotel room, like a substitute convent, letting her out only to practise her alarming profession. The bullring was small, poor and poorly attended. Juanita flung me her cape and dedicated the bull to me, a moment of intense self-importance, but I closed my eyes when I saw her running knock-kneed and not very fast from the oncoming bull. The bull though undersized was furious. Juanita's life worried me. I urged her to get a safe job as a waitress or salesgirl in El Paso but she said she was used to her work and had to support her family.

The trouble with the travelling life is that you never know the end of the stories. What became of the French prostitute's child who had such good pre-natal influences? What happened to Juanita? Did the East Texas oil millionaires end in Florida mansions or did they splurge their fortunes and end on the crumbling front porches? It saddens me to think how many stories I failed to understand even at their beginnings, and how many people I have forgotten.

Somehow my deal with the Missouri Pacific Railway got me to Mexico City. Mexico City is now one of the outstanding disasters of the world but in 1931 it was more magical than any European city I had seen. I wandered the streets in a daze of joy, admiring the strange old handsome buildings and the dignified brown-skinned people. The volcanoes shone in that clear light and the air smelled of flowers. The entire Federal District of Mexico, 570 square miles of which the city was only a part, had a population of 1,230,000. Now the population of Mexico City alone is 16 million. The fatal difference.

I wandered through a noble doorway into a great hall with a ceremonial stairway. Sitting on a plank, high up the wall by the stairway, a fat man in overalls was painting a mural. I thought such work went out with Michelangelo and stood transfixed. The huge wall was already half covered by brilliant agitated figures. He saw me and asked if I wanted to come up and presently, beside him on the plank, I was asking how he knew what to do next, while he went on painting as easily as he breathed. A voice from below shouted 'Hola!' The plank was lowered and a small dark Frenchman joined us with tacos and beer, a lunch party suspended in air. That plank in the Palacio Nacional was a meeting place for painter friends of the fat man with curly black hair and round happy face whose name, I learned, was Diego Rivera. They were a new breed to me, these men, I longed to be like them, geniuses in the art of living with friendship and laughter, poor and unworried, absorbed in their work, free.

The Frenchman, a painter named Jean Charlot, invited me to go south to the hacienda where Russians were making a movie. I was delighted to go anywhere until I saw the hacienda, a gloomy ruin set in oppressive fields of giant cactus. Furniture was minimal in two rooms; one a dormitory of beds, the other for eating, with table and chairs. You had to be careful not to put your foot through broken boards on the filthy floors and the place stank of dirt, drains and mildew. Two large fair-haired Russians, the camera crew, chased Mexican maidens through this chaos, whooping Russian war cries, and flung them on the beds, iron four-posters with torn mosquito nets. I became very stuffy on behalf of the maidens.

And nothing was happening. The movie was held up for lack of film or money or whatever. Meals were appalling. Sheathed in glittering black flies, we ate boiled cactus and boiled goat meat from unwashed plates on a tablecloth stained by months of such grim fodder. The boss man stayed in his neat ascetic room, behind a closed door, and read St John of the Cross. He received us briefly in audience, to discuss Catholicism with Jean. I gathered he was called Eisenstein; I thought him old and grumpy. In no time, I got ptomaine poisoning and clamoured to depart. Eisenstein told me, contemptuously, in French, that I was the sort of girl who went swimming and drowned. It is a cherished memory.

The world changes around us at desperate speed every day, for better (not enough), for worse (too much). The population explosion, the airplane, and tourism as a major international industry have changed travel, for an old traveller like me, from thrilling impetuous private discovery into a hassle of the deepest dye. Naturally I no longer love it as I did. To millions of latecomers travel today still brings newness of life, which is what travel is all about. Or anyway I hope crowding and organization do not flatten the surprise and dim the wonder. Nostalgia is foolish. There is no place to live except in the present. But what fun it was, what easy fun, long ago.

Cuba Revisited

The first morning in Havana, I stood by the sea-wall on the Malecon, feeling weepy with homesickness for this city. Like the exile returned; and ridiculous. I left Cuba forty-one years ago, never missed it and barely remembered it. A long amnesia, forgetting the light, the colour of the sea and sky, the people, the charm of the place.

The Malecon is a nineteenth-century jewel and joke. Above their arcade, the mini-mansions rise three storeys, each house exuberantly different from the next: windows garlanded with plaster roses, Moorish pointy windows of stained glass, caryatids, ornate ironwork balconies, huge nail-studded carved doors. The paint on the stone buildings is faded to pastel, a ghostly reminder of former brilliance: pink trimmed with purple, blue with yellow, green with cobalt. Whoever lived here, when Cuba was my home from 1939 to May 1944, had departed: fluttering laundry suggested that their rich private houses were now multiple dwellings.

A delightful little black kid bounced out of somewhere, in spotless white shirt and royal blue shorts. He smiled up at me with a look of true love and undying trust. '*Rusa?*' he asked. I was mortally offended. Russian women of a certain age, seen in Moscow, had bodies like tanks and legs like tree trunks.

'No,' I said crossly, '*Americana.*' I should have said '*Norteamericana.*' South of the US border, people do not accept Americans' exclusive ownership of the continent.

The loving smile did not change. *'Da me chicle,'* he said. Give me chewing-gum. Cuba does not manufacture chewing-gum. In due course, I gathered that kids admire gum chewing as seen in American movies, still the most popular.

The Prado is a stylish old street with a wide central promenade: live oak trees, big light globes on wrought iron lamp-posts, benches. The benches were occupied by old women knitting and gossiping, old men reading papers and gossiping, poor people by our standards, looking comfortable and content. Now in the lunch-hour, groups of school children—from gleaming black to golden blonde—romped about the promenade, healthy, merry and as clean as if emerged from a washing-machine. The little ones wear a uniform of maroon shorts or mini-skirts, short-sleeved white shirts and a light-blue neckerchief; the secondary school children wear canary yellow long pants or mini-skirts and a red neckerchief. The neckerchiefs show that they are Pioneers, blue for the babies, like Cubs and Scouts in my childhood.

Before, street boys would have drifted around here, selling lottery tickets or papers, collecting cigarette butts, offering to shine shoes, begging. They were funny and talkative, barefoot, dressed in dirty scraps, thin faces, thin bodies, nobody's concern. They did not attend school. Nor were they Afro-Cubans.

I had never thought of Cubans as blacks, and could only remember Juan, our pale mulatto chauffeur. Eventually I got that sorted out. A form of apartheid prevailed in central Havana, I don't know whether by edict or by landords' decision not to rent to blacks. Presumably they could not get work either, unless as servants. But of course there were blacks in Cuba as everywhere else in the Caribbean, descendants of African slaves imported for the sugar-cane plantations. In my day, they must still have been concentrated in the eastern provinces, still cutting cane. Roughly one third of Cubans are of African or mixed blood, two thirds Caucasian.

Calle Obispo, formerly my beat for household supplies, had been turned into a pedestrian street. At one of the cross streets I saw the only cops I noticed in Havana, trying to disentangle a jam of trucks, motorcycles and hooting cars. The shops were a surprise: bikinis and cosmetics, fancy shoes, jewellery, a gift shop with china and glass ornaments. Not high fashion, but frivolous. And many bookstores, a real novelty; I remembered none. And a neighbourhood store-front clinic.

Faces looked remarkably cheerful, unlike most city faces, and the street was enveloped in babble and laughter. Men met women, kissed them on the cheek, talked, moved on. That public friendly cheek-kissing astonished me; I had never seen it in a Latin American country, and never here in my day. Most of the women wore trousers made of a stretch material called, I think, crimplene; and most women were amply built. Their form-hugging pants were lavender, scarlet, emerald green, yellow, topped by blouses of flowered nylon. The young, boys and girls, wore jeans and T-shirts. T-shirts printed with Mickey Mouse, a big heart and LUV, UNIVERSITY OF MICHIGAN. Presents from relatives in the US? Grown men wore proper trousers of lightweight grey or tan material and white shirts. These people were much better dressed than average Cubans before, and much better nourished.

At the top of this street, Salomon, a very small tubercular man of no definite age but great vitality, sold lottery tickets. Salomon was a communist and lived with the certainty of a glorious communist future, when everyone would eat a lot and earn their keep by useful work. I remembered him out of nowhere, and hoped with all my heart that he lived to see his dream come true, but doubted it; Salomon didn't look then as if he had the necessary fifteen years left.

I was staying at the Hotel Deauville, a post-war, pre-Revolución blight on the Malecon. It is a plum-coloured cement Bauhaus-style tower. I came to dote on the hideous Deauville because of the staff, jokey and friendly with each other and the guests. The Deauville is classed as three-star, not suitable for rich dollar tourists. My room with bath cost $26. Like all tourist hotels, the Deauville has its own Duty-Free Shop. Tourists of every nationality pay for everything in US dollars. You are given your change, down to nickels and dimes, in American money. For practical purposes one dollar equals one Cuban peso, a parallel economy for natives and tourists. President Reagan has tightened the permanent US economic embargo to include people. Cuba is off limits to American tourists. But that year, 1985, 200,000 capitalist tourists, from Canada, Europe, Mexico, South America, uninterested in or undaunted by communism, had caught on to the idea of the cheapest Caribbean holiday.

At the Deauville, I had my first view of the amusing and economical national mini-skirt: above-the-knee uniform for women employees, different colours for different occupations. And was also plunged into the national custom of calling everyone by first names, beginning with Fidel who is called nothing else. I was rather testy, to start, hearing 'Marta' from one and all and the intimate *tu* instead of *usted*, a disappearing formality. But I quickly adjusted and was soon addressing strangers as *compañero* or *compañera*. You cannot say comrad (American) or comraid (British) without feeling silly, but *compañero* has the cosy sound of companion.

I wanted to be on my way. I had not come to Cuba to study communism but to snorkel. At the Cuban Embassy in London, I found some tourist bumf, describing a new glamorous hotel at Puerto Escondido, which included the magic word, snorkelling. I was going to Nicaragua, serious business, and meant to treat myself *en route* to two weeks mainly in the lovely turquoise shallows off the Cuban coast. A couple of days in Havana, to retrace my distant past; then sun, snorkelling, thrillers, rum drinks: my winter holiday.

You can go anywhere you want in Cuba, except to the American naval base at Guantanamo on the eastern tip of the island—an extraordinary piece of property which most foreigners do not know is held and operated by the United States. You can hire, with or without driver, a small Russian Lada sedan belonging to INTUR, the Ministry of Tourism. The Lada is as tough as a Land Rover, Third World model, with iron-hard upholstery and, judging by sensation, no springs. I asked INTUR for a car with driver, intending to look over the hotel at Puerto Escondido, the goal of

419

my Cuban trip.

The driver, rightly named Amable, said that Puerto Escondido was half an hour from Havana; my introduction to Cuban optimism. 'No problem' might be the national motto; it is the one English phrase everyone can say. We drove through the tunnel under Havana harbour, new to me, and along the superhighway, adorned with billboards, very depressing: progress. The billboards are exhortations not advertisements. A light bulb, with ENERGÍA in huge letters and a plea to save it. A bag of coins and a single-stroke dollar sign for the peso, recommending the public to bank their money at two-and-a-half per cent interest. Many patriotic billboards: 'WE WOULD DIE BEFORE WE GIVE UP OUR PRINCIPLES.' Two hours from Havana found us bumping on a mud road through lush jungle scenery. A solitary soldier stopped us where the track ended. Puerto Escondido was not finished; it would be ready next year. More Cuban optimism. The soldier suggested a tourist resort at Jibacoa further on.

Amable managed to find Jibacoa—small brick houses, newly landscaped—and a bar and a restaurant. At the bar two Canadian girls, secretaries from Toronto who had arrived yesterday, were full of enthusiasm and information. They had a nice double room; the food was 'interesting'; rape was punished by shooting; Cubans were lovely people; and they looked forward to a night out at the Tropicana, Havana's answer to the Paris Lido. Goody, but what about snorkelling? A man in a wet-suit was coming up from the beach; the girls said he was Luis, in charge of water sports. Luis guaranteed that the snorkelling was fine and we both stared to the north where clouds like solid black smoke spread over the sky.

'*Un norte?*' I asked with dismay. I remembered only perfect winter weather.

'Yes, come back in a few days when it is past.'

But it did not pass.

By morning, the sea was greenish black, matching the black sky. Waves smashed across the Malecon, closed to traffic, and drove sand and pebbles up the side streets. The wind was at gale force; it rained. A gigantic storm and worsening. I was cold and slumped into travel despair, an acute form of boredom. With no enthusiasm, I arranged to fill time, meeting people and seeing sights, until the storm ended.

The distinguished Afro-Cuban poet and I talked in the crowded lobby of the Hotel Nacional, an old four-star hotel. Suddenly she made a sound of disgust and said, 'I hate that stupid out-of-date stuff.' She spoke perfect American. The object of her disgust was a wedding party: bride in white with veil, groom in tuxedo, flower girls, bridesmaids, beaming parents and guests, headed for the wedding reception. I was pleased that the out-of-date could be freely practised by those who wanted it.

I had an important question to ask her but was very unsure of my ground. 'Something puzzles me,' I said. 'Fidel made a decree or whatever, as soon as the Revolución started, forbidding racism. I mean, he said it was over; there wouldn't be any more. And there isn't. Surely that is amazing?' It sure is. Even more amazing, it seems to work.

'Of course you can't change people's prejudices by law; you can't change what they feel in their hearts. But you can make any racist acts illegal and punish them. We hope that as we live together more and know each other better as human beings, the prejudices will disappear.'

We had no racist problem, she and I, just the wrong vibes. She thought me too light; I thought her too heavy.

I was interested in how writers earned their livings. Very few of the 600 members of the Writers' Union can live by books alone, like us. There are many publishing houses, state-owned but managed by distinct staffs for a varied public. You submit your manuscript; if accepted, you get sixty per cent of the retail price of the first edition, whether the books are sold or not; then forty per cent of further editions. Cubans love poetry, so poets abound and are widely read.

*

Feeling dull but dutiful, I went to look at Alamar—a big housing estate, white rectangular factories for living spread over the green land off the highway outside Havana.

'Marta, why do you say you do not like such a place? I have friends there. They have a very nice apartment.' Today's driver, called Achun, part Chinese, had served in Angola. He said he was truly sorry for those Africans; they were a hundred years behind Cuba.

I asked, 'How big?'

'Two bedrooms, three, four, depending on the number of the family.'

I told him about vandalism as we know it. Achun was dumbfounded.

'Why would people ruin their own homes?'

Close-up, Alamar was not bad; no graffiti on the white walls, no broken windows—on the contrary, shined and curtained—a skimpy fringe of flowers around each building, and thin new trees. The buildings are four storeys high, widely separated by lawn.

'The cinema is behind those buildings,' Achun said.

Here the bus stopped; a few weary people were piling out. The forty-minute ride to and from Havana in the always over-crowded buses has to be a trial. (Havana is about to get a needed metro system.) This central shopping area reduced me to instant gloom. I thought at first it was filthy. The impression of grime was not due to dirt but to unpainted cement. Of couse Cuba is poor and needs many things more vital than paint, yet it distresses me that these poeple, who adore bright colour, must be denied it.

The bookstore was attractive because of the gaudy book covers. A soldier and a child were the only customers in the middle of a chilly grey weekday afternoon. A corner of the room had been set aside for children's books. The paper is coarse, the covers thin, but books cost from forty-five to seventy-five cents.

'Every year we have a quota,' said the middle-aged saleslady. 'And every year we exceed it.'

'How can you have a quota? You can't force people to buy books, can you?'

'Oh no, it is not like that. Every year we are sent a quota of books and every year we must ask for more, because they are sold. All ages buy books. Fidel said, "Everything basic to the people must be cheap. Books are basics." '

'What is most popular?'

'Detectives and romantic novels.'

I drove around Havana, sightseeing, half-curious, and wholly sick of the miserable weather. I chatted in the dingy main market where the toy counter and meat and poultry counter were the busiest. I asked about fares at the jammed railroad station, learning that the best fast train to the other end of the island costs $10.50. I cruised through the stylish section of Vedado with the big hotels, airline offices, shops, restaurants, movies and the large Edwardian houses. I peered at the Miramar mansions. The rich departed Cubans left a bountiful gift to the Revolución, all their grand homes and classy apartment buildings. The big houses are clinics, kindergartens, clubs for trade unions, and whatever has no public use is portioned off for private living space.

Then I decided I needed some action and barged into a secondary school, announcing that I was a foreign journalist and would like to sit in on a class and see how they taught their students. This caused extreme confusion. (As it probably would if I barged into the Chepstow comprehensive.) The school sent me to the local Poder Popular office where I met the very cornerstone of bureaucracy: the woman at the door. Behind a desk/table/counter in every government office is a woman, preferably middle-aged; her job is to keep people out. Poder Popular sent me to the Ministry of Education. There the woman at the door said that Public Relations at INTUR, the Ministry of Tourism, must write to Public Relations at the Ministry of Education. I reported this to INTUR, decrying it as an absurd fuss about nothing. INTUR promised that a school visit would be arranged. 'Be patient, Marta,' said Rosa, an INTUR director. 'Everything is done through organizations here.'

To their credit, the Ministry of Education sent me to a very modest school in a poor suburb. The Secondary School of the Martyrs of Guanabacoa. The driver could not find it. We were twenty minutes late. I got out of the Lada and saw school kids in canary yellow lined up along the path to the front door and a greeting committee of adults. I apologized unhappily for keeping everyone waiting and walked past the honour guard, feeling absurd. Instead of a twenty-one gun salute, I got a shouted slogan. On the school steps a little Afro-Cuban girl stepped from the ranks, shouted something and behind her the official chorus shouted an answer. This went on for several minutes but I could not decipher a single shouted word. I was then presented with a sheaf of gladioli and lilies in cellophane and began to feel as if I were the Queen Mother.

The man in charge, whose position I never understood, presented the school principal, a large shy Afro-Cuban woman in dark blue crimplene trousers and white blouse. I was shown the school bulletin board with its smiling photographs of the 'Martyrs'—handsome girls and boys, not much older than the children here, killed by Batista's police for their clandestine work in the Revolución. Asked what I would like to visit, I said the English class. The school was unpainted cement inside and out, built on the cheap in 1979.

The English teacher was nervous and nice and desperately eager for his class to perform well. Each child read aloud a sentence from their textbook, dealing with Millie's birthday party. Offhand, I could not think of a deadlier subject. 'Toothbrush' and 'toothpaste' [Millie's birthday presents!] are very hard for them to say; also 'room'. His own accent was odd; the kids were choked with stage fright, rivalling mine.

A bell blessedly rang. Here, the children stay in one room, the teachers move. It was the history hour in another classroom. The children—the top form, aged fifteen—rose to their feet and shouted a slogan, led by the elected class prefect who was always a girl. Hard to understand, but it sounded like promising Fidel to study and be worthy of the Revolución. Each class devised its own slogan, a new one every month, and five times a day, at the start of their class periods, they shouted this at the teacher. The history teacher was a thin intense shabbily-dressed young man who described the sugar crisis of 1921, when prices fell and the people suffered despair and starvation though their work had enriched the bourgeoisie and the American capitalists. I wanted to say that American workers suffered too in times of depression and unemployment, but didn't feel that speech-making was part of my new role.

Biology was taught by a stout mulatta compañera in lavender pants, and taught brilliantly. The subject for the day was the renal system, up to that moment a total mystery to me. All the kids raised their hands, competing to answer. This subject—their bodies—clearly interested them much more than history or English. After class, the teacher explained that by the end of the term they would have studied the sexual organs, the nine months of pregnancy and birth. To finish, they would discuss 'the human couple, and the need for them to be equals and share the same ideals and interests.' She showed me their laboratory, a small room with a few Bunsen burners. Her only teaching-aid was a plaster human torso, open at the front, with all the brightly-coloured alarming organs in place.

There were 579 children, more Caucasian than Afro-Cuban, and fifty teachers, about equally divided as to colour and sex. School is compulsory through to the ninth grade, age fifteen. After that, children can choose to continue for three years in pre-university studies or technical schools, according to their grades. At eighteen, the boys do military service, but university students are exempt since Cuba needs all the professionals it can train.

Snacks had been laid out in the principal's office. I looked at these poorly-dressed men and woman and grieved to think of them chipping in for this party. They were so excited about me because the school had never received a visitor before, no Cuban personage, let alone a foreigner. They spoke of their students with pride; it must feel good to teach such lively and willing children. Never mind that they had no library, no workshop, no gym, no proper laboratory in this bleak building. The staff invented substitutes and got on with the job. I asked to meet the Head Prefect, elected by her peers. She was a lovely tall slim girl, almost inaudible from shyness, blonde with grey eyes. She said that the entire school went on two camping weekends a year and for a week to Varadero, Cuba's famous beach. The top student (this girl) joined all the other secondary school top-graders for a whole summer month at Varadero. Fun and sport as a reward for work. I remember winning a school prize, a richly-bound uninteresting book.

I liked everyone and told them they had a fine school, meaning it, and thanked them for the visit. In the Lada, returning to Havana, I gave my character a shake and became again a normal, not a Very Important, person.

That night, on the thirteenth floor of the Deauville, I listened to the howling wind. The storm had renewed itself with spiteful vigour and would never end. Snorkelling was a dead dream. I gave up. I had no choice; there was nothing left to do except cramp myself into a Lada, drive around the country and get a general idea of how communism works in Cuba.

For transport on this journey to the Cuban hinterland, I went to Rosa at INTUR, my sole contact with the Cuban government. She is small, brunette, very pretty, very bright and kind and patient above and beyond the call of duty. My manners to her were abominable and in no way deserved. I was rudely determined that nobody was going to show or tell me anything; I would see and question for myself. Rosa assigned Rafael as my driver. Rafael is grey-haired, mid-forties, overweight, racked by a cigarette cough, intelligent, good and a charmer. We drank a lot of delicious ice-cold Cuban beer and he laughed at my disrespectful jokes.

Rafael's story is one example of how the Revolución has changed lives. His wife works as an accountant in some ministry. Rafael is an official of the drivers' trade union, bargaining on his members' behalf with another ministry. 'Whoever gets home first cooks the dinner.' One son is reading English at Havana University. Another, having failed his exams, is doing military service and expects a place in medical school afterwards. Rafael pays thirty-five dollars monthly rent for an apartment in Vedado, formerly the chic section of Havana, and soon will own it. Rents pile up like down payments year after year, until the sale price of the flat is reached, whereupon bingo, you become an old-fashioned capitalist owner. Mrs Thatcher's vision of a home-owners' society coming true in communist Cuba.

Rafael left me strictly alone whenever we stopped. I stayed in several sumptuous hotels; these were the Mafia's legacy to Cuban tourism, built with Mafia money because they included casinos, now closed. It was all new to me; I had never bothered to travel in Cuba when I lived here and had no sense of its size—730 miles long by an average of fifty miles wide—or of the variety of the towns and the landscape. We drove without any previously arranged plan—wherever I felt like going—and covered 1,500 miles in the back-breaking Lada, a partial look at about a third of the country. Our first stop was Trinidad.

Trinidad is a beauty; Cubans are very proud of it. It is an unspoiled colonial town, most of it late eighteenth- and early nineteenth-century, but inhabited from the sixteenth century. The streets are cobbled, the houses one storey high, with vast, handsome wood doors, wide enough for a carriage, and bowed iron grill-work on the front windows. Every house is painted, and paint makes the difference—pale green, pink, blue, yellow. The Cathedral, at the top of the town, is yellow trimmed in white, and fronts a flowery square that descends in steps to the houses.

The Museo Historico was the home of a nineteenth-century sugar baron. The enchanting girl in charge, aged around twenty, with blonde hair in a pony tail, wore the museum uniform, immaculate white shirt, dark blue jacket and mini-skirt. 'He had thirty slaves,' she said. '*Thirty*. They lived in that one big room at the back.' The idea of slaves horrified her. Earlier, when she had collected my entry centavos, she said, 'Cuba was under Spanish domination for three centuries, until 1899. After that, it was under American domination until 1959.' It had sounded pat and off-putting, straight Party line, until I thought it over and decided it was true, no matter how it sounded.

The US actually ruled Cuba twice, and the Marines had been around in the usual Monroe Doctrine way. Until 1934, the United States government had the right by law to interfere in internal Cuban affairs. But American domination was mainly felt through its support of whatever useless Cuban government protected American investments. In my time, no one ever talked politics or bothered to notice which gang was in office and robbing the till. I cannot remember any elections, though I think the government did change, perhaps by palace coup. One day driving into Havana, I heard shooting and Salomon or the street boys advised me to settle in the Floridita and drink frozen daiquiris until it was over; the noise was farther down toward the harbour. This was taken lightly as a joke: who cared which crooks got in, the results would be the same. The poor would stay poor; the rich would stay rich; a different bunch of politicians would grow richer. After World War Two, during the Batista dictatorship, apart from the standard horrors of such rule—arrest, torture, executions—corruption must have been out of control, thanks to Batista's faithful friends, the Mafia.

At the Museo Romantico, said to be the former home of a Count, a bunch of noisy young people was clattering up the stairs to the salons and bedrooms. In the hall, a white-garbed nun waited, saying that she had seen it before. 'If you have lived in Spain,' said the little dark Spanish nun, 'there is nothing to look at in this country.' She seemed about thirty years old and had a sharp, severe face. She had come to Trinidad from Cienfuegos with the young people to attend the cathedral wedding of two of them, tomorrow. Her order has two houses, in Cienfuegos and Havana. There are eight Spanish, three Mexican and three Cuban nuns in all.

'People must be very brave to go to Mass,' she told me. 'We do not go out in the street with the young for fear of compromising them. There is much fear.'

'Fear? You mean fear of prison, fear for their lives?'

'No, no,' she said impatiently. 'Fear of losing their jobs or not getting a good one, if they are seen to be practising Catholics.' Mass is celebrated here in the Cathedral and in another church 'down there,' twice on Sundays and that is all. She felt outraged by this. 'No, nuns are not molested in any way but we are not allowed to do our pastoral work in the streets.' As far as I am concerned, that was great: I don't want anyone of any religion, secular or spiritual, haranging me in the streets. 'Still, people do talk to us.'

I pointed out that she had come here with these young people, a whole band of them, to take part in a church wedding.

'Yes, they are very loyal,' she said.

The stern Afro-Cuban museum lady, the ticket collector, stared at us with plain dislike. The nun remarked on it. 'She does not want me to talk to you.' Even so, it did not stop the nun from talking to me, an obvious foreigner.

Cuba is awash with museums. Museums for everything, past and present. The museums are scantily furnished—no great art treasures—and are visited with interest by all kinds of Cubans, young and old. I don't think I've ever raced through so many anywhere and I think I understand them. This is consciousness-raising on a national scale. The mass of Cubans had no education and no real sense of identity. Being Cuban meant being somebody else's underling, a subordinate people. I knew a few upper-class Cuban sportsmen; they spoke perfect English, had been educated abroad, and were considered honorary Americans or Europeans, not in words, nor even in thought, but instinctively: they were felt to be too superior to be Cubans. Now, through these innumerable museums, Cubans are being shown their history, how their ruling class lived and how the people lived, the revolts against Spanish 'domination,' and everything about the Revolución. They are being told that they have been here a long time: they are a nation and they can be proud to be Cubans.

Between Trinidad and Sancti Spiritus, the country looked like Africa: hump-backed, bony cattle, like Masai cattle; palms and ceibas, the handsomer Cuban form of the African Baobab tree;

jungle-green hills; brown plains; but where were we going to sleep? We had been turned away at two hotels, full up with Cubans, who travel joyfully and constantly. We set out again, hunting for rooms.

Suddenly loud horns and sirens. Motorcycle cops pushed the traffic to the roadside. Ten first-class buses flashed past, filled with excited kids, singing, shouting, waving. 'Pioneers,' Rafael said. They were primary-school children, the baby Pioneers of the light-blue neckerchief. 'They are going to camp at Asmaela. They go for a week with their teachers and continue with their lessons.'

Not that bunch, far too elated for lessons.

'Fidel started the idea of camping,' Rafael went on. 'Nobody in Cuba ever did that, live in a tent, cook over a fire. Now everybody does it. It is very popular.' Cubans have two paid vacations a year, two weeks each, and alternate full weekends. Besides camping, many new beach resorts dot the coasts. These resorts are simple, rudimentary—I don't want to give the impression of places like luscious photos in travel brochures—and so inexpensive that most Cubans must be able to afford them. And there are town parks with children's playgrounds, swimming pools, sports grounds. I like the government's decision in favour of pleasure: Cuba's Revolución is not puritanical. Outlawing drugs, gambling and prostitution eradicated crime as big business, hardly a bad idea. But there remain the delicious beer and rum, flowing freely, and cigarettes and cigars, since Cubans haven't yet heard of the horrors of smoking. But I think that the main cause of a different, open, pleasurable life-style is the change in women. The old Hispanic and Catholic custom of the women at home—isolated, the daughter guarded, the stiffness of that relation between men and women—is truly gone. Women are on their own at work, feeling equal to men, and showing this new confidence. Girls are educated equally with boys and chaperonage is dead. There is a feeling that men and women, girls and boys are having a good time together, in a way unknown before.

Bayamo, said the tourist map, offered historical sights; the church where the national anthem was first sung and other episodes of heroism against the Spanish overlords. I was not interested; I was interested in food. The food is ghastly, apart from breakfast. If Cuba means to earn millions of tourist dollars, it will have to make a culinary Revolución. On a corner of the main square, I saw an ice-cream parlour and bought a huge helping of delicious chocolate ice-cream.

I was enjoying this feast at an outside table when a boy came up, said his name was Pépé, shook hands, sat down and asked my name and where I came from. I thought he was eighteen; he was twenty-four, good-looking with light brown hair, blue eyes and a summery smile. He wanted to buy a pack of my cigarettes, Kools from a hotel Duty-Free; I said he could share mine. He wanted to see what a dollar looked like; I showed him. He wanted to know the price of cigarettes, gas lighters, dark glasses and trousers in England. He then brought out of his wallet a small colour print of a beautiful little bejewelled and bedecked doll, the Virgen de la Caridad de Cobre, patron of Cuba. He handed me this as if he were giving me a family photo.

A young Afro-Cuban in a dark business suit lurked nearby, listening. I said, 'Why do you stand there with a look of suspicion? Sit with us.' His presence at first annoyed Pépé, then he ignored the newcomer.

Pépé wished to talk about religion, absolutely not my subject. 'Are you a believer? Do you go to Mass? Do you believe in Jesus Christ?' By now we had another member of the seminar—an older Afro-Cuban—and slowly the waitresses pulled up chairs around our table.

Hoping to bring an end to this topic, I said, 'In our country, people are Protestants.' Easy misinformation.

'What religion is that?' said Pépé. 'Protestante?'

'They are not loyal to the Pope,' the older Afro-Cuban said.

'But you believe?' Pépé insisted.

As an untroubled unbeliever, I could not go into a long thing about Jesus as a man and a teacher, so I said, 'De vez en cuando'— which comes out as 'sometimes' and satisfied Pépé.

'There are churches in Bayamo?' I asked.

'Four,' they said in unison.

'People go to Mass?'

In unison, 'Yes.'

'They have trouble if they go to Mass?'

Again in unison, 'No.'

'I want to see a capitalist country,' Pépé said. 'I want to go to France. I met some Frenchmen here.'

'You want to leave?' the business suit asked, scandalized.

'No, not leave,' Pépé said. 'Visit. To see. But they will never give me a passport. Only to the socialist countries.'

The older Afro-Cuban said, 'Artists can go. Musicians, people like that.'

I didn't want Pépé to cherish hopeless golden dreams and could imagine the Frenchmen talking about France as the French do. 'You know, Pépé, everything is not perfect in our capitalist countries. We are not all rich and happy. We have great unemployment. There is also much crime.'

'There is no crime here,' said both Pépé and the business suit.

'No unemployment,' said the others.

Cubans believe that there is no crime in Cuba. They feel safe in their homes and on their streets. You see very small unaccompanied children going about their business in Havana, and women walking alone at night wherever they wish to go. No one fears mugging. Rape is too unimaginable to think about. But of course there are crimes since there are jails for common criminals.

We were now talking about education and the main members of the seminar, Pépé and the business suit, agreed that education was very good here. 'And free,' Pépé added, 'everything is free, even universities.'

Business suit, who was a serious young man employed as health inspector for hotel and restaurant kitchens, now departed: end of the lunch-hour. The rest of the seminar drifted back to work.

Pépé, it developed, was a night-watchman at a cement factory, scarcely a demanding job, and had only completed two years of secondary school. I began to realize that he was twenty-four going on sixteen, but no less sweet and interesting for that. 'Do people have servants in England? Not here, there are no servants here. Could I come to England and be your servant, chauffeur or something? I wouldn't want any money.' How he longed to see the mysterious capitalist world. 'If I was going about in France, just looking, doing nothing wrong, would they give me difficulties?' Cuban police are notably absent everywhere, and as Pépé had talked openly in front of his compatriots, strangers to him, he must have picked up some ominous news about police in the free world.

By now we were great friends and he said confidentially, 'I don't like dark girls.' I thought: gentlemen prefer blondes. But no. 'I only like girls with light skin.' He now produced two photographs from his wallet, almost identical Caucasian Cubans with a lot of brunette hair.

'Two *novias*, Pépé, isn't that one too many?'

He grinned, then said in a low voice, 'I have a brother who is a racist. He told me.'

I imagined an older brother and said, 'There is nothing much he can do about it, is there? You don't have to marry a dark girl. You aren't obliged to make any friends you don't want, are you?'

'No. Clearly no.'

'Well then. How old is your brother?' I disliked this tedious dummy brother, a bad example for young Pépé, and remembered the Afro-Cuban poet and the prejudices of the heart.

'Thirteen,' said Pépé. I shouted with laughter. At first he was bewildered; racism is no joke, an offence in law; then gradually he understood and the summery smile appeared.

I wandered into the square: live oaks, Ali Baba flower jars, benches of bright patterned tile, a design in the paving bricks—the Cubans had luck, architecturally, to be colonized by Spain. No sign of Rafael, so I sat on a bench in the shade, and an elderly lady sat beside me. She wore a neat, rather prissy cotton dress and a hat, unheard-of, a proper lady's hat; I felt she should have gloves. She said her husband had gone to the 'office' to speak about their pension. 'We are retired. Our pension is fifty-two pesos monthly.

What can you do with that? Some people get seventy pesos. If you have children, they could help. Or else you must do work at home, little work.' She was very worried and indignant. 'Ridiculous,' she said. 'Impossible. I hope they listen to my husband.'

In the car I asked Rafael about this. He said that pension depended on how long you had worked. His mother got sixty pesos a month, from his dead father's pension. I pointed out that his brother lived in the same village and would help her and so would he. 'Surely it is a bad system, Rafael, if people must depend on their children for money in their old age. It would be a reason to have as many children as possible.'

'But people do not want many children; they want few and to give them more. People do not have big families now. Every woman, girl, can get birth control assistance, whether married or not. There is no sense in big families.'

I abandoned pensions.

'Stop, Rafael. I want to take a photo.' This was a picture of rural poverty. Everywhere, in the villages, along the roads, the sign of new private prosperity was paint. If they could afford no more, people painted their door a brilliant colour and painted a band to outline their windows. Here three small, crumbling, unpainted wood houses stood on bare treeless ground in the middle of nowhere. They were typical peasants' homes; painted, beflowered, they would be picturesque cottages. They are box-shape, one room wide, with a porch on wood pillars. If very poor, the roof is palm thatch, less poor, it is corrugated tin. I chose the worst of the three.

'Did you see that?' Rafael pointed.

I had not. Each of the houses had a TV aerial.

'Marta,' Rafael said, 'have you seen anyone without shoes?'

'No.'

'You say everyone is too fat. When you lived here, how did the *campesinos* look?'

How did the *campesinos*, the peasants, look; how did everyone look? They looked abjectly poor or just everyday poor. Except for us, the narrow top layer. You could live in princely comfort on very little money in Cuba.

There was a farmhouse, barely visible beyond our land, east of the driveway. It was a bit larger than these houses, with peeling paint. The farmer was a bone-thin, unsmiling man; he kept chickens. If I saw him I said good morning. That is all I knew about him; I don't even know if the cook bought eggs there. The village below our place was a small cluster of houses like these; I knew nothing about the village except that it had a post office. The children waved when I drove by, I waved back, lots of smiles. They were in rags, barefoot, and everyone was unnaturally thin.

I did not say to myself: it isn't my country, what can I do? I didn't think about Cuba at all. Everything I cared about with passion was happening in Europe. I listened to the radio, bought American newspapers in Havana, waited anxiously for letters from abroad. I wrote books, and the minute I could break free, I went back to the real world, the world at war. Rafael had asked the wrong question. The right question would be: who looked at the *campesinos*? Who cared? Nobody, as far as I knew; including me.

'I know, Rafael. They were hungry and miserable.'

'Those people own their houses and prefer to stay there, not move themselves to a new co-operative building which is like an apartment block.'

'So would I.'

'Good, if they prefer television to making their houses beautiful, that is their business. When they get more money, maybe they will improve their homes. My mama lives in a house like that. I was born in a house like that. Clearly it is better repaired.'

'What is that thing, Rafael?'

He slowed the car.

'Back there, a sort of monument.'

It looked like a little cement obelisk, standing by the empty road among the hills, not a house in sight. I got out to read the inscription. MARTYR OF THE REVOLUCIÓN. TEACHER KILLED IN 1960. All those who were killed in the years of rebellion against Batista are called Martyrs of the Revolución.

'How can this be, Rafael? The Revolución won in 1959.'

'He would have been a volunteer teacher in the literacy campaign. Killed by the *campesinos* who had crazy ideas, maybe from propaganda by the priests. The *campesinos* thought the literacy campaign would take their daughters away and ruin them. Many young volunteers were killed at that time. It is very sad, very stupid.'

We were on a winding road, in pleasing green tree-covered hill country, that led down to a hotel by the sea. This hotel was post-Revolución, built for Cubans and lesser tourists. The site, on a bay surrounded by mountains, was lovely and the architects merit high marks. Otherwise, it had little to recommend it. The manager was always absent at Party meetings. They ran out of bread, and never had butter; when I ate the fish, I knew I was doomed. The bath towels had been washed to fragility. The front fell off the unwanted air-conditioning and barely missed my Russian vodka, the only booze I had left.

I settled grumpily at the snack bar which had nothing to offer except Cuban soft drinks, far too sweet, and had a heart-to-heart with the Afro-Cuban lady in charge. We shouted at each other over the din of the whiney-sugary anti-music that Cubans love. She was thirty with three children, divorced. The oldest, aged fourteen, was at school in Havana with his father, the others at school here. 'Oh *companera*, life has changed much, much. We have things we never had before. Furniture, frigidaire, television, and the right to work which women never had. We work, we have our own money.' And the pay? 'Women are paid equal to men, *igual, igual*.'

At lunch, a group of Polish tourists murmured to each other in whisper voices. They were the only non-capitalist tourists I saw. They looked bemused and pitiful, dressed in shades of grey, a non-colour, with grey skin. Lunch finished, their guide-nanny, a young, pretty Cuban woman, came to talk to them in Polish, no doubt the day's agenda; she raised a timid laugh. She had well cut and well set black shoulder-length hair and wore tight yellow pants, a brilliant poncho, big gold loop ear-rings, and lots of make-up. What on earth could these sad Poles think of communism, Cuban-style?

A man was watching TV in the hall; Fidel on the box. At this time, Fidel had been giving one of his marathon interviews to the *Washington Post* and it was broadcast like a serial on TV. The front desk receptionist beckoned to me. 'You should talk to him, Marta, the doctor on horseback.'

A fair-haired young man, with specs and a beard, tweed jacket, jeans, was telephoning. I waited and latched on to him. He had just finished his medical training, six years, and was now stationed in the mountains. 'They asked for volunteers, for two years. It is very dynamic work.' He lives alone in the Sierra Maestra and visits patients on horseback if they cannot come to his *consultorio*, a room in his three-room house. He is in charge of 117 families. This is a new idea, a doctor who stays in close touch with the same families over years, urban as well as rural preventive medicine. 'The main complaint is high blood pressure; maybe too much salt, maybe overweight. There is no tuberculosis, no cancer, no diabetes. Sometimes parasites. My work is to teach hygiene.' The people raise coffee and cattle in the mountains. The children go to primary school up there and come down to rural boarding schools for secondary education. I had seen a few of these, large buildings planted in the fields.

'Older women had as many as twelve children. Now women have two or three at most. There is every form of birth control, it is the physician's task to find what is best for each woman.'

'Don't you think the women are much too fat?'

'Yes, but it is the custom of the country and men like women to be fat. It is slow education, to teach them to eat less starch and sweets. They enjoy eating; you know, to be fat here was a sign of wealth. No, I am not lonely. I have many books and I like the people very much.'

Fidel announced somewhere, sometime, that he wished Cuba to be 'the greatest medical power in the world.' I dislike the form of words but applaud the ambition. The rule-of-thumb gauge of public health is the nation's infant mortality rate. I am using the figures given in the World Health Organization Statistics Annual for 1985. These figures are their estimate, arguably more accurate than the figures supplied by the nations concerned, and more recent. In 1985, Cuba's infant mortality rate was 19 per 1,000 live births. (Great Britain's was 11 per 1,000 births.) No other country in Latin America compares with Cuba by this standard: Mexico, 47; Guatemala, 57; Argentina, 32; El Salvador, 60; Chile, 36.

For a population of almost 10 million, there are 260 hospitals, of which 54 are rural. Public health depends on preventive medicine and quick early care, so they have 396 polyclinics—an outpatient service. General practitioners, neurologists, gynaecologists and paediatricians work in polyclinics, with X-ray machines and laboratory facilities in the building. There are 158 rural medical stations (the type I had seen in the villages) and 143 dental clinics. Most of the doctors and dentists, middle-class professionals, emigrated after the Revolución, but the number of physicians had tripled from 1958 to 1983 (increasing every year), the number of dentists quadrupled, and nursing staff, less than a thousand in 1958, numbered over 30,000 in 1983.

Apart from the grandiose hospital in Havana, which is Fidel's monument, hospitals and clinics are basic like everything else, but they are there, fully and willingly manned. They have eradicated malaria, polio and diphtheria; no deaths from tuberculosis since 1979 and the incidence of the disease in 1983 down to 0.7 per 100,000 population. Maybe they have finished it off by now. Tuberculosis, a poverty disease, is endemic in this part of the world. In health, as a single indicator of progress, Cuba is unique in Latin America. Ordinary people, which means the vast majority, from Mexico south to Tierra del Fuego would weep with joy to have the medical care that is free and routine for Cubans. Millions of North Americans would feel the same.

For a quarter of a century, everybody has heard how communism works in Cuba from successive American administrations. I do not believe anything that any governments say. Judge them by their deeds, by results, by what you can observe from yourself and learn from other unofficial observers. Apart from Jimmy Carter, all American presidents have hated Fidel Castro as if he were a personal enemy. They have done their varied powerful best to destroy him, and failed. Since it was politically impossible to accept that the monster Castro might be popular, even loved by his people, he had to be oppressing ten million cowed Cubans.

Whatever it is, Cuba is not a police state ruled by fear. You can sense fear at once, anywhere, whether the police are communist or fascist, to use the simplified terms. Fear marks the faces and manners of the people. It makes them suspicious, especially of strangers. And it is catching; fear infects the visitor. I know, for I have never been more frightened than in El Salvador, and I was shaking with relief to be safe inside the airplane leaving Moscow. No government could decree or enforce the cheerfulness and friendliness I found around me in Cuba. I haven't space to describe all the people I met in all the places but this is what matters: none of them was afraid to talk to a foreigner, to answer my questions, and they spoke their minds without hesitation.

The undeniable shame of the Cuban government is political prisoners. Sources that I trust estimate about one hundred men in jail for political reasons. The trials were secret, neither charges nor evidence published. The sentences, dating back to the early years of the Revolución, were crushing, twenty years and more. These prisoners call themselves *plantados*, firmly and forever planted in their loathing of Castro communism. They refuse to wear prison uniforms or be 're-educated' politically. Defiant to the end of their tremendous jail terms, released *plantados*—now abroad—have reported atrocious prison conditions, brutality from jailers, denial of family visits and mail, appalling malnutrition, periods of solitary confinement and barbarous medical neglect. These are terrible accusations and there is no reason to doubt them.

A book called *Against All Hope* by a former *plantado*, Armando Valladares, has recently appeared. Valladares served twenty-two years in prison and is now happily alive and well in Madrid. His charges against the Cuban prison regime are frightful, including torture, biological experiments, lightless cells and murder. The book should be studied with dispassionate care, especially by medical experts. The immediate question is: why did none of the many freed *plantados*—among them writers—provide such information earlier?

Amnesty has this year adopted five Cuban prisoners of conscience. Apparently four are long-term prisoners and one, a teacher of adult education, was arrested in 1981. Three of them are dissident Marxists; I don't know about the others. Amnesty is absolutely reliable. But whatever the remaining political prisoners are, I cannot understand why Fidel Castro does not release them all and allow them to go abroad. Or publish the charges and evidence that would justify the sentences. The secrecy about the *plantados* and the conditions of their imprisonment damage Cuba irreparably in world opinion. And, in the end, the *plantados* are released anyway. So what is the point? What is the Cuban government's need for this self-mutilation? The Revolución has triumphed. It has gone far beyond the threatened inexperienced violent early years. It has made an admirable record in social reform, in education, in public health; and, in its own way, it is an upwardly-mobile society where anyone can better his life through individual ability. Why spoil that record, why disgrace the Revolución by holding political prisoners?

You can name in minutes the few governments which hold no political prisoners. This ugly fact does not condone Cuba but puts it into perspective. My sources did not suggest that political arrests were a continuing frequent process in Cuba. But a small country existing under a relentless state of siege, persecuted by the strongest nation on earth, is not in the best shape for flourishing freedom. If any American administration truly cared about Cuban political prisoners and Cuban civil liberties, it would let up on Cuba, leave Cuba alone, give Cuba a chance to breathe for a while and feel secure enough to afford more and more freedom. I hope for the arrival, one day, of a sensible US administration which will come to sensible live-and-let-live terms with Cuba. I hope this for the sake of both America and Cuba.

I returned to Havana from Santiago de Cuba by air; the Lada had destroyed me. As I was about to leave Cuba, the sky cleared. On a sunny morning I collected Gregorio and we went to visit my former home, the Finca Vigía, fifteen miles outside Havana, now a museum or indeed a shrine. Gregorio is eighty-seven years old, the only link to my Cuban past and the only Cuban repository of Hemingway lore, as he was the sailor-guardian of Hemingway's boat, the *Pilar*, for twenty-three years. People come from far and wide to hear his verbatim memories, which he quotes like Scripture. Hemingway and he were the same age. His devotion to his patron-hero is genuine and time has added lustre to that devotion. The *Pilar* years were surely the best for Gregorio. He is a tall thin weather-beaten man, with calm natural dignity. He was liked and respected—thought, typically, to have the finest qualities of a Spaniard. Not that anybody troubled about his separate existence; I had never seen his house.

The Museo Hemingway, temporarily closed to the public for repairs, is wildly popular with Cubans. They come again and again, bringing picnics to spend the day, after a respectful tour of the house. The long driveway is flanked by towering royal palms and sumptuous jacaranda trees. I couldn't believe my eyes; I remembered nothing so imposing. The driveway curved to show the house, now glaring white and naked. 'It looks like a sanatorium,' I said. 'What did they do to the ceiba?'

Forty-six years ago, I found this house through an advertisement and rented it, for one hundred dollars a month, indifferent to its sloppiness, because of the giant ceiba growing from the wide front steps. Any house with such a tree was perfect in my eyes. Besides, the terrace beyond the steps was covered by a trellis roof of brilliant bougainvillaea. Flowering vines climbed up the wall behind the ceiba; orchids grew from its trunk. All around the house were acres of high grass, hiding caches of empty gin bottles, and rusty tins, and trees. The house was almost invisible but painted an unappetizing yellow; I had it painted a dusty pale pink; the Museo changed it to glaring white. The great tree was always the glory of the finca.

'The roots were pulling up the floor of the house. The Museo had to cut it down,' Gregorio said.

'They should have pulled down the house instead.'

I never saw a ceiba like it, anywhere. The enormous trunk, the colour and texture of elephant hide, usually dwarfs the branches of a ceiba. But this one had branches thick as other tree trunks, spreading in wide graceful loops; it was probably several hundred years old. The house is a pleasant old one-storey affair of no special style; the six rooms are large and well proportioned, full of light.

The members of the museum staff have their office in the former garage; they are earnest, devout keepers of the shrine. I recognized all the furniture I had ordered from the local carpenter, and lapsed into giggles over the later addition of stuffed animal heads and horns on every wall. In the master's bedroom, the biggest buffalo head I had ever seen, including hundreds on the hoof, glowered over the desk. True, I had never been so close to any buffalo, living or dead. 'He did not write here,' said one of the staff. He wrote *For Whom the Bell Tolls* at this desk, but that was pre-buffalo.

The house depressed me; I hurried through it, eager to get back to the trees. How had I taken for granted this richness? Then it struck me: time, the years of my life at last made real. The trees had been growing in splendour for forty-one years—the immense mangoes and flamboyantes and palms and jacarandas and avocates were all here before, but young then like me.

I had definitely forgotten the size and the elegant shape of the swimming-pool. Gregorio was interested in two large cement cradles, placed where the tennis court used to be. The *Pilar* was his inheritance, he had cared for it and given it to the state, and it was to be brought here and placed on these cradles.

'Like the *Granma*,' I said, and everyone looked slightly shocked at the irreverence. The *Granma* is the large cabin cruiser that bore Fidel and his followers from Mexico to Cuba in 1956: the transport of the Revolución. It is enshrined in a glass case in a small park in Old Havana. As an object of patriotic veneration, a lot jollier than Lenin embalmed. It seems that *Granma*, now the name of a province and of the major national newspaper, is simply a misspelling of Grandma, which is delightful.

The visit was as fast as I could make it—handshakes, compliments standing under a beautiful jacaranda by the garage—and we were off to Gregorio's house in the fishing village of Cojimar. The visit to the Museo had been a duty call; it was expected. I wanted to listen to Gregorio.

In the car, I began to have faintly turbulent emotions. I remembered with what gaiety I had come to this country and how I had left, frozen in distaste of a life that seemed to me hollow and boring to die. Looking after the finca ate my time, but was worth it because of the beauty. Then Cuba became worth nothing, a waste of time. Cuba now is immeasurably better than the mindless feudal Cuba I knew. But no place for a self-willed, opinionated loner, which is what I suppose I am. Never a team-player—though I wish this team, this people, well, and hope it improves, as it has, year by year.

'Gregorio, it is a comfort that nobody is hungry.'

Gregorio looked at me and smiled. 'You remember that?'

'Yes.'

'*Pues sí*, Marta, nobody is hungry now.'

Gregorio has owned his small cement house since 1936 and it is freshly painted, sky blue and white. Gregorio was still anxious about his wife, *mi señora* he calls her in the old way, who fell off a ladder weeks ago and broke her thigh. She was waiting for us indoors, in a chair, her leg in plaster. She kissed me, told me I was 'very well preserved,' and they both recounted the saga of the leg. They have a telephone; the ambulance came at once; she was taken to hospital and operated on. ' "A big operation," the doctor said.' Gregorio's turn: 'Very big. He said at our age the bones are like glass.' She stayed twenty days in the hospital, then the ambulance brought her home. The doctor from the local polyclinic came every day to check her condition, now he only comes once a week. 'Not a cent, Marta, you understand. It did not cost even one centavo.'

Gregorio has a monthly pension of 170 pesos (call it pre-inflation dollars); actually a large pension, due to his long work years. Still, I thought this a skimpy sum until they told me the price system: six dollars a month flat for the telephone, which is a luxury; three dollars flat for electricity—and they have an electric fridge and cooker and water heater; the colour TV is bought on the never-never, at ten per cent a month of salary or pension. The food ration is extremely cheap.

'Is it enough food?'

'Yes, yes, more than enough, but if you want different things you buy them. It costs more.' Clothes are also rationed and cheap; they would not need or want more than the yearly quota of shoes, shirts, underclothes etc. 'Young people care for clothes, they buy more off rations. And education is free too, Marta.'

His middle-aged daughter now arrived; she is volubly enthusiastic about the new Cuba. Then his grand-daughter appeared with a pink and white baby in her arms, Gregorio's great grandson, on her way to his weekly check-up at the polyclinic. Each generation owns its little house in this village.

I felt that Gregorio was getting a trifle restive among all these females so we moved to the front porch to smoke. He brought out a bottle of Cuban rum. 'As long as I have this,' he said, pouring me a hefty slug, 'and my cigars, I am content.' Now talking soberly he said, 'Marta, all the intelligentsia left, all of them.' I was baffled by that word: what would Gregorio know of intelligentsia? Then I guessed he meant the world he had known with Hemingway, the Sunday parties with the jai-alai players at the finca, parties at the Cojimar pub, the carefree company of the rich and privileged, the big-game fishermen, the members of the pigeon-shooting club, and though I had never seen the Country Club he meant that circle too, since the *Pilar* was berthed there in later years. He may have missed the glamour of a life he shared and did not share. But he had met Fidel. 'I think he is a good man,' Gregorio said. After Hemingway left in 1959, Gregorio returned to his old profession of fisherman, then retired and became unofficial adviser to the Museo Hemingway. 'I have never had any trouble with anyone'.

I asked about the few Cubans I could remember by name; they had all long decamped. I asked about the Basque jai-alai players, exiles from Franco's Spain, who had fought for their homeland and lost. I loved them, brave and high-spirited men who never spoke of the past, not expecting to see their country and families again.

'They left when Batista took power. They did not like dictatorship. There was much killing with Batista, in secret. I heard that Patchi died.'

'Patchi!' I was stunned. 'And Ermua?' Ermua was the great *pelotari* who moved like a panther and was the funniest, wildest of them all.

'Yes, he died too.'

'How could he? Why? So young?'

And suddenly I realized that Patchi was probably my age, Ermua maybe five years younger; they need not have died young.

'Gregorio, I am growing sad. Cuba makes me understand that I am old.'

'I too.' Gregorio laughed. *'Pues, no hay remedio.'*

My bag was packed, my bill paid and I had nothing to do until two a.m. when I took the plane to Nicaragua. I went back to Jibacoa where I had gone in hope of snorkelling on my first day. Now the weather was the way it ought to be, brilliantly blue cloudless sky, hot sun. I went to the Cuban resort, not the foreigners' tourist domain on the hill. There were dozens of small cabins for two or four people, a boat-yard with rentable pleasure craft, an indoor recreation room, ping-pong and billiards, a snack bar to provide the usual foul American white bread sandwiches and a restaurant. The main feature was a beautiful long white sand beach, bracketed by stony headlands. Where there are rocks there are fish. I was loaned a cabin to change in and a towel: No, no, you pay nothing, you are not sleeping here. I could never decide whether I was treated with unfailing kindness because I was a foreigner or because of my age.

There were many people on the beach, looking happy in the lovely weather, all ages, sunbathing, swimming, picnicking. A young man offered me his deck-chair so that I could read and bake comfortably between swims. I put on my mask and plunged in, feeling the water cold after the storm, but bursting with joy to see familiar fish, special favourites being a shoal of pale blue ovoid fish with large smiles marked in black on their faces. In my old Cuban days, I wore motorcyclist's goggles; masks and snorkels had not been invented.

When I returned to my deck-chair at the far end of the beach, I found two small fat white bodies lying face down near me. After a while they worried me, and I warned them in Spanish that they were getting a dangerous burn. A grey-haired man sat up and said, 'Spik Engleesh?' They were 'Greek-Canadians' from the tourist resort above; they liked the place, they even liked the food. He said, 'They work slow. No, lady, I don't think it's the climate. But they're happy. The guy who looks after our group is doing double time. For that, he gets a month off.' He smiled, he shrugged.

From nine to five, the tour guide would be on hand to interpret if needed, to coddle the old if they wanted it, swim with the girls, play table tennis, eat, drink. Maybe he would take them on a day sight-seeing tour of Havana. And then, from five to one in the morning, if anyone was still awake, he would do the same, except he would drink more than swim, and dance with the girls to radio music in the bar, and of course escort them all on the big night out at the Tropicana. The Greek-Canadian's shrug and smile said clearly that he did not consider this to be hardship duty. Here was a small-scale capitalist deriding the easy life of communists. Soft communism, a comic turn-around from the dreaded American accusation: 'soft on communism.' I thought it the best joke yet.

The Eighties

In my considered opinion, this decade is infuriating and shabby. I can think of at least six more adjectives but might then give the impression of foaming at the mouth. I am not making a world-wide judgement since for all I know this is the best decade of the century in Iceland and New Zealand or points between. My aversion to the eighties is caused by the governments of the two countries I do know something about, Britain and the US.

Nobody has a good word to say for politics but scorning politics is a waste of time. We are governed, that's all there is to it. Short of keeping house in a Tibetan cave, nobody can escape the ripple effect of politics; and even in Tibet, a Chinese cadre might show up. In the eighties, politics in the two great English-speaking democracies have been stamped hard by the personalities and prejudices of the tough handsome lady Prime Minister and the smiling waving President. We used to have the Tory Party in Britain, now we have Thatcherism; we used to have a Republican administration in the US, now we have Reaganism. It seems to me that we, the people, have never been more battered by politics than now when both leaders claim zealously to oppose government interference in the lives of the citizens.

As the Prime Minister and the President are soul-mates— she is smarter but he has wider power—Thatcherism and Reaganism are similar in views, values and aims. Vainglory is rampant in both regimes. President Reagan has made America stand tall. Apart from shuddering embarrassment, I cannot decipher this phrase. Was America supine until 1980? Mrs Thatcher orates frequently, given any excuse, about a strong Britain, 'respected in the world' because of its strength; she embodies that grandiloquent strength, having elevated stubbornness to the highest virtue. Both are infatuated with military might, especially nuclear military might. Both exalt wealth; acquiring money is righteousness. They are apostles of the belligerent Selfish Society.

My vehement distaste for Reaganism and Thatcherism is joined to 35.2 million Americans who voted against Reagan in 1980 (out of a total 76.5 million votes cast) and 37.5 million Americans who did likewise in 1984; and allied with 57.8 per cent of the British electorate who voted against Mrs Thatcher in 1987. Plus 56.1 per cent anti-Thatcherites in 1979 and 57.6 per cent in 1983. That is quite a lot of consensus repugnance.

The US has one priceless advantage over Britain: the Twenty-Second Amendment to the Constitution which forbids anybody to hold the office of President for more than two terms. If you cannot stand the type of government you are getting, you know there is an end in sight. And also the American president must be elected by popular majority. Not so in Britain. I was thinking that the British were as easily fooled by vainglory and as mercenary as Reaganite Americans until I realized that Mrs Thatcher has been an elected dictator for eight years.

Mrs Thatcher has never been the choice of the majority of British voters. She holds power because the formation of the constituencies and vote-splitting between the two Anti-Thatcher Parties produce a dominant Conservative majority in Parliament. Only proportional representation would give all the British a square deal in government. If the Prime Minister has a majority of well over a hundred MPs obediently voting as directed by the Party Whip, there is no Opposition. The Opposition can talk its collective head off and accomplish nothing. As an elected dictator, Mrs Thatcher has imposed a retrograde revolution. The rich get richer, the poor get poorer. The same is true in the US. If things keep up like this, we will have a large Third World bang inside our countries.

I find myself missing the old Tories. Rueful laughter. We don't choose the progress we get; we just get what comes. I cannot feel that national rejoicing is called for because 8.5 million Brits now own shares. Not only do I pine for the civilized manner and reading habits of Harold Macmillan, but I wish that America would mind its own business, instead of dangerously minding everybody else's. Foolish dreams. The unappealing narrow new Tories are here to stay and no American President is apt to renounce the heady excitements of being a Superpower Commander-in-Chief. Imagine the thrill of ordering the invasion of postage-stamp Grenada, the ecstasy of sending an armada to the Gulf. Poor Mrs Thatcher must content herself with memories of her glory as Britannia during the Falklands Campaign. I guess I am really sighing for the good old days when hubris in high places had better style.

But there are gallant generous-minded minorities, in both countries, who fight defensive actions against the worst abuses of Thatcherism and Reaganism, and I put my hope in them.

Since I wrote 'White into Black' in 1983, the Haitians have rid themselves of Baby Doc Duvalier. It does not sound as if they have rid themselves of traditional Haitian misrule. But anyway, the people revolted and that suggests they are no longer cowed and brain-damaged by Voodoo fears. Having lately seen a blood-curdling British TV documentary called 'The Sword of Islam,' I think Voodoo is wholesome compared to Shiite fundamentalism and Hizbollah. (Dear God, please don't let Mrs Thatcher, the Sword of Capitalism, destroy British TV by making it like American TV. Dear God, please lead Mrs Thatcher to understand that cultural assets are more enduring than here-today-bust-tomorrow commercial assets.) Fundamentalist Christianity, as also seen in TV documentaries, implies that Jesus has changed His mind; no longer the scourge of the money-changers in the Temple, He is all in favour of money now, especially for his preachers. The need of millions of people, in this decade, for entranced subjection to mullahs and evangelists is beyond my understanding; it scares and repels me, as long ago I was scared and repelled by Haitian Voodoo.

Racism—skin colour as a reason to take against people—is also beyond my understanding. It was not funny to be on the receiving end of racism in Haiti. I don't find the greyish-pink or greenish-grey, which is our average Caucasian complexion, all that superior. I take against people violently for what they proclaim and act out, irrespective of skin colour. Racism seems somewhat calmed in the US; or has distance blurred my sight? Racism is rife in Britain, from the National Front, a political party of slob losers, Paki-bashers, to the Immigration Laws. There are still enthusiastic Neo-Nazis in Germany. No cure has yet been found for cancer either.

The Women of Greenham Common are still there, three long bad winters after I visited them. The harassment I reported in 1984 has become spiteful persecution; they are driven from their 'benders' every night. I am dazzled by their fortitude. Thatcherism is authoritarian; the lady is a confirmed nuclear warrior and does not tolerate disagreement gladly. Hundreds of thousands of British people, and the whole Peace Movement, disagree with her resolutely. Nuclear weapons, militarism, the insistent political rhetoric of fear and war have had a sensational side effect: world-wide, they have created a citizens' opposition. They have taught people to think and act for themselves. Peace protesters will never again accept the statements of government as revealed truth. The triumphant word *why* has spread through the ranks. Citizenship on the march. I really believe in democracy, which has nothing to do with trust in the wisdom of governments. It has everything to do with the communal rights and responsibilities of each of us; we are not helpless and alone; we have a voice. Public opinion, though slow as lava, in the end forces governments towards more sanity, more justice. My heroes and heroines are all private citizens.

In 1983, I brought back from El Salvador a document of 23 single-spaced typed pages: the detailed account of the tortures suffered by a young Salvadoran. I read it in my Welsh cottage, remote from the horror of El Savador. After a few pages, I had to get up and walk and gulp air; I felt choked and sick. This testimony, like the sight of Auschwitz, is proof again of absolute evil. Torture continues in El Salvador; it is state-sanctioned routine. The US government last year gave over $390 million to the Salvadoran government, and as usual the best weaponry including napalm, and the beneficent assistance of American military advisers. According to President Reagan, El Salvador is a democracy, defending itself against Communist insurrection. Everybody in El Salvador knows about torture; every journalist there knows about CAIN; everybody in the US Embassy must know too. El Salvador is off the front pages and forgotten.

I have expanded the translation that appeared in *Granta*, but still you do not hear enough of the language of the torturers, coarse and obscene taunting; you do not realize that these subhumans were men in their twenties, who laughed and joked at their work. As the testimony is given in flat legal terms, it is hard to convey the sense of time; the exhaustion of Miguel, the young Salvadoran, blindfolded, naked, dragged like an animal from one torment to another. And these excerpts are not a complete account of all the torture. Miguel talked to himself to resist humiliation, for this is the filthiest purpose of torture; the destruction of identity, of self-respect. Many of the most disgusting outrages against Miguel are not translated; they are unprintable, but they happened. And these excerpts have not explained the prisoner, Miguel.

How can he be explained? From internal evidence, Miguel belonged to the small wealthy class for which El Salvador is ruled. His family had emigrated, and was evidently rich enough to support Miguel, who, by his own description, was adventurous, pleasure-loving, carefree, liking to travel, the author of 70 pages of an unpublished book, an epileptic, a very detached privileged young Latin American. After what seems to be ten years' absence,

Miguel showed his naïve ignorance of the real world by thinking he could safely return to San Salvador to visit the Psychiatric Clinic, presumably because of his epilepsy. Nothing more. He answered no questions that could involve others. When asked where he stayed in San Salvador he said he lived in pensions, hotels. How is it possible to explain the unbreakable courage and moral integrity of this man? Where did he find the strength of spirit that carried him through to the end, to the clear denunciation in court of his torturers and the whole system of torture?

There is no greater abomination in the world, though the world is oversupplied with cruelty, than the fact of torture. Many strong, healthy, well-fed men playing with one defenceless human being as if that human being were a tiresome insect. Sadism and sexual perversion are clear in this testimony; the torturers were the lowest, most debased creatures that our species produces. But Miguel, though nearly destroyed, was not defeated. His testimony could be a parable of the good and evil in man; one such parable would be enough. Neither Miguel nor his torturers are unique in our time. We do not know how many Miguels have died, nor how many torturers live.

It should be noted that doctors served in this torture prison. As a noble contrast, full documentation for 1982 alone shows that at least 32 doctors, nurses, medical students, known for assisting the poor, were murdered by Salvadoran security agents. In that debased society, compassion is communism, inimical to the state.

I have wished for fame a few times in my life, to use fame as a means of being heard. This was one time. I wished I had the VIP standing to call a press conference and talk of Miguel's testimony and of thousands of others who could not testify, condemning with all my force the Salvadoran government and its support by the American government. Condemning, while I was about it, official American hypocrisy on human rights: ignore their violation in capitalist regimes, upbraid their violation in communist regimes only. The British government is just as blandly dishonest but at least does not subsidize the violaters.

These few pages are in print and therefore on the record. I

do not know if any of the heroic young volunteers of the Salvadoran Commission of Human Rights are still alive or if the Commission is still operating. (A deceptive governmental Commission has been formed.) The aim of the genuine Commission of Human Rights was to keep the record of abuse 'for the eyes of the world.' The eyes of the world have been blind, or merely turned away.

President Carter introduced the revolutionary idea that respect for human rights should be linked to American military aid, which at least hampered Guatemala, if little more. President Reagan put an end to that nonsense. El Salvador is Vietnam in miniature, without Communist leadership. Salvadorans are Catholics; the Church, at its peril, is on the side of the poor and has always urged 'dialogue' with the insurgents. When poor people are driven to desperation by decades of unyielding social injustice, they take up arms because they have no other remedy. This does not prove that they are Communists, as President Reagan insists; it proves that they are human. The humanity of the Washington policy-makers is in doubt. I cannot comprehend these men. If you prick them, do they bleed?

Have they no imagination? Do they think only in terms of geopolitical claptrap? Do they know what they are doing? They are ensuring the hatred of hundreds of millions of poor non-white people around the world. America is seen as the friend of the rich, the enemy of the poor. Washington policy-makers, from the President down, should meet some of these non-white poor, listen to their stories, try to picture the misery in their lives. Washington deduces nothing from the fact that the civil war in El Salvador, a country the size of Massachusetts, has lasted for eight years. No matter what Washington says, there is no logistical means for the insurgents to be armed by Cuba or Nicaragua. And yet—despite over a million external and internal refugees, 60,000 casualties, the crushing power of military and civil repression—the war goes on. Will Washington never learn anything about real people and real life? When American anti-communism, in action, is simply anti-human, what does America stand for?

The great British miners' strike of 1984–85 was a festival of hatred. TV news thrives on action shots; the cameras, for safety, operated from behind the police lines. Week after week we saw a police phalanx, helmets, face guards, shields, heavy boots, advance in line abreast on a shouting unruly mob of pickets who were, however, not kitted out for combat. The pickets were fiercely blamed for violence. A two-second flash would show us four riot cops beating the hell out of a picket, truncheons flailing; or we might see a picket on the ground and a cop putting the boot in. Not much of that, though. Mrs Thatcher, now in the role of Boadicea, led the battle against these rabid dogs, these unpersons, this treacherous enemy within, the striking miners.

Apparently this island has enough coal to last to the year 3000. Nobody knows what to do with existing nuclear waste let alone all the poisonous muck that will pile up if Mrs Thatcher succeeds in commissioning more nuclear power plants to blight Britain's coasts. Can Britain afford to lose the skill of miners? No time for theoretical stuff like that. The country, whether it likes to or not, now marches behind a banner with the strange device: profitability.

The TV strike spectacular made me sick at heart. Britain was going down the drain, had become as mean and nasty as anywhere else. The new-look cops gave me the creeps; farewell to the friendly bobby. Compromise, civility, pleasantness, good humour, tolerance, all gone. Class is a fact of British life but this was class warfare. I think mining must be the hardest, dirtiest, most dangerous job there is; I was unwilling to believe that miners were monsters but I didn't know them. Then meet them.

I telephoned a newspaper in Newport to ask where the nearest mine could be found, got in my car and discovered that the famous Valleys with their mines are about an hour from the serene hilly farming country where I live. I introduced myself at the Miner's Club in Newbridge as a foreign journalist; they asked no questions and made me welcome. I liked the Welsh miners and their wives as much as any people I have met in the years I have lived in Britain. I wrote my little piece, was lucky to get it printed in the *Guardian* on the unimportant women's page, sent the modest pay cheque to the Abertillery Food Fund, and stopped watching the TV news or reading about the strike. Too sad. It was always clear that the miners would lose and they did, after fifty-one bitter weeks. Judging by the mine folk I met, they were starved out.

The estimated cost, to British taxpayers, of breaking the strike is £6 billion. Forty-two mines have been closed, fourteen merged; four more are at present threatened. 64,445 miners are no longer miners. The mines at Newbridge are shut down. The Union is split. Probably the surviving mines will be privatized in due course. Everything else is, bit by bit. Something has to be wrong if whiz kids can earn £100,000 and upwards, per year, for fiddling with computers at the Stock Exchange but people like the miners are on the dole. Is this profitability?

'Newness of Life' is a well-paid stroll down Memory Lane. In half a century, I seem to have trodden that path three times; once in the first article of this book, twice in this decade because I was asked to write about travel and had no useful ideas for recent travel tales. Poring over news of 1931, I thought: Crikey, you've been around so long you're practically an historical monument. Think of the amazing changes that have happened in your life. There followed a long pause while I tried to think what they were. You live in your time, in the present tense, the changes occur and you trundle along with them, they don't explode like bombs, they are dispersed and gradual. Each day keeps me too busy for lingering backward looks.

Since the question arises, I decided that the greatest changes were nuclear weapons, television and the airplane as public transport. I skip computers and the space age, too esoteric for me. When they invent a computerized baby robot for housework I will pay attention. In my own life, the change I feel most and deplore most is crowding; the sense of a world stuffed to bursting with people. (The Pope is not aware of this situation).

Rats, when overcrowded, go crazy and eat each other. I think something of this order is happening in our cities. But the young, who only know crammed cities, lollop happily around in their masquerade clothes and seem to accept people pressure as normal. Nor does noise rasp their nerves; they are addicted to their own noise, the music of their generation. I travel in the hope of escaping crowds, and the weary hordes of weary souls at Heathrow or Gatwick fill me with panic. Will any quiet uncluttered places be left on earth? Time-sharing in holiday complexes in Kathmandu, package tours to the Kalahari Desert?

When I read the estimated population for the year 2000—and five out of six of them predicted to exist in stages of hunger—I feel that I managed my birthdate just about right.

I had visited three communist countries before re-visiting Cuba in 1985. Poland as reported in this book; Russia in 1972; Hungary some time in the eighties, but I cannot remember when. I never wanted to see Russia, but had been pen pals with an extraordinary Russian writer for years, and felt obliged to grit my teeth and go because of her letters. 'I am old and cannot come to you, please come to me.' Within half an hour of arrival at Moscow airport, I was in a permanent black temper due to the bloody-minded boorishness of every Russian with whom I had to deal as a tourist. The general scruffiness and discomfort exasperated me; it cost a packet to be so wretched. The people in the streets looked whey-faced, dour and suspicious. Moscow was the dreariest capital I had ever seen. Though I refused to admit it, I felt frightened. I breathed in the sensation of being watched, the state like a great spider with many eyes weaving a web around everyone. I hated the place; the days stretched ahead like a long month.

I spent those boiling hot August days with Russians whom we would consider middle class liberal intellectuals; by Soviet standards, dissidents. Dissident in their thinking, because they thought for themselves. Their living conditions were unbelievably bad. They were marathon talkers, quick to laugh. I have written about my Moscow sojourn elsewhere[1] but there

[1] *Travels with Myself and Another*

is one point worth repeating often. Dissident thought does not touch their feelings; they adored Moscow and would not willingly live anywhere else or among any people other than Russians. Americans in particular do not understand this Russian blood patriotism; nor do I, but I know it is there.

I have not railed against the Soviet government because I am careful of the company I keep. Anti-communism, as a creed, links you to some of the world's most odious people; the governments of South Africa, Chile, El Salvador for example, and the fanatical Right and neo-Fascists everywhere. Not to mention the shame of agreeing with President Reagan's worldview. The Soviet government can only be reformed from within; let us hope that Gorbachev's *glasnost* becomes a reality. Genuine *glasnost* could not tolerate psychiatric hospitals as punishment for dissidents. A young Russian poet, a recent gulag emigré, says that there are 2,000 political prisoners though I do not see how she can know. Two thousand out of a population of 278 million. The Soviet government has condemned its rule, as no one else can, by its fear of so few critical voices.

I went to Hungary because I wanted to swim in Lake Balaton. My compulsive travels are often based on siren place names and often land me in hell holes. Lake Balaton was a vast greyish flat polluted body of water, shallow and crowded whenever you could get into it; I was bored blind. A Hertz or Avis car could be rented with a credit card, very surprising. I drove across the endless Hungarian plain, increasingly bored; I gave lifts to people and made no contact with them. German was an adequate lingua franca to supplement English but Hungarians were nothing like the Poles; I felt very much an isolated foreigner. Budapest has its own Bond Street where you could buy, at a price, cashmere sweaters from Jaeger, Dior perfumes, the entire luxury bit. You could eat well and be served by polite waiters. Communism is certainly not monolithic. Hungary was not frightening, it was dull.

Cuba must be the only communist success story. Perhaps the regime should be called Castroism, not communism. Since Khrushchev's reckless plan to site nuclear missiles in Cuba, without consulting Castro, the Soviet Union has bought Cuban sugar and let Cuba manage its own affairs. The implacable US economic embargo, meant to destroy Cuba, has instead helped it by obliging Cuba to manufacture for itself. And national pride gets a big boost from standing up alone to the Colossus of the North.

The Colossus of the North has been contemptible and myopic in its treatment of Cuba—and is doing the same with Nicaragua. Washington did not say a mumbling word against the Cuban dictator, Batista, a corrupt murderous thug, but cracked down at once on the new Castro regime. Castro was brought to power by a rebellion of the Cuban people. His mandate was social justice and the first step had to be a redistribution of wealth. Redistributing wealth annoys Washington as tyranny does not; Washington perceives social justice as communism. Cuba is communist thanks to Washington, not to any long-held ideological commitments of Castro and his bearded followers. Washington has done its best to force Nicaragua to become what it is not and does not want to be: communist.

Experience teaches the tunnel vision men in Washington nothing. One after the other, the dictators they chummily supported, from Chiang Kai Shek through to Marcos, have been turfed out. Who can teach those men in Washington that *capitalism* and *communism* are meaningless words to the desperate poor but justice means a chance for what they have never had. If Washington goes on equating social justice with communism, Washington is the most convincing missionary for communism.

After struggling through six decades of this retrospective survey, I think I should conclude something. But what? A writer publishes to be read; then hopes the readers are affected by the words, hopes that their opinions are changed or strengthened or enlarged, or that readers are pushed to notice something they had not stopped to notice before. All my reporting life, I have thrown small pebbles into a very large pond, and have no way of knowing whether any pebble caused the slightest ripple. I don't need to worry about that. My responsibility was the effort. Writers work alone but I do not feel alone. I belong to a global fellowship, men and women concerned in the welfare of the planet and its least protected inhabitants. I plan to spend my remaining highly privileged years applauding that fellowship, the young volunteers and the veterans together, cheering them from the sidelines, shouting: good for you, right on, that's the stuff, never give up. Never give up.

Kilgwrrwg, Wales
September 1987

ALSO FROM

GRANTA BOOKS

CLANDESTINE IN CHILE

Gabriel García Márquez

In 1973, a portly, dark-haired, bearded film director fled Chile after the military coup. Twelve years later he returned, slim, fair, clean-shaven, bringing with him a false passport, a false name, a false past and a false wife.

What kind of man trades his own identity for an invented one? What compels an exile to return to the country where he is on the wanted list?

This is the story of Miguel Littín, who risked his freedom to bring the world a truer picture of life under Pinochet. From eighteen hours of taped interviews, Gabriel García Márquez retells, in the voice we know from the novels, the adventures of Miguel Littín, Clandestine in Chile.

On 28 November 1986, in Valparaiso, the Chilean authorities impounded and burned 15,000 copies of this book.

ALSO FROM

THE USES OF ADVERSITY

Timothy Garton Ash

Ten years ago Timothy Garton Ash came to East Berlin to find out
from the archives what the Berliners had done under Hitler. Instead he
found out – from the streets – what the Berliners were doing under
Honecker. He observed the 'elections,' interviewed the local party
members and talked into the night with an actor ('Dr Faust') who also
worked for the State Security Service. He wrote about what he saw –
in German – and the authorities protested. When he tried to return to
East Berlin, he was turned back.

He went to Poland and wrote a history of Solidarity.
It was translated into Polish and became an underground bestseller.
He was blacklisted at the frontier.

He went to Prague to attend a Charter 77 meeting, but was met instead
by the secret police. His reputation now seems to arrive before him.
Ten years ago Timothy Garton Ash began to discover Central Europe.
The Uses of Adversity records what he found.

ALSO FROM

ONCE IN EUROPA

John Berger

In the mountains near the border between France and Italy, there is a
pasture and a wooden hut. It is in this pasture that a shepherd named
Boris burned sixty sheep, one by one, on a bonfire, and where, having
fallen in love with a woman who would not have his baby, he
eventually died. Down the road, there is Felix, who lives alone on the
farm his father left him and plays the accordion at weddings. Nearby,
there is a pasture called Peniel, where all but two of the wooden huts
once built by the shepherds are now deserted. In one is Danielle;
twenty-three years old and unaware that the old man she sees every
morning is in love with her. And, finally, below them, in the valley,
there is a factory, and this is where something happened that could
happen only once, only once in Europa...

'John Berger is writing one of the great works of fiction in this century.'
Booklist

'It is Berger's genius – and I don't use the word lightly – to reveal to us
how the process of history affects people we come to know as friends.'
Angela Carter, *Washington Post*